UNITED KINGDOM
Belfast
Isle of Man
Irish Sea
Blackpool
Leeds
York
Liverpool
Manchester
Nottingham
Chester
Snowdon 1085 m
England
Norwich
Galway
Shannon
Dublin
REPUBLIC OF IRELAND
Waterford
Cork
Birmingham
Rugby
Cambridge
Stratford-upon-Avon
Wales
Oxford
London
Swansea
Cardiff
Bristol
Bath
Thames
Canterbury
Dover
Folkestone
Euro-tunnel
Calais
SEALINK
Salisbury
Southampton
Great Torrington
Brighton
LANDS END
Plymouth
Isle of Wight
Land's End
English Channel
Scilly Islands
Channel Islands
0 50 100 miles
0 50 100 km

CAMDEN MARKET

2

Erarbeitet von
Ruth Barker, Michael Biermann, Otfried Börner,
Simone Collenberg, Hannelore Debus,
Phil Mothershaw-Rogalla, Peter Oldham,
Ingrid Preedy, Tanja Ripke und Jürgen Wrobel

unter Mitwirkung der Redaktion
Dr. Anne Grimm und Henriette Vahle

Herausgeber der bisherigen Reihe
und Berater der Programmleitung:
Otfried Börner, StD a.D.,
Dr. phil. h.c. Christoph Edelhoff, StD a.D.

Fachliche Beratung
Heidi Barucki, Sigrid Boinski, Bianka Gehler, Petra Günther,
Kathrin Hough, Holger Nürnberg, Susanne Quandt,
Alexander Schülting und Gisela Vogt

Diesterweg
westermann

CAMDEN MARKET 2

Materialien für Schülerinnen und Schüler

- Workbook 2 mit Lernsoftware und Audio-CD (ISBN 978-3-425-**73832**-1)
- Workbook 2 mit Audio-CD (ISBN 978-3-425-**73822**-2)
- Lernsoftware 2
  - Einzelplatzlizenz (ISBN 978-3-425-**73882**-6)
  - Schullizenz (ISBN 978-3-425-**73892**-5)
- Arbeitsheft Inklusion 2 mit Audio-CD (ISBN 978-3-425-**73782**-9)
- Kit 2 (ISBN 978-3-425-**73842**-0)
- Vocab-App 2 – kostenfreier Download unter https://verlage.westermanngruppe.de/diesterweg/landing/VocabApps
- Zoom-App 2 – Link zum Download unter www.zoom-app.de

Materialien für Lehrkräfte

- Lehrerfassung zum Textbook 2 (ISBN 978-3-425-**73983**-0)
- Workbook 2 mit Lösungen und Audio-CD (ISBN 978-3-425-**73812**-3)
- Teacher's Manual mit Lösungen 2 (ISBN 978-3-425-**73862**-8)
- Vorschläge für Lernerfolgskontrollen 2 (ISBN 978-3-425-**73912**-0)
- Audio-CD + DVD 2 für Lehrkräfte (ISBN 978-3-425-**73852**-9)
- Interaktive Whiteboard-Software 2
  - Einzelplatzlizenz (ISBN 978-3-425-**73932**-8)
  - Schullizenz (ISBN 978-3-425-**73992**-2)
- Folien 2 (ISBN 978-3-425-**73922**-9)
- Kopiervorlagen 2 (ISBN 978-3-425-**73872**-7)
- Differenzierendes Zusatzmaterial 2 (ISBN 978-3-425-**73952**-6)
- BiBox – Digitale Unterrichtsmaterialien
  - Lehrer-Einzellizenz (ISBN WEB-425-**73958**)

Weitere Lizenzen auch für Schülerinnen und Schüler sind verfügbar.Nähere Informationen unter www.bibox.schule

westermann GRUPPE

Druck A^6 / Jahr 2019
Alle Drucke der Serie A sind im Unterricht parallel verwendbar.

Redaktion: Dr. Anne Grimm, Demet Kömür und Henriette Vahle
Vokabelanhang: Lea Gonsior
Herstellung: Sandra Grünberg
Layout und Satz: Visuelle Lebensfreude, Hannover
Illustrationen: Ulf Marckwort, Kassel
Umschlaggestaltung: blum design und kommunikation, Hamburg
Druck und Bindung: Westermann Druck GmbH, Braunschweig

ISBN 978-3-425-**73802**-4

Mr Batson
Mr Lambraki
Mrs Lambraki
Mrs Collins
Mrs Batson
Mr Patel
Mrs Patel
Sheree Patel
Josephine Batson
George Lambraki
Rajiv Patel
Gillian Collins
Sharon Batson
Caroline Lambraki
Charlie Batson
Karla Marshall
Patch
Mrs Killmouskey

B BACK TO CAMDEN MARKET!

Gillian Collins

- 12 years old
- birthday is on 26th April
- lives with her mum, sees her dad at the weekend
- lives next door to Caroline
- has got a cat, Mrs Killmouskey
- likes animals, football and music

Rajiv Patel

- 12 years old
- birthday is on 8th February
- grandparents came to England from India
- parents have got a small shop
- sometimes helps his parents in the shop
- has got an older sister, Sheree (15)
- likes music, plays the guitar

Charlie Batson

- 12 years old
- birthday is on 22nd June
- family came to England from Barbados
- has got a younger sister, Sharon (7), and an older sister, Josephine (18)
- has got a goldfish, Fritz
- likes football, is an Arsenal fan

Caroline Lambraki

- 12 years old
- birthday is on 21st May
- moved from Manchester to Camden last summer
- lives next door to Gillian
- father came to England from Greece
- has got a twin brother, George
- has got a rabbit, Daisy, and a dog, Patch
- likes football and music

Karla Marshall

- 13 years old
- birthday is on 10th October
- has got a younger brother, Josh (6)
- has got a rabbit, Hoppity
- is in a wheelchair
- likes sports, plays wheelchair basketball

INHALT

Wortfelder	Sprachliche Mittel	Methodenkompetenz	Land & Leute
Ferien • Urlaubs-aktivitäten • Wetter • Gefühle	R: *be* • R: *Simple past* • R: *Simple past:* Verneinung • R: Fragen mit Fragewörtern	*How to read* • *How to give a talk*	Das Vereinigte Königreich
Schule • Freizeit-aktivitäten	R: *be* • R: *Simple present* • R: *There is/there are* • R: *Simple present:* Entscheidungsfragen, Kurzantworten • R: Fragen mit Fragewörtern	*How to work with others* • *How to work with words* • *How to talk* • *How to give a talk*	Schulalltag in Großbritannien
Ferien • Urlaubsaktivitäten • Wetter	R: *Simple past*	*How to help out*	
Schule • Freizeit-aktivitäten	R: *Simple present* • R: Fragen mit Fragewörtern	*How to help out*	
Ferien • Urlaubs-aktivitäten	R: *Simple past*	*How to listen* • *How to write* • *How to read*	
Schule • Freizeit-aktivitäten	R: *Simple present* • R: Fragen mit Fragewörtern	*How to read* • *How to talk*	
Londoner Sehens-würdigkeiten • Wegbeschreibung	R: *Simple past*	*How to listen* • *How to write*	Unterwegs in London
Tiere	R: *Present progressive* • R: *Simple past* • *Simple past:* Entscheidungsfragen, Kurzantworten • R: *Simple present:* Entscheidungsfragen, Kurzantworten	*How to work with others* • *How to talk* • *How to write*	
Wegbeschreibung	*Simple past:* Entscheidungsfragen, Kurzantworten	*How to help out*	
Tiere	R: *Simple present* • R: *Simple present:* Entscheidungsfragen, Kurzantworten • R: *Present progressive*	*How to help out*	
Londoner Sehens-würdigkeiten	R: *Simple present*	*How to give a talk*	
Tiere	R: *Simple present* • R: *Simple past*	*How to listen* • *How to read*	

Die Angebote in *Camden Market* sind nicht linear abzuarbeiten. Die Auswahl der Übungen und Übungsteile richtet sich nach den Schwerpunkten des schulinternen Curriculums.

R = *revision* (Wiederholung)

I

Wortfelder	Sprachliche Mittel	Methodenkompetenz	Land & Leute
Horoskope • Berufe • Zukunft	*will-future* • *will-future:* Entscheidungsfragen • *will-future:* Fragen mit Fragewörtern	*How to work with others* • *How to give a talk*	
Helden • Robin Hood	R: *Simple past* • Adverbien der Art und Weise	*How to read* • *How to work with grammar* • *How to talk*	Robin Hood
Berufe	*will-future* • *will-future:* Fragen	*How to help out*	
Menschen	R: *Simple present* • Adverbien der Art und Weise	*How to help out*	
Horoskope • Zukunft	*will-future* • R: *Simple past*	*How to listen* • *How to write*	
Helden	R: *Simple present*	*How to read*	
Gruselgeschichte	Adjektive • Adverbien der Art und Weise	*How to write*	
Feste • Bräuche	R: *Simple present* • R: Satzstellung • *going to-future*	*How to work with others* • *How to write* • *How to give a talk*	Traditionelle Feste in Großbritannien
Geburtstag • Essen und Trinken	Adjektive: Steigerung *(-er, -est)* • Mengenangaben	*How to work with others* • *How to work with grammar* • *How to write*	
Feste • Bräuche	*going to-future*	*How to help out*	
Essen und Trinken	Adjektive: Steigerung *(-er, -est)* • Mengenangaben	*How to help out*	
Feste • Bräuche	R: *Simple present*	*How to talk*	
Geburtstag • Essen und Trinken	R: *Simple present*	*How to write*	
Regeln • Meinungsunterschiede	Modalverben • Adjektive: Steigerung *(more, most)* • R: Imperativ	*How to listen* • *How to talk* • *How to write*	
Regeln • Schuluniformen / Kleidung	Modalverben • Adjektive: Steigerung *(more, most)* • R: Satzstellung • R: Imperativ	*How to read* • *How to work with others*	Schuluniformen

Die Angebote in *Camden Market* sind nicht linear abzuarbeiten. Die Auswahl der Übungen und Übungsteile richtet sich nach den Schwerpunkten des schulinternen Curriculums.

R = *revision* (Wiederholung)

Wortfelder	Sprachliche Mittel	Methodenkompetenz	Land & Leute
Regeln	Modalverben • Adjektive: Steigerung	*How to help out*	
Kleidung	Modalverben • Adjektive: Steigerung	*How to help out*	
Regeln	Bedingungssätze, Typ I • Modalverben	*How to listen* • *How to write*	
Regeln • Schuluniformen	Modalverben	*How to write a letter*	
Krankheit • Musik • TV	R: *going to-future* • *Present perfect*	*How to work with others*	Fernsehen in Großbritannien
Ferien • Urlaubs-aktivitäten	*Present perfect* • R: *Simple past*	*How to work with words* • *How to write*	
Musik • TV	R: *going to-future* • *Present perfect*	*How to help out*	
Gefühle	R: Adverbien der Art und Weise	*How to help out*	
Musik	*Past progressive*	*How to read* • *How to talk*	
Freizeitaktivitäten • Verkehrsmittel	Adverbien: Steigerung	*How to help out* • *How to work with others*	

Die Angebote in *Camden Market* sind nicht linear abzuarbeiten. Die Auswahl der Übungen und Übungsteile richtet sich nach den Schwerpunkten des schulinternen Curriculums.

R = *revision* (Wiederholung)

WEGWEISER

Aufbau der *Themes* 1–6

Basis-Teil mit zwei Themenkreisen	Erfüllt die Grundanforderungen für Klasse 6 Enge Verzahnung mit dem Übungsteil (**Practice-Teil**) und dem Differenzierungsteil (**More-Teil**): P6 p. 25 P – Hinweise auf passgenaue Übungen im **Practice-Teil** M4 p. 31 M – Hinweise auf passgenaue Aufgaben im **More-Teil** Jeder Themenkreis schließt mit einer farbig hinterlegten Zielaufgabe, wie z. B. **Choose an activity** oder **Project**.
Practice-Teil zu beiden Themenkreisen des **Basis-Teils**	Übungsteil zum Trainieren und Wiederholen mit Übungen zu Wortschatz, Aussprache und Strukturen sowie Sprachmittlung
More-Teil zu beiden Themenkreisen des **Basis-Teils**	Bietet Zusatzmaterial zur Differenzierung für mittleres und höheres Niveau Kennzeichnung von besonders anspruchsvollen Texten und Aufgaben
Camden Chronicle-Seite	Magazinseite mit Fragen zum *Theme*, interkulturellen Hinweisen und authentischen Texten

Anhang

Reading is Fun	Optionaler Lesestoff zu den *Themes*
Wordbanks	Thematische Wortschatzsammlungen
How to ...	Lern- und Arbeitstechniken
Language in Focus	Grammatikanhang zum Nachschlagen
Words W **Dictionary** D	Chronologisches und alphabetisches Wörterverzeichnis

Symbole

L xx	Dieser Text ist nur auf der **CD** für Lehrer.
L xx S xx	Dieser Text ist auf der **CD** für Lehrer und auch auf der **CD** für Schüler.
DVD	Das Video befindet sich auf der **DVD** für Lehrer.
10 p. 185	Hierzu gibt es eine Erklärung im Grammatik-Teil **Language in Focus**.
P6 p. 25 P	Hierzu gibt es Übungen im **Practice-Teil**.
M4 p. 31 M	Hierzu gibt es Aufgaben im **More-Teil**.
xx p. xx WB	Hierzu gib es im **Workbook** weitere Übungen.
portfolio	Das Ergebnis kann im **Portfolio**-Ordner abgeheftet werden.
How to ... read p. 168	Die Techniken auf den **How to ...-Seiten** helfen beim Englischlernen.
wordbank Celebrations p. 159	In den **Wordbanks** befinden sich die wichtigsten Wörter zu einem Thema.
	Die Sonne kennzeichnet schwierige Texte und Aufgaben im **More-Teil**.
	Kompetenz: Sprechen
	Kompetenz: Leseverstehen
	Kompetenz: Schreiben
	Kompetenz: Hörverstehen
	Kompetenz: Hörsehverstehen
	Kompetenz: Sprachmittlung

THEME 1

AFTER THE HOLIDAYS

In diesem *Theme* ...

» übst du, über deine Ferien und die Ferien anderer zu berichten.
» lernst du die Landesteile Großbritanniens kennen.
» findest du Unterschiede und Gemeinsamkeiten von britischen und deutschen Schulen heraus.
» arbeitest du an einem Projekt über deine Schule.

1 Holidays

a) Look at the pictures. What can you see?

L 1.1 S 1

b) Listen to some kids talking about their holidays. Which pictures in a) go with what you can hear?

5R p. 182

c) Talk about YOUR holidays.

1–4 p. 3/4

My holidays were great / boring / …

I was in …

I was at home.

The weather was …

I / We played …

I / We visited …

…

2 Back home

a) What do you think: What are Caroline, Gillian, Charlie and Rajiv talking about? Look at the title and the picture.

b) Now read the dialogue. Were you right in a)?

Caroline: Hi Gillian. How are you?
Gillian: Oh, hi Caroline. I'm fine. How was your holiday?
Caroline: It was great. The weather in Greece was fantastic. It was sunny and warm and sometimes a bit windy.
Gillian: Cool. How long did you stay in Greece?
Caroline: We stayed there for two weeks – with my grandparents, you know.
Gillian: Nice. So what did you do?
Caroline: We went swimming in the sea. We also visited some famous sights, for example Delphi and the Acropolis in Athens. It was amazing.
Gillian: Wow. Oh, look. There are Rajiv and Charlie. Hi guys.
Rajiv: Hi Caroline. Hello Gillian.
Charlie: Hi you two. You look fantastic.
Gillian: Thank you. How were your holidays, guys?
Rajiv: Well, I didn't have a very exciting holiday. I stayed in London. It was often wet and cloudy and I had to help in my parents' shop a lot.
Charlie: Oh, come on, Rajiv. I was here, too, and we had fun. We played football in the park when it was sunny.
Rajiv: Yes, we did. That was great. We also went to the cinema and to a concert for kids in Hyde Park.
Caroline: But Charlie, didn't you go to Cornwall? You sent me a postcard.
Charlie: Yes, I went to Cornwall. It was nice. The beaches were cool and I ate ice cream every day. We stayed on a campsite in a caravan – but only for one week.
Gillian: Well, I had a good holiday, too. First I went to Scotland with my dad. We visited the castle in Edinburgh and went on a ghost walk. That was spooky. Unfortunately it rained a lot in Scotland.
Caroline: Oh, that's a shame.
Gillian: Yes. But I was lucky. I also went to Majorca with my mum. It was so nice. We stayed in a hotel on the beach. The weather was great. We went swimming every day and I met this really nice boy …

c) Read the dialogue again. Take notes about the friends in a grid like this.

5R p. 182
WB 5 p. 5

who?	where?	what?	how?
Caroline	Greece, …	stayed with her grandparents, …	great, …
Rajiv	…	…	
…	…		

d) Check your notes with a partner.

e) Choose one of the friends. Use your grid to talk about his or her holidays.

Caroline was in Greece.
She stayed with …

P P1 – P3 p. 24
M M1 p. 28

3 Holiday activities

5R + 6R p. 182/183
WB 6 p. 6

What did Karla, George and Mrs Killmouskey do in the holidays?
What didn't they do? Write about them.

Karla played basketball but she didn't watch ... She ...

+ play basketball | – watch basketball on TV
+ read a lot of books | – go to the cinema

+ go to Greece | – write any postcards
+ eat lots of ice cream | – like his grandma's food

+ walk to the park | – catch any birds
+ play with some mice | – visit Patch

LAND & LEUTE

Das Vereinigte Königreich

Das Vereinigte Königreich Großbritannien und Nordirland *(United Kingdom of Great Britain and Northern Ireland, UK)* besteht aus England *(England)*, Schottland *(Scotland)*, Wales *(Wales)* und Nordirland *(Northern Ireland)*. England, Schottland und Wales liegen zusammen auf einer großen Insel *(Great Britain)*. Nordirland liegt im Norden der Insel Irland *(Ireland)*. Das Land Irland gehört nicht zum Vereinigten Königreich.
England ist der größte Landesteil des Vereinigten Königreiches. Hier liegt auch die Hauptstadt, London. Die anderen Landesteile haben aber auch jeweils eine Hauptstadt. In Wales ist das Cardiff, in Schottland Edinburgh und in Nordirland Belfast.
Vor allem die Waliser und Schotten sind sehr stolz auf ihre Herkunft. In Wales sind z. B. alle Straßenschilder zweisprachig auf Walisisch *(Welsh)* und Englisch. Schau dir mal den langen walisischen Ortsnamen auf dem Foto oben an. Viele Kinder lernen Walisisch in der Grundschule.
In Schottland gibt es einige Leute, die wollen, dass Schottland unabhängig wird und sich vom Rest des Vereinigten Königreiches trennt. Schotten sind sehr stolz auf ihre Kultur und ihre Landschaft. Zu besonderen Anlässen tragen schottische Männer oft einen Schottenrock, den *kilt*.
Waliser, Schotten und Nordiren mögen es nicht besonders, wenn man sie als Engländer bezeichnet. Wenn du dir also nicht sicher bist, aus welchem Teil des Vereinigten Königreiches jemand kommt, dann bezeichne ihn oder sie als Brite bzw. Britin *(British)*.

Auf der Karte vorne im Buch kannst du auf Entdeckungsreise gehen. Welche Gegend würde dich am meisten interessieren?

L 1.2

Höre dir mal an, wie *How are you?* auf Walisisch klingt und wie man den langen walisischen Ortsnamen ausspricht. Kannst du beides nachsprechen?

4 Chain game

Write one thing you did in your holidays on a card. Play a game like this:

5R + 6R p. 182/183

5 Rajiv's diary

a) Read Rajiv's diary entries. Why was Thursday a great day for Rajiv? Why was Friday a terrible day for him?

How to ... read p. 168

Thursday, 2nd August

Today was GREAT! In the morning I got a postcard from Caroline. She's so nice. I can't wait to see her again.
Later I phoned Charlie and we met at the market. I found a cool T-shirt. It was cheap so I bought it.
In the afternoon we went to a concert for kids in Hyde Park. The entry was free and there were two bands. They were really good. Charlie and I took some photos with our mobiles and danced to the music.
I felt so happy. ☺
When I came home, Sheree made pizza for us – yummy! I'm proud of my sister.

TERRIBLE Friday, 3rd August

In the morning I had to help in the shop. Dad asked me to clean the shelves. It was so boring and my jeans got dirty.
After that I had to help some customers. One man wanted to have kiwis. When I told him we don't sell kiwis, he got really angry. I can't stand unfriendly customers. 😕
Grandma phoned. She felt lonely and asked me to come to her house. She told me lots of stories. Some were funny but most of them were sad or boring.
On my way home I saw Charlie and his family with their caravan. Everyone is going on holiday and I have to stay in London. It's not fair!

b) Right or wrong? Correct what's wrong.

1. Rajiv met Caroline at the market.
2. There were four bands playing in Hyde Park.
3. Rajiv is proud of Sheree.
4. Rajiv's father got angry.
5. Rajiv visited his grandma.
6. Charlie and his family stayed in London.

c) Find all the words that describe feelings. What other words do you know? Make two lists.

great	terrible
...	...

d) Think about last week or your holidays. What was a good day for you? What was a bad day? How did you feel? Talk about it.

wordbank People p. 155
WB 7 p. 6/7
P4 + P5 p. 24/25
M2 p. 29

6 Talking about YOUR holidays

a) Think about your holidays. Make a word web like this:

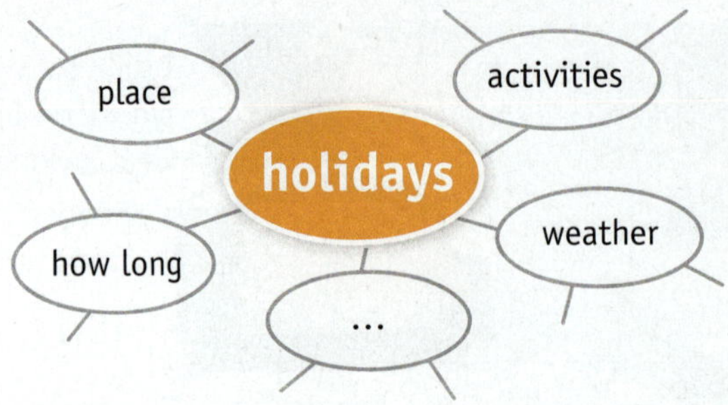

5R + 9R p. 182 + 184
P6 p. 25
WB 8 p. 7
wordbank Travelling p. 152 Weather p. 154

b) Talk about your holidays with a partner. Use your notes from a).

Where did you go on holiday?

I	went to stayed	Cologne / Berlin / Spain / … at home.

Where did you stay?

In a hotel / a holiday apartment.
On a campsite.
With some friends.

How long did you stay there?

One day / week / …
Two days / weeks / …

What was the weather like?

It was rainy / fantastic / …

What did you do?

I We	went played visited …	swimming to a museum. …

7 Choose an activity

portfolio
How to … write p. 171
How to … give a talk p. 169
WB 9 p. 7

You can …

- **write about YOUR holidays. You can use your notes from number 6.**
- **make a holiday collage and present it to the class.**
- **write a diary entry about a good or a bad day during your holidays.**
  You can look at number 5 for help.

<u>My holidays</u>

I stayed at home. It was great fun. The weather was very hot and it didn't rain. I went swimming and I met my friends. We played computer games. I stayed in bed late every morning.

8 Back to school

How to … work with others p. 174

Think – pair – share: How many school words do you remember?

- Make a list of school words.
- Now work with a partner and complete your lists.
- Then sit together with another pair and put your school words in groups (things in a schoolbag, people, …).

9 Wonderful world

wordbank At school p. 156

a) Look at the pictures. What school subjects do they stand for?

1 

2 

3 

4 

5 

6 

7 

8 

b) Now listen to the song *Wonderful World*. Which of the subjects from a) do you hear?

L 1.3 S 2

c) What other school subjects do you know?

P7 – P9 p. 26

WB 10+11 p. 8

10 At school

DVD

a) Watch the clip. What can you understand?

WB 12 p. 9

b) Watch the clip again. What is on Katie's timetable today?

A history
B registration
C maths
D English
E drama
F science
G RE
H food technology
I music
J PE
K geography
L ICT

c) What else do you remember?

Katie's favourite subject is …

Katie's favourite place in school is the …

d) Watch the clip a third time and check your answers.

11 Haverstock School

WB 13 p. 9

a) Look at the Haverstock School website. What is new or interesting to you?

News (230) ▾ Favourites ▾

WELCOME TO HAVERSTOCK

Haverstock School in central Camden is a secondary school with more than 1,000 students. Teachers, students and parents work closely together to get the best out of learning.

library

The school has got a large library. It is open until 4.30 pm. There is always a librarian to help students find the books they need.

cafeteria

Friendly staff serve students at morning break and lunchtime. During the morning break you can buy drinks, snacks, sandwiches and fruit in the school cafeteria. At lunchtime there is also a selection of healthy dishes with lots of fresh vegetables.

sports

In the gym students can take part in basketball, indoor cricket, badminton and indoor football. There are also classes in table tennis, dance and wall climbing. There is also an outdoor basketball court.

clubs and activities

Haverstock School offers many different clubs and activities in the morning and afternoon, for example ICT clubs, games clubs (chess, darts, snooker) and of course many sports clubs. Every morning students can come to the breakfast club from 8.00 – 8.30.

uniforms

Students have to wear school uniforms: a grey shirt with the school logo, a dark blue blazer with the school logo and a tie, black trousers (not jeans or tracksuit trousers) or a black skirt (knee length or longer). Students also have to wear black shoes.

homework

Students use the 'Havafax' which is a personal diary and planner to note down homework and set learning goals.

How to ... work with words p. 165

b) Read the website. Can you guess the meaning of new words? Look up words you can't guess in your dictionary (pages 243 to 267).

12 What's different, what's the same?

a) Make a grid like this. Find the information for the grid on the website. Then add information about YOUR school.

	Haverstock School	our school
number of students	…	…
uniforms	…	
…		

b) Talk to a partner about what is different and what is the same.

At Haverstock School there is / are …

There is / are … at our school / Haverstock School, too.

We don't have …

…

P10 p. 26
M3 p. 30
1R + 2R + 8R p. 178 – 180 + 184

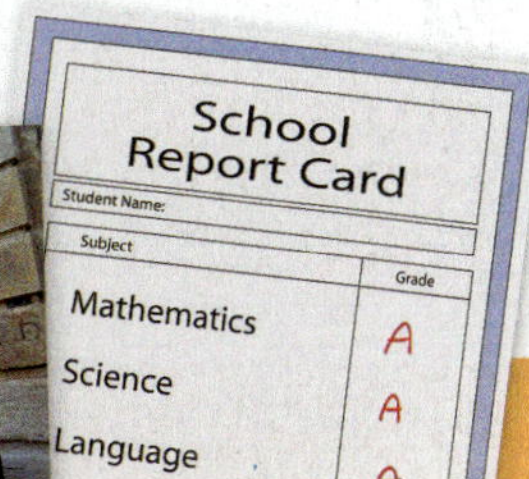

LAND & LEUTE

Schulalltag in Großbritannien

Für britische Kinder beginnt die Schulpflicht an einer Grundschule *(primary school)*, wenn sie fünf Jahre alt sind. Die *primary school* wird sechs Jahre besucht.

Anschließend geht es auf eine weiterführende Schule *(secondary school)*. Die meisten Schüler besuchen dabei eine staatliche Schule, z. B. eine Gesamtschule *(comprehensive school)*. Auch Haverstock ist eine Gesamtschule.

Es gibt in Großbritannien allerdings auch viele Privatschulen und Internate *(boarding schools)*, für die man oft eine Menge Geld bezahlen muss. Der wahrscheinlich berühmteste britische Internatsschüler ist Harry Potter.

In vielen Schulen beginnt der Tag mit der *registration*. Hier wird die Anwesenheit überprüft. Eine weitere Besonderheit ist die *assembly*. In dieser Schulversammlung werden einmal in der Woche Ankündigungen gemacht, z. B. über Projektwochen, Sportveranstaltungen und Theateraufführungen.

Anders als in Deutschland sind die Zensuren keine Zahlen, sondern Buchstaben (A ist die beste Note, F die schlechteste). In Großbritannien gibt es jedoch kein Sitzenbleiben – alle Schülerinnen und Schüler werden automatisch in die nächste Klassenstufe versetzt.

Welche Schulen gibt es in deiner Gegend?
Was weißt du über das Schulsystem in anderen Ländern?

13 School sounds

L 1.4

Listen to the sounds. Can you tell where these people are at Haverstock School?
Write down the names of the different places at the school.
Look at the photos on the website (page 20) for help.

M4 M p. 31

14 A new classmate

M5 M p. 31

3R + 9R p. 180 + 184

14 + 15 WB p. 10

a) There is a new boy in the kids' class at Haverstock. Charlie is talking to him. What are his questions? Put the words in the correct order.

Hi, I'm Charlie. your – what's – name – ?

Hello, I'm Nick.

are – from – where – you – ?

I'm from Cardiff. My mother got a new job in London so we moved here.

do – now – you – where – live – ?

Only five minutes from here, on Eton Road.

London – do – like – you – ?

Yes, I do. It's cool.

you – have – brothers and sisters – got – ?

No, I haven't.

hobbies – what – your – are – ?

Music, playing computer games, reading and lots more.

like – sports – you – do – what – ?

I like judo, basketball, swimming and football, of course.

school – a game of – after – what about – football – ?

That's a good idea!

wordbank Free time p. 151

b) Think of more questions to ask Nick. Write them down and make up possible answers.

How to ... talk p. 170

c) Work with a partner. One of you is a new classmate. Ask each other questions and answer them. Think about:

name • age • brothers and sisters • hobbies • pets • favourite food / ... • ...

P11 – P13 P p. 27

Then make a plan for what you can do in your free time.

15 A project – YOUR school

portfolio

wordbank
At school
p. 156

PLAN IT

- **You can work:**
  - on your own
  - with a partner
  - in groups
- **What do you want to write / talk about?**
  Think about:
  - students and teachers
  - different places / rooms
  - activities
  - school times
  - …
- **Think about how to present it:**
  - flyer
  - poster
  - interview
  - computer presentation
  - …

DO IT

- **Think about what you already know, then collect more information:**
  - look at the noticeboard in your school
  - interview classmates, your teacher, the headteacher, …
  - visit the home page of your school
  - …
- **Make notes.**
- **Write about your topic(s).**
- **Find material (pictures, things, …).**
- **Prepare your presentation.**

CHECK IT

- **Is the English OK?**
- **Is it interesting?**
- **Show your text to other classmates and your teacher.**
- **Edit it.**
- **Practise what you want to say.**

PRESENT IT

- **You can:**
  - use your notes to talk about your topic(s)
  - show your computer presentation
  - put up your poster and talk about it
  - …

How to …
give a talk
p. 169

WB test yourself
p. 11/12

P1 Holiday weather

a) What are these weather words? Write them down.

1  2  3  4  5 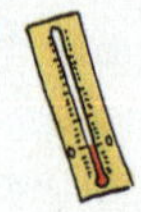 6 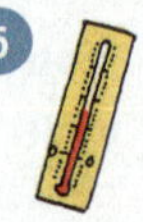

b) What other weather words do you know?

P2 Sound check

L 1.5

a) Listen and sort the words.

help • yes • sea • we • Edinburgh • her • beach • be • get • Greece • sent • were • see • meet • went • wet • Berlin

/iː/	/e/	/ɜː/
sea	help	her
...	...	...

b) Check your list with a partner and say the words.

P3 Verb search

5R p. 182

a) Look at number 2b) again and find the *simple past* forms of these verbs:

be – was / were, visit – visited, send – ..., go – ..., do – ..., stay – ..., have – ..., play – ..., eat – ..., meet – ...

How to ... work with grammar p. 173

b) Sort the simple past forms in a) in a grid like this. Then try to find more verbs for your grid.

verbs with the same ending	other verbs
visit<u>ed</u>	was / were
...	...

P4 Charlie's holidays

5R p. 182

Complete the sentences with *was* or *were*.

Charlie's holidays XX great. He XX in Cornwall with his family and the weather XX really good. It XX sunny and warm. They stayed on a campsite in a caravan. There XX lots of other nice families. Charlie and Sharon often went to the beach with the other kids. They often had some ice cream at the beach because it XX so good.

P5 David's holidays

5R
p. 182

Gillian's cousin David sent her some pictures from his holiday in Wales. Look at the pictures. What did David do in his holidays?

1. be – Wales

2. stay – hotel

3. visit – castle

4. go to – the top of Mount Snowdon

5. see – dolphins

6. take photos of – football stadium

P6 Getting active

Es geht um ... Dort können Kinder ...

How to ...
help out
p. 176

You are on holiday with your parents and see this poster. Your parents don't speak English. Tell them what the poster is about.

Kayak Adventure Day!

Are you between 10 and 14 years old?
Then come to the *Kayak Adventure Day!*
You will learn to kayak, make lots of friends and HAVE FUN!

WHEN ›› Wednesday 21st June
TIME ›› From 9.30 am until 4.30 pm
WHERE ›› The Lake
COST ›› £10 per person

PLEASE BRING ›› Swimwear | Towel | Lunch

If you are interested, please call
05197 413675

Come and join the fun!

P7 School poems

portfolio

Read the examples and write YOUR school poem.

students
pen
schoolbag
books

SCHOOL
nice classmates
small classroom
boring biology
long breaks
school

wordbank
At school
p. 156

P8 A word game

a) How many words can you make out of "school subject"?

she, …

b) Compare your words with a partner. Who found more words?

P9 Sound check

a) Look at these words and say them. Make lists.

afternoon • book • classroom • come • do • does • club • look • other • school • too • two • foot • wonderful • you • food • brother • took

/uː/	/ʊ/	/ʌ/
afternoon	book	come
…	…	…

L 1.6

b) Listen and check your words. Say the words again.

P10 School days

2R + 9R
p. 179/180 + 184

Work with a partner and talk about YOUR school day. Ask and answer the questions.

When What How many lessons What subjects …	do does don't is are …	school start? school finish? you have every day? new this year? your favourite subjects? you like? …

P11 More about Nick

Read about Nick. Complete the sentences with the correct verbs.

2R p. 179/180

does • has got • is • is • is • likes • listens • lives • lives • loves • sees • works • plays

Nick XX from Cardiff in Wales but he XX in London now. Nick's mother XX in a bank. His father XX in France so Nick only XX him in the holidays. Nick XX 12 years old. He XX a hamster and a budgie. Music XX one of Nick's favourite hobbies. He XX the drums and XX to music as often as possible. But he also XX football and other sports. Nick XX Chinese food. At the weekend he sometimes XX the cooking.

P12 Getting to know somebody

Find out what Nick asked Charlie. Read Charlie's answers and make questions.

9R p. 184

1. My name is Charlie.
2. I'm from London.
3. I'm 12 years old.
4. Yes, I've got two sisters.
5. Yes, I love pets. I've got a goldfish.
6. His name is Fritz.
7. I play football and I like music.
8. I love burgers, pizza and chips.

Have you got ... ?

How ... ?

What ... ?

Where ... ?

P13 In der Schulkantine

Du isst in der Schulkantine zu Mittag. Bei dir sitzt eine Schülerin aus der Parallelklasse mit einer englischen Austauschschülerin. Die eine spricht kaum Englisch, die andere kaum Deutsch. Kannst du den beiden helfen?

How to ... help out p. 176

M1 Gillian's story

a) **Look at the pictures. Describe them to a partner. Take turns. What differences can you find?**

In the first picture I can see a boy. He is …

L 1.7 S 3

b) **Now listen to Caroline and Gillian. Which picture in a) goes with Gillian's story?**

How to … listen p. 167

c) **Listen again and complete the sentences.**

M1 WB p. 15

1. Gillian is looking at …
2. In Majorca she met …
3. They played …
4. The dog …
5. Noah was …
6. Gillian hopes to …

d) **Make a fact file about Noah.**

Name: Noah
Age: …
Town: …
…

How to … write p. 171

e) **Gillian wants to send an email to Noah. What can she write about? Collect ideas (school, her friends, …). Then write Gillian's email. You can start like this:**

portfolio

M2 + M3 WB p. 15/16

Send Chat Attach Save draft

To:

Subject: Hi Noah!

Hi Noah,

How are you?
I'm back in London. School started three days ago. …

M2 A mysterious tale

a) Hugo from Mexico is spending his holidays at Lake Titicaca in Bolivia. Look at a map of South America and find Bolivia and its famous lake.

b) Read Hugo's blog entry. What do you learn about Lake Titicaca?

How to ... read p. 168

News (230) Favourites

Hi guys! [Friday, August 3rd]

I'm writing this blog at Lake Titicaca in Bolivia - it's the highest lake in the world! I'm on holiday here with my family. Yesterday something really mysterious happened.

Late last night my brothers and I decided to go on an adventure. Mum and Dad were asleep, so we snuck out of the hotel. We wanted to go to the top of Cerro Calvario, a big hill by the lake. On our way we suddenly heard strange and angry voices in foreign languages. We also saw the shadows of huge cats in the moonlight. We were really scared. So we walked quicker and quicker until we were at the top of the hill. There we found an old man with a white beard. He was looking over the lake. We told him about the voices and the huge cats but he wasn't surprised.

"In the beginning," the old man said, "the Gods gave the Inca people this beautiful place. But the Gods also said 'There is one rule. You must not climb to the top of the mountain. A sacred fire always burns there.' But the Devil said to the people 'Don't listen to the stupid Gods. Go and find the fire.' The people believed the Devil and went up the mountain. But the Gods saw them and sent hungry pumas to eat the people. When Inti the Sun God heard about this, he cried and cried. His tears created a huge lake. And when his tears touched the hungry pumas, the pumas became stone. Only two people survived. They called the lake Titicaca, which in their language means 'Lake of the stony pumas'."

That was the end of the man's mysterious tale. Together we watched the sunrise on the other side of the lake - maybe it was Inti the Sun God saying good morning! In the light of day we didn't feel scared anymore. Now all that seems to be a very strange dream.

c) What happened in the story? Why is it a mysterious tale?

d) Read the story again. What do you think: How did Hugo and his brothers feel?

glad • tired • scared • excited • happy • cold • ...

WB M4 p. 16

wordbank People p. 155

How did they feel ...

1. when they snuck out of the hotel?
2. when they heard the voices and saw the shadows?
3. when they found the old man?
4. when they listened to the mysterious tale?
5. when they watched the sunrise?

e) Do you know any other mysterious tales? Write or talk about them.

M3 Kids around the world

How to ... read p. 168

M5 WB p. 17

a) Read Michelle's text for a website from kids around the world. What is it about?

It's interesting to see what school days are like in other countries. I go to a *collège* in Paris. This is a kind of comprehensive school that all kids in France go to for four years right after primary school *(école primaire)*.

My school starts at 8 am and ends between 4 pm and 6 pm. We have a school cafeteria and I eat there every day. I think the food is OK. On Wednesdays school ends early - at 12 o'clock.

I think our teachers are quite strict because if you are even a little bit late for school, you get into trouble ...

Between the lessons we have a 5-minute-break to change to another room. You mustn't be late for the next lesson. Otherwise you have to repeat that lesson another time. We also have two 15-minute-breaks and a long lunch break.

In our lessons our teachers talk most of the time and we take notes. Students don't say a lot during the lessons. I like it that students in other countries are allowed to say more in class and can sometimes work in teams. But I prefer our marks - we have 20 (20 is the best, 0 the worst).

I like my school a lot. I can see my friends all day. But after school we have to do our homework. So there is not a lot of time for hobbies or other things. That's too bad because I would really like to learn to play the piano.

b) What is different and what is the same at YOUR school?

M6 WB p. 17

c) What do you like about Michelle's school? What don't you like? Why? Make notes first, then write about it. Here is some help:

I like that Michelle's school ends early on Wednesdays.
She can meet her friends ...

I also like ... because ...

What I don't like about Michelle's school is that the teachers ...

I think ...

I prefer ...

M4 Lots of information

L 1.8 S 4

WB M7 p. 18

a) Listen and find out: What kind of school event is it?

registration • school club • assembly

b) Read the students' notes. Then listen again. Which notes are correct?

A

- Havafax and PE clothes!!!
- Mondays: drama club (Oliver), 3.45 – 5.45
- Thursdays: football (3.20) and skateboarding (4.30)
- Wednesdays: book club in library during morning break
- Friday: Japan evening (5 – 7)

B

- don't forget: Havafax + PE clothes
- Mondays drama club from 3.45 pm to 5.45 pm
- football at 3.30 pm on Thursdays and skate-boarding club at 4.30 pm
- book club during lunchtime on Wednesdays
- this Friday from 5 to 7 pm: Japan evening (video)

C

- *bring Havafax and PE clothes*
- *drama club on Mondays (3.45 – 5.45)*
- *Thursdays: football (3.20) and skateboarding (4.30)*
- *new book club, Wednesdays at lunchtime*
- *Japan evening, Friday 5 – 7 pm*

M5 Meeting somebody new

Work with a partner. Partner B is a new classmate. Make a dialogue.

How to … talk p. 170

wordbank Free time p. 151

WB M8 p. 18

Partner A	Partner B
1 Begrüße B, nenne deinen Namen und frage B nach seinem / ihrem Namen.	2 Begrüße A und beantworte seine / ihre Frage.
3 Befrage B zu folgenden Dingen und beantworte auch seine / ihre Fragen: – Alter – Herkunft – Geschwister – Haustiere – Hobbys – Lieblingsessen / … – …	4 Antworte und befrage auch A zu folgenden Dingen: – Alter – Herkunft – Geschwister – Haustiere – Hobbys – Lieblingsessen / … – …
5 Schlage B eine gemeinsame Aktivität vor: – Let's … – What about … ?	6 Sage, dass du einverstanden bist, oder mache einen anderen Vorschlag.

CAMDEN CHRONICLE
LEARN ENGLISH THE CAMDEN WAY

DID YOU GET IT ALL?

- Where do Caroline's grandparents live?
- Who went to Edinburgh / Scotland with Gillian?
- Where did Charlie go on holiday?
- What kind of concert did Charlie and Rajiv go to?
- What is Katie's favourite subject?
- What is a "Havafax"?
- What are the colours of the Haverstock School uniform?
- Where is Nick from?

GOOD TO KNOW ...

In Großbritannien ist an den meisten Schulen das Tragen einer Schuluniform Pflicht. An vielen Schulen gibt es aber auch einmal oder öfter im Jahr einen *Non-uniform day*. An diesem Tag dürfen die Schülerinnen und Schüler ausnahmsweise in ihrer normalen Kleidung zur Schule kommen. Oftmals wird an diesem Tag Geld für wohltätige Zwecke gesammelt.

"Yech... I hate when they put that sauce on."

She sells seashells by the seashore.
The shells she sells are surely seashells.
So if she sells shells on the seashore,
I'm sure she sells seashore shells.

SUMMER IS OVER,
CLASS HAS BEGUN,
HOLIDAYS WERE GREAT,
OH YES, THEY WERE FUN!
OUT OF THE POOL,
LET'S RUN BACK TO SCHOOL!

THEME 2

AROUND LONDON

In diesem *Theme* ...

» lernst du viele Londoner Sehenswürdigkeiten kennen.
» schreibst du über deine Favoriten unter den Sehenswürdigkeiten.
» erfährst du etwas über Verkehrsmittel in London und den Londoner Zoo.
» übst du, Wegbeschreibungen zu verstehen und zu geben.
» sprichst du über Tiere.

1 Kids' London A to Z

1+2 p. 19

a) What do you know about London? Do you know any of these famous sights?

WELCOME TO LONDON!

Buckingham Palace

The Queen lives here when she is in London. There are 775 rooms, 760 windows and 1514 doors! In summer you can visit the palace but you can't have tea with the Queen! Come and watch the Changing of the Guard.

Covent Garden

Shops and stalls, music, jugglers and clowns – you can find them all at Covent Garden. Enjoy an exciting afternoon, have an ice cream and watch, watch, watch!

The London Dungeon

Travel back in time to learn about the dark side of London's history. It's scary – so don't go alone! Open: 10 am – 4.30 pm

King's Cross Railway Station

Platform 9 ¾ is a 'must-see' for all Harry Potter fans – that's where Harry takes the train to Hogwarts! In real life King's Cross is the station where trains leave for Scotland and Wales.

London Zoo

What's new at the zoo? Come and see the baby giraffes and about 12,000 more animals. Here the animals are the stars! Open: 10 am – 5.30 pm

Hyde Park

The perfect place to relax. Sit on the grass or in a boat and enjoy the sun. On Sundays you can listen to all kinds of people at Speaker's Corner.

P P2 p. 46
M M1 p. 50

b) Read about the sights and match them with the pictures.

I think picture number 1 is London Zoo.

VISIT LONDON'S FAMOUS SIGHTS!

Tower Bridge

This amazing bridge is next to the Tower of London. It is 60 metres long and opens up when tall ships are passing.

The Tower of London

Visit London's famous castle. Come and see the towers, the cannons and the uniforms.
And don't forget to look at the Crown Jewels.
Open: 9 am – 6 pm

The Sherlock Holmes Museum

Visit the museum and travel back in time to learn all about the life of London's most famous detective.
Open: 9.30 am – 6 pm

Piccadilly Circus

Meet your friends at the statue in the middle of Piccadilly Circus. This is the ideal place to sit and watch people, cars and buses.

The London Eye

Ride 135 metres to the top and enjoy a great view of London. You can see three airports, 13 football stadiums and 36 Thames bridges.
Open: 10 am – 9 pm

Madame Tussauds

Meet the famous people of the world – in wax. Kings, queens, pop stars, sportspersons – even Jack the Ripper is waiting for you!
Open: 9 am – 5.30 pm

I ❤ LONDON

2 London sounds

L 1.9

Imagine you are in London now. Listen to the sounds. Where are you? Look at the photos for help.

3 Sightseeing in London

DVD

a) Watch the clip. Where are Leanne, Rebecca and Daniel? Which sights do they visit/see? Look at the photos for help.

First they are … Then they … After that they …

b) Watch the clip again and match the sentence parts. There is one more ending than you need.

1 Each tower of Tower Bridge
2 The HMS Belfast
3 The Gherkin
4 Tower Bridge

A is a museum.
B opens up 1000 times every year.
C is 135 metres high.
D is 65 metres high.
E looks like an egg made of glass.

c) What else can you understand?

Globe Theatre

The Gherkin

London Underground

The London Eye

Big Ben

fish & chip shop

Tower Bridge and HMS Belfast

London City Hall

Tate Modern and Millennium Bridge

St Paul's Cathedral

Covent Garden

The Tower of London

Changing of the Guard at Buckingham Palace

4 Where to go in London

Look at the sights in number 1 and on pages 36 – 37 again.
Ask and answer questions with a partner.

Where can you go	and see	animals? jugglers? famous people? …
	when it is sunny? when it is rainy? when you have no money? …	

Where can you go and see animals?

You can go to London Zoo.

My top three London sights:
1. …
2.
3.

5 YOUR favourite sights

a) Make a list of your top three London sights. Why did you choose them? Tell a partner.

M2 M p. 50

3+4 WB p. 20/21

b) Write about your top three sights. What can you do there? Look at pages 34 – 35 for help.

My day in London

First I want to see London Zoo because I love animals. I think it is interesting to watch …
Then …
After that …

LAND & LEUTE

Unterwegs in London

London ist eine sehr große Stadt. Sie ist mehr als zweimal so groß wie Berlin. Zum Glück gibt es dort ein weit verzweigtes U-Bahnnetz – die *London Underground*, sodass man überall gut und schnell hinkommt. Die Londoner haben ihrer *Underground* einen lustigen Namen gegeben, nämlich *tube* (Röhre). Weltberühmt ist die *tube map*, auf der die U-Bahnlinien und Haltestellen mit farbigen Linien dargestellt sind. Diese besondere Karte wurde 1933 von Harry Beck erfunden. Sie war damals völlig neuartig. Inzwischen verwenden Städte überall auf der Welt solche Karten.

Willst du mehr von London sehen, solltest du unbedingt den Bus nehmen. Die roten *double-deckers* (Doppeldeckerbusse) bieten dir vom Obergeschoss eine wunderbare *sightseeing tour* (Stadtrundfahrt).

Weltberühmt, aber natürlich auch wesentlich teurer als Bus oder *tube*, sind die meist schwarzen *cabs* (Taxis). Fahrradfahren ist ziemlich gefährlich, denn die Straßen sind extrem voll. Viele Sehenswürdigkeiten sind aber auch gut zu Fuß zu erreichen.

Welche Verkehrsmittel gibt es in deinem Ort? Welche benutzt du?

6 Where is Rob?

George's friend Rob lives in Manchester. He is in London for the weekend. Today George, Caroline and Gillian want to show him the Sherlock Holmes Museum.

a) Look at the pictures and talk about them.

b) Listen to the kids. What happened?

L 1.10

Gillian: Hi George.
George: Hi girls. Have you seen Rob? I've lost him.
Caroline: What? I thought you went shopping in Oxford Street together.
George: Of course we did. Then we took the tube to Baker Street. It was really full and when we got off, I suddenly couldn't see Rob anymore.
Gillian: I don't believe it! Did you phone Rob?
George: Yes, I did … well, I tried to phone him but my mobile is dead. I forgot to charge it.
Caroline: Oh great! Have you got Rob's number?
George: Yeah, it's here on my hand: 07700 900 325.

Rob: Hello?
Caroline: Hi Rob, it's Caroline.
Rob: Caroline, where is George? I couldn't reach him on his mobile.
Caroline: We'll explain that later. Where are you?
Rob: I don't really know. Five minutes ago I walked past a building on the left. There was a long queue.
Caroline: That was Madame Tussauds. So you walked along Marylebone Road.
Rob: Yes, well, then I turned right because I thought I saw George but it wasn't him. So I walked straight on to the next street and turned left.
Caroline: Can you see a street name? I've got a map here. I can tell you how to get to the museum then.
Rob: Just a minute, it says Nottingham Street and right in front of me is Marylebone High Street …

c) Listen again and read along. Find out: Where and how did Rob lose George? Where is Rob now? Find the place on the map below.

P4 p. 47

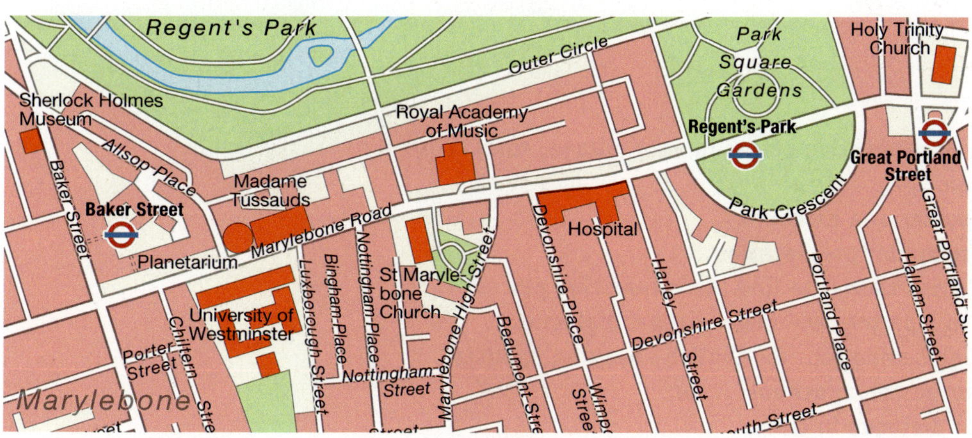

7 Directions

wordbank
Travelling
p. 153

a) Match the expressions with the symbols.

1. walk straight on
2. turn left
3. turn right
4. walk past …
5. walk on until you get to …
6. on your right
7. on your left
8. cross the street

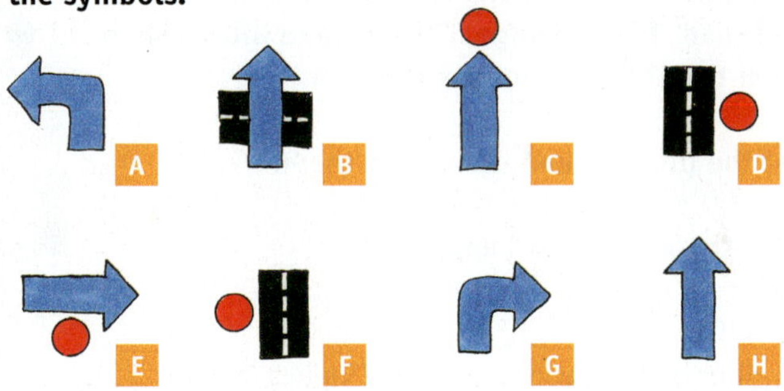

L 1.11
M3
p. 51

**b) With a partner tell Rob how to get to the museum.
Use the map on page 39 and the expressions from a).
Then listen to Caroline. Which way did she choose?**

P1 + P3
p. 46
5 – 7
p. 22/23

**c) Work with a partner. Use the map on page 39 and say where you are.
Your partner gives you directions but he / she doesn't say where you are going.**

8 A sightseeing tour

The next day Rob went sightseeing with George. They visited six places.

L 1.12

**a) Listen and find out where they went.
Look at the map on pages 34 – 35
and follow with your finger.**

5R
p. 182

**b) Listen again and write about the friends' day
in London.**

First they looked at …
Then they were at …
After that they visited …
Later they saw … and …

9 Choose an activity

portfolio
P5 + P6
p. 47
wordbank
Travelling
p. 152/153

**Make a list of interesting places in your village / town / city.
Then you can …**

- **make a poster or a brochure.**
- **make a computer presentation.**
- **help a British tourist to find the interesting places.
Work with a partner and make a short dialogue.**
- **plan a sightseeing tour for English-speaking tourists.**

**Present your poster / brochure / … or
act out your dialogue in class.**

10 Gillian is frightened

a) Get together in buzz groups. Look at the picture. What can you see? What do you think is happening? Then choose a member of your group to present your results to the class.

How to ... work with others p. 174

WB 8+9 p. 24

b) Listen to the story. Why is Gillian so frightened?

L 1.13

WB 10 p. 25

Gillian is at home. Her mother is at work. Gillian is doing her homework and listening to the news on the radio. The newsreader is talking about a tiger from London Zoo. But the tiger isn't in the zoo now – it is walking in the streets of London! Gillian is very frightened.

Newsreader: *... and the police are looking for it now. The keeper went to the cage at five o'clock and the tiger wasn't there. It must be somewhere in the streets of London.*
Gillian: Help! Perhaps it's in our street! Perhaps it's walking outside our house! ... Oooh, where's Mum? Why isn't she back yet? And where are George and Rob?
Newsreader: *The keeper says that the tiger ate at three thirty and it's always sleepy after its meal ... so perhaps it's sleeping in a garden somewhere.*
Gillian: Oooh, perhaps it's sleeping in our garden ... Oh dear! What's that noise?
Mrs Collins: Hello, Gillian. What's the matter? You look frightened.
Gillian: Oh, Mum. Quick! Close the door! They're looking for a tiger from the zoo. It's in our street!
Mrs Collins: Oh, Gillian, don't be silly!
Newsreader: *It's six fifteen. News just in – the tiger is in Kensington Gardens. It is sleeping under a tree. The police are trying to catch it now ...*

c) Listen again and read along. Then find out:
Where was the tiger at 3.30 pm / 5 pm / 6.15 pm? Take notes.

3.30 pm: ...
5 pm:
6.15 pm:

d) Write about what is happening.

4R p. 181

P10 p. 48

1. Gillian is listening to ...
2. The newsreader is talking about ...
3. The police are looking for ...
4. Perhaps the tiger is walking ...
5. Perhaps it is sleeping ...
6. Now the police are trying to ...

11 The tiger's walk through London

4R p. 181
P11 p. 49
11 p. 25

A runaway tiger – the people in London are very frightened. A tiger is dangerous! Everyone is calling the police. Look at the pictures and say what the people are telling the police officers.

The tiger is running away …

1. run away from the zoo
2. swim in the canal
3. run after people in the park
4. buy a ticket for …
5. eat a tourist's sandwich
6. look in the shop windows
7. sleep in Kensington Gardens
8. …

12 The tiger's adventure

When the tiger is back at home, it tells its friends about its adventure.

a) Listen to the tiger and act out the animals' reactions. L 1.14

1. I felt bored this afternoon. I thought "What about a walk around London?" I opened the door of the cage and walked away!
2. Then I went swimming in the canal – but the water was so dirty, ugh!
3. I walked to the park but that was terrible. There were a lot of people there. I wanted to say hello but everyone ran away.
4. Then I wanted to go to Madame Tussauds. I tried to buy a ticket but they didn't let me in.
5. Suddenly I was very hungry and I ate a tourist's sandwich. I asked him first, of course.
6. Then I looked at the lovely shops.
7. After that I felt really tired so I slept in Kensington Gardens. Then the police brought me back to the zoo.

That's too bad.

Oh, did you?

Cool!

Oh dear!

Exciting!

What a day!

Really?

b) Work in a group. One of you is the tiger, the others are its friends. Think about questions to ask the tiger. Think about possible answers. Then act out your dialogue in class.

How to … talk p. 170
7R + 9R p. 183/184
M4 p. 52

Did you … ?

How did you … ?

What did … ?

Where did the police … ?

Why did … ?

… ?

Yes, I did. / No, I didn't.

I / They felt / went / …

…

13 Tigers

a) Think about tigers. Which of these words go with tigers? Write a list.

run · a cat · four paws · tall · predator · a long nose · wild · Asia · clever · a zoo · grey · a long tail · black stripes · two long teeth · India · beautiful · strong · fast · jump · dangerous · a cage · eat meat · orange fur · large ears · big

b) Talk about tigers.

Tigers live in …
Tigers have got …
Tigers are (always / sometimes / …) …
Tigers can be …
Tigers …
They …

P7 – P9 P
p. 48

c) Look at the other words in a). They fit another animal. Can you find out which one?

14 Lunch for the animals

3R
p. 180

a) What do these animals eat? Test your partner. You can ask funny questions, too.

grass • meat • eggs • mice • chocolate • fish • pizza • insects • apples • carrots • …

Do spiders eat meat?

I'm not sure. I think they eat …

Yes, they do. / I think they do.

No, they don't. They eat …

zebra · gorilla · lion · tiger · penguin · hippo · snake · spider

M5 M
p. 52

b) Think about more animals and talk about their food.

15 Working at a zoo

a) What kind of people work at a zoo?

b) Listen to Sam, a keeper at London Zoo. What does he say about his work?

L 1.15

c) Listen again. Which colleagues does Sam talk about?

P12 p. 49
M6 p. 53

Mary • Simon • Pete • Sonya • Mrs Miller • Mr Perkins

What jobs do they do?

ice cream seller • vet • gardener • zoo director

d) Would YOU like to work at a zoo? Why / Why not? What would you like to do there?

WB 12 p. 26

16 A project – YOUR animal book

Make an animal book in your class. Write about an animal at the zoo. Each student finds out about a different animal and makes one page for the animal book.

Think about:

- Where does the animal come from?
- What does it look like?
- What does it eat?
- What is interesting about it?
- …

portfolio
How to … write p. 171
wordbank Animals p. 157
WWW

WB test yourself p. 27/28

P1 Odd one out

a) Find the odd one out.

1. tube • skateboard • bus • train • taxi
2. park • museum • street • bridge • history
3. singers • actors • music • clowns • jugglers
4. left • right • between • never • in front of
5. clean • visit • watch • enjoy • see
6. exciting • famous • great • cold • amazing

b) Write a new 'odd one out' for your partner.

P2 Sound check

a) What are these sights in London? Write them down.

1. /ˈtaʊə ˌbrɪdʒ/
2. /ˌkɒvənt ˈgɑːdən/
3. /ðə ˌlʌndən‿ˈaɪ/
4. /ˌbʌkɪŋəm ˈpæləs/
5. /ˌpɪkədɪli ˈsɜːkəs/

L 1.16

b) Listen and check.

P3 Giving directions

L 1.17

a) Listen to the directions and follow them on the map. Where do you go?

wordbank
Travelling
p. 153

b) Work with a partner. Tell your partner where you are. Then ask him/her for directions.

Excuse me, can you tell me the way to …, please?

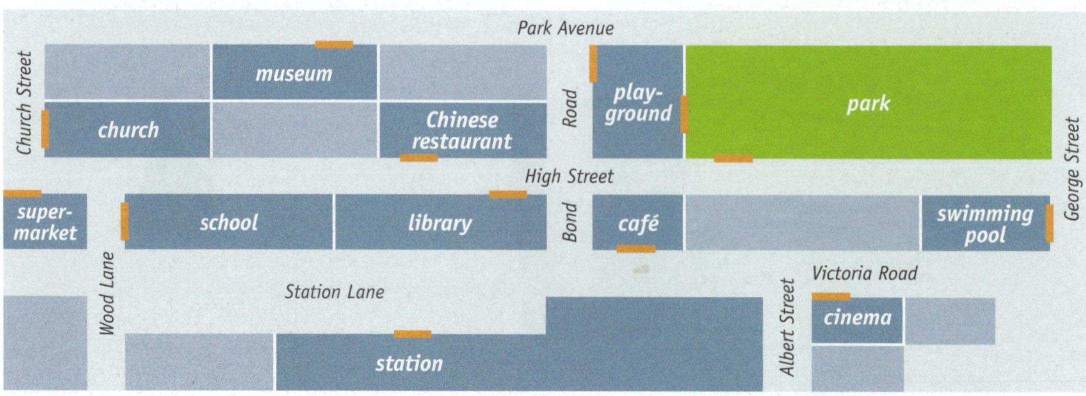

= entrance

P4 Looking back

7R p. 183

**What do you remember? Look at number 6 again.
Ask and answer questions with a partner.**

1. Did Rob and George go shopping together?
2. Did Rob reach George on his mobile?
3. Did the girls have Rob's mobile number?
4. Did Gillian phone Rob?
5. Did Rob walk past Madame Tussauds?
6. Did Caroline have a map?
7. …

Yes, he / she did.

Yes, they did.

No, he / she didn't.

No, they didn't.

P5 Say it in English

How to … help out p. 176

Match the German and the English sentences.

Wie sagst du einem englischen Touristen bei einer Führung durch deinen Heimatort, …

1. dass er / sie sich etwas angucken soll?
2. was er / sie auf der linken Seite sieht?
3. was dein Lieblingsort in der Stadt ist?
4. wie teuer eine Eintrittskarte ist?
5. dass sich etwas auf der rechten Seite befindet?
6. dass die Führung nun zu Ende ist?

A. A ticket costs …
B. On your right there is …
C. Take a look at …
D. On your left you can see …
E. This is the end of our tour.
F. My favourite place in town is …

P6 Can you help?

How to … help out p. 176

**You are at a tube station in London.
A German tourist is looking at this sign
and doesn't understand everything on it.
Tell him / her what it is about in German.**

Dort steht, dass …

Sie müssen …

… ist nicht erlaubt.

P7 An animal quiz

a) What are the animals?

1. It is small with grey, white or brown fur. It has got a tail. It can run fast. It is scared of cats.
2. It is long and thin with little black eyes. It doesn't have legs or fur. People often hate it.
3. It has got brown fur and long legs. It jumps around a lot. It carries its babies in a special pocket.

wordbank Animals p. 157

b) Now make a quiz for your partner.

P8 Which animal is it?

wordbank Animals p. 157

3R p. 180

Work with a partner. Your partner thinks of his / her favourite animal. Ask questions to find out about the animal.

Is it big / small / dangerous / … ?

Yes, it is. / No, it isn't.

Does it have four legs / a long nose / … ?

Yes, it does. / No, it doesn't.

Can it jump / swim / fly / … ?

Yes, it can. / No, it can't.

P9 Rhyming pairs

a) Find the rhyming pairs.

zoo • strong • wild • nose • ear • cage • now • street • house • walk • think • park • took • catch • more

zoo – shoe

here • how • mouse • door • talk • child • dark • toes • pink • page • match • shoe • wrong • book • feet

L 1.18

b) Listen and check your pairs.

P10 The London tiger

Look at number 10 again. Right or wrong? Correct what's wrong.

1. Gillian's mother is at the supermarket.
2. Gillian is listening to the news.
3. The newsreader is talking about the tigers in London Zoo.
4. The police are looking for a tiger now.
5. The keeper went to the tiger's cage at 5.35 pm.
6. The tiger is always tired after its meal.
7. It is eating its lunch.

P11 The animals' holidays

2R + 4R p. 179 – 181

Look at the pictures. What do the animals normally do and what are they doing now?

1. The tiger usually **stays** in its cage but now it **is walking** around London.
2. The giraffe normally ... (drink / water) but today it is drinking cocktails on the beach.
3. The rabbit usually sits in a field but now it ... (fly / to Mexico).
4. The turtle normally walks on the ground but at the moment it ... (go / inline skating).
5. The monkey usually ... (eat / in its cage) but today it is eating in a snack bar.
6. The penguin normally swims in the swimming pool but now it ... (play / football).

P12 London Zoo

How to ... help out p 176

Your friend doesn't speak English. Tell him / her about London Zoo in German.

News (230) ▾ Favourites ▾

LONDON ZOO NEEDS FRIENDS LIKE YOU!

Adopt an animal

When London Zoo opened its doors in 1828, it was not like a zoo today. The cages were very different. For example, there were grass huts for African animals. Many of the 12,000 animals in London Zoo today were born in zoos. They do not know Africa, Asia, America or the North Pole. London Zoo also has some very rare animals: the Komodo dragon, for example, or the tiger and the Asian lion.

A zoo has always got money problems. You can adopt an animal at London Zoo for a year. For £20 you can adopt a guinea pig, a hamster, a mouse or a rabbit, a gecko or a small snake. You can share bigger animals with other people: the food for a giraffe is £1,500 - for a tiger it is £3,000.

M1 More London sights

a) Look at the tips for sightseeing in London on pages 34 – 35. Read them again and collect adjectives and phrases from the texts that make a place sound interesting.

enjoy an exciting afternoon; …

WB M1 p. 31

b) Choose one of the sights below and look at the information. Use adjectives and phrases from a) to write a short text about them. Present it to the class.

Westminster Abbey
- large and famous church
- William and Kate got married here
- many kings and queens are buried here

Harrods
- biggest department store in Europe
- sells everything
- 35,000 people visit every day

Arsenal museum
- in the stadium in North London
- see shirts, caps, medals from former players
- do a tour of the stadium

M2 Talking about your home town

a) Look at the photo. What can you say about the building? Perhaps you know where it is.

L 1.19 S 5

b) Listen to Oleg talking about his city. What did you understand?

c) Listen again and find out:
- What does Oleg like about his city?
- What doesn't he like?
- What sights does he mention?

Take notes.

WB M2 – M3 p. 32

d) Compare your notes with a partner.

How to … give a talk p. 169

e) Prepare a short talk about YOUR village / town / city. Present it to the class.

M3 At the Sherlock Holmes Museum

wordbank People p. 155

a) **Look at the picture and describe the man in it. What do you know about him? Make notes.**

b) **Now read about the children's visit to the Sherlock Holmes Museum. Add any new information about Holmes to your notes from a).**

George: Look, there he is. Hi Rob!
Rob: Well, it's not my fault. You didn't answer your mobile!
Caroline: Let's forget about it now and go into the museum.
Rob: So this is the house that belonged to Sherlock Holmes!
Gillian: Don't be stupid! Sherlock Holmes isn't a real person. The writer Sir Arthur Conan Doyle created Sherlock Holmes. Sherlock Holmes lived at 221b Baker Street in Doyle's stories.
George: Wow, these stairs are really dark and narrow.
Caroline: And the lights are not very strong.
Rob: This looks like Sherlock Holmes' study.
George: Yeah, and this must be Doctor Watson's medical bag.
Caroline: And here's the bedroom. Look at all these photos of the criminals who lived at that time.
Gillian: Come upstairs! You must look at the man with a snake around his head. And over there you can see a dead body in a coffin. And all these weapons. This is better than the London Dungeon!
Caroline: Ugh! That's horrible. Look at this poor man in a cage! And this one is falling through a trapdoor.
George: They are all people who Sherlock Holmes met in the stories. Look! It says so in the brochure.
Gillian: Let's go to the museum shop. Perhaps Rob can find a souvenir to take home to Manchester.
Rob: Good idea! Perhaps I can get a magnifying glass or …

c) **Match the sentence parts about Sherlock Holmes and the museum. There is one more ending than you need.**

1 Sir Arthur Conan Doyle is the man
2 The house in Baker Street is now
3 One of the rooms is
4 The museum shows
5 You can see people

A a museum.
B who Sherlock Holmes met in the stories.
C who lived at 221b Baker Street.
D criminals from that time.
E who wrote stories about Sherlock Holmes.
F Sherlock Holmes' study.

d) **Find out more about Sherlock Holmes or Sir Arthur Conan Doyle or the museum. You can ask your parents, go to the library or search the Internet. Present your information to the class.**

WWW

M4 On the radio

L 1.20 S 6

How to ... listen p. 167

M4 p. 33

a) Listen to two people from London, John and Hilda. They are talking about the runaway tiger on the radio. Find out:
- Where did they see the tiger?
- What did they do?
- How did they feel?

What else can you understand? Take notes in a grid.

	where?	what?	how?	other information
John	...	...		
Hilda	...			

b) Compare your notes with a partner.

M5 Animal information

a) Look at the information about different animals in London Zoo. What information is new for you? What do you find interesting?

GIRAFFES
FROM: Africa
FEEDING TIME: 2.45 pm
EAT: leaves
LIVE: 25 years
BABIES: one or two in their life

TORTOISES
FROM: Galapagos Islands
FEEDING TIME: 10 am
EAT: vegetables, grass
LIVE: 150 years
BABIES: 20 every year

PENGUINS
FROM: South America
FEEDING TIME: 3.30 pm
EAT: fish
LIVE: 20 years
BABIES: one every year

MEERKATS
FROM: Africa
FEEDING TIME: 1.15 pm
EAT: insects
LIVE: 6 years
BABIES: 10 every year

M5 p. 33/34

b) Work with a partner. One of you is a tourist, the other works at the information point in London Zoo. Ask questions and give answers.

M6 Goldie the golden eagle

a) Look at the pictures. What do you think happened? Put the pictures in the correct order.

1

2

3

4

b) Now read the newspaper article. Were you right in a)?

How to ... read p. 168

WB M6 p. 34

28th February 2012 **THE DAILY POST** 50 p

LONDON ZOO: THE GREAT ESCAPE!

On this day ... in 1965, Goldie the golden eagle escaped from his home at London Zoo. A keeper was cleaning Goldie's cage, when Goldie flew away. Maybe the keeper left the door open. Goldie left his good friend Regina behind – but he was free!

Goldie the escaped eagle is looking at ducks in Regent's Park

He went to Regent's Park and he visited Tottenham Court Road, Euston and Camden Town, too. Lots of Londoners came to see him in the park. The people at London Zoo tried very hard to get Goldie back. They even asked the British Navy to help.

Goldie was happy. He spent time in the park and avoided capture ... until he got very hungry. He saw a tasty rabbit and went to eat it ... but it was a trap! A keeper jumped on Goldie and finally caught him. After 12 days of freedom in London, the keepers took Goldie home – back to London Zoo. He had a great holiday and was happy to see his friend Regina again!

Naughty Goldie escaped again in December 1965, but only for 4 days this time.

c) Tell the story in your own words.

d) Do you know any other animals who escaped from people's homes or a zoo?

WWW

CAMDEN CHRONICLE
LEARN ENGLISH THE CAMDEN WAY

DID YOU GET IT ALL?

- What can you do on the London Eye?
- How did Leanne, Rebecca and Daniel get to the Tower of London?
- Where is the Sherlock Holmes Museum?
- What building is in Luxborough Street?
- Why did Gillian ask her mum to close the door?
- What did the tiger do in Kensington Gardens?
- How did the tiger get back to the zoo?
- What is Sam's favourite animal?

GOOD TO KNOW ...

In Großbritannien herrscht Linksverkehr. Touristen sehen oft automatisch in die falsche Richtung. Als Warnung steht in London daher meist *Look right* auf den Straßen eines Fußgängerübergangs.

Geraldine Giraffe
The longest ever woolly scarf was worn by Geraldine Giraffe. Around her neck the scarf she wound, but it still trailed upon the ground.

Ten tiny tigers take twelve tomatoes to town.

Seven sweet snakes sang some stupid songs.

There was a young woman from Riga,
who smiled as she rode on a tiger.
They came back from the ride,
with the woman inside,
and the smile on the face of the tiger.

An animal quiz
What can you see here?

1. 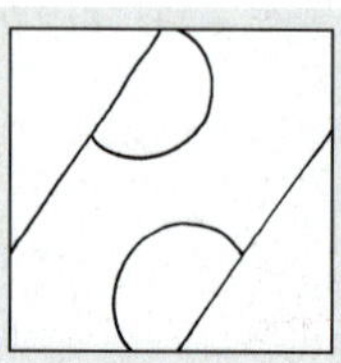
2. 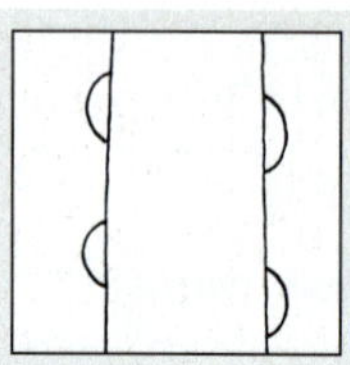
3. 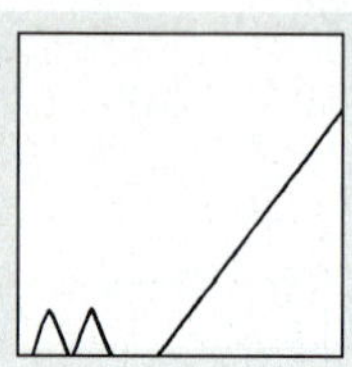

1. A giraffe in front of a mirror.
2. A cat going up a tree.
3. Someone with a dog.

3

THEME 3

DREAMS

In diesem *Theme* ...

» lernst du, über die Zukunft und deine Zukunftsträume zu sprechen.
» berichtest du über Berufe und Berufswünsche.
» erzählst du von deinen Vorbildern und Helden.
» beschäftigst du dich mit Robin Hood.

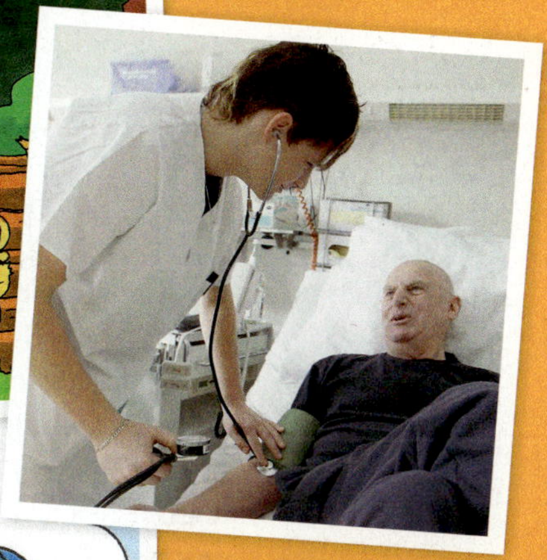

1 Star signs

WB 1 p. 35

a) What is your star sign?

b) Do you read horoscopes?
Do you believe in them?

2 A phone call

a) Look at the pictures. Who can you see? Where are they? What are they talking about?

L 1.21 S 7

b) Listen to the story. Were you right in a)?

How to ... listen p. 167

WB 2–4 p. 35/36

Caroline: Hello?
Rajiv: Hi Caroline, it's Rajiv. What are you doing?
Caroline: Hi Rajiv. Nothing special. I'm looking at some magazines.
Rajiv: Anything new or exciting?
Caroline: No, not really. But wait – here's a page with horoscopes.
Rajiv: Oh, no! I don't believe in horoscopes. They are for old ladies.
Caroline: Come on! What star sign are you?
Rajiv: Aquarius.
Caroline: OK. Now listen: This is your lucky month. Take part in a competition and you'll get a big surprise.

Rajiv: Wow! There's this maths competition at school next week. Maybe I should take part and I'll be the winner.
Caroline: Wait, there's more. Your horoscope also says that you'll be a very good boy this month. You'll help your parents in the shop every day, you'll always do your homework and you won't have any problems.
Rajiv: Ha, ha, very funny! Now it's my turn. I'm Rajiv, the best fortune-teller in the world. Are you ready?
Caroline: Yeah, tell me my fortune. Will I be happy? Where will I live?

Rajiv: Well, you'll marry a tall, dark, good-looking man and you'll have two children and lots of pets but you won't have a pony.

Caroline: Children? That's stupid. I won't marry anyone. I'll find a good job – I'll be a doctor one day. And I'll have a lot of fun with my friends.

Rajiv: Are you sure? I know that I'll find a nice woman. And I'll have a fast car. I'll be a famous guitar player and I'll be rich …

c) Listen again and read along. What does Rajiv say about horoscopes?

3 Ideas about the future

Look at number 2 again. What are Caroline's and Rajiv's ideas about the future?

10 p. 185
P2 + P3 p. 66
M1 p. 70
WB 5 p. 37

I will / won't …

be rich •
be a doctor •
have a fast car •
…

I will / won't …

4 Fortune-telling

a) Think of eight different fortunes and write them down in a list. Here are some ideas.

b) Make a fortune-teller and play this game. Tell your classmates their fortune.

1. You will be poor but happy.
2. You will be a pop star.
3. You won't be famous but you will have many friends.
4. …

10 p. 185
WB 6 p. 37

5 Dream jobs?

wordbank
Jobs
p. 158

a) Look at the photos. What do these people do?

A pilot flies planes.

firefighter

bus driver

pilot

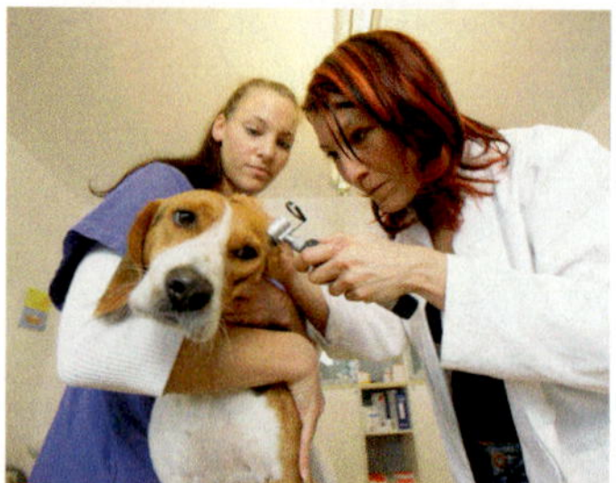
vet

cook

hairdresser

gardener

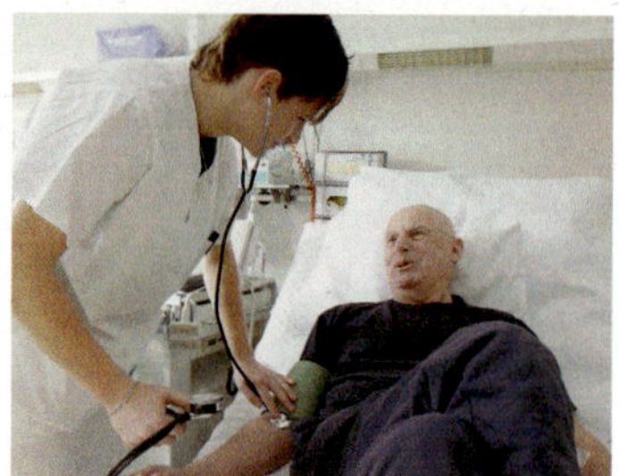
nurse

shop assistant

car technician

builder

police officer

cut and style people's hair • take care of ill people • repair cars • sell things • fight fires • cook meals in a restaurant • drive people • help people in trouble and catch gangsters • work with flowers and plants • build things • take care of ill animals • fly planes

WB 7+8
p. 38

b) What jobs are YOU interested in?

c) **Walk around the classroom and interview your classmates about their future jobs. Take notes.**

What will you be when you grow up?

I think I'll be a police officer. Then I'll catch gangsters.

Perhaps I'll be a / an …

How to … work with others p. 174
P1 p. 66
WB 9 p. 39

6 I'll live in Hollywood

a) **Listen to Jason talking about the future. What will his future job be?**

b) **Listen again and take notes. Then talk about Jason.**

Jason
- will …
- won't …
- …

L 1.22
How to … listen p. 167
10 p. 185

7 YOUR ideas about the future

Collect ideas and talk about your future.

I think Perhaps / Maybe I hope I'm sure …	I'll … I won't …

… work as a / an …

… have a horse.

… be my own boss.

… live in a big city.

… have a robot to work for me at home.

…

… fly to the moon.

wordbank Jobs p. 158
10 p. 185
P4 p. 67
M3 + M4 p. 70/71
WB 10 p. 39

8 Whatever will be

L 1.23 S 8

a) Listen to the song. What do you think "Qué será" is in English? What language is it?

b) Listen again and sing along.

When I was just a little girl,
I asked my mother: "What will I be?
Will I be pretty? Will I be rich?"
Here's what she said to me:

"Qué será, será.
Whatever will be, will be.
The future's not ours to see.
Qué será, será.
What will be, will be."

When I grew up and fell in love,
I asked my sweetheart: "What lies ahead?
Will we have rainbows, day after day?"
Here's what my sweetheart said:

"Qué será, será.
Whatever will be, will be.
The future's not ours to see.
Qué será, será.
What will be, will be."

Now I have children of my own,
They ask their mother: "What will I be?
Will I be handsome? Will I be rich?"
I tell them tenderly:

"Qué será, será.
Whatever ..."

P5 + P6 P
p. 67
M2 M
p. 70

c) Who asks the questions in the song? Who answers them?

a teacher • a mother • a girl • a lover • ...

9 Choose an activity

portfolio

You can ...

- think about the next two weeks. Write down what you think will happen. Give your notes to your teacher. After two weeks you will get them back. Were you right?

Kevin
I will play football.
We will visit my grandma.
I won't go to the zoo.
I will do my homework.

Michelle
I will go to the cinema.
I won't eat popcorn.
We will win the football match.
I won't be angry with my sister.

How to ...
give a talk
p. 169

- make a poster about your future in 20 years. Present it in class. Think about:
  - what you will be or do
  - where you will live
  - what the world will be like
  - ...

- look at number 2 again and act out your own scene.

10 Daydreams

a) Look at the pictures. What are Charlie's daydreams?

b) Now listen. Were you right in a)?

L 1.24

c) Read about Charlie's daydreams. Who are his heroes?

How to … read p. 168

WB 11 p. 40

Charlie likes reading and watching films. Then he starts to daydream …
When he watches a western, he wants to be a cowboy. "One day I'll ride horses. They run really fast! I'd love to live in New Mexico and look after cattle."
When he reads his Donald Duck comics, he wants to be rich like Donald's uncle Scrooge. "I'll work hard and make lots of money. Then I'll buy a chocolate factory."
When he watches science fiction films, he wants to be an astronaut. "Then perhaps I'll be the first man on Jupiter."
When he reads his sports magazines, he wants to be a famous football player. "I want to play really well and score a lot of goals. Then Arsenal will want to buy me for a billion pounds."
Sometimes he reads books about heroes from the past. "Robin Hood. He was a cool guy! He took money from the rich and gave it to the poor people. When I grow up, perhaps I'll be a hero like Robin Hood. It would be great to live in the forest and have adventures."

d) Which of Charlie's heroes do YOU like best? Why?

I like Uncle Scrooge best because …

e) Who is YOUR hero or favourite person? Why? Tell your partner about him / her.

P P9 p. 68

M M5 + M6 p. 72/73

WB 12 p. 40

My hero / favourite person is …

He / She lives in …

He / She is …

He / She can …

I like him / her because he / she …

11 Robin Hood

a) Read the story.

One day the Sheriff of Nottingham took a lot of money from an old farmer. Robin Hood and his men were in Sherwood Forest …

But then the Sheriff had an idea …

A moment later they found the Sheriff.

b) Find out who did what. Robin Hood • the farmer • the Sheriff • Robin Hood and his men

P7 p. 68
WB 13–14 p. 40/41

1. ... took a lot of money.
2. ... shouted loudly for help.
3. ... had an idea.
4. But ... caught the Sheriff easily.
5. ... was very angry.
6. ... got on his horse and rode home quickly.
7. ... gave the old woman some money.
8. ... took back his money happily.

LAND & LEUTE

Robin Hood

Viele Geschichten werden über die Abenteuer von Robin Hood erzählt. Es gibt Lieder, Romane und Filme über ihn. Robin Hoods echter Name soll Robert Earl of Huntingdon gewesen sein. Er lebte im 12. Jahrhundert und war ein Untertan von König Richard Löwenherz. Als der König das Land für einige Zeit verließ, regierte sein Bruder Prinz John. Er war sehr habgierig und nahm den Anhängern von Richard Löwenherz ihr Land und ihr Geld weg. Da sammelte Robin Hood eine Gruppe von Freunden um sich. Sie wollten den Verrätern das Geld wieder wegnehmen, um es den Armen zu schenken. Bald waren Robin Hood und seine Freunde berühmt. Jeder erkannte sie an ihren grünen Jacken und ihren Pfeilen und Bogen. Sie lebten gemeinsam und gut versteckt in einem Wald namens Sherwood Forest bei Nottingham. Noch heute steht der Name Robin Hood für Gerechtigkeit und Mut.

Finde heraus, wo Nottingham und der Sherwood Forest liegen.
Welche Geschichten oder Filme über Robin Hood kennst du?

12 The story

What did Robin tell his people in Sherwood Forest?
Use the keywords to finish the story.

P12 P p. 69
M7 + M8 M p. 73

1. Sheriff – took money – old farmer
2. I – wanted to – get the money back
3. Sheriff – took clothes – old woman
4. old woman – told – me
5. My men and I – found – Sheriff
6. I – took money and clothes – Sheriff
7. Sheriff – rode away – no clothes
8. I – gave clothes and money – old woman
9. I – gave money back – old farmer

13 Robin's adventure – a dramatic reading

L 1.25
13 p. 187

a) Listen to these people from the story. How do they talk?

Robin Hood The Sheriff The farmer The old woman	talks speaks shouts	angrily. loudly. happily. excitedly. quickly.

b) Look at these sentences. Say each sentence in five different ways: angrily, loudly, happily, excitedly, quickly.

There's Robin Hood.

This is my forest.

You helped us to catch the Sheriff.

Don't worry, my friend.

Ha, ha!

c) **In groups of five practise reading the story in number 11.**
- Think about how your character feels. Is he / she happy, sad or angry?
- Then try to learn your role by heart.

How to ... work with others p. 174

14 Do this carefully

a) **Words like *angrily*, *quickly* or *loudly* are called adverbs.**
What are the adverbs of these adjectives?

angry – angrily | excited – ... | easy – ... | quiet – ... | slow – ...

b) **Some adverbs are special, for example the adverbs of *fast*, *hard* and *good*.**
Can you find them in the story in number 10?

c) **When do you use adverbs? Tell your classmates in German.**

13 p. 187
How to ... work with grammar p. 173
P P8 + P10 + P11 p. 68/69
WB 15 + 16 p. 42

15 Choose an activity

You can ...

- **record your dramatic reading from number 13.**
- **work in groups and act out the story from number 11.**
  You will need:
  - a narrator,
  - people to play the characters,
  - people to make the noises.

  Record your play and then listen to it.
- **make a WANTED poster for Robin Hood.**
- **find out more about Robin Hood. Look in books, watch films or look on the Internet. Present your information to the class.**

portfolio
How to ... talk p. 170
How to ... give a talk p. 169
WB test yourself p. 43/44

P1 Jobs, jobs, jobs

Name the people's jobs. This person …

1. … helps cats when they can't get down from a tree.
2. … takes care of your pet when it is ill.
3. … uses his or her hands and tools to build things.
4. … works in the kitchen of a restaurant.
5. … drives lots of children to school every day.
6. … often wears a uniform and catches criminals.
7. … flies you on holiday to far away places.
8. … helps you when you want to buy something in a shop.
9. … helps your father or mother with their car.
10. … works in a park and looks after the plants and trees in it.
11. … washes and cuts your hair.
12. … looks after you when you are in hospital.

P2 Sound check

L 1.26

a) Listen and repeat the words. Is it 'w' /w/ or 'v' /v/?

■isit ■ill ■ait ■iew ■ery ■ork ■egetable ■oman

b) Make two lists. Write the words in the correct list.

c) Do you know more words with 'w' and 'v'? Add them to your lists. Then read your lists to a partner.

/v/	/w/
visit	…
…	…

P3 When I am 25

10
p. 185

a) Look at Karla and George. Write down what they think about their future. Use *will* or *won't*.

Karla: I think I will/won't …

George: I think I will/won't …

b) And YOU? Draw your ideas and write about them.

P4 What will happen?

10 + 12 p. 185/186

a) Write about your future.

1. What will you buy when you have your first job?
2. When will you get married?
3. How many children will you have?
4. Where will you live when you are 25?
5. What car will you have?
6. What will you do on this day in 5 years?

1. I will buy …

b) Ask your partner and find out about his / her future. Take turns.

P5 Rap-a-dap-a-do

11 p. 186

Make a rap about YOUR future.
First think of questions about the future.

Will I	be live in have meet travel to	New York? happy? my dream partner? a film star? a motorbike? …

Then work with a partner. Ask and answer your questions. Take turns.

P6 A horoscope

How to … help out p. 176

Read this horoscope from a teen magazine. A friend who doesn't speak English wants to know what it says. Tell him / her in German.

GEMINI
21 MAY – 20 JUNE

This is the perfect month for new ideas and new projects. Get into action and your days will be full of excitement. Also look into the faces of the people around you. Are there any sad people? You are just the right person they can talk to. It will help them a lot and it will also put a smile on your face. Yellow is the colour of the month. It will bring luck and happiness and you will be cheerful the whole month.

P7 Words, words, words

a) **Look at these words. Write them with your finger on the desk or on your partner's back. Can he / she guess the words?**

forest • worry • clothes • recognize • woman • catch • angry • remember • loud • steal

b) **Now spell the words for your partner. Can he / she write them down correctly? Use other words from this Theme, too.**

P8 Tongue twisters

L 1.27

Listen to the tongue twisters. Then say them yourself.

Can Charlie catch Caroline's crazy chocolate cake carefully?

One-one was a race horse,
Two-two was one, too.
One-one won one race,
Two-two won one, too.

P9 YOUR favourite person

wordbank
People p. 154/155

a) **Copy the grid. Then read the words in the box and fill them in. Try to find more words for your grid.**

What is a favourite person like?	What does a favourite person do?
clever	helps others
…	…

clever • funny • helps others • runs fast • cool • works hard • rich • happy • sings well • goes on adventures • …

portfolio

b) **Write about your favourite person. You can add a photo or draw a picture, too.**

My favourite person is my cousin Paula. She lives in Darmstadt. She is funny and she can play the guitar really well. I like her because she always has lots of good ideas.

P10 A word snake

a) Find 14 adverbs in the snake.

13 p. 187

b) Find the adjectives for the adverbs and write them down like this:

quickly – quick, …

P11 You can do this easily

a) Read the sentences and say how these people are doing things.

13 p. 187

carefully • dangerously • slowly • fast • hard • loudly

1. The man is driving XX.
2. The boy is running XX.
3. The young man is working XX.
4. The girl is walking XX.
5. The old man is moving XX.
6. The dog is barking XX.

b) Find more sentences. You can do this crazily!

The cat is singing beautifully.
…

P12 The Major Oak

Look at this information from the Internet. What do you learn about the Major Oak? Tell a classmate in German.

How to … help out p. 176

News (230) ▾ Favourites ▾

The Major Oak in Sherwood Forest was Robin Hood's favourite tree. He hid from his enemies inside the Major Oak. He and his men also slept there.
The oak tree is between 800 and 1,000 years old and is England's most famous tree. The footpath that leads up to the Major Oak is called Robin Hood Way.

M1 Caroline's horoscope

L 1.28 S 9

How to … listen p. 167

WB M1 p. 47

a) Listen to Caroline. She is talking to her friend Claire about her horoscope. Find out:
- Does Caroline like her horoscope?
- What about Claire?

b) Listen again and take notes on their ideas about the future.

	Caroline	Claire
ideas about the future	…	…

c) Compare your notes with a partner.

M2 A horoscope for a friend

How to … write p. 171

portfolio

WB M2 + M3 p. 47/48

Write a horoscope for a friend. Look at the horoscope in P6 and the horoscopes on page 145 for help.

M3 My spaceship

L 1.29

a) Be very quiet. Close your eyes and listen.

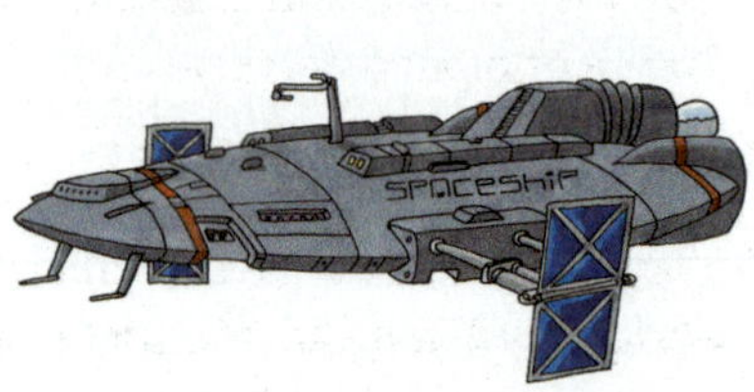

b) Now you have time to draw and write about your trip as an astronaut.

M4 A timewatch

a) What do you think life will be like in the year 3013? Talk to a partner.

b) Read about Cerys and her trip to the year 3013. What do you learn from the text?

How to ... read p. 168

L 1.30

BANG! Cerys looked at her timewatch. Year 3013. She looked around excitedly. Where were the robots, the spaceships, the aliens in silver clothes? She felt disappointed – there weren't any. She was in a strange, quiet forest. Each tree was taller than a skyscraper and there were tree houses on each one. Hundreds of long thin wires went between the houses. Suddenly a boy ran past her.

"Wait!" Cerys said. "Where are you going?"
"It's time for the Old Car Race, of course!" said the boy. "A thousand years ago everyone had a car, but it was bad for our planet. So now we go around with zip wires between the tree houses. It's great fun and the world is much greener and quieter now. Each year we think about the old times and we have a race in the forest. I'm in the race but I don't understand old cars! So I'm quite worried."

At home, Cerys' hobby was go-karting and she wanted to have an adventure.
"I think it's your lucky day", she said to the boy. "I come from the twenty-first century and I know a lot about old cars. I can help you. Would you like that?"

At first the boy looked very surprised but then he smiled. "We haven't got much time. Follow me!" They ran through the forest and soon they were at the race. Cerys was amazed – there was so much to see! Lots of people wanted to have lunch before the race. In a small tree house next to the road, there was food for everyone. But this food wasn't normal. Cerys saw blue bananas, flower-flavoured milkshakes and 'leaf pizza'. She wanted to try all of it but the boy said "We've only got five minutes! Come on, we have to go to our car."

When Cerys saw the old car, she was a bit scared because it looked dangerous. It was brown and dirty, the windows were broken and the wheels were flat.

"Isn't it beautiful?" said the boy happily. "I think we're going to win. OK, you're the driver. Let's go!" Cerys looked at her timewatch. One minute to go. Should she take a chance? It was now or never! So she got into the car and the adventure began.

c) Read again and complete the sentences.

WB M4 p. 48

1. Cerys felt disappointed because ...
2. The trees around her were ...
3. Instead of cars the people ...
4. Once a year the people ...
5. For lunch they could have ...
6. The car Cerys got into was ...

d) Imagine YOU have a timewatch. What year do you want to travel to? Then write about what you can see there, whom you meet and what else you experience there.

How to ... write p. 171

portfolio

M5 Big heroes?

a) What do you think of when you hear the word 'hero'? Collect ideas in a word web.

How to ... read p. 168

b) Read the website and find out about the children's heroes.

News (230) ▾ Favourites ▾

Sarah

Sarah
I love science fiction stories. They're really good adventure stories. I'd like to be an astronaut and fly in a spaceship. It won't be an easy life because astronauts live dangerously. I'd like to explore the universe, find new planets and meet strange aliens. Astronauts like Buzz Aldrin are my heroes.

Murat

Murat
I've got two big heroes. The first is Tarzan. He lived in Africa and protected the jungle and the animals in it. Well, in books and films he did. There are lots of real people who really do that. I'd like to live in a rainforest in South America when I grow up. Then I can protect the rainforest, too. My second hero is Terry Pratchett. He's an author and he writes the best books in the world. When I started school, I didn't like reading. But then I discovered his books and became a big fan.

Antonia

Antonia
I've got two heroes and they're both real. One of them is Amelia Earhart. She was a pilot in the 1930s. She was the first woman to fly solo across the Atlantic and the Pacific. She was very brave. My other hero is my aunt Ulrike. She is a nurse and works in a children's hospital. She looks after kids who are seriously ill. Although it's a really hard job, Ulrike loves doing it.

Oleg

Oleg
I'm a sports fan. I enjoy skateboarding, riding my bike and swimming. I also play basketball a lot and often watch it on TV. There are lots of great American basketball players but my favourite player is Vitaly Fridzon. He's from Russia and with his team he won the bronze medal in the London 2012 Olympic Games. So I think Vitaly Fridzon is a kind of hero for me.

c) Read again and match the heroes' names with the pictures.

1 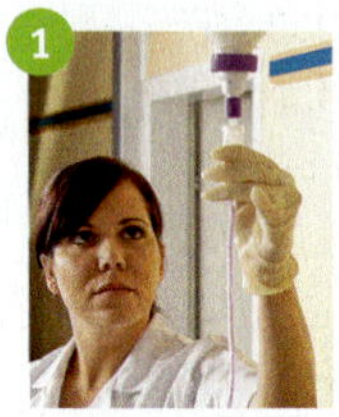
2 
3 
4 
5 
6 

WB M5 p. 49

d) Why do the children like the heroes?

M6 An interview with Karla

Last week there was an interview with Karla for the school magazine.

a) Listen to the interview. What is Karla talking about?

her favourite pop star • her favourite film star • her favourite sportsperson

L 1.31 S 10

WB M6 p. 49

b) Listen again:
- What do you learn about Karla's favourite person?
- What do you find interesting? Why? Talk to a partner.

M7 Supermouse

a) Look at the comic strip. What can you see? Talk to a partner.

b) Write speech bubbles and captions for the comic strip.

M8 Presenting a hero

a) Think about a book or a film that you like. Is there a person or an animal in it that is a kind of hero for you?

b) What do you want to tell your class about your hero? Make notes. Then practise what you want to say.

c) Bring a picture of your hero and show it to the class. Then use your notes to talk about your hero.

Matilda
- book by British writer Roald Dahl
- also a film and a musical
- Matilda: very intelligent girl, started reading at the age of three
- parents not interested in her, watch TV all day
- headteacher at Matilda's school hates clever girls

WB M7 p. 50

How to ... give a talk p. 169

CAMDEN CHRONICLE
LEARN ENGLISH THE CAMDEN WAY

DID YOU GET IT ALL?

- What star sign is Rajiv?
- Who says she will be a doctor one day?
- Who works with flowers and plants?
- What job does Jason dream of?
- What is the name of Donald Duck's rich uncle?
- Where did Robin Hood and his men live?
- What did the Sheriff of Nottingham take from the farmer?
- What was the Sheriff of Nottingham wearing when Robin Hood found him?

GOOD TO KNOW ...

Freitag, der 13. gilt in Deutschland, aber auch in Großbritannien, als Unglückstag. Abergläubische Menschen trauen sich an diesem Tag nicht aus dem Haus. In Deutschland verbreitet auch eine schwarze Katze, die einem von links über den Weg läuft, bei Abergläubischen Angst und Schrecken. In Großbritannien dagegen gelten schwarze Katzen allgemein als Glücksbringer.

I WANNA BE A STAR

I wanna be a star.
I wanna go far.
I wanna drive around
in a big red car.
I said yeah yeah yeah
I wanna be a star.

I wanna be a hit.
I wanna be it.
I wanna see my name
all brightly lit.
I said yeah yeah yeah
I wanna be a hit.

I wanna be the scene.
I wanna be on screen.
I wanna make the
cover of a magazine.
I said yeah yeah yeah
I wanna be a scene.

I wanna be a star.
I wanna be a star.
But I've only got a job
in a burger bar –
so far ...

Op1 The Concert at Coldy

a) Listen to the story and read along.

L 1.32

It was a dark and cold evening. The large clock at Coldy School showed 7 pm. The children in the choir were waiting nervously in the warm classroom. They had to learn the difficult words of their school song before 7.30 pm, the start of the concert.
"Students of Coldy, young and old. Good education is better than gold ... What's the next line? I'm so bored," said Bobby. "Can we play a game or something?"
"How about hide-and-seek?" said Louis. "All the corridors and classrooms are dark and empty, it would be so fun!"
"Yeah, that sounds like a cool idea," said Bobby. "OK, you can hide and I will count. Ready? ONE – TWO – THREE ..."
Louis ran out of the classroom and Bobby counted up to one hundred.
"NINETY-NINE – ONE HUNDRED! Coming, ready or not!"

Bobby ran out of the classroom to find Louis. The corridors were dark and quiet and soon Bobby was lost. He didn't know this old part of the school.
"Louis? Louis? OK, game over. I'm scared and I want to go back to the concert. Louis?"
No answer. Suddenly there was singing. "Oh no!" thought Bobby. "The concert has started!" He went towards the music. After a minute he found an old wooden door. The singing was behind it. "I'm sure this isn't usually the door to the concert hall," thought Bobby. But he opened it anyway.

The door led to a very old classroom, full of cobwebs and shadows. There was a cold wind and then Bobby saw something terrible: a choir of ghostly children in school hats and ties. They were singing in high, spooky voices. *"Students of Coldy, young and old. Good education is better than gold. Look back through time and you will see how important your days at school can be."*
The ghosts looked at Bobby coldly, and then he saw the most scary thing of all. He knew one of the ghosts ... it was Louis!
"Louis!" cried Bobby. "What's happened? Is this a joke?" But Louis the ghost only sang and the ghosts walked slowly towards Bobby. *"Never run around in your school at night. If you do, the ghosts will come out to bite."*

It was too much for Bobby and he ran out of the room. He heard the singing behind him but soon he was back with the other children in the warm, bright classroom. But Louis wasn't there. "Have you seen Louis?" Bobby asked his friends. They all said no. Bobby wanted to speak with friends about the ghost choir but at that moment Mrs Smale the music teacher came in. "Time to sing, boys and girls! This way to the concert hall!"
On the way to the concert hall Bobby saw a black and white photo on the wall. It was from the year 1863. And there, in the school hat and tie, was his best friend Louis.

b) The story has four parts. Choose a good heading for each part.

An old photo • A choir of ghosts • Getting lost • The music teacher • Getting ready for the concert • Cobwebs and shadows

Op2 How to make a story interesting

a) **Look at these two texts. What is different?**

1 It was evening. The clock at Coldy School showed 7 pm. The children in the choir were waiting in the classroom. They had to learn the words of their school song before 7.30 pm, the start of the concert.

2 It was a dark and cold evening. The large clock at Coldy School showed 7 pm. The children in the choir were waiting nervously in the warm classroom. They had to learn the difficult words of their school song before 7.30 pm, the start of the concert.

b) **Which words make the second text more interesting? Write them down. What kind of words are these?**

c) **Which words describe these people or things? Collect ideas.**

my friend:
frightened • clever • silly • ...

ghost:
white • angry • strange • ...

house:
spooky • cold • empty • ...

weather:
rainy • dark • grey • ...

d) **Read the beginning of this story and make it more interesting. Write an ending to the story, too. These words can help you:**

big • old • black • dark • spooky • cold • bright • old • warm • interesting • loud • strange • slowly • carefully • ...

There was a house in a forest. It was night but there was a light at the window. A woman was sitting by the fire in the living room. She was reading a book. Suddenly the light went out. There was a noise. The woman went to the door, opened it and ...

Op3 A different ending

a) **Read the last part of the story "The Concert at Coldy" in number 1 again. Think of a different ending. Collect ideas with a partner and make notes.**

How to ... write p. 171

b) **Now write YOUR ending.**

c) **Read your ending to the class.**

Op4 YOUR story

Make up a story. You can look at the pictures for ideas.

How to … write p. 171

PLAN IT

- Collect ideas first. Make notes on "who", "where", "when" and "what", for example:

WHO?	WHERE?	WHEN?	WHAT?
- I	- old castle	- last weekend	- weather
- two friends	- dark tower	- two years ago	- noises
- ghosts	- …	- …	- lights
- …			- …

DO IT

- Write your story.
  Here is an example of a beginning:

> Last weekend Julian and Lana got lost on a hiking trip. It was late and the weather was … Suddenly …

- Use adjectives and adverbs to make your story interesting.
- Use *time words* and *linking words*:
  Time words help to show when something happened.
  Linking words help you to connect ideas and sentences.

time words (when?)
last weekend / … • first • then • at … o'clock • in the morning / … • before • after (that) • finally • …

linking words (connect sentences)
and • because • so • but • …

- Think of a good title, too.

How to … talk p. 170

CHECK IT

- Is the English OK?
- Is your story interesting enough for others to read or listen to it?
- Swap stories with a partner and give each other feedback on your texts.
- Edit your story.

PRESENT IT

- Show your story to the class: Read it, record it or put it up in the classroom.

A ghost story – Part one

Last year two poltergeists from London were on holiday in Scotland.

The night was dark and they were tired: "Oh, look. This hotel looks good." "Yes, it does. Let's go in."

A grey ghost was in the hall. "Hello. I'm Mrs MacHowl." "Hello. Do you have a double[1] room for one night?"

"The house is full and only one bedroom is free. It's under the roof[2] but it's cheap."

"It's a terrible mess[3]!" "And it's cold, windy and wet!" "Yes, there's a hole[4] in the roof. That's why the room is so cheap."

"No, thank you, Mrs MacHowl." "We like nice, warm and dry[5] rooms!"

"I'm very sorry. Come into the living room. There's a warm fire and you can meet my other guests[6]."

"This is Mrs Griff. And that is Mrs Mutt." "Nice to meet you. I'm Mo." "And I'm Joe."

"Mrs Mutt is asleep[7], I think." "But she doesn't have a head!" "Oh, she always loses her head after a glass of wine[8]. It's in her bag."

Anna and Tom were outside. "Let's go in here out of the rain[9]. I think the house is empty."

"What was that?" "What?" "There was a noise." "Mrs MacHowl, there are people in the hall!"

"Let's look around the house." "I don't know. I don't think we are alone!" "But no one[10] lives here!" "Really? Then why is it so warm here?"

to be continued ...[11] (page 146)

[1]double – *Doppel-*; [2]roof – *Dach*; [3]mess – *Unordnung*; [4]hole – *Loch*; [5]dry – *trocken*; [6]guest – *Gast*; [7]be asleep – *schlafen*; [8]wine – *Wein*; [9]rain – *Regen*; [10]no one – *keiner, niemand*; [11]to be continued – *Fortsetzung folgt*

THEME 4
CELEBRATIONS

In diesem *Theme* ...
» berichtest du über Feste und Feiern.
» erfährst du etwas über traditionelle Feste und über Feste anderer Kulturen in Großbritannien.
» sprichst du über Pläne und Vorhaben in der Zukunft.
» lernst du, Gegenstände und Personen zu vergleichen.

1 Festivals

a) Look at the pictures of different festivals. What can you see? Then match the pictures with the correct names. Which pictures were easy to match?

New Year's Eve • Halloween • Eid • Christmas • Hanukkah • Easter

In picture A I can see …

I think picture A is …

wordbank
Celebrations
p. 159
Time
p. 160
14R
p. 188
WB 1
p. 51

b) What other celebrations do you know? What festivals do YOU celebrate?

c) What is YOUR favourite festival? Think about it and make notes. Then talk about it with a partner.

What's your favourite festival?

When is it?

How do you celebrate it?

We I …	usually often sometimes …	go to / have a party. have a big meal. visit friends. decorate the house. go to church. set off fireworks. go to bed early / late. wear special clothes. …

How to …
work with others
p. 175

d) Form a double circle in class and tell each other about your favourite festivals.

My favourite festival is … It is in … We usually …

2 Let's celebrate

a) Listen to the people. What are they celebrating?

L 1.33

b) Write down the languages in the order you hear them.

WB 2 p. 51

CHINA

Chinese

TURKEY

Turkish

GREAT BRITAIN

English

ITALY

Italian

RUSSIA

Russian

FRANCE

French

LAND & LEUTE

Traditionelle Feste in Großbritannien

Die meisten Briten feiern Ostern *(Easter)* und Weihnachten *(Christmas)*. Allerdings wird Weihnachten erst am 25. Dezember gefeiert – die Geschenke gibt es morgens. Den Weihnachtsfeiertag am 26. Dezember nennen die Briten *Boxing Day*.

In Großbritannien gibt es auch einen Muttertag *(Mother's Day)*, der jedoch nicht wie bei uns im Mai, sondern im März stattfindet. Wie inzwischen auch in Deutschland, ist der Valentinstag *(Valentine's Day)* am 14. Februar zu einem wichtigen Fest für alle Verliebten geworden. Allerdings schenkt man sich in Großbritannien nicht nur Blumen oder Pralinen, sondern verschickt auch Karten, und zwar anonym. Je mehr Karten man bekommt, desto mehr Verehrerinnen oder Verehrer hat man.

Ein Fest im Herbst ist *Halloween*. Es entstand vor über eintausend Jahren in der Keltenzeit auf den Britischen Inseln. An *Halloween* gehen die Kinder verkleidet von Haus zu Haus. Sie fordern mit „Süßem oder Saurem" *(trick or treat)* die Bewohner auf, ihnen Süßigkeiten zu geben.

Neujahr wird in London zwischen November und März gefeiert. Das kommt daher, dass in London Menschen aus aller Welt leben. Sie haben ihre Bräuche und Feste mitgebracht.
In den meisten anderen Gegenden Großbritanniens wird am 31. Dezember Silvester so gefeiert, wie ihr es auch in Deutschland kennt. Allerdings wird auf der Straße weniger Feuerwerk gezündet als bei uns. Um Mitternacht singen viele Menschen das traditionelle Lied *Auld Lang Syne* (auf Deutsch: „längst vergangene Zeit"). Dabei stehen sie im Kreis und halten sich an den Händen. Dieses Lied und der Brauch stammen aus Schottland. Mittlerweile gibt es diesen Brauch auch in vielen anderen englischsprachigen Ländern.

Kennst du noch andere Neujahrsfeste? Wie feierst du Neujahr?

M M1 p. 96

3 At the Chinese New Year parade

L 1.34

a) Read about the Chinese New Year parade. What do you find interesting about it?

WB 3 p. 52

It is the end of January and Rajiv and Charlie are in London's Chinatown. They are watching the Chinese New Year parade. There are many people, and there is a lot to see: colourful costumes, scary dragons and a lot of bands playing music. In the evening there are even fireworks. All the shops are decorated with little red flags. Food stalls are selling Chinese prawn crackers, noodles and other delicious things.
"Look, Charlie. We can buy shrimp dumplings! ... Oh no, they're too expensive."

The boys follow the parade. Rajiv suddenly stops. "Hey, I stepped on something. Hm, what's this?" It is something red, an envelope.
Rajiv opens the envelope. "Wow, there're £30 in it! You know what? I'm going to keep it." Charlie is quiet for a minute. "Ah, no, Rajiv. You can't keep it. It belongs to a Chinese boy or girl. You know that Chinese children get red envelopes from their family and friends with good-luck money for the New Year. We're going to give the money back."

"But Charlie, there's no one to give it back to! And I can buy a cool T-shirt. And you can buy a new computer game." "Rajiv, what if someone sees us? Look, there's a police officer over there. I think he's looking at us." The boys don't know what to do. After a minute Rajiv says, "OK. Let's see if we can find the owner."

P1 + P2 P p. 92

b) What is the boys' problem? What would YOU do?

4 What to do?

15 p. 189

a) Look at the pictures. What are the boys going to do?

Rajiv Charlie The boys	is are	going to	look for the owner. ask ... go to ... give back ...

b) **The Chinese girl's dad gives Rajiv and Charlie £5. What are the boys going to do with it?**

The boys are going to …
Charlie is …
Rajiv …

P P3 + P4 p. 92/93
WB 4 p. 52

5 The Chinese calendar

WB 5 p. 53

a) **Look at the Chinese calendar. What is your birth year? Which animal are you? Also find out for your friends, parents, sister, brother, …**

I was born in …
My sign is the …

My brother's birth year is … He's a / an ….

Animal	birth years	
RAT	…, 1960, 1972, 1984, 1996, 2008, …	creative, charming, loves parties
OX	…, 1961, 1973, 1985, 1997, 2009, …	quiet, reliable, a good friend
TIGER	…, 1962, 1974, 1986, 1998, 2010, …	brave, optimistic, interested in lots of things
RABBIT	…, 1963, 1975, 1987, 1999, 2011, …	very friendly, generous, good to talk to
DRAGON	…, 1964, 1976, 1988, 2000, 2012, …	full of energy, self-confident, friendly
SNAKE	…, 1965, 1977, 1989, 2001, 2013, …	intelligent, likes to learn new things, loves reading
HORSE	…, 1966, 1978, 1990, 2002, 2014, …	independent, strong, doesn't like rules
SHEEP	…, 1967, 1979, 1991, 2003, 2015, …	patient, doesn't like to tidy up, likes to work in a team
MONKEY	…, 1968, 1980, 1992, 2004, 2016, …	very active, clever, loves sports
ROOSTER	…, 1969, 1981, 1993, 2005, 2017, …	hard-working, proud, loves music
DOG	…, 1970, 1982, 1994, 2006, 2018, …	honest, friendly, hates it when something is unfair
PIG	…, 1971, 1983, 1995, 2007, 2019, …	tolerant, peaceful, doesn't like arguments

b) **What are the animals like?**

I'm a snake. A snake is intelligent, … and …

My mother is a …
A … is …

6 Talking about festivals

DVD

WB 6 p. 53

a) Watch the clip. Rebecca, Daniel and Leanne are talking about special celebrations in their families. What can you understand?

Rebecca

Daniel

Leanne

b) Watch the beginning of the clip (0:00 – 0:25). Who celebrates what?

Rebecca and her family celebrate …

Daniel and his family …

Halloween • weddings • Valentine's Day • Easter • birthdays • Christmas • New Year's Eve

c) Copy the grid. Then watch the rest of the clip. Find out the teenagers' favourite festivals, why they like them and how they prepare for them. Take notes.

	favourite festival	why?	how do they prepare?
Rebecca	…	…	…
Daniel	…		
Leanne	…		

d) Use your grid to talk about the teenagers' favourite festivals.

Valentine's Day

birthday

Christmas

wedding

Mother's Day

Chinese New Year

St Martin's Day

carnival

7 St Patrick's Day

L 1.35

P5 P
p. 93

7 WB
p. 54

a) Andrew from Ireland is talking about St Patrick's Day, an important Irish festival. Listen to the interview on Radio Junior Europe. Take notes on these questions:
- When is St Patrick's Day?
- What happens on St Patrick's Day?

Then check your notes with a partner.

WWW

b) Who was St Patrick? Find out more about him.

8 YOUR favourite festival

How to ... write
p. 171

M2 + M3 M
p. 97

8 + 9 WB
p. 55

Write about your favourite festival. You can look at number 1 for help.

Diwali

My favourite festival is Diwali.
It is the Hindu festival of lights.
We celebrate Diwali in autumn.
My family always sets off fireworks
and goes to the temple.
We eat Indian food like samosas
and pakoras.
We always have a great time and
hope that Lakshmi, the goddess
of wealth, comes to our house.

9 Choose an activity

portfolio

wordbank Celebrations
p. 159

How to ... give a talk
p. 169

You can ...

- make a calendar for your classroom with all the special days and festivals that you and your classmates celebrate.
- make a collage about a festival with texts and pictures. Present it in class.
- show pictures of a family celebration and talk about them.
- make quiz cards about festivals. Then quiz your classmates.

10 Birthday presents

You want to find a present for your mum's birthday. Think – pair – share: What would be a good present for her? Write down your ideas.

Things you can buy	Things you can make or do
...	...

How to ... work with others p. 174

WB 10 p. 56

11 A chat

a) It is Mrs Lambraki's birthday in two days. Caroline wants to find a present for her mum. Caroline, Gillian and Charlie are chatting on the Internet. Who is who?

WB 11 p. 56

Add Subject Call Video More

Gi11i@n: So what are you going to buy for your mum?
Coco12: I don't know. Maybe gloves or a book ... No, it must be something nicer.
Gi11i@n: Why don't you go to Selfridges on Oxford Street? You know that it's one of the biggest and finest department stores in London. I just love Selfridges. You can get the nicest things there.
Batcha: Yeah, but a lot of them are really expensive. There's this new shop on Camden High Street called *Presents & More*. It has got lots of good stuff and it's cheaper than most of the other shops.
Coco12: That's a good idea. Maybe I can get a small bottle of perfume for my mum there. A perfume that smells better than the one she uses every day.
Batcha: Or a big box of chocolates and some flowers. All women love that.
Gi11i@n: Don't talk nonsense! Anyway, perfume is fine but expensive, too. I think earrings would be ...

b) Read the chat again. What ideas do the kids have? Are they similar to your ideas in number 10?

12 A great idea

a) Listen and read along. Find out what Caroline bought for her mum.

L 1.36 S 11

P6 p. 94

M4 p. 98

WB 12 p. 56

Gillian: So what did you buy?
Caroline: I thought the scarf was the best present, much nicer than a box of chocolates and much cheaper than perfume. And here, look at this birthday card.
Gillian: Fantastic. It's as pretty as the card you gave me for my birthday. And it smells of roses – lovely.
Caroline: Thanks. Oh Gill, I've got a brilliant plan for my mum's birthday. My dad is on a business trip in Greece. So can you come and help me? I want to ...

b) What could be Caroline's plan? What does she want to do?

13 Lots of presents

16a + 16c p. 190/191
P7 p. 94

a) When Caroline was at *Presents & More* she looked at these presents. Work with a partner and compare the presents.

I think the scarf is as nice as the gloves.

But maybe the scarf is cheaper than the gloves.

I think Maybe	the scarf the sunglasses the … birthday card …	is are	nicer than prettier than cheaper than better than	the …
			as nice as as pretty as as good as	

b) Now look at your list of presents in number 10 and compare them in a group. Which is the best / the cheapest / … present?

How to … work with grammar p. 173
WB 13 + 14 p. 57

c) You can use adjectives to compare things and people. What rules can you find? Write down the adjectives in a) like this:

nice → nicer → the nicest
pretty → … → …
good → … → …
…

d) How can you say that things are the same?

14 A poem

L 1.37
16a + 16c p. 190/191
P8 – P10 p. 94/95

a) Listen to the poem and read along.

b) Write one more verse about a birthday present. You can use these words:

- book: funny, …
- voucher: great, …
- kiss: sweet, …

What's prettier than a card?
A card with a smell.
And the prettiest card of all?
That's the card you made so well.

What's lovelier than a cake?
A larger cake.
And the loveliest cake of all?
That's the cake you baked for me.
I'm sorry but there's only a little left.

15 A message

a) Listen and find out: Who is talking first? And then?

b) Listen again. What is the plan? Where and when are they going to meet?

L 1.38
How to ... listen p. 167

16 A birthday plan

a) Look at the picture. Where are Caroline, Gillian and Charlie? What are they doing?

b) Listen and read along. What food have the friends already got? What haven't they got? Look at the picture, too.

L 1.39 S 12
17 p. 192
WB 15 p. 58

They have got some broccoli but they haven't got any …

Caroline: … Now what do you think?
Charlie: Great idea, but have you got everything?
Gillian: Have you got a chicken? Have you got any broccoli? And what about cream?
Caroline: Don't worry. How much cream do we need?
Charlie: Hey, don't ask us. You're the cook.
Caroline: Well, let me see. Here's some broccoli … and the potatoes are in the cupboard. But I can't find any cream in the fridge.
Gillian: And what about the birthday cake? We need sugar, flour, chocolate, butter, milk and some eggs. How many eggs are there in the fridge?
Caroline: Well, we've always got sugar and flour in the cupboard. But milk and eggs? Let me see … No, we haven't got any milk but here are some eggs … two, three. Are three eggs enough? Oops, are two eggs enough?
Gillian: Oh, Caroline! We need five or six eggs. And what about candles? Did you look for candles? Are there any?
Charlie: Not in the fridge!
Gillian: Ha, ha!
Caroline: I'm sure Mum has got some candles.
Charlie: Hey, why don't we go to the Patels' shop and buy everything we still need for tomorrow? I know that Rajiv is there. He'll be happy to see us.

c) What are they going to buy at the Patels' shop? Write a shopping list.

P P11 + P12 p. 95
M M5 p. 99

17 A special birthday

L 1.40 S 13

How to ... read p. 168

a) Read about Mrs Lambraki's birthday.
Find out:
- What was the special meal?
- How did Mrs Lambraki like her presents?
- How good was the meal?

The next day Gillian and Charlie came to wish Mrs Lambraki a happy birthday and to help Caroline with her birthday idea.

Charlie was the waiter and Gillian was the waitress. Caroline cooked a fantastic meal – chicken with cream sauce and broccoli – and George made a chocolate cake while the waiter and the waitress set the table. They used the best knives, forks, spoons and plates. Mrs Lambraki waited in the living room.

Then the waiter asked her to come to the dining room. Mrs Lambraki opened her children's presents. She loved Caroline's scarf and George's flowers. But she thought the birthday card smelled of oranges.

Then the waitress brought the chicken to the table. Mrs Lambraki said it was a delicious meal – as good as in a top-class restaurant. Everyone was so polite! Afterwards Mrs Lambraki said, "What a pity I can only celebrate my birthday once a year."

b) Mrs Lambraki told her husband about her special birthday. What did she say?

M6 p. 99 **M**

c) What did you like best about Caroline's birthday idea? What would YOU do to surprise your mum / dad / best friend on their birthday?

18 A birthday song

L 1.41 S 14

a) Listen to the song and sing along.

For he's a jolly good fellow,
for he's a jolly good fellow,
for he's a jolly good fellow,
and so say all of us,
and so say all of us,
and so say all of us.
For he's a jolly good fellow,
for he's a jolly good fellow,
for he's a jolly good fellow,
and so say all of us!

b) What other birthday songs do you know?

WB 16 p. 58

19 Choose an activity

portfolio

You can ...

- **write about your best birthday present.**

How to ... write p. 171

My best birthday present was my bike. I like it because it has 24 gears and it is green. That is my favourite colour. I ride my bike to school and to the sports club. Now my bike is one year old. It still looks very good because I often clean it.

- **draw your best birthday present and tell your partner about it.**

How to ... talk p. 170

- **work in groups. Act out the stories in numbers 16 or 17.**
- **make a crossword puzzle or a wordsearch with birthday / celebration words for your classmates.**

WB test yourself p. 59/60

P1 A festival ABC

Make an ABC of festival or celebration words.

A – activities, …
B – big meals, …
C – celebrate, …
D – …
…

P2 Sound check

L 1.42

a) Listen to the words and repeat them.

b) Which words are spoken like *celebrate* (Ooo)?
Which words are spoken like *remember* (oOo)?
Make two lists.

Ooo	oOo
celebrate	remember
…	…

expensive • festival • decorate • exciting • envelope • family • delicious • colourful • evening • computer

c) Listen again and check your lists.

P3 Plans for a party

15
p. 189

Gillian and her mother are going to have a New Year's Eve party at their house.
Look at the pictures and write about their plans.

Gillian / Mrs Collins is going to …

Gillian and her mum are going to …

wear her new T-shirt • go to the hairdresser's • write invitations • make pizza • decorate the house • buy lemonade and crisps

A

B

C

D

E

F

P4 A good party?

15
p. 189

Look at the picture. What is going to happen?

eat the pizza • fall on the sofa • spill their drinks • climb up the curtains • get hurt • get ill • drop the plates • fall off their chairs • go through the window

Patch is going to eat the pizza. …

P5 Valentine's Tea Dance

Look at the poster. A friend who doesn't speak English wants to know what it says. Tell him / her in German.

Die Haverstock Schule lädt ein zu …

Dort gibt es …

…

Valentine's Tea Dance for senior citizens

with live band & tea
with home-baked cakes served by our students

Saturday
February 14th
3 pm – 5 pm
£ 3 (including entertainment and all refreshments)

Haverstock School
24 Haverstock Hill
London NW3 2BQ

How to …
help out
p. 176

P6 Presents

a) What are these presents? You can look at numbers 11 and 12 for help.

1. You wear them on your hands.
2. You put them in water and they look very pretty.
3. You can eat them but they are bad for your teeth.
4. You can read it.
5. It is expensive and smells very nice.
6. You can send it to a friend.

b) Write a quiz for your partner. Describe three more presents.

P7 Sound check

a) Say these words. Watch out for their endings. Which one is the odd one out?

1. presents • bikes • parks • dresses • skirts
2. sandwiches • buses • roses • sunglasses • shirts

L 1.43

b) Listen and check.

P8 Good, better, best

16a + 16c p. 190/191

a) Put these adjectives in alphabetical order and add the comparative and superlative forms.

big, bigger, the biggest
...

funny • big • small • short • clever • tall • good • strong • happy

b) What about the adjective *bad*? Can you find its comparative and superlative forms, too?

P9 I'm as strong as you!

16a + 16c p. 190/191

Use the adjectives from P8 to write comparisons with *than* or *as ... as*. Write about yourself or about famous people. You can write funny comparisons, too.

Robin Hood is as clever as Tarzan.
My feet are bigger than Onur's feet.
...

P10 Different people

Look at the picture and compare the people.

old • young • tall • short • long • funny • …

Daniel is taller than Olivia.
Tariq is the tallest.
Olivia is as short as …
…

16a + 16c p. 190/191

P11 What have we got?

Talk about what you can see on the breakfast table. Use *some* or *any*.

17 p. 192

We've got some … but we haven't got any …
There is / are … on the table.
There isn't / aren't … on the table.

milk? • sugar? • toast? • cornflakes? • honey?
tea? • juice? • eggs? • sausages? • bread? • …?

P12 A recipe from India

Look at the recipe for cucumber raita. What do you need? What do you have to do? Tell a classmate in German.

How to … help out p. 176

CUCUMBER RAITA

- half a cucumber
- 2 tablespoons fresh mint
- 300 g yoghurt
- pinch cumin
- pinch black pepper
- pinch salt

- Peel and slice cucumber.
- Chop mint finely.
- Put yoghurt in bowl and beat with fork.
- Mix in cucumber, mint, cumin, pepper and salt.
- Put raita in fridge to cool. Tastes great with fresh bread!

Für dieses Rezept braucht man …

Man muss …

M1 Christmas

a) Read Karla's text for the Haverstock school project "Christmas celebrations". What do you like about her Christmas? What don't you like?

Christmas

About a week before Christmas we buy a Christmas tree. We put it up in our living room and decorate it. We also write Christmas cards and send them to friends and relatives. We hang the cards we get on our living room door or put them on the mantelpiece.

The 24th December, Christmas Eve, is a normal working day. In the evening we put mince pies for Father Christmas and some carrots for his reindeer in front of the chimney. We also put presents under the Christmas tree and hang stockings from the mantelpiece. When Father Christmas comes through the chimney at night, he puts the presents for the children in their stockings.

On Christmas Day, the 25th December, my little brother Josh and I open our presents in the morning. There is always a big family meal, it's usually turkey for lunch. Everyone gets a Christmas cracker that you pull open with your neighbour. In our crackers there are some small plastic toys and a paper crown. Then everyone wears the paper crown on their head – it looks really funny. We play lots of silly games and have a great time.

The 26th December is also a holiday. It is called Boxing Day because on that day the rich people gave the poor people boxes of food. On this day we always have the leftovers from the Christmas meal, go for a walk and visit relatives.

Karla Marshall, year 8

M1 + M2 p. 63 WB

b) Read Karla's text again and compare Christmas in Germany with Christmas in Great Britain: What is similar? What is different?

similar	different
…	…

c) Give Karla information about how people celebrate Christmas in Germany.

M2 Diwali celebrations

**a) Rajiv and his family are Hindus. Their favourite festival is Diwali.
Read the information from the Internet to find out how Hindu families celebrate Diwali.**

News (230) ▾ Favourites ▾

A FESTIVAL OF LIGHTS

Diwali is a five-day celebration in late October or early November. It is a festival of lights. The people celebrate the god Rama and the victory of light over darkness, of good over evil. It's a time to visit friends and relatives, give presents and have fun. The lights, the presents, the sweets, the fireworks and the singing and dancing make Diwali a highlight for everybody.

In Britain the biggest Diwali festival is in Leicester. People set off wonderful fireworks and there is a big parade where young girls in colourful saris dance, sing and give sweets to people in the street. The girls dance for the goddess Lakshmi.

In Indian homes Diwali is a very busy time for women and young girls. They have to clean all the rooms in the house and then decorate them with fresh flowers and lots of little candles and oil lamps. They also make delicious meals and traditional Indian sweets.

During Diwali people send cards to their friends. They visit each other and exchange presents and sweets. Young girls and boys wear traditional clothes and perform Indian songs and dances.

b) Read again and collect information about Diwali in a grid like this:

name	when?	why?	how do they prepare?	how do they celebrate?
Diwali	…	…	…	…

c) Use your grid to tell your classmates more about Diwali.

WB M3 p. 64

M3 Rajiv's surprise

a) Rajiv and his classmate Nick are in Rajiv's room. Listen to them and take notes on these questions:
- What does Rajiv want to do for Diwali?
- Where are his parents?
- Why didn't Rajiv tell his parents?

L 1.44 S 15

WB M4 p. 64

b) Rajiv's parents got a surprise when they came home – but not a nice one! Listen to the end again. Then finish the dialogue between Rajiv and his parents and act it out.

How to … talk p. 170

M4 Birthdays around the world

An international teen magazine wanted to know how its readers celebrate their birthdays. Lots of readers sent emails.

a) Here are some of the emails. Which countries are they from?

Mexico — Russia — Australia — China — India

I think the first email is from …

Send Chat Attach Save draft
To:
Subject: Birthdays around the world

We get new clothes for presents. We usually get up at six o'clock and then we go to the temple. We always wear our colourful new birthday clothes. In the afternoon our family eats a birthday meal: a delicious curry and a sweet rice pudding. 1

My birthday is in December. I often go to the beach with my friends. We go surfing or swimming. I usually get my presents then. Or we have a barbecue in the garden and play fun games. Young children often eat "fairy bread" at their birthday parties. "Fairy bread" is white bread with hundreds of colourful sprinkles on it. It's yummy! 2

In my country we usually don't have birthday parties with cakes and presents because it is not a tradition to celebrate birthdays. In fact, some people do not celebrate their birthdays until they turn 60! But we often eat long noodles on our birthdays – long noodles for a long life! 3

I usually invite lots of friends and have a big party. There is always a piñata with lots of sweets and other nice things in it. And I have to eat birthday cake without using my hands – it's a big mess but it's very funny for everybody! 4

When we have our birthdays, we get small presents at school. Teachers often give students flowers, pencils or books. After school we usually have a birthday party at home. We play a game where prizes hang down from a rope. Each guest can cut down a prize and take it home. 5

M5 + M6 WB p. 65

wordbank Celebrations p. 159

How to … write p. 171

b) Read the emails again. Which birthday party do you like best? Say why.

c) Write about how you celebrate YOUR birthday. Think about:
food – activities – presents – guests – …

M5 A special present

a) **Listen to Gillian and Karla. What are they talking about?**

b) **Listen again. What does Karla need to make the present? Write her shopping list.**

c) **Write down YOUR favourite recipe.**

L 1.45

wordbank Food and drink p. 161

WB M7 p. 66

M6 Party games around the world

a) **Read about some party games from around the world. Which game do you like best?**

On one knee (Australia)

You need two or more players. Throw a tennis ball to each other. When someone drops the ball, you say "Down on one knee!" If the same person drops the ball a second time, then you say "Down on two knees!" If the same person drops the ball again, you say "Down on one elbow!", and again, you say "Down on two elbows!", and then "Down on your chin!", and then "You're out!" Remember you have to stay in the position you're in to catch and throw the ball.

Lion and Mouse Tag (South Africa)

Stand in a circle. Two players are in the circle. Both wear blindfolds. One of them is the lion and the other is the mouse. The lion tries to catch the mouse. When the lion roars, the mouse must squeak. When the lion catches the mouse, the game stops. The mouse then becomes the lion and a new player becomes the next mouse. Then the game continues.

Chicken Market (Italy)

In this game one person is the customer, one person is the grocer and the others are chickens. The players who are chickens stand behind the grocer. They have to act like chickens! The customer and the grocer say:

Customer: Have you got any good chickens?
Grocer: Yes, we've got some delicious chickens. Would you like to try any of them?
Customer: Yes, please.

Then the customer can go to the chickens and touch them and make any comments such as "this chicken is too old ... too thin," etc. If any chicken giggles, he or she is out of the game. Now a new customer starts. The game is over when there are no chickens left.

b) **What games do YOU enjoy playing at parties? Choose one and write down the rules.**

c) **Explain YOUR game or one of the games above to your class. Then play the game.**

CAMDEN CHRONICLE
LEARN ENGLISH THE CAMDEN WAY

DID YOU GET IT ALL?

- What was in the red envelope?
- How many animals are there in the Chinese calendar?
- What animal is somebody who was born in 1974?
- What is Rebecca's favourite festival?
- What did Caroline buy for her mum's birthday?
- Why didn't Mr Lambraki celebrate with his wife?
- Where did Caroline buy the things she needed for her birthday surprise?
- What did the birthday card smell of?

GOOD TO KNOW ...

Ein beliebter britischer Feiertag ist der Faschingsdienstag *(Shrove Tuesday)*. An diesem Tag backen die meisten Leute Pfannkuchen. Auch in den Schulkantinen gibt es sie zum Mittagessen. Dieser Tag wird daher auch *Pancake Day* genannt. In vielen Orten gibt es lustige Pfannkuchenrennen *(pancake races)*, bei denen mit einer Pfanne mit Pfannkuchen in der Hand um die Wette gelaufen wird.

A PARTY GAME:
Bed Sheet Ping-Pong (USA)
Players stand and hold a bed sheet at opposite ends. A ping-pong ball is put in the middle of the sheet. The players raise or lower the sheet. The aim is to get the ping-pong ball to fall off the other team's side.

RAINBOW CAKE

- 250 g flour
- 2 tsp baking powder
- 175 g butter
- 175 g sugar
- 3 eggs
- 30 g cocoa
- red food colouring
- 175 g chocolate
- sweets

1. Mix the flour, baking powder, butter, sugar and eggs together.
2. Divide the mixture into three bowls. Add cocoa to one bowl and food colouring to another bowl.
3. Put all the mixtures into a baking tin.
4. Stir the mixtures together.
5. Bake the cake at 180°C for about 45 minutes, then melt the chocolate.
6. When the cake is cool, decorate it with chocolate, sweets and candles.

5

THEME 5

DOS AND DON'TS

In diesem *Theme* ...

- » beschäftigst du dich mit Regeln daheim und in der Schule.
- » berichtest du, was du tun musst und was du (nicht) tun darfst.
- » stellst du Vergleiche an.
- » erfährst du mehr über Schuluniformen in Großbritannien.
- » äußerst du deine Meinung zu Schuluniformen und Regeln.

1 Problems

a) Look at the picture. What problems are there between the girl and her father?

I think the father doesn't like …

The girl is wearing a … / has got …

1 WB p. 67

b) Work with a partner. Can you think of more problems between parents and children? What are they?

coming home …

spending money on …

playing computer games …

? …

2 Rajiv and his mum

a) What does Rajiv ask his mum? What does she answer?

Mum, can I play computer games?

No, you can't. You must study for the maths test.

1. Can I wear these jeans when we go to Grandma's birthday party?
2. Can I watch the film at 10 o'clock tomorrow night?
3. Can I do my homework when I come back from Charlie's house this evening?
4. Can I go shopping on Oxford Street after school?
5. Can I go to the youth club disco with Charlie?

A No, not after school. You can go there on Saturday afternoon.

B You must do your homework before you leave.

C OK, but you have to be back by eight o'clock.

D No, it's a horror film and it's too late.

E Sorry, no jeans for Grandma's birthday.

2 WB p. 67

b) Work with a partner and act out the dialogues. You can make your own dialogue, too.

3 Rajiv's diary

Read Rajiv's diary entry. What is he angry about?

18 p. 193/194
M1 p. 116
WB 3+4 p. 68

Wednesday, 27th March

Why can't I do what I want? Mum always knows better. I've got cool new jeans but I must wear those ugly trousers for Grandma's birthday.

I bet Sheree doesn't have to wear what Mum says. Charlie can watch TV after ten, I can't. Rules, rules, rules in our house – I hate them!!! I can go to the youth club disco – great. But I always have to be home by eight. ☹

Then there's homework! Mum says that I must not listen to music when I do my homework. And I have to do it before I can go out or play computer games. I wonder what Sheree could do when she was twelve. I think Mum is worse than most of my teachers!

4 Parents

L 1.46 S 16
WB 5 p. 69

a) Listen. Who is talking?

b) Right or wrong? Listen again and correct what's wrong.

1. Mrs Patel has an argument with her husband.
2. Rajiv wants to wear his new jeans to his grandmother's birthday party.
3. Mrs Patel doesn't like the jeans because they have holes.
4. Mrs Patel likes the black trousers.
5. Sheree is going to school.
6. Sheree is wearing a long skirt.

5 YOUR rules at home

18 p. 193/194
6 + 7 WB p. 69/70

a) Work in a group. Talk about your rules at home.

I must … / I have to …	I don't have to …	I mustn't …	I can …	I can't …

watch TV after … o'clock. | have a pet. | wear what I want when I go to school. | do my homework before I can … | play computer games before I do my homework. | put on make-up. | take out the rubbish. | eat sweets before dinner. | …

P2 – P4 P p. 112/113
M2 + M3 M p. 117

b) Now write about your rules at home.

6 Different opinions

L 1.47

a) Listen to Rajiv and Charlie and read along. What are they talking about?

Charlie: Hey, what's the matter with you?
Rajiv: I can't stand my mum. It's always: 'Do this, don't do that'. My mum has too many rules!
Charlie: My mum is strict, too – and strange. You know that she loves talking about healthy food. Today at lunch she said that salad is more delicious than a hamburger. I can't believe she thinks that. Nothing is better than a hamburger!
Rajiv: Yeah, and all this stuff my parents say about school, for example that German is more important than PE. Or listen to this: My father thinks maths is the most interesting subject at school.
Charlie: Ha, ha! Well, let's play football now and forget about our parents.

P1 P p. 112

b) What do YOU think: What is the most delicious food? What is the most interesting subject?

7 YOUR opinion

a) What do you like? What don't you like? Make top three lists. The pictures and the words can give you some ideas.

WB 8 p. 70

difficult subjects
1. German
2. ...
3. ...

delicious food
1. pizza
2. ...
3. ...

difficult · boring · delicious · beautiful · expensive · exciting · dangerous · famous · fantastic · interesting · wonderful · ...

sports

clothes

computer games

singers / bands

books / comics

films / TV series

b) Work with a partner. Discuss your top three lists and compare them. You can look at the words in the box for help.

difficult / ...
more difficult / ...
most difficult / ...

16b + 16c p. 190/191
P5 p. 113

I think pizza is the most delicious food. What about you?

I think so, too.

8 Don't

L 1.48 S 17

19R p. 195

a) Listen to the poem and read along.

Why do people say "don't" so much
whenever you try something new?
It's more fun doing than don'ting!
So why don't people say "do"?

Don't slurp your spaghetti!
Don't kiss your cat!
Don't butter your fingers!
Don't walk like that!

Don't wash your books!
Don't bubble your tea!
Don't jump on your sister!
Don't goggle at me!

Don't climb up the curtains!
Don't feed the chair!
Don't sleep in the wardrobe!
Don't cut off your hair!

Don't draw on the pillow!
Don't change all the clocks!
Don't water the phone!
Don't hide my socks!

Don't cycle upstairs!
Don't write on the eggs!
Don't chew your pyjamas!
Don't paint your legs!

Oh, why do people say "don't" so much
Whenever you try something new?
It's more fun doing than don'ting!
So why don't people say "do"?

b) Work with a partner and find the rhyming words.

P6 p. 113

c) Make seven groups. Each group learns one verse by heart. Act out your verse.

9 Choose an activity

portfolio

You can ...

- **make a poster with rules for your family / pet / ...**
- **draw pictograms or make signs for rules that are important to you. Then tell your class about them.**

- **write your own verse for the poem in number 8. These words can help you:**
  – bed / head – brother / mother – floor / door – ...

10 Haverstock school rules

> The student in picture A is breaking rule number …

a) Read the school rules. Then look at the pictures and say which rules the students are breaking. Who is not breaking a rule?

A

B

HAVERSTOCK SCHOOL RULES

1. Be polite and show respect for other students.
2. School starts at 8.50 am. Students who are late must first report to the deputy head.
3. Students must not run in the school building.
4. Students must wear the correct school uniform.
5. Students must not leave the school grounds at break or at lunchtime.
6. Eat and drink in the right place and at the right time.
7. Students must not chew gum at school.
8. Students must not bring mobile phones to school.
9. Students must wear sports kit for PE.
10. Students can only listen to their MP3 players at break and at lunchtime.
11. Students can buy school meals at the cafeteria or bring a packed lunch.
12. This is your school, so look after it. Look after property and put litter in the bins.

C

D

b) Read the school rules again and answer the questions.

WB 9 + 10 p. 71

1. Ken's alarm clock did not work. He arrives at school at 9 am. What does he have to do?
2. Nasaar wants to wear her new miniskirt at school. Can she wear it?
3. Mark is in the school football team. What does he have to wear for football training?
4. Tim wants to phone a friend on his mobile phone at lunch. Why can't he make the call?
5. Samantha wants to go home for lunch. Can she leave the school grounds?
6. Kate doesn't like the meal at the cafeteria on Tuesday. What can she bring?

c) Which three rules do you think are the most important? Which one is the least important?

> I think rules number … are the most important.

P P8 p. 114

11 Rules at YOUR school

18 p. 193/194
WB 11 p. 72

a) Work with a partner. Think of the rules at your school or in your class and write them down. Start like this:

We must …
We must not …

Rules in our class
1. We must clean the board.
2. We must not talk.

P12 p. 115
M4 p. 118

b) What do you think about the rules? Are they OK or not OK? Give reasons.

Rules in our class
1. We must clean the board. OK
2. We must not talk. not OK

12 What to wear?

14R p. 188
wordbank Clothes p. 162

a) What do YOU and your friends wear when you go to school?

I We	always usually often sometimes never	wear …

P7 p. 114

b) What must the students at Haverstock School wear? Look at the pictures in number 10 and the words in the box.

grey shirt with the school logo • black trousers • black shoes • dark blue sweatshirt with the school logo • black skirt • dark blue blazer with the school logo • tie

Girls must wear …
Boys must wear …
Students must also wear …

16 p. 190/191
P9 + P10 p. 114/115
WB 12 p. 73

c) What do you think about the clothes students wear at school?

I think it's	better worse cheaper more expensive nicer more boring …	to wear	jeans a uniform skirts ties …	at school.

LAND & LEUTE

Schuluniformen

An den meisten britischen Schulen tragen Schülerinnen und Schüler eine Schuluniform. Für Mädchen ist das oft ein dunkler Rock und eine Bluse mit Schulkrawatte. Jungen tragen in der Regel eine dunkle Hose und ein helles Hemd mit Krawatte. Auch die Schuhe sind vorgeschrieben. Die Schüler und Schülerinnen dürfen keine Sportschuhe tragen.

An den meisten Schulen kommen Pullover und Blazer mit dem Abzeichen der Schule hinzu. So kann auf dem Schulweg jeder sofort erkennen, zu welcher Schule man gehört. Es gibt auch keinen Streit über die „richtige" Jeans- oder Sportschuhmarke oder das coolste Sweatshirt.

Welche Vor- und Nachteile einer Schuluniform fallen dir noch ein?
Gibt es an deiner Schule Schulkleidung? Falls ja, wie sieht sie aus? Falls nein, habt ihr schon einmal darüber nachgedacht? Wie könnte sie aussehen?

13 What other students say

a) Read what these students say about their school uniforms. Do they like them?

Hannah, 15, Fairfield High School, Bristol

I think my school uniform is ugly and horrible. I hate wearing it. I would love to go to school in clothes that look nice on me.

Joel, 13, Denbigh School, Milton Keynes

I think my school uniform is cool and I'm proud to wear it. It just makes me feel good. We're going to have a new logo on our sweatshirt soon. It's going to be better and even smarter!

b) Listen to Will and find out: L 1.49

- What does he think about his school uniform?
- What does it look like?

c) Now have a vote in your class:
Hands up: Who is for / against school uniforms?

… students are for school uniforms.
… students are against school uniforms.

M M5 p. 119

14 At the bus stop

wordbank People p. 155

a) Look at the picture. What do you think is happening?

- What does the big boy say?
- How does the small boy feel?
- What do the other children think?
- Why don't they help?

b) What do you think is going to happen?

15 No bullying!

WB 13 p. 74

a) Look at the picture in number 14 again. Then read the article from a school magazine.

THERE IS SOMETHING YOU CAN DO!

Tom was a good student. But one day he started arriving late for lessons. He told his teacher that he wasn't able to get up early enough and so he always missed the bus. At the next parent-teacher meeting Tom's teacher talked to his parents about this. They were very surprised. Tom always left home early enough to get to school by bus.

The teacher talked to some students who took the same bus to school. They told him that Tom didn't go to school by bus anymore. He walked the three miles to school! They didn't know why. Perhaps he liked going to school on foot.

The teacher talked to Tom again – but not in front of the class. At first Tom didn't want to tell him anything. Then he started to cry because he was so embarrassed. There was an older boy from school who waited for him at the bus stop every morning. He was big and mean and Tom was afraid of him. The bully took Tom's bus money and so Tom had to get to school on foot.

The teacher reported everything to the headteacher. Now this boy doesn't bully Tom anymore!

JOIN OUR ACTION CAMPAIGN NOW!

Don't be like those kids at the bus stop. Say 'no' to bullies!
Don't be afraid of them!
Don't look away!
Don't be afraid to tell someone!

P P11 p. 115

b) Were you right with your answers and ideas in number 14?

16 Bullying: No chance!

a) What can YOU do when someone bullies you?
Work in groups of four and make a placemat.

I can call friends for help.

I can talk to ...

I can ...

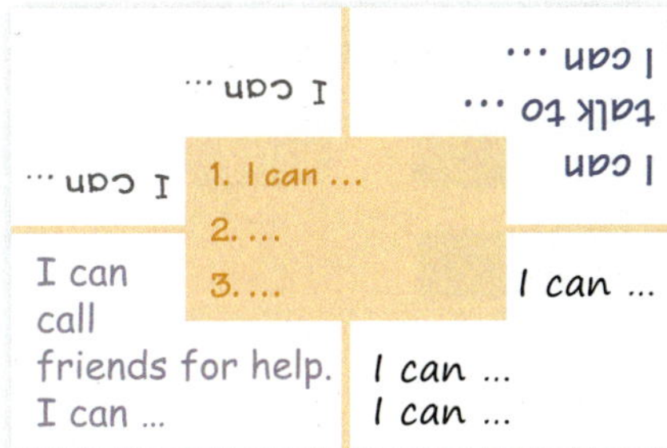

How to ... work with others p. 175

b) Talk about your ideas. Then decide on the three most important ideas and write them down in the middle of the placemat.

c) Compare your placemat results in class.

d) *ChildLine* offers help to children and young people in the UK.
Read the tips from *ChildLine's* website. What do you think about them?
Are they similar to your ideas?

M M6 p. 119

News (230) ▾ Favourites ▾

How to beat bullying – *ChildLine*'s top tips

- Don't ignore bullying. It won't go away on its own.
- Tell someone – for example a teacher, your parents or a friend.
- Contact *ChildLine* for free on 0800 1111.
- Remember: It's not your fault.
- Stay away from the bullies.
- Stay with a group when you don't feel safe.
- Don't fight back. You could get into trouble.

17 Choose an activity

You can ...

- make a poster with rules for your class, your school or your teachers.
- write a blog entry with anti-bullying rules for your school.
- design your dream school uniform. Draw it or make a collage. Then label it and present it in class.
- practise the rap on page 120 on your own, with a partner or in a group and present it in class.

portfolio

How to ... give a talk p. 169

WB test yourself p. 75/76

P1 Opposites

Find the opposites of these words.

before – … | early – … | like – … | interesting – … | today – …

better – … | can – … | always – … | have to – …

P2 Sound check

L 1.50

a) Copy the words. Then listen: Which letters can't you hear? Underline them.

mustn't • answer • listen • grandma • talk • autumn • knee • write • know

b) Listen again and say the words.

P3 Rules – rules – rules

18 p. 193/194

Look at the pictures and write down the rules at Caroline's house.

Caroline	has to mustn't	have any more pets. tidy up her room. go to bed at 10 pm. put her feet on the table. be back by 7.30 pm. …

1 "Be back by 7.30 pm!"

2 "No feet on the table!"

3 "No more pets!"

4 "Bed time!"

5 "Tidy up your room!"

6 …

P4 Rules for Mrs Killmouskey

18 p. 193/194

a) What are Gillian's rules for her cat? can • has to • mustn't

1. Mrs Killmouskey sleep all day.
2. She bring home any mice.
3. She play with Caroline's dog Patch.
4. She drink enough water every day.
5. She stay away from the fridge.
6. She steal Gillian's lunch from the kitchen table.

b) Do YOU have a pet? What are your rules for it? Write them down.

P5 The most interesting ...

16 p. 190/191

Think about the last two or three weeks. What was ...

- the most interesting film / TV series you saw?
- your biggest problem?
- your nicest day?
- your most boring day?
- the most fantastic surprise you had?
- your funniest moment?
- your most delicious meal?
- ... ?

Make notes. Then talk about them with a partner.

P6 Signs

How to ... help out p. 176

Look at the signs. Tell a friend who doesn't speak English what they mean.

1

2

3

4

5

P7 Different clothes

wordbank Clothes p. 162

Look at the pictures. What does Charlie wear for school? What does he usually wear in his free time?

T-shirt • trainers • grey shirt • jacket • dark blue sweatshirt • black shoes • jeans • dark blue blazer • black trousers • tie

For school Charlie always wears ...

In his free time Charlie usually wears ...

P8 Sound check

a) Read what the students say.

L 1.51

b) Listen and check.

P9 Let's compare

16 p. 190/191

a) Look at the adjectives in the box. Write down their comparative and superlative forms.

small • boring • cheap • difficult • interesting • easy • expensive • good • delicious • nice • bad

	COMPARATIVE	SUPERLATIVE
small	smaller (than)	(the) smallest
boring	more boring (than)	(the) most boring
...	...	...

b) Check your results with a partner. Then quiz your partner. Take turns.

P10 It's YOUR turn

Use the adjectives from P9a) and write what you think.

16 p. 190/191

1. our school – Haverstock School
2. school uniforms – regular clothes
3. a meal at the cafeteria – a packed lunch
4. a mobile phone – an MP3 player
5. a shirt – a T-shirt
6. music – biology
7. …

1. I think our school is smaller than Haverstock School.
2. …
…

P11 By bike?

How do you get to these places? Talk to your partner.

school • the swimming pool • your friend's house • the sports centre • your mum's workplace • the cinema • the train station • …

by bus

by train

by car

by bike

by underground

on foot

I go to school on foot. What about you?

I go to …

P12 School cafeteria rules

How to … help out p. 176

Your British epal sends you the cafeteria rules at his or her school. Your mother looks at them and doesn't understand everything. Tell her in German.

Man muss / soll …

Man darf nicht / soll nicht …

CAFETERIA RULES

- Silently enter and exit the cafeteria.
- Be polite to the cafeteria staff.
- Choose a seat and don't run around.
- Only eat food from your own lunch.
- Talk quietly.
- Keep your table and eating area clean.

M1 The next day

M1 + M2 WB p. 79

a) Read Rajiv's next diary entry. How does he feel?

Thursday, 28th March

I'm still angry. If I can't wear my new jeans, I'll phone Grandma and tell her about my problem. I guess she will say that I can come to her birthday party in jeans. Grandma is cool. She likes my clothes and sometimes gives me money for a new T-shirt.

But maybe I should talk to Dad first. He is often more relaxed than Mum. If he understands me, he will try to convince Mum that those ugly black trousers are not the right clothes for me.

If I have children one day, I won't tell them what to wear. I'm sure about that. If they go to parties or weddings in miniskirts or jeans with holes, I won't say a word. And if I earn enough money and they like music, I'll buy them guitars and we will become a famous family band. I'm feeling so much better now.

b) Read again and find out:

- What does Rajiv say about his grandma and his dad?
- What are Rajiv's plans?

c) Match the sentence parts.

1. If Rajiv can't wear his new jeans,
2. If Mr Patel understands his son,
3. If Rajiv has children one day,
4. If he doesn't like his children's favourite clothes,
5. If Rajiv earns enough money,

A he won't say a word.
B he will buy guitars for his children.
C he will phone his grandma.
D he will talk to his wife.
E he won't tell them what to wear.

20 p. 195/196
M3 WB p. 80

d) What will or won't YOU do if this happens to you?

1. If I can't wear my favourite clothes to my friend's party, I will/won't …
2. If I have children one day, …
3. If I earn enough money, …

M2 The morning radio show

L 2.1

How to ... listen p. 167

a) Listen to three students from London. They are talking about the dos and don'ts at their homes. Find out:
- What do they say about their families?
- What rules do they mention?

What else can you understand? Take notes in a grid.

	family?	rules?	other information
Zoe	...	...	...
Selim	...		
Mena	...		

b) Compare your notes with a partner.

M3 The room

WB M4 p. 80

a) Look at the pictures. What can you see? Talk to a partner.

18 p. 193/194

How to ... write p. 171

b) Imagine YOU are the girl <u>or</u> the mother. Tell her story. Make notes first.
You can start like this:
My room is always a mess but I like it. ... Yesterday when I was at school, ...
<u>or:</u>
My daughter's room is always a mess. I just hate it. ... Yesterday when she was at school, ...
Then read your story to the class.

c) What do you think: What could the girl and her mother do to solve the problem?

M4 A letter

M5 WB p. 81

a) Nina is Caroline's friend from Hamburg. Read Caroline's letter to her about classroom rules at Haverstock. How many rules does Caroline mention?

99 Arlington Road
London
NW1 7HT

Dear Nina, 5th April

Thanks so much for your letter! It was great to read about your school.

You asked me about classroom rules at Haverstock. There are lots of rules! First of all, we are not allowed to put our bags and blazers on the tables. That is OK because the desks are small. Then we are not allowed to eat or drink. Only water is allowed. We are also not allowed to chew gum in the classroom. I don't really understand that because chewing gum helps me to concentrate. Sometimes I do chew gum and then my teacher says: "Caroline, chewing gum is against the classroom rules. Please take out your gum and put it in the bin. This is your first warning." If you get three warnings, the teacher can send you outside to 'cool down'. But you needn't stay outside for more than two minutes.

We must wear the correct school uniform, of course. I don't really like the colour black or dark blue. I wish I could wear regular clothes like you in Hamburg. But I'm glad we needn't wear those ugly dresses we had in primary school.

In the lessons we must listen to the teachers and do what they tell us to do. If we want to say something, we must put our hands up. That is OK and I guess it's the same at your school. Oh, and I nearly forgot: We are not allowed to use swearwords. What a stupid rule!

What classroom rules are there at your school?
Hope to hear from you soon.

Love,
Caroline

18 p. 193/194

b) Read the letter again and complete the sentences.

Caroline and her classmates are allowed to …
They are not allowed to …
They must …
They needn't …
The girls needn't …

c) What does Caroline think about the rules?

How to … write a letter p. 172

d) Imagine YOU are Nina. Write a letter to Caroline and tell her about your classroom rules.

- What are you allowed / not allowed to do?
- What must you do? What needn't you do?
- What do you think about the rules?

M5 Uniform or no uniform?

a) Here are some arguments for and against wearing a school uniform. Sort them in a grid. Can you think of more arguments?

You see no differences between rich and poor kids.

They can be expensive for parents to buy.

It makes us feel that we belong together.

People like to look different and individual.

It's easy to decide what to wear in the morning.

SCHOOL UNIFORMS

for	against
…	…

b) Have a discussion in class. You need three groups:
- Group one speaks for school uniforms.
- Group two speaks against school uniforms.
- Group three listens to the arguments and can take notes.

c) At the end of the discussion group three decides: Which group had the best arguments?

M6 Calling *ChildLine*

L 2.2 S 18

WB M6 + M7 p. 82

a) Jennifer and Austin call *ChildLine* about their problems with bullying. Listen to the two children and find out:
- Why does Jennifer / Austin call *ChildLine*?
- What do other children do to them?
- What does Jennifer's mother / Austin's friend say?

Jennifer
…

Austin
…

b) What could Jennifer, Austin and their friends do against bullying? Talk to a partner and write down some tips.

I think Jennifer could …

Austin should …

CAMDEN CHRONICLE
LEARN ENGLISH THE CAMDEN WAY

DID YOU GET IT ALL?

- » What kind of film did Rajiv want to watch?
- » When does Rajiv have to be back from the youth club disco?
- » What is Charlie's favourite food?
- » What did Rajiv say about his mum?
- » How many rules are there at Haverstock?
- » What does Hannah's school uniform look like?
- » What did Tom's teacher do to help him?
- » What does *ChildLine* do?

A Rap

You know who they are,
you know what they do.
There's no way to ignore them,
they might bully you, too.

You should tell your friends,
parents and teachers, too,
about the bullies at school
before they bully you.

So let's get together,
come on, let's make some noise.
Don't let them bully you.
Stand up, let's hear your voice.

GOOD TO KNOW ...

Die Briten sind bekannt für ihre Höflichkeit und Rücksichtnahme. Die Wörter *please* und *thank you* werden für deutsche Ohren auffällig oft gebraucht. So ist es auch selbstverständlich, dass Menschen sich höflich begrüßen. Wenn man jemanden versehentlich anstößt, entschuldigt man sich mit *I'm sorry*. Drängeleien sind nicht üblich. Die Briten stellen sich geduldig in eine Schlange *(queue)* im Supermarkt, am Postschalter oder wenn sie auf den Bus warten.

THEME 6

LET'S GO!

In diesem *Theme* ...

» erzählst du, was du am Wochenende vorhast.
» lernst du, jemandem gute Besserung zu wünschen.
» sagst du, wie du welche Fernsehprogramme findest.
» lernst du weitere Urlaubs- und Freizeitaktivitäten in Großbritannien kennen.
» arbeitest du an einem Projekt über deine Ferienpläne.

1 Weekend plans

15 p. 189
P2 p. 132
WB 1 p. 83

Talk about your plans for the weekend with your classmates.

at the weekend:
- listen to …
- visit …
- read …
- meet friends in the park
- sleep over at a friend's house
- play …
- …

What are you going to do this weekend?

This weekend I'm going to sleep over at a friend's house.

2 A weekend in Camden

WB 2 p. 83

a) Read about the friends.

It is one of the last weekends before the summer holidays. It is warm and sunny. Gillian and Karla are in Regent's Park. All their other friends are busy.
Caroline, George and their parents have gone to Manchester to visit friends and family. They have taken Patch with them.
Their classmate Nick is at home. His mother wants to build a shed in the garden. Nick has promised to help her.
Rajiv and his sister Sheree have gone to a concert by the Magic Boys. They are Rajiv's favourite band. Rajiv has already been to a concert for kids. But this is a real concert so Sheree has to go with him.
Charlie can't go anywhere this weekend because he is in bed with chickenpox. He has been ill all week. He is feeling a little better but the doctor said he may not go out until next Wednesday. Charlie feels bored. He has already watched a lot of TV and has listened to the radio for hours.
Now Gillian and Karla are talking about what they could do this weekend. Perhaps they could go shopping or they could …

21 p. 196/197
P1 + P3 p. 132

b) What can you say about the friends?

Caroline and George	has	been	to a concert before.
Nick	have	taken	in bed all week.
Rajiv and Sheree		listened	to help his mum.
Rajiv		gone	their dog with them.
Charlie		promised	to Manchester.
		watched	to a concert by the Magic Boys.
			…

M1 + M2 p. 136/137

c) Whose weekend activities do YOU like best? Why?

3 Cheering up Charlie

a) Gillian and Karla want to do something to cheer up Charlie. What could they do?

They could …

… call him

… write him a get well card

…

b) Listen to the girls and read along. What are their plans?

L 2.3

Karla: That's it! Let's send a music request.
Gillian: A music request? What do you mean?
Karla: Well, we can write an email to the radio station. We'll ask them to play a song by Linus May for Charlie. He's his favourite singer, isn't he?
Gillian: He is! Hey, what a great idea! Have you ever sent a music request?
Karla: Yes, I have. For my uncle. It's easy: You just have to write an email to DJ Rasta at Radio Camden.
Gillian: Good idea! Let's do it!
Karla: But we'll have to phone Charlie and tell him to listen to the radio.
Gillian: OK, here is what we'll do: First we'll write the email, then we'll phone Charlie and tell him to listen to Radio Camden tomorrow afternoon.
Karla: And we can send him a get well card, too.
Gillian: Great, let's do that!

4 A get well card

Make a get well card and write a message.

WB 3+4 p. 84

Get well soon.

I hope you will …

We are missing you a lot.

You haven't missed much at school.

Cheer up!

…

5 The music request

a) Read the email. Who is the music request for? Why?

Send Chat Attach Save draft

To:

Subject: music request

From:

Dear DJ Rasta,

We'd like to make a music request for Charlie Batson. He's ill with chickenpox. We miss him and we hope he'll get well soon. Charlie is a big fan of Linus May. We want to cheer him up. So could you please play one of Linus May's songs tomorrow afternoon? Thanks a lot!

Best wishes
Karla Marshall and Gillian Collins

PS: We really love your radio show!

How to ... write p. 171
P4 p. 133
WB 5 + 6 p. 85

b) Write YOUR music request to Radio Camden. These questions can help you:

- Who do you want to say hello to?
- What music do you request?
- Why?
- When?

6 Radio Camden

**It is Sunday afternoon. Charlie is still in bed.
He is listening to Radio Camden.**

L 2.4

a) Listen to DJ Rasta. What song does he play for Charlie?

b) What do you remember? Match the sentence parts.

1. Linus May is
2. He is
3. Linus May will give
4. You can win
5. DJ Rasta met
6. He thinks that "Monkey" is

A. the singer last month.
B. a concert in London next week.
C. 17 years old.
D. a great song.
E. in the top ten this week.
F. two tickets for his concert.

M3 p. 137

c) Listen again and check.

7 TV programmes

a) When Charlie is ill, he may watch a lot of TV. There are many different programmes on TV. Match the words with the pictures.

a soap opera • a talk show • a film • a music show • a quiz show • a sports programme • the news • a cartoon

Picture … is a soap opera.

A

B

C

D

E

F

G

H

b) Work with a partner. What kind of programmes do / don't YOU like? Why?

My favourite programme is … because …

I like … but I don't like …

I think … is more boring / interesting than …

I (don't) agree. I think …

P6 p. 133
M4 p. 137
WB 7 p. 86

LAND & LEUTE

Fernsehen in Großbritannien

Wie bei uns gibt es auch in Großbritannien ein großes Angebot an nationalen und privaten Fernsehsendern. Man zahlt einmal pro Jahr eine Gebühr *(TV licence)* und kann dann verschiedene Fernsehprogramme empfangen. Dazu gehören die beiden werbefreien Programme *BBC1* und *BBC2* der britischen Rundfunkgesellschaft, der *British Broadcasting Corporation*.
Die *BBC* sendet viele beliebte Programme. Manche von ihnen laufen schon seit vielen Jahren, wie z. B. seit 1985 die *soap opera* (Seifenoper) *EastEnders* auf *BBC1*. Sehr bekannt ist auch *Doctor Who*, eine Science-Fiction-Serie. *Doctor Who* handelt von einem mysteriösen Zeitreisenden, der mit seinen Begleitern in seiner Raum-Zeit-Maschine, der TARDIS, durch das Universum reist. Die Raum-Zeit-Maschine sieht wie eine typisch britische Polizeinotrufzelle aus.
Speziell für Kinder gibt es *CBBC*, the *Children's BBC*. Eine bekannte Sendung der *CBBC* heißt *Newsround*. Sie ist eine der weltweit ersten Nachrichtensendungen für Kinder. Eine beliebte Unterhaltungssendung für Kinder heißt *Blue Peter*. Sie läuft schon seit 1958 im Fernsehen!

Welche speziellen Sendungen für Kinder gibt es bei uns?

8 Have you ever ...?

L 2.5 S 19

Listen to the song and sing along.

Have you ever been to Paris?
Have you ever been to Rome?
Have you ever been to London?
No, I've just been here at home.

Have you ever met a stunt man?
Have you ever met the Queen?
Have you ever met a T. Rex?
No, I've just seen them on screen.

Have you ever eaten snails?
Have you ever eaten snake?
Have you ever eaten frogs' legs?
No, I've just had too much cake.

Have you ever done a backflip?
Have you ever done things wrong?
Have you ever done a marathon?
No, I've just done a song and the last line got too long.

9 And YOU?

How to ... work with others p. 174
21 p. 196/197
P5 p. 133
8 p. 86

Walk around the classroom and interview your classmates.

Have you ever	had chickenpox/...? been to a concert/...? met a film star/...? done a backflip/...? played ...? ...

Yes, I have.

No, I haven't.

10 Choose an activity

portfolio

You can ...

- **collect information about your favourite TV programme and quiz your classmates. Think about:**
  - type of programme
  - channel
  - day
  - time
  - people in it
  - ...

wordbank Free time p. 151

- **write about what you and your friends or family are going to do this weekend. You can add pictures, too.**
- **write more verses for the song in number 8 and present them.**

My favourite TV programme is a cartoon.

It's on ProSieben every day at ... pm.

Is it "The Simpsons"?

The people in it are yellow and ...

...

11 Holidays in Britain

a) Look at the brochures. What are they about?

Welcome to SNOWDONIA NATIONAL PARK!

Do you love nature and being active?
Then spend your holidays in the beautiful
Snowdonia National Park in Wales!

You won't be able to decide what to do first:
Go hiking, for example up Mount Snowdon!
But you can also go up the mountain by train
with Britain's highest railway.
Or go riding and enjoy the fantastic views
from the back of a horse!
Or go on a treasure hunt and go geocaching!
Or get wet and go river-rafting!
Or go mountain biking or fishing or ... !

Snowdonia National Park is a great place
for nature lovers of all age groups.

Beam House Adventure Centre

What can you do there?

There is never a boring moment on a *Beam House* holiday. There are lots of fun activities you can do at the beach, like surfing or sailing.
You can also try other exciting activities, like mountain biking and abseiling.
In the evenings you can chat to friends or enjoy our evening programme.

Who can come?

We offer fun activities, sports and games for young people from 10 to 18.

Where can you find us?

Near Great Torrington in North Devon, near to some of the best beaches in the UK.

FOOTBALL CAMP
for boys and girls from 6 to 16

Spend your holidays at our exciting football summer camp in Manchester. A fantastic chance to learn new techniques from Manchester United coaches.

Morning sports programme:
3 hours with a Manchester Football School coach

Afternoon sports programme:
2 hours with a Manchester Football School coach

Other activities:
The evenings and weekends are free. Every evening there are activities, for example a Friday night disco plus karaoke and quiz nights. Or you can just chat to friends, listen to music or watch TV.

How to ... work with words p. 165

P7 p. 134

WB 9 p. 87

b) Read the brochures. Can you guess the meaning of new words?
Look up words you can't guess in your dictionary (pages 243 to 267).

12 Interesting places

a) Copy the grid and fill in the information from the brochures in number 11.

	Snowdonia	Beam House	Football Camp
where?	…	…	…
activities?	…		
age?	…		

P9 + P10 + P13 P
p. 134/135

b) Where would YOU like to go? Why? Present your number one to the class.

M5 M
p. 138

My number one is …

I like it because it's exciting / …

13 Holiday plans

Charlie, Nick and Caroline are in Charlie's garden. They are talking about their holiday plans.

L 2.6

a) Listen to the kids. What did you understand? Who is going to do what?

b) Listen again and find out:

- Who has already packed his or her suitcase?
- Who has never been to Scotland?
- Who wants to take lots of photos?

14 Our trips

5R + 21
p. 182 + 196/197
WB 10
p. 87

Ask and answer questions with a partner.

Have you ever visited Greece / Munich / Turkey / Poland / …?

Yes, I have.

No, I haven't but I've been to …

Have you ever been to an adventure centre / a sports camp?

Have you ever gone on a class trip?

What did you do there?

I went … / played … / …

What was it like?

It was great / boring / …

15 The dog in the fog

a) Look at the title and the pictures. What do you think happens in the story?

b) Listen and find out about the dog in the fog.

L 2.7
P8 p. 134
WB 11 p. 88/89

Last summer Gillian's cousin David, his parents and his dog Kenny Hoover went to Wales on holiday. One day they decided to walk to the top of Mount Snowdon, the highest mountain in Wales. Mrs Williams didn't like the idea.
"It's a very difficult walk," she said. "Let's take the train to the top."
David and his father thought that was out of the question! So they took their rucksacks and a picnic and started walking.
It wasn't a sunny day but the weather was OK. Mrs Williams was right – it was a difficult walk. At one o'clock they were hungry and tired. So they stopped for lunch. Suddenly it became dark.

"Oh no!" said Mr Williams. "The last thing we need – fog." "It's scary. We won't be able to find our way back," David said. "It's OK," Mr Williams answered. "Let's just wait here until we can see better." They sat there for a long time. David felt cold.
"What about the train next time? I knew ...," Mrs Williams started to say. "Shhh," whispered Mr Williams. "Look at our dog! What's up, Kenny Hoover?" Suddenly a big black dog came out of the fog. Now they were really scared. But the dog only barked at them and started to run away. Kenny Hoover barked back and quickly followed the dog.

"Kenny Hoover, stay here!" shouted David. But Kenny Hoover ran after the dog and so they followed, too.
They followed the black dog for about two hours and then suddenly they saw the village. They were so glad. "Look, there's our hotel!" David shouted happily. They turned round to say 'thank you' to the dog but it wasn't there. Kenny Hoover barked but there was no answer.
At the hotel they met Mrs Jones, the landlady. "Oh, thank goodness, you're back," she said. "It's very foggy. How did you find your way?"
"Oh, a big black dog helped us," David answered. "It was incredible. I don't know how, but the dog knew the way back to the village."

Mrs Jones looked very surprised. "A big black dog? So it's true," she said.
"What's true?" David and his parents asked.
"The story of Gerret, the dog. I guess you haven't heard it yet. His master, Mr Perrin, was a very good walker but he was old and one day he died in the mountains. Gerret came back to the village for help but he was too late. People say Gerret lives in the mountains now. Of course, I never thought the story was true ..."

16 The hiking trip

L 2.7

Right or wrong? Listen to the story in number 15 again and correct what's wrong.

1. David, his parents and his dog went on holiday to Scotland.
2. It was a sunny day.
3. They took a picnic with them.
4. The last thing they needed was snow.
5. David was really scared.
6. They met Mrs Jones in the mountains.
7. She told them about Mr Perrin and Gerret.

17 What a day!

a) Now read the story in number 15. How did David feel …

1. at one o'clock?
2. when the fog came?
3. when the big black dog barked at them?
4. when they could see the village again?
5. when he told the landlady about the hiking trip?

He was / felt …

excited cold glad scared tired

P11 + P12 P
p. 135
M6 M
p. 138

b) What do you think: Was it a good day or a bad day for David? Say why.

I think it was a good / bad day for David because …

18 Kenny Hoover's adventure

How to …
write
p. 171
M7 – M9 M
p. 138/139
portfolio
12 WB
p. 89

Imagine YOU are David's dog Kenny Hoover.
What did you experience during the hiking trip? How did you feel?
Tell your story. You can start like this:

Woof! Yesterday we walked up Mount Snowdon.
The weather was … Suddenly …
Then … After that …
Later … Finally …

Here is some more help:

it became dark and foggy → waited for a long time →
a big black dog came out of the fog → followed the dog →
saw the village → the dog was no longer there →
met the landlady → told her about the dog →
the landlady told the story of Gerret and his master

19 A project – YOUR holiday

How to … give a talk p. 169

wordbank Travelling p. 152/153

WB 13 p. 90

PLAN IT

- **You can work:**
  - on your own
  - with a partner
  - in groups
- **Think about:**
  - where you would like to go on holiday
  - how you can get there (by train / plane / …)
  - how long you are going to stay
  - what you can do there
  - what you should take with you
  - why you want to go there
  - …
- **Think about how to present it:**
  - poster or brochure
  - interview or discussion
  - computer presentation
  - …

DO IT

- **Think about what you already know, then collect more information:**
  - interview classmates, your family, …
  - go to the library
  - go to a travel agency
  - search the Internet
  - …
- **Make notes.**
- **Write about your holiday plans.**
- **Find material (pictures, things, …).**
- **Prepare your presentation.**

CHECK IT

- **Is the English OK?**
- **Is it interesting? Add details.**
- **Show your text to other classmates or your teacher.**
- **Edit it. Use a dictionary.**
- **Practise what you want to say.**

PRESENT IT

You can:
- use your notes to talk about YOUR holiday plans
- show your computer presentation
- put up your poster and talk about it
- …

WB test yourself p. 91/92

P1 Strange words

a) What are these words from the text in number 2?

1. i■l
2. s■■d
3. b■■y
4. r■■■o
5. d■■■■r
6. f■■■■y
7. c■■■■■t
8. p■■■■■s
9. a■■■■■y
10. c■■■■■■■■x

b) Take other words from number 2. Turn them into "strange words" and test your partner.

P2 Sound check

a) What are the children's plans? Read what they say.

Serkan

I'm going to go to the /ˈsɪnəmə/ on /ˈsætədeɪ/.

Sue

I'm going to meet some /frends/ and play /ˈfʊtbɔːl/ with them.

I'm going to /ˌsliːp ˈəʊvə/ at a friend's /haʊs/.

Grace

I'm going to help my /ˈmʌðə/ with the /ˈkʊkɪŋ/.

Martin

L 2.8 **b) Listen and check.**

P3 Three go together

21 p. 196/197

a) Find the three verb forms that go together. Write them down.

speak • met • **be** • gone • took • spoke • made • **meet** • was • been • read • **take** • slept • found • slept • **go** • taken • **make** • read • **find** • went • made • spoken • **read** • met • **sleep** • found

1. **speak** – spoke – spoken
2. …

L 2.9 **b) Listen and check your verb forms. Then learn them by heart.**

P4 Ready or not?

21 p. 196/197

DJ Rasta is late for his radio show today. It is only five minutes before the show starts. What has he already done and what hasn't he done yet?

DJ Rasta has read the music requests.
He hasn't found …
…

- read music requests ✓
- find CDs
- interview Magic Boys ✓
- make notes for show ✓
- make coffee
- tidy up desk
- find questions for music quiz

P5 Spot the differences

a) Look at the pictures of Charlie's room. Find the differences.

b) Write about what has changed in picture number 2. Use these verbs:

make • put • clean • tidy up • put away • close • …

21 p. 196/197

Charlie has made his bed.
He …

P6 What's on TV today?

Look at these programmes. Tell a friend who doesn't speak English what they are about.

How to … help out p. 176

BBC1		BBC2		Channel 4	
8.00 pm	**Match of the Day** Live: Denmark v England. Gary Lineker presents coverage from the Parken Stadium in Copenhagen.	8.30 pm	**The life of Sherlock Holmes** A film about the world-famous detective and his friend Watson – you have to watch it!	8.15 pm	**Emergency Room (ER)** Dr Pratt is angry with Neela and Abby has problems.

P7 Odd one out

Find the odd one out. Then make your own for a partner.

1. activity • mountain • river • beach
2. summer • football • autumn • spring
3. wet • fantastic • active • horse
4. sailing • hiking • evening • abseiling

P8 Finding words

Look at pages 122 to 131. Find more words for the list.

places	people	sports	things you can do (verbs)	what people / things are like (adjectives)
park	friend	swimming	go	ill
…	…	…	…	…

10 to 20 words: Look again! **21 to 30 words:** Good! **more than 30 words:** Great!

P9 Sound check

L 2.10

a) Listen and sort the words.

end • family • chat • bed • tennis • programme • had • man • sad • send • head • men • bad • festival • said • friend • match • sand • red • pet • black

/e/	/æ/
end	family
…	…

b) Check your list with a partner and say the words.

P10 A closer look

a) Write down the questions in the correct order.

1. do – can – What – you – at the beach – activities – ?
2. Who – at – teaches – the football camp – ?
3. can – you – go up – How – Mount Snowdon – ?
4. you – in Snowdonia – get – When – do – wet – ?
5. a Friday night disco – Where – you – go – to – can – ?
6. near – find – can – Great Torrington – you – What – ?

**b) Work with a partner. Ask and answer the questions.
You can look at number 11 for help.**

P11 How do YOU feel?

wordbank
People
p. 155

Choose an adjective and complete the sentences.

1. When I can't meet my friends, I feel …
2. When I'm ill and no one is there to visit, I feel …
3. When people smile at me, I am …
4. When I win a race, I …
5. When I wake up at night, I …
6. …

tired
happy
glad
sad
scared
proud
bored
… ???

P12 Happily or sadly?

13
p. 187

Read about David's adventure in Wales again. Pick the right adverb.

1. David and his parents walked up Mount Snowdon slowly / easily / quickly. It was a difficult walk.
2. "It's getting dark," Mrs Williams said well / nervously / happily.
3. "What's Kenny Hoover doing?" Mr Williams asked loudly / quietly / gladly.
4. They followed the big black dog sadly / angrily / quickly.
5. "Look, there's our hotel!" Mrs Williams shouted quietly / happily / proudly.
6. "Please tell us about Gerret, the dog," David said excitedly / angrily / sadly.
7. That night David didn't sleep tiredly / terribly / well.

P13 Say it in English

How to …
help out
p. 176

a) What do you say when you make new friends on holiday? Match the sentences.

1 Wie sagst du, wie du heißt?	A What are your hobbies?
2 Wie fragst du, wo jemand herkommt?	B Where are you from?
3 Wie fragst du, wie jemand heißt?	C Where are you staying?
4 Wie sagst du, wo du herkommst?	D What's your name?
5 Wie sagst du, dass es dir hier gut gefällt?	E My name is …
6 Wie fragst du, wo jemand wohnt?	F I'm from …
7 Wie fragst du, ob jemand das erste Mal hier ist?	G I really like it here.
8 Wie machst du einen Vorschlag?	H Is this the first time you've been to …?
9 Wie fragst du, was jemand gerne macht?	I Why don't we …? / What about …?

b) Work with a partner. Use the sentences from a) for a dialogue.

M1 The backstage report

WB M1 p. 95

A few days after the Magic Boys concert there was an interview with Rajiv and Sheree for the school magazine.
Read the article and find out: Why were Rajiv and Sheree allowed to go backstage? What could they do backstage?

Backstage with the MAGIC BOYS

Everybody at our school has probably heard of the Magic Boys but very few have had the chance to meet the band. Last Saturday Haverstock students Rajiv and Sheree Patel went to see the Magic Boys live and also met the famous boy group before the concert. The two were allowed to go backstage after Rajiv won a contest on the band's home page.

The students arrived at the concert hall at about five o'clock and a lot of fans were already waiting outside. The lucky fans made their way through the crowd and showed their backstage passes at the door. A young woman then took them through the backstage rooms.

The band was practising their new hit song when Rajiv and Sheree walked into the room. "It was amazing! I'll never forget it," said Rajiv. The members of the band then talked to the two fans. "At first I didn't know what to say because I was so excited," laughed Sheree. "They asked about our favourite songs and our hobbies, and it turned out that lead singer Rick and I both like horses."

The band members gave both fans a copy of their new CD and also wrote their autographs on Rajiv's T-shirt. He thought it was great and was laughing the whole time. When asked what he will do with the T-shirt, Rajiv answered: "I'll never wash this T-shirt again!"

The students were still talking to the band when reporters suddenly came into the room. "It was crazy," explained Sheree. "The reporters were asking questions and running around until the manager finally shouted 'time's up!'. Then the band had to go for make-up. They were getting ready for the concert so the manager had time to show the fans the tour bus. Rajiv really liked the bus. "It's so cool, not like a normal bus. It's a living room with a big TV and a stereo!"

Rajiv and Sheree then got another surprise: The band invited them to stand at the front and watch the show. Sheree was very excited. "When the band came on stage, all the girls were screaming. I was screaming, too. What an incredible feeling!"

The concert was fantastic and everybody had a lot of fun. The band came back on stage three times. "Everybody was still cheering when they came back the third time," said Rajiv. "We didn't want it to end, we had a great time!"

M2 Who was doing what?

a) Read the article in M1 again and complete the sentences.

22 p. 198

WB M2 + M3 p. 95/96

O When Rajiv and Sheree arrived at five o'clock, a lot of fans were already waiting outside.

A When the manager showed them the tour bus, …

G When the band came on stage, …

E When the band came back the third time, …

S When the band wrote their autographs on Rajiv's T-shirt, …

N When the students walked into the room, …

T When reporters suddenly came into the room, …

b) Put the sentences in the right order. What words do you get?

M3 Be a radio DJ!

L 2.4

a) Listen to DJ Rasta on Radio Camden again (number 6). What expressions and phrases does he use to talk about Linus May?

b) Prepare a short talk as a radio DJ about YOUR favourite singer or band. You can use expressions and phrases from a).

c) Now be a radio DJ and talk about your favourite singer or band.

M4 A couch potato

WB M4 p. 96

a) What do you think is a 'couch potato'?

A a potato that you keep near your couch

B a person who watches a lot of TV

C a couch or cushion that looks like a potato

b) Listen and find out if you were right in a).

L 2.11

c) Listen to Tom and Alex again and take notes to answer the questions.

1. What do Alex's friends want to do tonight?
2. Why does Alex want to stay at home tonight?
3. Why does Tom think Alex is strange?
4. How many hours of TV does Alex usually watch a day?

M5 A holiday brochure

How to … help out p. 176

You are on summer holiday with your parents and see this brochure. Your parents don't speak much English. Answer their questions.

Welche Fahrgeschäfte gibt es dort?

Was kostet der Eintritt?

Das ist aber ganz schön teuer. Gibt es auch Ermäßigungen?

Wie sind denn die Öffnungszeiten?

Da steht "FRIGHT NIGHT". Was ist das?

OK. Und wie kommen wir da am besten hin?

THORPE PARK
is the place to go!

Are you tough enough for our 26 thrilling rides?
For example: the fantastic *Samurai Ride*, the exciting *Looping Roller Coaster*, the amazing *Action Horror Ride* and many, many more?

ENTRANCE FEES

Adults (12+ years)
On the day: **£ 43.20**
Online: **£ 30.24**

Children under 12 years
On the day: **£ 33.60**
Online: **£ 23.52**

Children under 1 metre
FREE!

Special prices for families and groups!

TIP Buy your tickets online and save money!

HOW TO GET THERE

By car
From the M25 take junctions 11 or 13 and follow A320 to **THORPE PARK**

By train
5 trains run per hour to and from London Waterloo station, with a journey time of 30 to 50 minutes. Special ticket prices available if you travel with South West Trains.

OPENING TIMES
Open daily from 10 am

March – May **until 5 pm**
June & July **until 6 pm**
August **until 7 pm**
September – November **until 5 pm**

SPECIAL EVENTS
Have a FRIGHT NIGHT and enjoy our rides in the dark and scary surprises!
On FRIGHT NIGHTS our park is open until 11 pm.
Look online for the dates.

The park is closed for winter from December to February.

Come and visit one of the UK's most popular parks!

THORPE PARK
Staines Road, Chertsey, KT16 8PN

M6 The dog in the fog – a dramatic reading

How to … work with others p. 174

Read the story in number 15 in groups of five. Think about how your character feels. Read your role with feeling.

M7 All about the adventure

M5 p. 97 WB

a) Imagine YOU are a reporter for the village newspaper. You want to interview David about his adventure. Work with a partner. Think of possible questions. Here are some examples:
- Who was with you?
- Why didn't you take the train?
- What was the weather like?
- When … ?

b) Write down David's answers. Then practise the interview with your partner and present it to the class.

M8 Holiday postcards

a) Rajiv, Caroline and Charlie get postcards from their friends. Who are they from? Where were they?

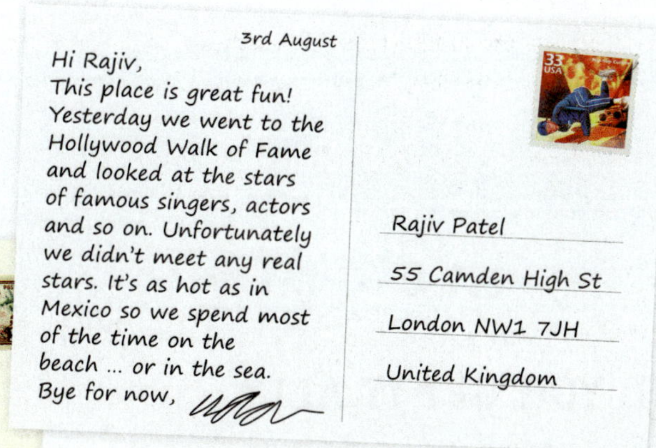

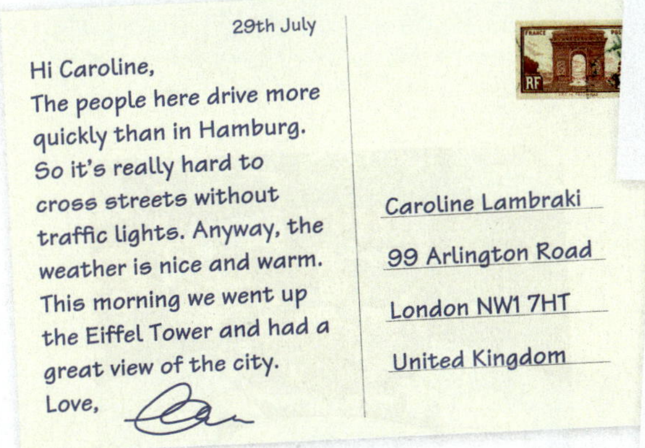

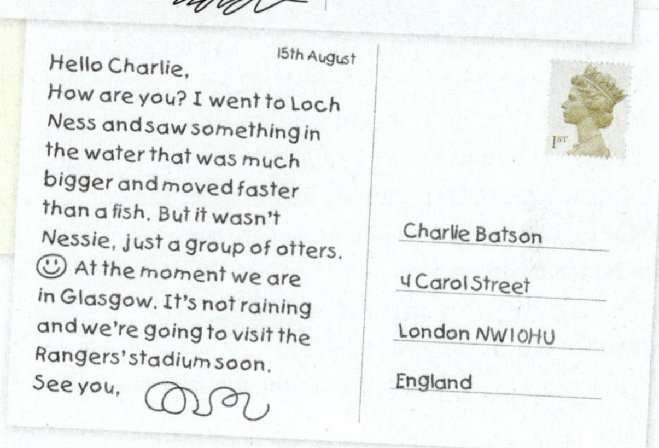

b) Work with a partner. How can you get to Paris, Los Angeles and Glasgow from your home town? Look at an atlas for help.

WB M6 p. 97

by bike • by bus • by train • by plane • by car • by motorbike • by boat • by ferry • on foot

c) Look at the means of transport in b). Put them in order from slowest to fastest. Then talk about them like this:

23 p. 199
WB M7 p. 98

A bike A plane …	goes travels moves	more slowly faster	than a …

M9 YOUR holiday postcard

Write a postcard in English from your holiday or from home. Write about:

portfolio
WB M8 p. 98

- where you are
- what the weather is like
- what you are doing now
- what you did yesterday
- what you are going to do tomorrow or next week
- …

CAMDEN CHRONICLE
LEARN ENGLISH THE CAMDEN WAY

DID YOU GET IT ALL?

» Where did Gillian and Karla meet to make plans for the weekend?
» What did they do to cheer up Charlie?
» What is the new song by Charlie's favourite singer?
» What radio station does DJ Rasta work for?
» What can you do in Manchester in the summer holidays?
» Who is going to Scotland?
» What is Mount Snowdon?
» What did Kenny Hoover do when he saw the other dog?

GOOD TO KNOW ...

Wie in Deutschland ist Fernsehen auch in Großbritannien eine beliebte Freizeitbeschäftigung nach der Schule oder der Arbeit. Die Briten haben viele verschiedene Bezeichnungen für den Fernseher, z. B. *telly* (als liebevolle Kurzform von *television*), *box* (Kiste), *small screen* (kleiner Bildschirm – der Gegensatz dazu ist der *big screen* im Kino) oder auch *goggle-box* (Glotze).

YOUR YEAR

Your year with Camden Market 2 is over.
What was ...

- your favourite Theme?
- your favourite page?
- your favourite photo or picture?
- your favourite story?

Going for a swim

On hot summer days, after school,
we go for a swim in the swimming pool.

As soon as I'm ready, I jump straight in.
I gasp as cold water splashes my skin.

I paddle across and cling to the side,
then pull myself out to go on the slide.

I check if it's safe, then let myself go,
with a splash I crash into the water below.

I go underwater, but I don't care.
I come to the surface and breathe in some air.

Then I swim as fast as I can to the side
and I climb back up for another slide!

A time-saving postcard

Dear Gillian,

Greetings from Greece!
The weather is
☑ great. ☐ terrible.
The food is
☑ delicious. ☐ awful.
The people are
☑ friendly. ☐ unfriendly.
I can't wait to
☑ come back next summer!
☐ go home soon!

Bye! Caroline

Gillian Collins
101 Arlington Rd
London NW1 7HE
United Kingdom

A The legend of Gelert

There is a Welsh[1] legend[2] about a Prince of Wales and his big black dog.

L 2.12

Long, long ago there was a Prince of Wales called Llewellyn. He and his beautiful wife, Merfanwi Goldenhair, loved each other and were very happy. Merfanwi laughed, "Soon we'll have a child." It was a boy and the prince and the princess were very happy. Then Merfanwi became very ill. She kissed her son and looked at Llewellyn for the last time. "Goodbye, my love. Look after our son." She died[3] and Llewellyn was heartbroken[4].

One morning Llewellyn and his men and their dogs went hunting[5]. The prince took his baby son with him. In the evening they camped near a river. The next morning was cold and wet, so Llewellyn left[6] his son in the tent[7] with Gelert, his favourite dog. "Look after my son, old friend. We'll be back in the afternoon." When Llewellyn and his men came back, Gelert didn't run out to meet them. Something was wrong! Llewellyn ran into his tent. The baby's bed and blanket[8] were on the ground[9] and there was blood[10] on them. There was blood everywhere! The men behind Llewellyn shouted: "Gelert went crazy[11] and killed your son!"

Llewellyn was very angry and he killed Gelert with his spear[12]. And then the baby cried[13]. It was under the blanket. There was a big wolf next to it. It was dead[14]. The blood wasn't from the baby, it was from the wolf and from Gelert. "Gelert killed the wolf! I made a mistake[15] and killed my best friend!" Llewellyn was happy about his son but sad about Gelert. He felt ashamed[16]. He and his men collected stones[17] from the river and made a big grave[18] for Gelert.

The grave is still there. In Welsh it's called Beddgelert – Gelert's grave.

There is also a Welsh village called Beddgelert. Find out more about it on the Internet.

[1]Welsh – *walisisch;* [2]legend – *Sage, Legende;* [3]die – *sterben;* [4]heartbroken – *todunglücklich;* [5]hunt – *jagen;* [6]leave – *hier: lassen;* [7]tent – *Zelt;* [8]blanket – *Decke;* [9]ground – *(Erd)boden;* [10]blood – *Blut;* [11]go crazy – *durchdrehen;* [12]spear – *Speer;* [13]cry – *weinen; schreien;* [14]dead – *tot;* [15]mistake – *Fehler;* [16]feel ashamed – *sich schämen;* [17]stone – *Stein;* [18]grave – *Grab*

B Cliffhanger

These postcards are from a book called "Cliffhanger" by Jacqueline Wilson.

**Look at the postcards on this page and the next page:
Where is Tim? How does he feel?**

POST CARD

Dear Mum and Dad
I am at the Adventure Centre. Well. You know that. You took me here.
I have only been here half an hour. I am not enjoying it so far. Not one bit.
With love from
Tim
xxxxxxxx to Mum
x to Dad

Mr and Mrs R. Parsons,
10 Rainbow Street,
Didcot,
Oxon

POST CARD

Dear Mum and Dad
I promised to write you lots of postcards. So I am. I keep my promises. Not like some people.
Maybe this will be the last postcard you will get though. Because we are going abseiling today. It is very dangerous. I could easily fall to my death. But if you'd only come and collected me last night you'd still have your only son alive and well.
From Tim

Mr and Mrs R. Parsons,
10 Rainbow Street,
Didcot,
Oxon

POST CARD

Dear Mum and Dad
I went abseiling!!!
I didn't like it. (Understatement of the century.) I let go of the rope and was in MORTAL DANGER. But I managed to grab it again. I survived. Just.
With love from
Tim
P.S. It's canoeing today. I could still drown.

Mr and Mrs R. Parsons,
10 Rainbow Street,
Didcot,
Oxon

biscuit – *Keks*; I have only been here half an hour – *ich bin erst seit einer halben Stunde hier*; so far – *bisher*; sheer drop – *steiles Gefälle*; promise – *Versprechen*; though – *allerdings*; fall to one's death – *in den Tod stürzen*; collect – *hier: abholen*; alive and well – *gesund und munter*; understatement of the century – *Untertreibung des Jahrhunderts*; I let go of the rope and was in mortal danger – *ich ließ das Seil los und war in Todesgefahr*; I managed to grab it again – *ich habe es wieder zu fassen gekriegt*; survive – *überleben*; drown – *ertrinken*

POST CARD

Dear Mum and Dad
Us Tigers all got into Mega-Trouble last night. But it was good fun all the same. And then Kelly gave me a Kit Kat before we went to bed. I shared it with Biscuits. I had the Kit and he had the Kat. Biscuits is my friend. And Kelly. Even though she's a girl.
With love from
Tim xxxxx
P.S. We're doing the Crazy Bucket race today. Weird! How can you race buckets????

Mr and Mrs R. Parsons,
10 Rainbow Street,
Didcot,
Oxon

POST CARD

Dear Mum and Dad
Guess what! We won the bucket race!!! And it was all because I sussed out how to do it. Honest. The other Tigers all think I'm Mega-Brilliant. Even Giles. Wonders will never cease.
I can think of another Wonder. I'm quite enjoying my adventure holiday now. In fact I almost wish we weren't going home tomorrow!
With love from
Tim
xxxxx to Mum
xxxxx to Dad

Mr and Mrs R. Parsons,
10 Rainbow Street,
Didcot,
Oxon

POST CARD

Dear Biscuits-Boy
I wish we were still having Adventures! My dad is ever so chuffed we won. My mum is just glad I'm back safe. She says to ask your mum if you can come and stay. Kelly might be coming too. Has she written to you? She's written to me twice already!
How many biscuits have you consumed since I saw you?
Is it A) 10 B) 100 C) 1000 ???
Your pal
Super-Tim

Mr 'Biscuits' Baker,
39 Marlow Road,
Market Harborough,
Leicestershire

Which postcard do you like best? Why?
Have you ever been to a summer camp? What was it like? Were you homesick?

us – *hier: wir*; get into trouble – *Schwierigkeiten bekommen*; all the same – *trotzdem*; share – *teilen*; even though – *obwohl*; crazy bucket race – *verrücktes Eimerrennen*; weird – *merkwürdig*; Guess what! – *Ihr werdet es nicht glauben!*; I sussed out how … – *ich habe herausgefunden, wie …*; honest – *ehrlich*; brilliant – *hier: genial*; Wonders will never cease. – *Es geschehen noch Zeichen und Wunder.*; quite – *ziemlich*; in fact – *eigentlich*; almost – *fast*; ever so chuffed – *total stolz*; might be coming too – *kommt vielleicht auch*; Has she written to you? – *Hat sie dir geschrieben?*; twice – *zweimal*; consume – *hier: essen*; since – *seit*; be homesick – *Heimweh haben*

C The Shard

THE SHARD

A SPECIAL LANDMARK

Paris has the *Eiffel Tower*, New York has the *Empire State Building* and London has *The Shard* – a tall and very special landmark[1] for a beautiful and special city.

SOME FACTS

The Shard is 309.6 metres high, which makes it the tallest building in Western Europe. Before *The Shard* was opened in July 2012, the tallest building was a tower in Frankfurt. The building looks a bit like a pyramid that is covered[2] entirely[3] in glass. This is the reason[4] for its name: "shard"[5]. The design of the building is environmentally friendly[6]: 95% of construction[7] materials used were recycled. There are 72 floors[8] that can be used for offices[9], restaurants, a 5-star hotel and flats[10]. And from the top floor you can enjoy a spectacular 360° view[11]. You can see all the famous London sights from there. On a sunny day you can see for 64 kilometres.

THE VIEW FROM THE SHARD – OPENING TIMES

Every day from 9 am to 10 pm (last entry[12] at 9 pm)

THE VIEW FROM THE SHARD – PRICES

Adults[13] and children over 16: £24.95
Children (under 16): £18.95; Children (under 3): free

HOW TO GET THERE

Nearest tube station: London Bridge
It's a 2-minute walk from the tube station to the entrance[14] of *The View from The Shard*. The entrance is on Joiner Street, near St Thomas' Street.

Choose an activity

- **Read the information and present *The Shard* to your class.**
- **Choose another sight in London or somewhere else[15] in the world (for example in YOUR village / town / city). Then make a brochure like this one.**

[1]landmark – *Wahrzeichen*; [2]covered – *bedeckt, überzogen*; [3]entirely – *ganz*; [4]reason – *Grund*; [5]shard – *Scherbe*; [6]environmentally friendly – *umweltfreundlich*; [7]construction – *Bau*; [8]floor – *hier: Stockwerk*; [9]office – *Büro*; [10]flat – *Wohnung*; [11]view – *Aussicht*; [12]entry – *Einlass*; [13]adult – *Erwachsene/r*; [14]entrance – *Eingang*; [15]somewhere else – *irgendwo anders*

D A horoscope

Aries
21 March – 19 April
Think before you buy or you won't have any money for something you really want.

Lucky number: **7**
Lucky colour: **pink**

Taurus
20 April – 20 May
Be nice to someone in your family and they will do something nice for you!

Lucky number: **3**
Lucky colour: **black**

Gemini
21 May – 20 June
You watch too much TV. But this month you will go out more and meet someone new.

Lucky number: **10**
Lucky colour: **gold**

Cancer
21 June – 22 July
You are always happy when you are with your friends, so you won't be sad this month!

Lucky number: **8**
Lucky colour: **white**

Leo
23 July – 22 August
You worry about the future. Just listen to your heart[1], it will tell you what to do.

Lucky number: **4**
Lucky colour: **orange**

Virgo
23 August – 22 Sept.
Wear your lucky colour on the 15th and you will get an invitation to something special.

Lucky number: **12**
Lucky colour: **green**

Libra
23 Sept. – 22 Oct.
You usually say what you really think but watch out[2] this month or you won't have many friends.

Lucky number: **11**
Lucky colour: **blue**

Scorpio
23 Oct. – 21 Nov.
This is your lucky month. Take part in a competition. You will get a big surprise.

Lucky number: **2**
Lucky colour: **yellow**

Sagittarius
22 Nov. – 21 Dec.
You'll have an unusual[3] weekend. It won't be what you planned but you'll enjoy it!

Lucky number: **5**
Lucky colour: **red**

Capricorn
22 Dec. – 19 Jan.
Someone wants to meet you. Don't be shy[4] and you will make a very special friend.

Lucky number: **1**
Lucky colour: **grey**

Aquarius
20 Jan. – 18 Feb.
Be nice to a boy or girl who looks sad at school. You will soon have a new friend.

Lucky number: **9**
Lucky colour: **brown**

Pisces
19 Feb. – 20 March
Life is boring at the moment[5] but don't worry. Something amazing will soon happen.

Lucky number: **6**
Lucky colour: **silver**

Choose an activity

- **What do you think of YOUR horoscope? Would you like to be a different star sign? Why?**
- **Write a horoscope for a friend or for someone in your family. You can decorate it, too.**

[1]heart – *Herz;* [2]watch out – *aufpassen;* [3]unusual – *ungewöhnlich;* [4]shy – *schüchtern;* [5]at the moment – *im Moment*

E A ghost story – Part two (Part one on page 78)

"Oh no! Cold rooms and people in the hall! What kind of hotel is this?"

"We hate cold rooms and my friend is afraid[1] of people. They are scary!"

"Don't be silly! We can scare[2] them, like real ghosts do!"

"Mrs Griff, put down your glass. Mrs Mutt, wake up and put on your head. Let's scare those people in the hall!"

The ghosts hide[3] behind the sofa.

"Hm, there is no one here." "That's strange[4]."

"Look, there is light under the door! I think there's somebody in the living room. Let's have a look."

"Boohoo! Boo!" "And boo to you! Good evening. Nice to meet you."

"What? You are not afraid of ghosts?" "Afraid? No, we have ghosts at home, too."

"At home? Where do you live?" "We live over there in the small house." "Oh, the small house? It looks very nice and warm. Do you have a room for us? This hotel is terrible."

"Yes, of course. You can come with us. Let's go."

Tom, Anna, Joe and Mo went to the children's house. The ghosts stayed for a week. They had a wonderful holiday in Scotland.

[1]be afraid (of sth/sb) – *(vor etw/jdm) Angst haben*; [2]scare – *erschrecken*; [3]hide – *(sich) verstecken*; [4]strange – *seltsam*

F The Chinese calendar

Look at the titles and the pictures. What do you think the story is about?

L 2.13

The story of the Jade Emperor

In the beginning[1] of time, the Jade Emperor[2] invited all the animals to come to see him in his home, the Jade Palace[3]. Different things happened on their way to the palace.

Before arriving at the Jade Palace, the animals had to cross a river.

The rat, the cat and the ox came early. The friendly ox invited the rat and the cat to ride on his back. When they were in the middle of the river, the greedy[4] rat pushed[5] the cat into the water.
When the ox and the rat reached[6] the other side of the river, the rat jumped off the back of the ox. Because of that, the rat arrived at the palace first. The ox arrived second.
The cat was swept away[7] and couldn't get to the palace. That's why cats don't like rats.

The next animal that arrived was the tiger, followed by[8] the rabbit. The helpful[9] dragon arrived later because it stopped on the way to help some people who didn't have enough water.

The horse arrived next[10]. But the clever snake had hidden[11] under its foot, which startled[12] the horse. It got scared[13] and started to run backwards[14]. The snake jumped ahead[15], making it the sixth to arrive, just before the horse.

The sheep, the monkey and the rooster arrived at the Jade Palace after working together to solve[16] some problems. They were followed by the dog. The last animal to arrive was the pig.

As a reward[17] for coming to see him, the Jade Emperor named[18] a year in the calendar after each[19] animal in the order[20] in which they arrived.

In which order did the animals arrive? What do you learn about them?

[1]in the beginning – *am Anfang, zu Beginn*; [2]Jade Emperor – *Jadekaiser (chinesische Gottheit)*; [3]palace – *Palast*; [4]greedy – *gierig*; [5]push – *schubsen*; [6]reach – *erreichen*; [7]sweep away – *fortspülen*; [8]followed by – *gefolgt von*; [9]helpful – *hilfsbereit*; [10]next – *als Nächstes*; [11]hide – *(sich) verstecken*; [12]startle – *erschrecken*; [13]get scared – *Angst bekommen*; [14]backwards – *rückwärts*; [15]ahead – *voraus*; [16]solve – *lösen*; [17]reward – *Belohnung*; [18]name – *(be)nennen*; [19]each – *jede(r, s)*; [20]order – *Reihenfolge*

G The story of Cinderella

L 2.14

What can you remember about the story of Cinderella[1]? Talk about the fairy tale[2] to a partner. Then read this modern Cinderella story.

Cindy lives with Mrs Scritch, her stepmother[3], and her two stepsisters[4], Daisy and Maisy. Cindy works in the kitchen of her stepmother's restaurant in Soho, London. Daisy and Maisy don't like Cindy because she is pretty and they aren't. Her stepmother gives Cindy all the hard jobs. One Saturday Mrs Scritch and her daughters put on their best clothes. They have tickets for the big rock concert in Hyde Park. But Cindy can't go with them because she has to clean the kitchen.

Cindy looks at the kitchen and starts to cry. Today is her 15th birthday! Just then there's a bright[5] flash[6] and suddenly a very strange man is standing next to her!

"OK. Here I am! Let's start!"

"Wh..., wh..., who are you? And what do you want?"

"I'm a good spirit[7], Cindy. My name is Roy and I'm here for you on this special day! You're going to that rock concert!"

"I can't! I have to clean the kitchen! Look at it!"

"Oh, that's no problem! Watch! Hocus pocus!"

There is another bright flash and four small men run into the kitchen. They clean everything very quickly and soon the kitchen looks like new.

"But I haven't got anything to wear! And look at my hair!"

"Oh, don't worry! Hocus pocus!"

FLASH! Two other small men come into the kitchen ...

"Oh, I look wonderful! I can't believe it! But I'll need a ticket for the concert, Roy. Can you get a ticket for me, too?"

"I can do even better than that. Hocus pocus!"

FLASH!

"This is Russel. Isn't he cool? He's a roadie[8] with the band Cool Ice. You can go with him. He'll look after you. Here – take this mobile phone. Take some photos with it."

"Thanks, Roy. Thanks for everything!"

[1]Cinderella – *Aschenputtel;* [2]fairy tale – *Märchen;* [3]stepmother – *Stiefmutter;* [4]stepsister – *Stiefschwester;* [5]bright – *hell;* [6]flash – *(Licht)blitz;* [7]spirit – *Geist;* [8]roadie – *Begleiter einer Band, zuständig für Auf- und Abbau*

"Now listen carefully, Cindy. You have to be home before midnight. It's important, so don't forget!"
"I won't, Roy. Come on, Russel. Let's go!"

At the concert...
Russel takes Cindy to the front row[9] so she can see the band and their singer, Stud Stains, really well. Cindy is very excited. She loves the concert and she takes pictures of Stud with her new mobile phone. Then Stud sings the most romantic[10] song and looks at Cindy. He takes off[11] his jacket, which has COOL ICE in big letters on the back, and gives it to Cindy. It fits perfectly.
Suddenly Cindy's phone rings[12]. Then she remembers – it's 11.30 and she has to go home quickly! She promised! But then Cindy runs into[13] her stepsisters. The girls are angry that she is at the concert and they start a fight[14]. Cindy loses her phone but manages[15] to run away.

Later...
Cool Ice have just finished the concert. A young woman walks on stage[16] and says: "Ladies and gentlemen! Has anyone seen a pretty young girl in a Cool Ice jacket? She has won a prize[17] – an evening with Stud Stains. If you know who she is or where she lives, call us. Thank you."
Mrs Scritch and her daughters are very excited.
"I'd love to spend an evening with Stud Stains!"
"Me, too! Call the number and give my name, Mum."
"Give my name, too!"
"OK, girls, but first we must find that horrible Cindy."

When they get back to the house, Cindy is watching TV. Mrs Scritch starts to shout at her but then she sees that Stud Stains is on TV.
"... We now have more information about the pretty girl with the Cool Ice jacket. We found her mobile phone. If you know who she is, please tell us. I really hope I can see this girl again!"
Suddenly Daisy and Maisy see that Cindy has a Cool Ice jacket.
"You're the girl that Stud wants to meet! It isn't fair!"
Cindy stays very calm[18] and looks at her stepsisters.
"You both[19] love Stud, don't you? Well, I don't. I think his music is cool but I don't want to go on a date[20] with him. So I have an idea. I'll give you the jacket, but only if your mum gives me some money. And I don't want to live with you or work in the restaurant kitchen again. Is that OK?"
"Yes! Yes! Of course!"
Mrs Scritch wants to help her daughters so she pays Cindy for the jacket. Now Cindy can leave London and start her own rock band. She becomes the youngest rock star ever and is very famous. But Daisy and Maisy are still unhappy. They can't decide who can have the jacket and meet Stud Stains so they fight about it for the rest of their lives.

Do you like this modern Cinderella story? Why / Why not?

[9]front row – *erste Reihe;* [10]romantic – *romantisch;* [11]take off – *ausziehen;* [12]ring – *klingeln;* [13]run into – *über den Weg laufen;* [14]fight – *Streit; (sich) streiten;* [15]manage – *es schaffen;* [16]stage – *Bühne;* [17]win a prize – *einen Preis gewinnen;* [18]calm – *ruhig;* [19]both – *beide;* [20]date – *Verabredung*

H Are you fit and healthy?

Do the test and find out.

1. Do you have breakfast before school?

- ▲ Sometimes.
- ● No, never.
- ■ Yes, every day.

2. Walk up and down[1] 20 stairs[2] quickly. Are you out of breath[3]?

- ■ No, I'm not. That's easy.
- ● Yes, I am!
- ▲ Just a little.

3. How often do you laugh every day?

- ■ Very often.
- ▲ Often.
- ● Sometimes.

4. A friend wants to go to the sports centre with you. What do you do?

- ▲ You stay at home and watch TV.
- ■ You go with him / her. Sport is great.
- ● You think it's a joke[4].

5. Which meal would you choose for lunch?

- ● A sausage with chips.
- ▲ Chicken with potatoes and carrots.
- ■ A salad.

6. What do you drink?

- ▲ Sometimes water, sometimes sweet drinks.
- ● Only sweet drinks.
- ■ Mostly[5] water.

7. How much time do you spend in front of the TV or computer every day?

- ● More than 3 hours.
- ■ Less[6] than an hour.
- ▲ 1 to 3 hours.

You have answered mostly …

■ **Fantastic! You're fit and healthy. Keep up[7] the good work!**

▲ **Not bad! You're quite[8] fit and healthy but you can do better.**

● **Oh dear[9]! Turn off[10] the TV or computer, eat an apple and go outside.**

[1]up and down – *auf und ab*; [2]stair – *(Treppen)stufe*; [3]out of breath – *außer Atem*; [4]joke – *Witz*; [5]mostly – *hauptsächlich; meistens*; [6]less – *weniger*; [7]keep up sth – *etw fortführen*; [8]quite – *ziemlich*; [9]Oh dear! – *Du meine Güte!*; [10]turn off – *ausmachen*

A Free time

Activities

meet (my) friends • listen to music • watch TV / a film • play the guitar / piano / … • play computer games / board games / chess • go to the cinema / zoo / youth club / a party / concert • dance • relax • visit a museum / castle / … • take photos • sleep over at a friend's house • phone / call a friend • chat to friends / on the Internet • read books / magazines • collect stickers / football cards / … • go shopping • be in / join a club • …

watch TV

listen to music

read a book

go shopping

dance

play the guitar

go to the cinema

play computer games

Sports

play table tennis / basketball / football / … • do judo / gymnastics • go swimming / dancing / inline skating / hiking / wall climbing / … • ride a bike / horse • …

What can we do this afternoon?

Let's go to the swimming pool.

What about a lemonade at the snack bar?

play basketball

play football

What are you going to do this weekend?

I'm going to go to the cinema.

What do you do in your free time?

I meet my friends.

do judo

go swimming

What's your hobby?

I do judo.

B Travelling

Where did you go on holiday?

I stayed at home.

I went to Spain.

Countries

Germany • Spain • France • Italy • Greece • Turkey • Russia • Poland • Ireland • Great Britain • the USA • Africa • Australia • …

stadium

park

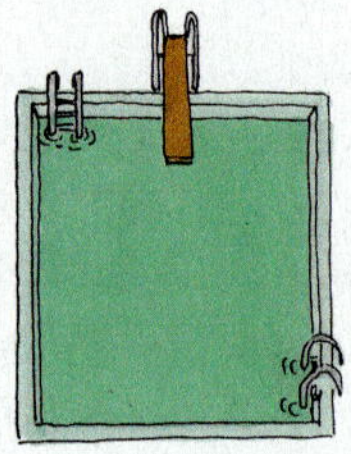

swimming pool

playground

cinema

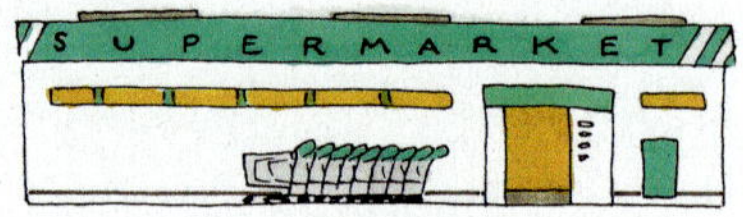

supermarket

Places and buildings

city • town • street • road • shop • supermarket • market • restaurant • snack bar • school • library • playground • sports centre • sports ground • skate park • swimming pool • cinema • park • zoo • river • house • flat • room • hotel • holiday apartment • campsite • beach • the sea • church • castle • museum • theatre • tower • bridge • department store • airport • train / underground station • football stadium • statue • adventure centre • sports camp • …

Where did you stay?

In a holiday apartment.

On a campsite in a caravan.

In a hotel.

With my grandparents.

Holiday activities

take photos of famous sights • go to the park / beach / … • visit a museum / castle / … • have a barbecue • eat ice cream • go shopping / hiking / swimming / … • relax in the sun • enjoy the weather • meet new people • write postcards • buy souvenirs • …

What did you do?

I went to the zoo.

I visited a museum.

Getting around

by bus / train / car / bike / motorbike / plane / underground / boat / ship / … • on foot • take the bus / train / car / … • walk / drive / fly to … • miss the bus / train / …

How did you get to Berlin?

We went there by train. In Berlin we took the underground.

I went on holiday by plane. I flew to Turkey.

Giving directions

walk past … • cross the street • on the / your left • on the / your right • walk straight on • walk on until you get to …

turn left • turn right

Walk past the museum and then turn left.

Turn right at the next corner.

Excuse me, can you tell me the way to …, please?

Cross the street, it's on your right.

Excuse me, how can I get to …, please?

Turn left into Victoria Road.

Can you show it to me on the map, please?

It's the second street on the left.

Walk straight on. It's next to the cinema.

Talking about places / sights

On your left / right you can see … • In front of you there is / are … • Take a look at … • You can go inside and see … • … is the oldest / tallest / … • … is famous because … • My favourite place in town is …

C Weather

What's the weather like today?

It's cold / warm / hot / wet / ...

It's nice / terrible / wonderful / ...

What a lovely day!

sun • sunny

snow • snowy

Brrr ... I'm cold!

What can we do on a sunny day?

On a sunny day we can go swimming.

rain • rainy

What can we do on a rainy day?

On a rainy day we can play games.

cloud • cloudy

wind • windy

fog • foggy

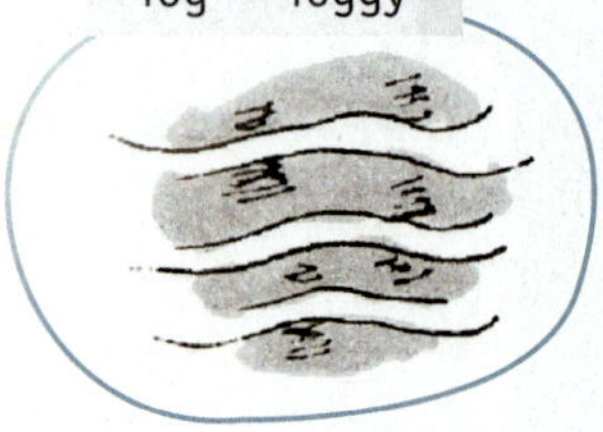

What was the weather like in Wales?

It was a bit windy and it rained a lot.

D People

family members	other people
• mother – father (parents)	• woman – man
• daughter – son	• wife – husband
• sister – brother	• girl – boy
• grandmother – grandfather (grandparents)	• child, teenager
• aunt – uncle	• friend, classmate
• cousin – cousin	• neighbour
• relative	• ...
• ...	

Describing people

positive	neutral	negative
good-looking • beautiful • strong • pretty • brave • polite • active • honest • clever • hard-working • self-confident • creative • charming • funny • optimistic • nice • friendly • …	small • large • tall • thin • long • short • blond • dark • old • young • strict • rich • poor • careful • slow • fast • ill • quiet • …	angry • strange • unfriendly • ugly • terrible • mean • silly • stupid • crazy • …

My friend Rajiv is tall and good-looking.

I like him because he is friendly and often funny.

Feelings

be afraid of big dogs • be nervous before a test • cry because you are very sad • laugh about a joke • love your pet • be scared of spiders • miss a friend • be proud of your sister • be angry with your brother • feel embarrassed because … • hate cleaning your room • …

positive	negative
happy • good • great • surprised • proud • wonderful • excited • glad • fantastic • safe • …	bad • terrible • angry • sad • lonely • frightened • scared • embarrassed • bored • cold • tired • hungry • nervous • worried • surprised • …

Hey, are you OK?

Don't worry. I can come with you.

I'm sad because Sally doesn't want to go to the party with me.

The body

tooth (two teeth) • face • hand • foot (two feet) • arm • leg • ear • eye • hair • back • finger • head • mouth • toe • nose • elbow • chin • neck

E At school

People and places at school

teacher • student • classmate • secretary • headteacher • librarian • deputy head • school building • classroom • cafeteria • library • gym • sports ground • basketball court • playground • office • …

In the classroom

door • window • bookcase • desk • chair • bin • paper • book • schoolbag • computer • poster • calendar • map • classroom rules • board • (interactive) whiteboard • …

Timetables and subjects

lesson • break • lunchtime • homework • registration • assembly • food technology • English • German • drama • history • art • ICT (information and communication technology) • maths • science • geography • biology • chemistry • RE (religious education) • PE (physical education) • …

Things in a schoolbag

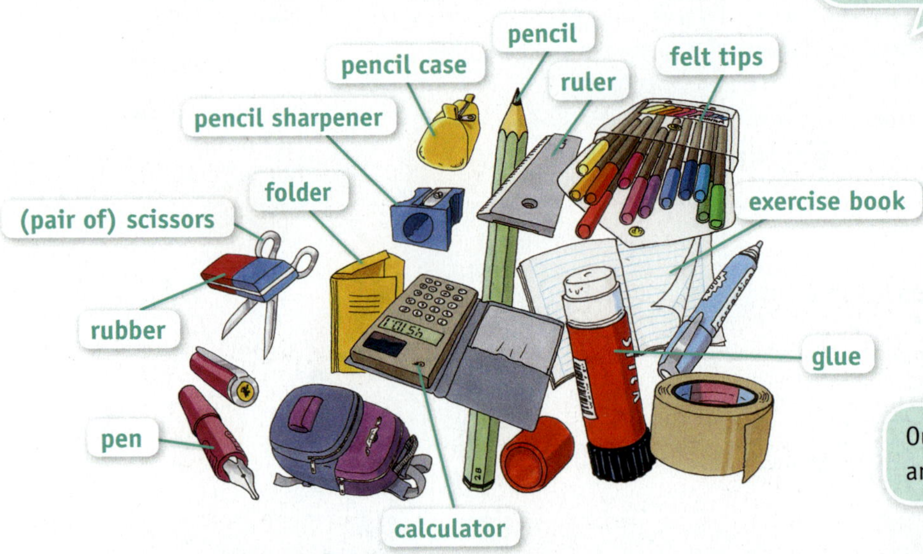

I go to Haverstock School.

I have to wear a school uniform.

School starts at 8.35 am and finishes at 3 pm.

Our library opens at 7.30 am and closes at 4.30 pm.

Today I must study for the maths test.

I'm very good at biology. It's my favourite subject. I also enjoy PE and art.

I'm in the film club. Do you join a school club?

F Animals

Wild animals

lion • tiger • kangaroo • fish • giraffe • hippo • elephant • meerkat • bird • eagle • tortoise • monkey • gorilla • zebra • rat • penguin • snake • spider • otter • …

Pets

budgie • parrot • dog • cat • mouse • goldfish • guinea pig • hamster • turtle • rabbit • …

Farm animals

duck • chicken • goat • sheep • pig • cow • lamb • horse • pony • …

Looking after a pet

feed it • talk to it • go for a walk with it • clean the cage • play with it • pet it • …

animals can …	**animals eat / drink …**	**animals are …**	**animals live / sleep in a …**
• swim	• fruit	• clean	• barn
• run	• vegetables	• cute	• cage
• catch …	• meat	• sweet	• basket
• fly	• cat / dog / fish food	• friendly	• fish tank
• eat	• water	• funny	• zoo
• drink	• milk	• fast	• …
• do tricks	• grass	• dangerous	
• bite	• leaves	• strong	
• jump	• insects	• clever	
• climb	• …	• …	
• bark			
• …			

My favourite animal is the kangaroo.

It has got strong legs and a long tail.

It is beautiful and can jump.

G Jobs

jobs	what these people do
actor / actress	act in films or plays
astronaut	fly in a spaceship; explore the universe
author	write articles or books
builder	repair and build houses
bus driver	drive people
car technician	repair cars
cook	cook meals in a restaurant
doctor	take care of ill people
farmer	work on a farm; feed farm animals
firefighter	fight fires; help people
football player	play football in a team; score goals
gardener	work in a park; look after flowers, plants and trees
hairdresser	wash, cut and style people's hair
keeper	look after animals, for example in a zoo
nurse	take care of ill people; look after you when you are in a hospital
pilot	fly planes
police officer	catch gangsters / criminals; keep people and the streets safe
secretary	make phone calls; prepare / write letters
shop assistant	work in a shop; help customers; sell things
teacher	teach at school
vet	take care of ill animals
waiter / waitress	serve customers in a café or restaurant

I think I'll work as a secretary.

Perhaps I'll be a pilot. Then I'll make lots of money.

I'd like to work with my hands / with people / …

jobs can be …
- boring
- creative
- dangerous
- easy
- exciting
- fun
- great
- hard
- interesting
- special
- terrible
- …

I hope I won't have a boring job.

Jobs at home

make the / your bed • tidy up the / your room • take out the rubbish • hoover the floor • do the shopping • do the cooking • make breakfast • set the table • empty the dishwasher • clean the kitchen / bathroom • …

I usually make my bed.

I sometimes clean the bathroom.

H Celebrations

Celebrations and festivals

New Year's Eve • Halloween • Eid • Christmas • Hanukkah • Easter • wedding • Valentine's Day • birthday • carnival • Mother's Day • Diwali • St Patrick's Day • Chinese New Year • ...

Presents

a box of chocolates • a scarf • a card • a bottle of perfume • flowers • a kiss • sweets • a cake with candles • a book • earrings • a voucher • a special meal • a poster • a game • a nice surprise • ...

Activities

go to / have a party • have a big meal • cook a special meal • make / bake a cake • go out for dinner • visit friends • celebrate with family and friends • give / get presents • write invitations • send cards • decorate the house • go to bed early / late • wait for the midnight countdown • watch the fireworks • have a great time • set off fireworks • make / wear a costume • wear special / traditional clothes • go to church • look for Easter eggs • dance to music • play games • sing songs • watch a parade • ...

presents

a box of chocolates

sweets

flowers

a cake with candles

cards

a book

a bottle of perfume

a scarf

My favourite festival is Easter. It is in spring. We look for eggs on Easter Sunday. Afterwards we always have a big family breakfast.

Would you like to come to my party?

Sure. Thanks for the invitation.

birthday

New Year's Eve

Christmas

I Time

What time is it, please?

My birthday is on the twenty-third of May.

What time do you go to bed?

I go to bed at half past eight.

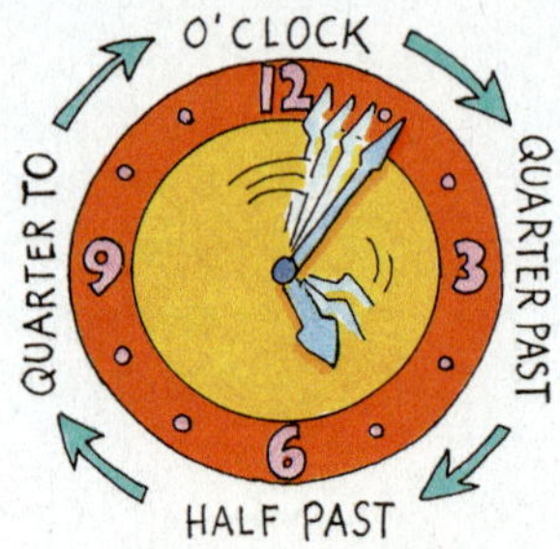

You say:
the twenty-third of May
You write:
23rd May *or* 23 May

When do you get up on Sundays?

I get up at ten o'clock.

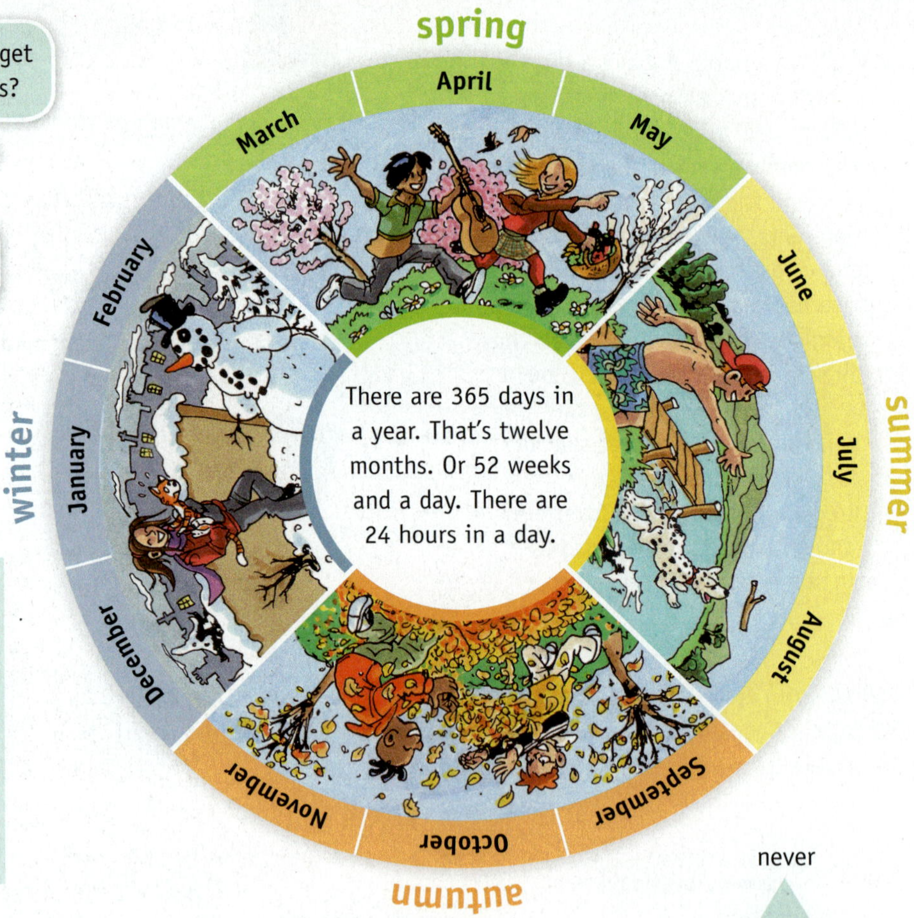

days of the week
- Monday
- Tuesday
- Wednesday
- Thursday
- Friday
- Saturday
- Sunday

When?

in the morning / afternoon / evening • at the weekend • last Monday / … • once a day / week / … • (three days) ago • before • first • then • after (that) • afterwards • later • finally • …

How often?

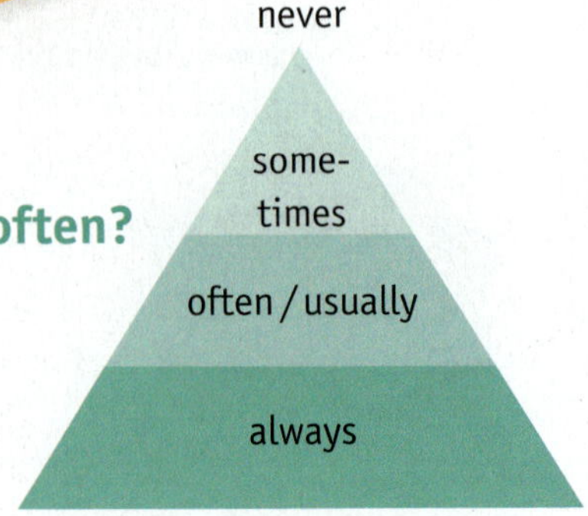

J Food and drink

breakfast	lunch	fruit and snacks	dinner
butter • jam • marmalade • honey • sausage • egg • cheese • ham • sandwich • yoghurt • muesli • cornflakes • bread • toast • …	pizza • burger • salad • chips • beans • chicken • vegetables • cream sauce • broccoli • potatoes • rice • meat • …	sandwich • orange • apple • banana • yoghurt • cake • chocolate • sweets • crisps • ice cream • …	tomatoes • broccoli • vegetables • potatoes • chicken • meat • cream sauce • cheese • chips • bread • sandwich • salad • beans • …

bread

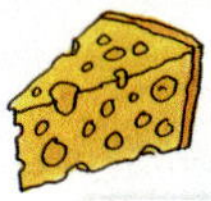
cheese

egg

crisps

chips

jam

Drinks

hot drinks	cold drinks
• tea • hot chocolate • …	• milk • lemonade • milkshake • orange juice • water • …

a cup of tea

a bottle of water

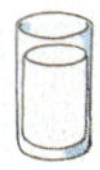
a glass of milk

food can be …
- hot
- cold
- delicious
- yummy
- sweet
- traditional
- healthy
- fresh
- old
- good
- bad
- …

For a cake

sugar • flour • eggs • milk • butter or oil • …

For the table

knives • forks • spoons • plates • cups • glasses

Would you like a glass of lemonade?

I feel really hungry!

Can I have some milk, please?

Of course. Here you are.

have tea • set the table • bake / make a cake • cut fruit • make a salad • put something in the fridge • clean the kitchen • use a knife and fork • feed the baby • eat in a cafeteria at lunchtime • go to a restaurant • …

make have cook eat	breakfast lunch a meal dinner

K Clothes

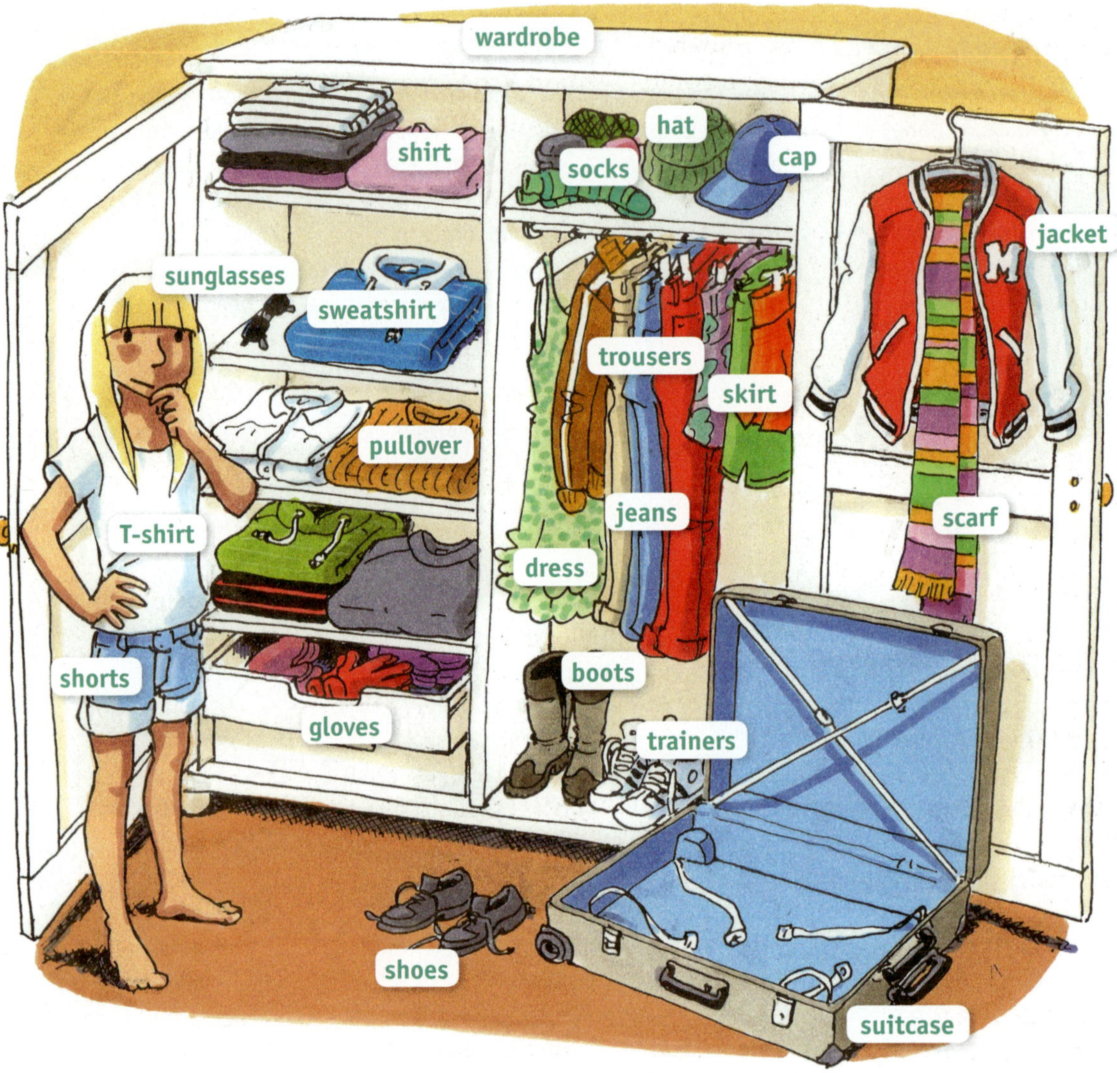

Clothes (free time)

hat • cap • sunglasses • scarf • gloves • jacket • pullover • shirt • sweatshirt • T-shirt • trousers • jeans • shorts • dress • skirt • socks • boots • shoes • trainers • …

School uniform

shirt • pullover • sweatshirt • trousers • skirt • blazer • tie • school logo • shoes • …

Wenn man ankommt oder geht

Good morning.	Guten Morgen.
Sorry, I'm late.	Tut mir leid, dass ich zu spät komme.
Sorry, I don't have my exercise book with me.	Tut mir leid, ich habe mein Heft nicht dabei.
Sorry, I don't have my homework with me.	Tut mir leid, ich habe meine Hausaufgaben nicht dabei.
What's for homework?	Was haben wir als Hausaufgabe auf?
See you tomorrow.	Bis morgen.

Wenn es ein Problem gibt

What's the matter with you?	Was ist mit dir los?
I'm fine. / I feel sick.	Mir geht's gut. / Mir ist schlecht.
I've got a headache.	Ich habe Kopfschmerzen.
Can I open the window, please?	Kann ich bitte das Fenster öffnen?
Can I go to the toilet, please?	Kann ich bitte zur Toilette gehen?

Wenn man Hilfe braucht

Can you help me, please?	Können Sie / Kannst du mir bitte helfen?
I've got a question.	Ich habe eine Frage.
I don't understand this.	Ich verstehe das hier nicht.
How can I do this exercise?	Wie mache ich diese Aufgabe?
What's ... in English / German?	Was heißt ... auf Englisch / Deutsch?
What does ... mean?	Was bedeutet ... ?
Can you write it on the blackboard, please?	Können Sie / Kannst du das bitte an die Tafel schreiben?
Can you say it again, please?	Können Sie / Kannst du das bitte noch einmal sagen?
Sorry, I don't know.	Tut mir leid, das weiß ich nicht.
What page, please?	Auf welcher Seite bitte?

Wenn man zusammen arbeitet oder spielt

Whose turn is it?	Wer ist dran?
I (don't) like this story.	Diese Geschichte gefällt mir (nicht).
I think it's good / interesting / funny.	Ich finde ... gut / interessant / komisch.
I think it's terrible / boring / sad.	Ich finde ... schrecklich / langweilig / traurig.
Do you want to work with me?	Möchtest du mit mir arbeiten?

CLASSROOM PHRASES

Wenn man mit dem Computer arbeitet

What's your email address? – Was ist deine E-Mail-Adresse?
You can click on this link. – Du kannst auf diesen Link klicken.
Can I print it out / download it? – Kann ich das ausdrucken / herunterladen?
I saved it. – Ich habe es abgespeichert.
My computer has crashed. – Mein Computer ist abgestürzt.

Was die Lehrerin oder der Lehrer sagt

Open your books at page ... – Öffnet eure Bücher auf Seite ...
Turn to page ... – Blättert zu Seite ...
Look at line ... – Seht euch Zeile ... an.
Read the text on page ... – Lies / Lest den Text auf Seite ...

Work in pairs. – Arbeitet zu zweit.
Work in groups of four / five / ... – Arbeitet zu viert / fünft / ...
Sit in a circle. – Bildet einen Sitzkreis.

Listen to the CD / MP3 / ... – Hör / Hört die CD / MP3 / ... an.
Write about ... – Schreibe / Schreibt über ...
Talk about ... – Sprich / Sprecht über ...
Ask questions about ... – Stelle / Stellt Fragen zu ...
Answer the question, please. – Beantworte / Beantwortet bitte die Frage.
Match the sentences. – Ordne / Ordnet die Sätze zu.
Who wants to read the text? – Wer möchte den Text vorlesen?
Write down the answers. – Schreibe / Schreibt die Antworten auf.

Act out the dialogue. – Spiel / Spielt den Dialog vor.
Change roles. – Tauscht die Rollen.
Make your own dialogue. – Entwirf / Entwerft selbst ein Gespräch.
Take a card. – Nimm / Nehmt eine Karte.

Come to the blackboard, please. – Komm / Kommt bitte zur Tafel.
Collect the exercise books, please. – Sammle / Sammelt bitte die Hefte ein.
Do this exercise at home, please. – Mach / Macht diese Aufgabe bitte zu Hause.

Please be quiet. – Sei / Seid bitte ruhig.
Please sit down. – Setz dich / Setzt euch bitte.
Please speak up. – Sprich / Sprecht bitte lauter.

You can do better. – Du kannst das besser.
Try again. – Versuch es noch einmal.
That's it. – Das ist alles.
Well done. – Gut gemacht.

A ... work with words

So arbeitest du mit dem Wörterbuch in Camden Market

- Wie du sicher schon weißt, befindet sich ganz am Ende deines Englischbuches ein *dictionary* (Wörterbuch). Dort findest du alle Wörter aus deinem Englischbuch. Wenn du ein englisches Wort nicht verstehst, kannst du es im *English-German dictionary* ab Seite 243 nachschlagen. Wenn du etwas auf Englisch sagen willst und dir ein Wort fehlt, kannst du es im *German-English dictionary* ab Seite 268 nachschlagen.

- Sieh dabei gut hin: Die Wörter sind alphabetisch geordnet. Du musst nicht nur auf den ersten Buchstaben achten, sondern auch auf den zweiten oder sogar dritten. Das Wort *wash* steht zum Beispiel vor *watch*.

wardrobe /ˈwɔːdrəʊb/ Kleiderschrank I
warning /ˈwɔːnɪŋ/ Warnung 5/M4
was /wɒz/ *Vergangenheitsform von „be"*
wash /wɒʃ/ (sich) waschen I
watch /wɒtʃ/ beobachten; anschauen; zusehen I
watch out (for) /wɒtʃ‿ˈaʊt/

- Manche Wörter stehen mehrmals in der Liste, zum Beispiel *water*. Einmal ist es ein Nomen und einmal ein Verb. Schau dir also den ganzen Abschnitt genau an, damit du die richtige Übersetzung findest.

Welche Bedeutungen hat das Wort *water* in den folgenden Sätzen?

water *(no pl)* /ˈwɔːtə/ Wasser I
water /ˈwɔːtə/ gießen 5/8

I water the plants every day.
Jim drinks lots of water.

So lernst du mit den *wordbanks*

- Es ist leichter, Wörter zu lernen, die zusammengehören. Deshalb findest du in den *wordbanks* (Seite 151 bis 162) Wörter nach Themen sortiert. Hier begegnen dir auch Fragen, Satzteile oder Redewendungen, die zum Thema passen.

- Sieh dir die *wordbanks* in deinem Buch genau an und gestalte deine ganz persönlichen *wordbanks*. Manche *wordbanks* sind wie ein Bildwörterbuch angeordnet. Mache dir eigene Bildwörterbuch-Seiten zu einem Thema. Schneide dafür Bilder aus Katalogen und Zeitschriften aus. Klebe sie auf ein Blatt Papier und beschrifte sie. Ergänze deine Seiten, wenn du neue Wörter zu dem Thema lernst.

So kannst du Wörter notieren und besser behalten

- Erstelle Bildwörterbuch-Seiten für dich oder als Poster für das Klassenzimmer. Wie das funktioniert, hast du bereits auf der vorherigen Seite erfahren (So lernst du mit den *wordbanks*).

- Sammle Wörter, die zu einem Oberbegriff passen, in einer Tabelle.

SCHOOL			
people	**places**	**subjects**	**schoolbag**
classmates	library	maths	pencil case
teachers	cafeteria	music	folders
...	...	...	...

- Du kannst auch ein Wortnetz (*word web*) zu einem bestimmten Thema anlegen. Ergänze dein Wortnetz, wenn du neue Wörter zu dem Thema lernst.

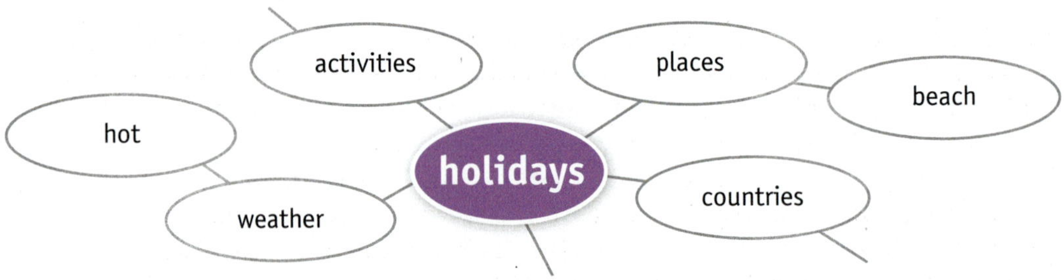

- Sammle Gegensatzpaare und schreibe sie auf.

  great ↔ *terrible*　　　*cold* ↔ *warm*

- Bilde Sätze mit den Wörtern, die du dir merken willst. Sie können auch lustig sein oder sich reimen.

  My mum can make a yummy cake.

- Schreibe Wörter auf Klebezettel und hänge sie zu Hause an verschiedenen Stellen auf. So hast du sie immer im Blick.

- Wenn du gerne am Computer arbeitest, dann benutze die Lernsoftware.

TIPP

- Deine Bildwörterbuch-Seiten, Tabellen, Wortnetze und vieles mehr kannst du in einem Vokabelordner abheften und dort beliebig ergänzen.
- Übe Vokabeln immer nur fünf bis zehn Minuten, aber dafür regelmäßig!
- Zu zweit macht das Vokabellernen mehr Spaß. Fragt euch gegenseitig ab. Ihr könnt auch selbst Lückentexte, Kreuzwort- oder Buchstabenrätsel für den Partner / die Partnerin erstellen.

B ... listen

Ohren auf! Worum geht es überhaupt?

Du kennst ja schon einige Tricks, wie du einen Hörtext besser verstehen kannst:

1. Vor dem Hören

- Wie lautet die Überschrift des Hörtextes? Welche Hinweise gibt sie dir?
- Gibt es Bilder zum Text? Was ist zu sehen?
- Überlege: Worum könnte es wohl gehen? Was weißt du schon über das Thema? Was erwartest du?

2. Beim Hören

- Höre dir das Gespräch oder die Geschichte einmal ganz an. Du musst nicht jedes einzelne Wort verstehen. Versuche herauszufinden, worum es geht. Wer ist beteiligt? Was passiert? Achte auch auf die Geräusche. Sie geben dir oft Hinweise auf den Ort und das Geschehen. Wie klingen die Stimmen der Personen? Begeistert? Aufgeregt?
- Lies dir die Höraufgabe im Buch genau durch. Was sollst du herausfinden? Höre dir das Gespräch oder die Geschichte ein zweites Mal an. Kannst du die Höraufgabe im Buch jetzt lösen? Wenn nicht, dann höre dir den Text noch ein weiteres Mal an.
- Wenn es zu einem Hörtext keine Aufgabe gibt, können dir diese Fragen weiterhelfen:

Who? (Wer spricht? Um wen geht es?)	**Where?** (Wo findet das Gespräch / die Geschichte statt?)	**When?** (Wann findet es / sie statt?)	**What?** (Worüber wird gesprochen? Was passiert?)

- Mache dir Notizen zu den Fragen, auf die du eine Antwort weißt.

3. Zu guter Letzt

- Vergleiche deine Ergebnisse mit einer Partnerin oder einem Partner. Was habt ihr herausgefunden? Haben sich eure Erwartungen bestätigt?

TIPP

Nutze jede Gelegenheit, um Englisch zu hören!
- Mit der *Camden Market*-CD kannst du zu Hause dein Hörverstehen trainieren.
- Höre dir englische Musik an und achte auf den Text. Was kannst du schon verstehen?
- Sieh dir einen Film, den du schon kennst, auf DVD an. Auf einer DVD kannst du fast immer den englischen Ton (mit oder ohne Untertitel) einschalten.

C ... read

Lesen leicht gemacht

Es gibt viele Tricks, die dir helfen, einen englischen Text leichter zu verstehen. Probiere doch einmal die folgenden Tipps beim Lesen aus:

1. Was verrät das Bild? Worum könnte es in der Geschichte gehen?

2. Was erfährst du aus der Überschrift?

3. Überfliege den Text erst einmal. Versuche herauszufinden, worum es geht. Was passiert? Wer ist beteiligt? Dafür brauchst du nicht jedes Wort zu verstehen.

4. Lies den Text noch einmal gründlich. Mit den *wh*-Fragen kannst du die wichtigsten Informationen herausbekommen:
Who?
Where?
When?
What?

The orienteering trip

Last summer a group of twenty boys went camping and orienteering in Scotland for two days. They had small tents and sleeping bags in their rucksacks. Every pair had a map, a compass, food and drink and warm pullovers and trousers.

Jim and Kevin were partners. The two boys walked and walked and talked and laughed about lots of things. But they didn't look at their maps and they didn't look at their watches.

It got dark and foggy. They looked for the others but couldn't find them, so they put up their tent, ate some chocolate and told ghost stories.

Suddenly there were strange noises. And then a big dark thing came to their tent. It opened the tent and said, "Ah, it's you two! The others are all here, too. But they're still putting up their tents, so you're the winners. Congratulations!"

It was the guide, John. Jim and Kevin were at the campsite!

TIPP

So kannst du die Bedeutung eines Wortes ohne Wörterbuch herausfinden:

- Oft kennst du ein deutsches Wort, das ganz ähnlich aussieht, z.B. *orienteering* oder *congratulations*.
- Überlege, ob du ein englisches Wort aus der gleichen Wortfamilie, also einen „Verwandten", kennst, z. B. *sleep – sleeping bag*.
- Häufig kannst du die Bedeutung eines unbekannten Wortes aus dem Satzzusammenhang erschließen. Dabei helfen dir die Wörter, die vor oder nach dem unbekannten Wort stehen. Was könnten die Wörter *tent* und *guide* in der Geschichte oben bedeuten?

D ... give a talk

Wenn du etwas vor der Klasse präsentierst

Wenn du Arbeitsergebnisse präsentieren möchtest oder einen Vortrag halten willst, können dir folgende Tipps dabei helfen:

1. Bevor du etwas vorträgst

- Überlege: Was ist dein Thema? Was möchtest du sagen? Wie viel Zeit hast du für deinen Vortrag?
- Sammle deine Gedanken und schreibe sie in Stichpunkten auf, z. B. in einem *word web* oder auf Karteikarten.
- Entscheide, in welcher Reihenfolge du die Dinge sagen und wie du anfangen möchtest.
- Fertige ein Poster oder eine Folie an, um deinen Vortrag anschaulich zu machen. Du kannst aber auch eine *PowerPoint*-Präsentation gestalten.
- Übe deinen Vortrag vor dem Spiegel, vor Freunden oder deiner Familie – oder nimm deinen Vortrag zur Probe auf, z. B. mit einem Handy oder einem Easi-Speak-Mikrofon.

TIPP

So sieht ein gelungenes Vortrags-Poster aus:

- ansprechende Überschrift
- interessante Informationen
- verständliche Sätze, aber: nicht zu viel Text
- große Bilder und Schrift: → Jeder im Raum muss sie sehen und lesen können.
- saubere Schrift
- Bilder mit Bildunterschriften

2. Bei deinem Vortrag

- Sprich langsam und deutlich.
- Sieh deine Zuhörer an, wenn du sprichst.
- Versuche, frei zu sprechen. Du kannst die wichtigsten Punkte von deinen Notizen oder deinem Poster / deiner Folie ablesen.
- Zeige deinen Zuhörern auf deinem Poster oder deiner Folie, worüber du gerade sprichst. So wird dein Vortrag für die Klasse noch interessanter.

3. Nützliche Redewendungen

- **Zu Beginn deines Vortrags:** *Hello, everybody.*
  My talk is about ... / I'd like to talk about ...
- **Im Hauptteil:** *On my poster you can see ...*
  Look at this picture. It shows ...
  Another thing I want to tell you about is ...
- **Wenn du mal den Faden verlierst:** *Just a moment, please. / Wait a second.*
- **Zum Schluss:** *Thank you for listening. Have you got any questions?*

E ... talk

Du kannst reden!

Im Englischunterricht arbeitest du oft mit einem Partner oder in einer Gruppe zusammen. Auch wenn es dir vielleicht komisch vorkommt, solltest du mit deinen Mitschülerinnen und Mitschülern Englisch sprechen – so lernst du besser Englisch und kannst deine Arbeitsergebnisse leichter vorstellen. Hier findest du dazu einige nützliche Redewendungen und Tipps:

Wenn du mit jemandem zusammenarbeitest

- *Can I be ...?*
- *Whose turn is it? – It's your turn.*
- *Sorry, have you finished? Can I say something now?*
- *Can you explain that, please?*
- *Can you say it again, please?*

Wenn du einen Vorschlag machen möchtest

- *Let's do it like this.*
- *You/We could write something different here.*
- *Why don't you/we change this?*

Wenn du Rückmeldung geben möchtest

- **Zu einem Vortrag:** *Your presentation was/wasn't easy to understand. It was/wasn't really interesting. You spoke/didn't speak loudly and clearly.*
- **Zu einem Poster:** *Your poster looks/doesn't look attractive/interesting. The letters are/aren't big enough. The text is (not) too long.*
- **Zu einer Geschichte:** *I (don't) like your story because it is ...*
- **Zu einem Rollenspiel:** *André was/wasn't very good as Rajiv because he ...*

- Wenn dir ein Wort mal nicht einfällt, versuche es zu umschreiben. Du kannst aber auch deine Hände zu Hilfe nehmen.
- Im Gespräch solltest du immer höflich sein. Verwende deshalb *sorry*, *please* und *thank you*.

TIPP

Sprich Englisch, sooft du kannst!

- Höre dir die *Camden Market*-CD an und lies die Texte laut mit. Versuche, die Aussprache der Sprecher nachzuahmen. Du kannst auch englische Lieder mitsingen.
- Lies einen Text aus dem Buch laut vor oder sprich Englisch und nimm dich auf. Dann kannst du dich selbst anhören und überprüfen, wie dein Englisch klingt.
- Sprich Englisch mit jemandem, der ebenfalls Englisch sprechen kann.

F ... write

Tipps und Tricks zum Schreiben

1. Plane deinen Text

- Überlege: Was für einen Text willst du schreiben – einen Text über dich, eine E-Mail, ein Gedicht oder eine (Fantasie-)Geschichte?
- Sammle Ideen und Wörter zum Thema deines Textes, z. B. in einem *word web* oder einer Liste.
- Bringe deine Ideen und Wörter in eine sinnvolle Reihenfolge.

2. Schreibe den Text

- Sieh dir Texte im Buch an, die sich mit dem Thema beschäftigen. Du kannst sie als Muster benutzen, um deine eigenen Texte zu schreiben. Übernimm nützliche Satzanfänge und Ausdrücke und ersetze die Wörter, die nicht zum Thema passen.
- Schreibe erst einmal kurze, einfache Sätze auf.
- Fange deine Sätze unterschiedlich an:
  Charlie likes football. Charlie is an Arsenal fan. → *Charlie likes football. He is an Arsenal fan.*
- Verbinde deine Ideen und Sätze mit *linking words* wie *and, or, but, so, because*:
  Caroline often goes to Manchester. Her friend Claire lives there. → *Caroline often goes to Manchester because her friend Claire lives there.*
- Benutze *time words*, um zu sagen, wann etwas geschieht, z. B. *in the morning, then, later, after (that), yesterday*:
  I went shopping. I met some friends. → *Yesterday I went shopping. Later I met some friends.*
- Adjektive und Adverbien machen deinen Text interessanter.
  Suddenly a man opened the door and looked at us. → *Suddenly a tall man opened the door and looked at us angrily.*
- Überlege dir eine passende Überschrift.

3. Überarbeite deinen Text

- Sieh dir deinen Text noch einmal genau an. Hast du alles richtig geschrieben? Schlage schwierige Wörter im *English-German dictionary* ab Seite 243 nach.
- Bist du bei der Grammatik unsicher? Schau im LiF-Teil ab Seite 177 nach.
- Tauscht eure Texte untereinander aus. Sprecht darüber, was euch an dem Text gefällt, was noch ergänzt werden könnte und was verbessert werden sollte.
- Wenn du deinen Text fertig hast, schreibe ihn ins Reine.

4. Präsentiere deinen Text

- Du kannst deinen Text nun präsentieren, indem du ihn z. B. vorliest, aufnimmst, aushängst oder in einem *class book* veröffentlichst. Danach heftest du deinen Text in deiner Portfolio-Mappe ab.

G ... write a letter

So kannst du einen persönlichen Brief schreiben

Auch hier gehst du am besten Schritt für Schritt vor:

1. Deine Adresse (ohne deinen Namen) gehört in die rechte obere Ecke.

2. Das Datum folgt unter der Adresse auf der rechten Seite.

3. Beginne deinen Brief an einen Freund oder eine Freundin mit *Dear ...*, oder *Hi ...*,

4. Fange die erste Zeile mit einem Großbuchstaben an.

5. Worüber möchtest du schreiben? Vielleicht darüber, was du am Wochenende erlebt hast? Dann benutze die Vergangenheit (*simple past*): *I went, I played, ...* Denke auch an *linking words* und *time words* (siehe *How to ... write* auf Seite 171).

6. Am Ende deines Briefes kannst du deinem Freund oder deiner Freundin Fragen stellen. Du kannst ihn oder sie auch bitten, dir zurückzuschreiben.

7. So kannst du deinen Brief beenden: *Best wishes, Love, Lots of love, Yours, All the best, ...*

Waldschmidtstraße 39
60316 Frankfurt
Germany

22nd May 20..

Dear Helen,

How are you?

I'm fine. I had a great weekend. On Friday after school my friend Jasmine came to my house. We made pizza and watched a funny film on TV.

On Saturday the weather was warm and sunny. So my parents made some sandwiches and we all went swimming. The water was still cold but I liked it.

On Sunday I stayed in bed until 12.30 pm.
I listened to my favourite music and finished a book. In the afternoon I met some friends in the park. We played basketball and had a lot of fun.

What did you do last weekend? What was the weather like?

Please write back soon.

All the best,
Ella

TIPP

- Sieh dir deinen Brief noch einmal genau an. Hast du alles richtig geschrieben?
- Hast du die richtige Zeitform verwendet?
- Ist dein Ton höflich und freundlich?
- Schreibe die Adresse gut leserlich auf den Briefumschlag – und ab geht die Post!

H ... work with grammar

Grammatikregeln auf der Spur

Versuche, Grammatikregeln selbst aufzuspüren. Auf diese Weise kannst du sie nämlich besser behalten. Das folgende Beispiel soll dir zeigen, wie das gehen kann.

1. Sammeln

Schaue dir englische Texte an. Sammle mehrere Beispiele für eine Grammatikregel, z. B. für die Zeitform *simple past*.

2. Sortieren

Schreibe die Beispiele untereinander.
Was sieht hier ähnlich aus?
Unterstreiche die Stellen.

visit<u>ed</u>	was / were
stay<u>ed</u>	went
walk<u>ed</u>	had
ask<u>ed</u>	ate

3. Beschreiben

Sieh dir deine Beispiele gut an.
Was kannst du erkennen?
Welche Veränderung tritt immer wieder auf?
Beschreibe und notiere dann deine Regel.

Manche Verben werden im simple past mit -ed gebildet, manche nicht.

4. Überprüfen

Schaue nun im LiF-Teil ab Seite 177 nach, ob du richtigliegst. Ändere oder ergänze deine Regel falls nötig.

TIPP

- Auf den Seiten 284 und 285 findest du alle Verben, die eine unregelmäßige *simple past*-Form haben. Diese Verben musst du dir gut einprägen. Aber keine Sorge: Viele Verben werden ähnlich gebildet, z. B. *bring – brought, buy – bought, think – thought* oder *sleep – slept, keep – kept, leave – left*. In den Wortlisten zu den *Themes* und in den *dictionaries* erkennst du die unregelmäßigen Verben daran, dass sie mit *(irr)* gekennzeichnet sind.
- Schreibe Grammatikregeln in deinen eigenen Worten auf und ergänze Beispiele und Merksätze. Umrande die Grammatikregeln farbig und schreibe den Grammatikbegriff (z. B. *simple past*) auf den Blattrand. So findest du die Regeln beim Nachschlagen schnell wieder.
- Versucht, euch gegenseitig Grammatikregeln zu erklären.

I ... work with others

Zusammen seid ihr stark!

Think – pair – share

Um Ideen zu einem Thema zu sammeln, kannst du in drei Schritten vorgehen:

1. *Think:* Sammle deine Gedanken und Ideen und mache dir Notizen.
2. *Pair:* Tausche dich mit einem Partner / einer Partnerin aus. Ergänze neue Ideen in deiner Liste.
3. *Share:* Teilt dann eure Gedanken und Ideen mit einem anderen Paar. Nun habt ihr schon Ideen und Meinungen von vier verschiedenen Leuten kennengelernt.

Buzz groups

Bei dieser Arbeitsform sprecht ihr alle mit leiser Stimme, damit sich die verschiedenen Gruppen nicht gegenseitig stören. *Buzz* heißt summen oder brummen und beschreibt den Geräuschpegel, der dabei im Raum entsteht.

1. Bildet *buzz groups* mit drei bis fünf Gruppenmitgliedern. Sprecht über das vorgegebene Thema. Ein Gruppenmitglied macht Notizen.
2. Wählt einen Sprecher / eine Sprecherin, der / die die Ergebnisse eurer *buzz group* in der Klasse vorstellt.

Milling around

Mit der Methode *milling around* (auf Deutsch: umherlaufen) kannst du dich mit deinen Klassenkameraden zu einem Thema (z. B. *jobs* oder *rules at home*) austauschen.

1. Gehe durch die Klasse, ohne dass du dabei sprichst.
2. Wenn dein Lehrer / deine Lehrerin ein Zeichen gibt oder „Stop!" sagt, sprich mit der Person, vor der du gerade stehst. Tauscht euch über die Aufgabe aus.
3. Notiere deine Ergebnisse und gehe weiter.

Dramatic reading

Um einen Text mit verschiedenen Rollen lebendig vorzutragen, bietet sich *dramatic reading* an:

1. Lies den Text zu deiner Rolle mit leiser Stimme mehrmals durch.
2. Schaue dir jeden Satz einzeln an und präge ihn dir ein. Sieh dann hoch und sprich den Satz nach. Schaue deine Gruppenmitglieder dabei an. Arbeite den ganzen Text auf diese Weise durch.
3. Überlege, wie sich die Person gerade fühlt, deren Rolle du liest. Ist sie verärgert, fröhlich, ...? Versuche, die Sätze entsprechend zu lesen und zu betonen.

Double circle

Auch dies ist eine Arbeitsform, bei der du die Ideen und Gedanken von vielen verschiedenen Leuten in deiner Klasse erfährst.

1. Bildet in der Klasse zwei Kreise: einen Innenkreis und einen Außenkreis.
2. Diejenigen von euch, die sich gegenüberstehen, unterhalten sich über ein vorher bestimmtes Thema (z. B. *favourite festivals*).
3. Wenn dein Lehrer / deine Lehrerin ein Zeichen gibt, dreht ihr euch in den beiden Kreisen in entgegengesetzte Richtungen weiter. Nun tauscht ihr euch mit einem neuen Partner / einer neuen Partnerin über das Thema aus.

Placemat

Auf einer *placemat* (auf Deutsch: Tischvorlage, Platzdeckchen) sammelst du mit deinen Gruppenmitgliedern zu einem Thema gleichzeitig Ideen.

1. Jede/r von euch macht auf einem Teil eines großen Bogens Papier Notizen.
2. Anschließend dreht ihr die *placemat* so lange, bis jede/r alle Beiträge gelesen hat.
3. Einigt euch dann in der Gruppe auf die wichtigsten Punkte und notiert sie in der Mitte des Blattes.
4. Schließlich stellt ein Gruppenmitglied das Ergebnis in der Klasse vor.

J ... help out

So kannst du jemandem sprachlich aushelfen

Du kannst anderen Menschen helfen, die kaum Deutsch oder Englisch verstehen.
Hier erfährst du, wie das funktioniert:

1. Gib den Sinn wieder

Stell dir vor, du bist mit einer englischen Austauschschülerin und einem deutschen Freund unterwegs. Sie spricht kaum Deutsch, er kaum Englisch. Du musst jetzt nicht Wort für Wort übersetzen. Wichtiger ist es, den Sinn wiederzugeben. Das kannst du auch in deinen eigenen Worten machen.

2. Benutze Redewendungen

Versuche, dich an Redewendungen aus dem Unterricht zu erinnern.

3. Bilde kurze Sätze

Bilde einfache, kurze Sätze, wenn du den Sinn wiedergibst.

4. Umschreibe Wörter

Wenn dir ein wichtiges Wort nicht einfällt, kannst du es umschreiben. Du weißt z. B. nicht, was „Geschenk" auf Englisch heißt. Du kannst dann sagen: *You give it to a friend. It's for a birthday.* Natürlich kannst du auch Hände und Füße benutzen, um deutlich zu machen, worum es geht.

LiF steht für *Language in Focus*. Das ist der Grammatikteil von *Camden Market*, in dem die englische Sprache genauer unter die Lupe genommen wird. Du findest in LiF die grammatischen Regeln. Wenn vorne im Buch zum Beispiel 10 p. 185 steht, kannst du in LiF unter Nummer 10 die passenden Regeln nachschlagen.
Das „R" hinter manchen Nummern steht für *revision* (Wiederholung). So gekennzeichnete Regeln kennst du bereits aus dem letzten Jahr.
Auf dieser und der nächsten Seite findest du die grammatischen Begriffe auf Englisch und auf Deutsch.

Grammatical terms

Englisch	LiF	Deutsch	Beispiel
adjective	16	Adjektiv	a perfect day, a big house
adverb		Adverb	
adverb of frequency	14R	Häufigkeitsadverb	often, sometimes, never, …
adverb of manner	13	Adverb der Art und Weise	James sings badly.
article		Artikel	
definite article		bestimmter Artikel	the
indefinite article		unbestimmter Artikel	a / an
comparison		Vergleich	
comparative	16	Komparativ (1. Steigerungsform)	Anne is taller than Tom. The film was more interesting than the book.
superlative	16	Superlativ (2. Steigerungsform)	Steven is the oldest boy. Sue is the most beautiful girl.
comparison of adjectives	16	Steigerung von Adjektiven	London is bigger than Berlin.
comparison of adverbs	23	Steigerung von Adverbien	Greg runs faster than his brother.
conditional clause	20	Bedingungssatz	If it rains, I will stay at home.
future		Futur (Zukunft)	
going to-future	15	Futur mit *going to*	She's going to buy a book.
will-future	10-12	Futur mit *will*	I'm sure he will be a pop star.
genitive		Genitiv	
genitive with of		Genitiv mit *of*	the name of the ship
s-genitive		*s*-Genitiv	Bob's dog
imperative	19R	Imperativ (Befehlsform)	Please sit down! Don't shout!
infinitive		Infinitiv (Grundform)	walk, read, go, …
linking word		Bindewort	and, because, but, so, …
long form	1R	Langform	I am, he is, they are, …
modal verb	18	Modalverb	can, must, need, should, …
noun		Nomen (Hauptwort, Substantiv)	song, ball, car, dog, …
object	14R	Objekt	We've got a car.
past participle	21	Partizip Perfekt	eaten, gone, started, …
past tense		Vergangenheit	
simple past	5R-7R	einfache Vergangenheit	They played football yesterday.
past progressive	22	Verlaufsform der Vergangenheit	Emma was reading a book.

personal pronoun		Personalpronomen	
object pronoun		Objektpronomen	me, you, him, her, it, us, them
subject pronoun		Subjektpronomen	I, you, he, she, it, we, they
plural		Plural (Mehrzahl)	
regular / irregular		regelmäßig / unregelmäßig	cars, books, ... / children, men, ...
possessive determiner		Possessivbegleiter	my, your, his, her, its, our, their
preposition		Präposition	in, on, next to, behind, ...
present perfect	21	Perfekt	David has cleaned the kitchen.
present tense		Präsens (Gegenwart)	
present progressive	4R	Verlaufsform der Gegenwart	It's raining.
simple present	2R	einfache Gegenwart	I often walk to school.
question		Frage	
question word	9R	Fragewort	who, where, what, how, ...
yes / no question	1R, 3R	Entscheidungsfrage	Are you from Germany?
short answer	1R, 3R	Kurzantwort	Yes, I am. / No, I'm not.
short form	1R	Kurzform	I'm, he's, they're, ...
singular		Singular (Einzahl)	dog, friend, house, ...
statement		Aussagesatz	She's from Camden. /
positive / negative		bejaht / verneint	I don't like football.
subject	14R	Subjekt	School is great. / Jo and I like tea.
verb		Verb	
regular / irregular	5R, 21	regelmäßig / unregelmäßig	look, walk, ... / meet, see, ...
word order		Satzstellung	
subject – verb – object	14R	Subjekt – Verb – Objekt	Sarah likes popcorn.

1R Das Verb *be* (The verb *be*)

Die Formen des Verbs *be* gibt es als Kurzformen und als Langformen. Die Kurzformen (*short forms*) verwendet man oft beim Sprechen. Beim Schreiben verwendet man die Langformen (*long forms*).

Langform	Kurzform		
I **am**	I'**m**	I'**m** eleven.	*Ich bin ...*
you **are**	you'**re**	You'**re** my friend.	*Du bist ...*
he **is**	he'**s**	He'**s** from Manchester.	*Er ist ...*
she **is**	she'**s**	She'**s** my sister.	*Sie ist ...*
it **is**	it'**s**	It'**s** late.	*Es ist ...*
we **are**	we'**re**	We'**re** hungry.	*Wir sind ...*
you **are**	you'**re**	You'**re** nice.	*Ihr seid ...*
they **are**	they'**re**	They'**re** in the garden.	*Sie sind ...*

*They **are** from Manchester.*

Die Formen von *be* kannst du ganz einfach verneinen, indem du ***not*** einfügst:
*He **is** from Camden.* → *He **is not** from Camden. / He **isn't** from Camden.*
*They **are** friends.* → *They **are not** friends. / They **aren't** friends.*

Wenn du eine Entscheidungsfrage mit *be* stellen möchtest, vertauschst du einfach das **Subjekt** und die Form von ***be***:

Gillian is from Camden.
Is Gillian from Camden?

Auf Entscheidungsfragen antwortet man meist nicht mit einem ganzen Satz. Es ist aber unhöflich, nur mit „*Yes.*" oder „*No.*" zu antworten. Deshalb verwendet man häufig Kurzantworten:
Is Peter from London? – ***Yes, he is.* / *No, he isn't.***

2R Die einfache Gegenwart (The simple present)

Das *simple present* verwendest du, ...

- um über Gewohnheiten oder regelmäßige Handlungen zu sprechen:
  *They **play** football every Tuesday.*
- um über aufeinander folgende Handlungen zu sprechen:
  *First Caroline **gets** up. Then she **has** breakfast. After that she **goes** to school.*
- um über Zustände zu sprechen, die längere Zeit andauern:
  *Emma and Gillian **live** in London.*

***simple present:* Aussagesätze**		
I often	play	football.
You sometimes	play	tennis.
He never	plays	basketball.
She	plays	the guitar.
It always	plays	with other dogs.
We	play	basketball every Monday.
You always	play	hockey.
They	play	games at the weekend.

Bei *I, you, we* und *they* hat das *simple present* dieselbe Form wie der Infinitiv.
Bei *he, she* und *it* (in der 3. Person Singular) hängst du ein *-s* an.

! Endet das Verb mit *-ss, -sh, -ch* oder *-x*, hängst du bei *he, she, it* ein *-es* an:
He washes his face in the morning.
She often watches TV.

! Auch bei *do* und *go* fügst du in der 3. Person Singular *-es* an.
Achte auf die unterschiedliche Aussprache:
do / duː / – she does / dʌz /,
go / gəʊ / – she goes / gəʊz /.

! Bei Verben, die auf *-y* enden (z. B. *tidy up* und *empty*), gilt folgende Regel:
Kommt ein Konsonant vor dem *-y*, so wird das *-y* zu *-ies*:
She often tidies up her room.
He sometimes empties the dishwasher.

Sätze im *simple present* kannst du mit ***don't*** verneinen. Bei *he, she, it* (also in der 3. Person Singular) verwendest du ***doesn't***. Dabei verliert das Verb das *-s* am Ende. *Don't* und *doesn't* sind die Kurzformen von *do not* und *does not*. Meistens verwendet man diese Kurzformen:

	simple present: **Verneinung**		
Singular	I	don't play	football.
	You	don't like	tennis.
	He	doesn't work	in London.
	She	doesn't live	in Manchester.
	It	doesn't look	like a dog.
Plural	We	don't walk	to school.
	You	don't know	Peter's sister.
	They	don't go	to Manchester.

Gillian ***doesn't like*** *rubbish.*

! Bei der Verneinung von Sätzen mit *be, can* oder *have got* brauchst du *don't* oder *doesn't* nicht:
He ***is not*** *from Camden.*
I ***can't*** *play an instrument.*
I ***haven't got*** *a computer.*

3R Die einfache Gegenwart: Entscheidungsfragen und Kurzantworten

(The simple present: Yes/no questions and short answers)

Entscheidungsfragen sind Fragen, auf die man mit „Ja" oder „Nein" antworten kann.

Entscheidungsfragen und Kurzantworten mit *be, can, have got*		
Are you eleven?	Yes, I am.	No, I'm not.
Can you play an instrument?	Yes, I can.	No, I can't.
Has Emma got a new book?	Yes, she has.	No, she hasn't.

Wenn du Entscheidungsfragen im *simple present* mit einem anderen Verb wie *play, like* oder *know* stellen möchtest, verwendest du einfach ***do*** oder ***does*** am Satzanfang und in der Kurzantwort:

Entscheidungsfragen und Kurzantworten mit *do* + Verb		
Do you play volleyball?	Yes, I do.	No, I don't.
Do they like pizza?	Yes, they do.	No, they don't.
Does George know Gillian?	Yes, he does.	No, he doesn't.

! Bei *he, she, it* verwendest du in den Entscheidungsfragen *does*.
Dabei verliert das Verb das *-s*:
George knows Gillian.
Does *George know Gillian?*

4R Die Verlaufsform der Gegenwart (The present progressive)

a) Bejahte und verneinte Aussagesätze

Das *present progressive* verwendest du, wenn du sagen möchtest, was jemand gerade tut oder was gerade passiert – also für Vorgänge, die gerade ablaufen und noch nicht abgeschlossen sind:

	present progressive: **Aussagesätze**	
Singular	I **am watching** TV. You **are writing** an email. He **is drinking** orange juice. She **is sitting** on the sofa. Oh no, it **is raining** again!	*Ich sehe (gerade) fern.* *Du schreibst (gerade) eine E-Mail.* *Er trinkt (gerade) Orangensaft.* *Sie sitzt (gerade) auf dem Sofa.* *Oh nein, es regnet schon wieder.*
Plural	We **are eating** pizza. You **are playing** football. Listen, they **are singing** a song.	*Wir essen (gerade) Pizza.* *Ihr spielt (gerade) Fußball.* *Hör mal, sie singen (gerade) ein Lied.*

Im Deutschen gibt es keine Verlaufsform. Mit Wörtern wie *gerade, im Moment* oder *jetzt* lässt sich die Verlaufsform aber gut wiedergeben:
*Caroline **is reading** a book.* – Caroline liest **gerade** ein Buch.

*Caroline **is reading** a book.*

So bildest du das *present progressive:*
Form von *be (am, is, are)* + **Infinitiv des Verbs** + **Endung *-ing***:
*He **is drinking** orange juice.*

! Endet das Verb auf *-e*, dann fällt das *-e* in der Verlaufsform weg.
write → *writ**ing*** — *Caroline is writ**ing** a letter.*
dance → *danc**ing*** — *Rajiv is danc**ing**.*

! Endet das Verb auf einem kurzen betonten *Vokal* + *Konsonant*, wird der Konsonant verdoppelt.
sit → *sit**ting*** — *George is sit**ting** in the kitchen.*
run → *run**ning*** — *Charlie is run**ning**.*

Für die Verneinung fügst du einfach ein ***not*** hinter die Form von *be* ein:
*Caroline is **not** writing a letter.* *George is**n't** reading a book. He's watching TV.*

b) Fragen und Kurzantworten

Auch in der Verlaufsform kannst du Entscheidungsfragen bilden:

*Charlie **is** reading a book.*
Is Charlie reading a book?

Is George **helping** his mum? – **Yes, he is. / No, he isn't.**
Are Caroline and George **playing** basketball? – **Yes, they are. / No, they aren't.**

Bei Fragen mit Fragewort stellst du das Fragewort an den Satzanfang:

***What are** you **doing**? **Where are** you **going**?*

5R Die einfache Vergangenheit (The simple past)

Das *simple past* verwendest du, wenn du über etwas sprechen willst, das in der Vergangenheit liegt und abgeschlossen ist – z. B. wenn du berichtest, was du erlebt hast, oder wenn du eine Geschichte erzählst.

Infinitiv + ed

watched | walked
helped | started

a) Regelmäßige Verben (Regular verbs)

Das *simple past* der regelmäßigen Verben bildest du, indem du die Endung *-ed* an den **Infinitiv** anhängst:
watch + *ed* ➔ *watched*

***simple past:* regelmäßige Formen**	
Yesterday I **watched** a film about elephants.	*Gestern habe ich einen Film über Elefanten gesehen.*
Last Monday Rajiv **helped** his parents in the shop.	*Letzten Montag hat Rajiv seinen Eltern im Laden geholfen.*

! Achte auf folgende Besonderheiten in der Schreibung:
Endet das Verb auf *-e*, dann wird nur *-d* angehängt.
like ➔ *liked*
Endet das Verb auf einem kurzen betonten *Vokal* + *Konsonant*, wird der Konsonant verdoppelt.
stop ➔ *stopped*
Endet das Verb auf *Konsonant* + *-y*, dann lautet die Endung im *simple past* *-ied*.
try ➔ *tried*

b) Unregelmäßige Verben (Irregular verbs)

Bei unregelmäßigen Verben wird das *simple past* nicht mit *-ed* gebildet. Du musst ihre Formen wie neue Vokabeln lernen. Auf Seite 284 – 285 findest du eine Liste der unregelmäßigen Verben.

Be hat als einziges englisches Verb zwei Formen im *simple past*, *was* und *were*:
I / he / she / it was – *you / we / they were*

Weitere unregelmäßige Verben findest du in diesen Sätzen:

Infinitiv	***simple past***	
be	was / were	I **was** very hungry after school. They **were** in London last week.
have	had	Sarah **had** a great holiday.
go	went	She **went** to Spain with her family.
find	found	She and her sister **found** many nice postcards.
do	did	They **did** lots of interesting things together.

6R Die einfache Vergangenheit: Verneinung
(The simple past: Negation)

Wenn du sagen willst, was in der Vergangenheit nicht geschehen ist, verwendest du ***not*** oder die Kurzform ***n't***, die an *was/were* angehängt wird.

simple past: **bejahter Satz**	***simple past:*** **verneinter Satz**
I **was** at school on Monday.	I **wasn't** at school on Monday.
They **were** friendly at the hotel.	They **weren't** friendly at the hotel.

Wenn im Satz kein *was/were* steht, musst du ***didn't (did not)*** vor das Verb stellen. *Didn't* ist die Vergangenheitsform von *don't* und *doesn't*. *Didn't* ist bei allen Personen gleich. Das Verb selbst bleibt im **Infinitiv**, weil *didn't* schon die Vergangenheit anzeigt.

simple past: **bejahter Satz**	***simple past:*** **verneinter Satz**
George **talked** to Gillian yesterday.	George **didn't talk** to Gillian yesterday.
I **went** to Paris last year.	I **didn't go** to Paris last year.

7R Die einfache Vergangenheit: Entscheidungsfragen und Kurzantworten
(The simple past: Yes/no questions and short answers)

Entscheidungsfragen im *simple past* bildest du, indem du ***did*** an den Satzanfang stellst. Du antwortest, wie bei allen Entscheidungsfragen, nicht nur mit *„Yes."* oder *„No."*, sondern fügst eine zusätzliche Bestätigung oder Ablehnung hinzu.

simple past: **Entscheidungsfragen und Kurzantworten**		
Did you **go** on holiday?	**Yes, I did.**	**No, I didn't.**
Did Claire **visit** Caroline in London?	**Yes, she did.**	**No, she didn't.**

Bei Entscheidungsfragen mit *was/were* stellst du ***was*** oder ***were*** an den Satzanfang.

simple past: **Entscheidungsfragen und Kurzantworten mit *was/were***		
Were you at the party yesterday?	**Yes, I was.**	**No, I wasn't.**
Was it good?	**Yes, it was.**	**No, it wasn't.**

Did *Rajiv* ***buy*** *a new football yesterday?*
– ***Yes, he did.***

8R *There is … / There are …*

Wenn du sagen möchtest, dass eine Sache oder eine Person vorhanden ist, benutzt du ***there is***. Bei mehreren Sachen oder Personen benutzt du ***there are***.
Wenn du fragen möchtest, ob etwas vorhanden ist, vertauschst du einfach die Wortstellung:

There is a market in Camden.
Is there a market in Camden?

There are posters in the classroom.
Are there posters in the classroom?

Auf solche Fragen antwortet man häufig mit Kurzantworten:
Yes, there is / there are oder ***No, there isn't / there aren't***.

9R Fragen mit Fragewörtern (Questions with question words)

Who, what, when, where, why und *how* sind Fragewörter.
Wenn du eine Frage mit einem Fragewort stellen möchtest, stellst du das Fragewort an den Satzanfang.

Who?	Wer?
What?	Was?
When?	Wann?
Where?	Wo?
Why?	Warum?
How?	Wie?

Fragen mit Fragewörtern mit *be, can, have got*	
Where is George?	*Wo ist George?*
What was the weather like?	*Wie war das Wetter?*
When can I call you?	*Wann kann ich dich anrufen?*
Who has got an idea?	*Wer hat eine Idee?*

! Mit *who* fragst du nach Personen, mit *where* nach Orten.
Ein Merkspruch: *Who, who, who* – **wer** bist du?
Where, where, where – **wo** kommst du her?

Auch bei Fragen mit *do* stellst du das Fragewort an den Satzanfang:

Fragen mit Fragewörtern mit *do* + Verb	
Why does Amy **like** the film?	*Warum mag Amy den Film?*
Where do you **go** on holiday?	*Wo machst du Urlaub?*
When do you **leave**?	*Wann gehst du?*
What did you **do** this summer?	*Was habt ihr diesen Sommer gemacht?*
How long did you **stay** there?	*Wie lange warst du da?*

Bei Fragen mit *who* braucht man kein *do* oder *does*, wenn *who* Subjekt ist:
***Who** lives in Camden?*
***Who** empties the dishwasher?*

10 Die Zukunft mit *will* (The *will*-future)

Wenn du über die Zukunft sprechen willst, benutzt du das *will-future*. Mit dem *will-future* kannst du Vermutungen aussprechen und Vorhersagen oder Versprechen äußern.

Das *will-future* bildest du mit ***will*** und dem **Infinitiv des Verbs**.
Auch ***will*** hat eine Kurzform. Sie lautet *'ll*. Die Kurzformen verwendet man meistens beim Sprechen, die Langformen verwendet man meist, wenn man etwas schreibt. *Will* ist in allen Personen gleich.

	Langform	Kurzform		
Singular	I **will**	I'**ll**	I'**ll** **help** you.	*Ich werde dir helfen.*
	you **will**	you'**ll**	You'**ll** **be** a pilot.	*Du wirst Pilot werden.*
	he **will**	he'**ll**	He'**ll** **be** rich.	*Er wird reich werden.*
	she **will**	she'**ll**	She'**ll** **be** happy.	*Sie wird glücklich werden.*
	it **will**	it'**ll**	It'**ll** **rain** soon.	*Es wird bald regnen.*
Plural	we **will**	we'**ll**	We'**ll** **fly** to Mars.	*Wir werden auf den Mars fliegen.*
	you **will**	you'**ll**	You'**ll** **have** children.	*Ihr werdet Kinder haben.*
	they **will**	they'**ll**	They'**ll** **live** in France.	*Sie werden in Frankreich leben.*

! ***Will*** sieht aus wie das deutsche Wort „will". Aber es bedeutet „werden", nicht „wollen".
Im Deutschen kannst du es oft weglassen, aber niemals im Englischen:

*Next time I'**ll** catch you.* – Das nächste Mal krieg' ich dich!
Das nächste Mal werde ich dich kriegen!

Für die Verneinung fügst du einfach ein ***not*** hinter *will* ein.
Die Kurzform von ***will not*** ist ***won't***.
Won't ist für alle Personen gleich.

*On Wednesday it **will** be sunny. It **won't** be cold.*

*I think the boys **won't** win the football match.*
Ich denke, dass die Jungen das Fußballspiel nicht gewinnen werden.

*I'm sure you **won't** be a cook.*
Ich bin mir sicher, dass du kein Koch wirst.

11 Die Zukunft mit *will*: Entscheidungsfragen mit *will* und Kurzantworten

(The *will*-future: Yes / no questions with *will* and short answers)

Entscheidungsfragen mit *will* bildest du, indem du *will* an den Satzanfang stellst. Du verwendest *will* auch in der Kurzantwort.

Entscheidungsfragen und Kurzantworten mit *will*		
Will I **be** a famous pop star?	**Yes, I will.**	**No, I won't.**
Will you **live** in America?	**Yes, you will.**	**No, you won't.**
Will Tom **get** rich?	**Yes, he will.**	**No, he won't.**

12 Die Zukunft mit *will*: Fragen mit Fragewörtern

(The *will*-future: Questions with question words)

Bei Fragen mit Fragewörtern stellst du auch beim *will-future* das Fragewort an den Satzanfang (➔ LiF 9R).

Fragen mit Fragewörtern mit *will* + Verb	
Who will win the match?	*Wer wird das Spiel gewinnen?*
What will I **be**?	*Was werde ich sein?*
Where will you **live** in ten years?	*Wo wirst du in zehn Jahren leben?*
When will you **get married**?	*Wann werdet ihr heiraten?*
How many children **will** you **have**?	*Wie viele Kinder wirst du haben?*

13 Adverbien der Art und Weise (Adverbs of manner)

Wenn du eine Person, ein Tier oder eine Sache beschreibst, benutzt du ein Adjektiv.

The boys are **loud**. The garden is **big**. The sky is **blue**.

Wenn du beschreiben möchtest, wie jemand etwas tut oder wie etwas geschieht, benutzt du ein Adverb der Art und Weise. Adverbien der Art und Weise bildest du, indem du an das Adjektiv die Endung *-ly* anhängst:

Adjektiv	Adverb	
loud	loud**ly**	The boys speak very **loudly**.
bad	bad**ly**	Susan sings **badly**.
slow	slow**ly**	Tom walks **slowly**.

*He sings **badly**.*

Bei manchen Adverbien ändert sich die Schreibweise, wenn *-ly* angehängt wird. *-y* wird zu *-ily*; *-le* wird zu *-ly*; *-l* wird zu *-lly*.

Adjektiv	Adverb	
happy	happ**ily**	Caroline laughed **happily**.
angry	angr**ily**	He called the police **angrily**.
terrible	terrib**ly**	Simon dances **terribly**.
beautiful	beautiful**ly**	Mona sings **beautifully**.

! Einige Adverbien haben Sonderformen, die du wie Vokabeln lernen musst.
Manche Adjektive und Adverbien sind gleich:

Adjektiv	Adverb	
good	**well**	Rajiv is a good guitar player. He plays the guitar **well**.
fast	**fast**	Jack is a fast runner. He runs **fast**.
hard	**hard**	Gillian is a hard worker. She works **hard**.

Adverbien der Art und Weise stehen nach dem Verb.
In Sätzen mit Objekt stehen sie nach dem Objekt.

Subjekt	Verb	Objekt	Adverb.
Gillian	works		**hard**.
Rajiv	plays	the guitar	**well**.

*Rajiv dances very **well**.*

14R Die Satzstellung (Word order)

a) Satzstellung Subjekt – Verb – Objekt (S – V – O)

Die Satzstellung ist so etwas wie der „Bauplan" eines Satzes.
Im englischen Aussagesatz ist die Satzstellung meist: Subjekt – Verb – Objekt (S – V – O):

Subjekt *(subject)* **S**	**Verb** *(verb)* **V**	**Objekt** *(object)* **O**
I Charlie and his friends	like play	ice cream. football.

b) Aussagesätze mit Häufigkeitsadverbien

Wörter wie *always, sometimes* oder *never* nennt man Häufigkeitsadverbien *(adverbs of frequency)*.
Mit ihnen kannst du ausdrücken, wie häufig etwas geschieht:

never	sometimes	often	usually	always
nie	manchmal	oft	normalerweise	immer

! Im Englischen stehen Häufigkeitsadverbien meist zwischen Subjekt und Verb:

Subjekt	Häufigkeitsadverb	Verb		
I Leon	**sometimes** **never**	help walks	at home. to school.	*Ich helfe manchmal zu Hause.* *Leon läuft nie zur Schule.*

! Häufigkeitsadverbien stehen hinter den Formen von *be*:
She's ***always*** *late.*

! Häufigkeitsadverbien stehen hinter *can*:
We can ***sometimes*** *get up late on Saturdays.*

15 Die Zukunft mit *going to* (The *going to*-future)

Die Zukunft mit *going to* verwendest du, wenn du sagen willst, was jemand für die Zukunft plant oder vorhat. Im Deutschen gibt es keine Zeitform, die dem *going to* entspricht.
Du hast aber verschiedene Möglichkeiten, es wiederzugeben:

We're going to fly to London tomorrow.	*Wir werden morgen nach London fliegen.* *Wir möchten/wollen morgen nach London fliegen.* *Wir planen/haben vor, morgen nach London zu fliegen.*

Du bildest die Zukunft mit *going to* mit
einer **Form von *be*** + ***going to*** + **Infinitiv des Verbs.**

Zukunft mit *going to*: Aussagesätze			
I'm	going to	fly	to Spain next week.
Rajiv is	going to	help	his parents in their shop.

He is going to buy an ice cream.

Für die Verneinung von *going to* verwendest du die verneinte Form von *be*. Hier steht *not* immer hinter *am, is* oder *are*.

Zukunft mit *going to*: Verneinung			
I'm not	going to	call	her tomorrow.
She isn't	going to	go	to the party.
They aren't	going to	visit	Emma's aunt.

Bei Entscheidungsfragen rückt auch beim *going to-future* die Form von *be (am, is, are)* an den Satzanfang.

Zukunft mit *going to*: Fragen und Antworten	
Are you going to watch the film tonight?	Yes, **I am.** / No, **I'm not.**
What are you going to do?	I'm going to read a book.

16 Steigerung und Vergleich von Adjektiven
(Comparison of adjectives)

Mit Adjektiven lassen sich Personen oder Sachen näher beschreiben.
Wenn du Personen oder Sachen miteinander vergleichen möchtest, kannst du ein Adjektiv steigern.
Die Steigerungsformen heißen ***comparative*** (Komparativ) und ***superlative*** (Superlativ).

a) Steigerung von Adjektiven mit *-er* und *-est*

Einsilbige Adjektive (z.B. *cheap, old, young)* werden durch das Anhängen von *-er* und *-est* gesteigert.

Adjektiv	Komparativ	Superlativ
cheap	cheap**er**	(the) cheap**est**
old	old**er**	(the) old**est**
young	young**er**	(the) young**est**

Bei zweisilbigen Adjektiven, die auf *-y* enden, wird aus dem *-y* ein *-i*.

Adjektiv	Komparativ	Superlativ
pretty	prett**ier**	(the) prett**iest**
easy	eas**ier**	(the) eas**iest**
friendly	friendl**ier**	(the) friendl**iest**

! Bei manchen Adjektiven ändert sich die Schreibweise.

Adjektiv	Komparativ	Superlativ
nice	nic**er**	(the) nic**est**
hot	hot**ter**	(the) hot**test**
big	big**ger**	(the) big**gest**

Einige Adjektive haben unregelmäßige Steigerungsformen.
Diese Formen musst du wie Vokabeln lernen.

Adjektiv	Komparativ	Superlativ
good	**better**	(the) **best**
bad	**worse**	(the) **worst**
much / many	**more**	(the) **most**

b) Steigerung von Adjektiven mit *more* und *most*

Mehrsilbige Adjektive werden mit ***more*** und ***most*** gesteigert.
Du stellst dabei ***more*** oder ***most*** vor das Adjektiv. Das Adjektiv bleibt unverändert.

Adjektiv	Komparativ	Superlativ
interesting	**more** interesting	(the) **most** interesting
beautiful	**more** beautiful	(the) **most** beautiful

c) Vergleichssätze

Willst du ungleiche Dinge miteinander vergleichen, benutzt du den Komparativ mit ***than***.

Vergleichssätze	
The blue cap is **cheaper than** the green cap.	*Die blaue Kappe ist billiger als die grüne.*
The jacket is **more expensive than** the white T-shirt.	*Die Jacke ist teurer als das weiße T-Shirt.*

*Today it's **windier than** yesterday.*

*Rabbits are **smaller than** cats.*

Sind die Eigenschaften von zwei Dingen oder Personen gleich, benutzt du ***as … as***.

Vergleichssätze	
Mike's brother is **as old as** Finn's brother.	*Mikes Bruder ist genauso alt wie Finns Bruder.*
Sarah is **as tall as** Anne.	*Sarah ist so groß wie Anne.*

17 Mengenangaben (Quantifiers)

Mit *some* und *any* werden Mengen wie z. B. „etwas" oder „einige" bezeichnet.
Die Mengenangabe *not ... any* bedeutet „kein" oder „keine".
Some und *any* werden aber oft nicht übersetzt.

In bejahten Aussagesätzen verwendest du *some*, in verneinten Aussagesätzen und in Fragen *any*.

Bejahte Aussagesätze mit *some*	**Fragen und verneinte Aussagesätze mit *any***	
There are **some** apples in the kitchen. *In der Küche sind (ein paar) Äpfel.*	Are there **any** apples? *Gibt es Äpfel?*	We haven't got **any** apples. *Wir haben keine Äpfel.*
I need **some** milk for my cornflakes. *Ich brauche (etwas) Milch für meine Cornflakes.*	Have you got **any** milk? *Hast du (etwas) Milch?*	There isn't **any** milk. *Es gibt keine Milch.*

! Wenn du jemanden höflich um etwas bittest oder ihm etwas anbietest, benutzt du *some* auch in Fragen:
*Can I have **some** milk, please?*
*Would you like **some** tea?*

Mit *how much* fragst du nach unbestimmten, nicht zählbaren Mengen (z. B. *water, milk, time, chocolate, ...*):
***How much** money have we got?*
– We've got £12.

Mit *how many* fragst du nach der Anzahl von Dingen:
***How many** books have you got? – I've got twenty books.*
***How many** eggs are there? – There are two eggs.*

***How much** time has she got?*
– Only a little.

18 Modalverben (Modal verbs)

Du kennst bereits einige Modalverben wie *can*, *must*, oder *need*.
Die meisten Modalverben haben nur Formen für das *simple present*.
Im *simple past* und im *will-future* verwendest du deshalb die Ersatzformen.

a) Fähigkeit: *can / can't – be able to / not be able to*

Mit ***can*** kannst du sagen, …
- was jemand tun kann
- was jemand tun darf

He **can** swim.	*Er kann schwimmen.*
You **can** watch TV.	*Du darfst fernsehen.*

Can steht mit dem Infinitiv und bleibt in allen Personen gleich.

! Die Ersatzform von *can* ist ***be able to***. Im *simple past* kannst du aber auch ***could*** benutzen.

Emma and Charlie **were able to** help Mr Miller.	*Emma und Charlie konnten Herrn Miller helfen.*
Rajiv **couldn't** do his maths homework because it was too difficult.	*Rajiv konnte seine Mathehausaufgaben nicht machen, weil sie zu schwierig waren.*

Could benutzt du auch für höfliche Bitten und Aufforderungen.

Could I take your pencil, please?	*Könnte ich bitte deinen Bleistift nehmen?*

b) Erlaubnis: *can / can't – be allowed to / not be allowed to – must not*

Can / can't, ***be allowed to*** und ***must not*** benutzt du, wenn du …
- um etwas bittest
- um Erlaubnis fragst oder jemandem etwas erlaubst
- etwas verbietest.

You **can** swim in the swimming pool but you **are not allowed to** swim in the lake.	*Du kannst im Pool schwimmen, aber du darfst nicht im See schwimmen.*
Kenny Hoover **is allowed to** sleep in David's bedroom.	*Kenny Hoover darf in Davids Schlafzimmer schlafen.*
In Germany cars **mustn't** drive on the left.	In Deutschland dürfen Autos nicht links fahren.

! ***Must not*** oder die Kurzform ***mustn't*** klingt wie im Deutschen „muss nicht", heißt aber „etwas nicht dürfen".

You **mustn't** talk now.

Ihr dürft jetzt nicht mehr sprechen.

c) Notwendigkeit: *must/have to – needn't/don't have to*

Must klingt wie das deutsche Wort „muss“ und heißt auch *müssen*.
In der Regel kannst du ***must*** auch durch ***have to/has to*** ersetzen.

Claire **must** tidy up her room. *oder* Claire **has to** tidy up her room.	*Claire muss ihr Zimmer aufräumen.*

Must hat keine eigene Vergangenheitsform. Daher wird die *simple past*-Form von ***have to*** benutzt.

Before there were lights, people **had to** use candles.	*Bevor es Lampen gab, mussten die Menschen Kerzen benutzen.*

Wenn du sagen willst, was jemand *nicht* tun muss, benutzt du ***don't/doesn't have to***.

Auch mit ***need not*** oder ***needn't*** kannst du ausdrücken, dass etwas nicht notwendig ist.

You **needn't** do your homework now. You can do it later.	*Du brauchst deine Hausaufgaben nicht jetzt zu machen. Du kannst sie später machen.*

19R Imperativ (The imperative)

Mit dem Imperativ (der Befehlsform) kannst du Bitten, Befehle oder Anweisungen ausdrücken:
*Please **open** the window, Lisa.*

Im Englischen hat der Imperativ dieselbe Form wie der Infinitiv und bleibt im Singular und Plural gleich.
***Help** me, please.* – Bitte **hilf** mir. / Bitte **helft** mir.

Wenn jemand etwas nicht tun soll, stellst du einfach *do not* oder *don't* vor das Verb.
***Don't forget** your keys.*

! Wenn du nur den Imperativ verwendest, kann das im Englischen sehr unhöflich klingen. Höflicher ist es, wenn du ***please*** hinzufügst.

20 Bedingungssätze, Typ I (Conditional clauses, type I)

Ein Bedingungssatz besteht aus einem *if*-Satz *(if-clause)* und einem Hauptsatz *(main clause)*:

- Der *if*-Satz nennt eine Bedingung. Der Hauptsatz drückt aus, was passiert, wenn die Bedingung erfüllt ist.
- Im *if*-Satz steht das *simple present*, im Hauptsatz das *will-future*.

***if*-Satz** (Bedingung: *Wenn …*)	**Hauptsatz** (Folge: *dann …*)	
If you **miss** the bus,	you **will be** late.	*Wenn du den Bus verpasst, kommst du zu spät.*
If it **rains**,	they **won't go** outside.	*Wenn es regnet, werden sie nicht rausgehen.*

Bedingungssätze können entweder mit dem *if*-Satz oder mit dem Hauptsatz beginnen. Wenn sie mit dem *if*-Satz beginnen, werden sie mit einem Komma getrennt. Wenn sie mit dem Hauptsatz beginnen, verwendest du kein Komma:

***If** you go to the cinema, **I'll** come with you.*
***I'll** come with you **if** you go to the cinema.*

*They **won't** go to the beach **if** it rains.*

Im Hauptsatz kannst du auch Modalverben (z. B. *can*, *must*) oder den Imperativ verwenden:

If it snows, we ***can go*** *inside.* – Wenn es schneit, können wir reingehen.
If you like her, you ***must call*** *her.* – Wenn du sie magst, musst du sie anrufen.
If you need help, ***ask*** *Lisa.* – Wenn du Hilfe brauchst, frag Lisa.

! *If* und *when* kannst du beide mit „wenn" übersetzen.
Sie werden aber unterschiedlich verwendet:

- ***If*** *I see Ben on Monday, I'll give him the book.*
  Der Sprecher verwendet *if*, weil er nicht sicher ist, ob er Ben am Montag sieht.
  Du kannst *if* hier mit „wenn" oder „falls" übersetzen.

- ***When*** *I see Ben on Monday, I'll give him the book.*
  Der Sprecher hat fest vor, Ben am Montag zu sehen.
  Du kannst *when* hier mit „wenn" übersetzen, aber nicht mit „falls".

21 Das Perfekt (The present perfect)

a) Present perfect: Verwendung

Das *present perfect* verwendest du, …
- wenn etwas irgendwann, noch nie oder noch nicht geschehen ist:
  Holly ***has*** *never* ***eaten*** *fish.*
  Holly hat noch nie Fisch gegessen.
- wenn ein Vorgang in der Vergangenheit noch Auswirkungen auf die Gegenwart hat:
  David ***has cleaned*** *the kitchen.*
  David hat die Küche geputzt (sie ist noch sauber).

She ***has bought*** *new clothes.*

b) Present perfect: Aussagesätze

Das *present perfect* bildest du mit ***have / has*** + **Partizip Perfekt (past participle)**.
Die Verneinung bildest du mit ***haven't / hasn't*** + **Partizip Perfekt.**

***present perfect*: Aussagesätze und Verneinung**			
I	**have**	**cleaned**	the kitchen.
He	**has**	**gone**	to London.
We	**have**	**seen**	the Queen.
She	**hasn't**	**been**	to Scotland.
They	**haven't**	**helped**	him.

The boys ***have tidied up*** *their room.*

Das *present perfect* kannt du mit Adverbien der unbestimmten Zeit verwenden, z. B. mit *already, just, ever, never*. Es ist in solchen Sätzen nicht wichtig, wann genau etwas geschehen ist.
Die Adverbien stehen dann direkt vor dem Partizip Perfekt:
*I have **already** done my homework.* – Ich habe meine Hausaufgaben schon gemacht.
*Angela has **just** seen the Queen.* – Angela hat eben / gerade die Queen gesehen.

! Beachte die Ausnahme: *yet* steht am Satzende.
*I haven't been to Berlin **yet**.* – Ich war noch nicht in Berlin.

c) Present perfect: Fragen und Kurzantworten

Entscheidungsfragen im *present perfect* bildest du, indem du das Subjekt und ***have / has*** vertauschst. Bei Fragen mit Fragewörtern steht das Fragewort am Satzanfang:

***present perfect*: Fragen und Kurzantworten**					
	Have	you	**finished**	your homework?	**Yes, I have. / No, I haven't.**
	Has	Jill	**bought**	a new book?	**Yes, she has. / No, she hasn't.**
What	**have**	you	**done?**		
Why	**hasn't**	she	**come?**		

d) Das Partizip Perfekt

Bei regelmäßigen Verben bildest du das Partizip Perfekt *(past participle)* mit dem **Infinitiv** + ***-ed***.

Infinitiv	*simple past*	*past participle*
clean	cleaned	clean**ed**
help	helped	help**ed**
play	played	play**ed**

Unregelmäßige Verben haben unregelmäßige Formen. Diese solltest du wie Vokabeln lernen. Auf Seite 284 – 285 findest du eine Liste der unregelmäßigen Verben.

Infinitiv	*simple past*	*past participle*
be	was / were	**been**
do	did	**done**
have	had	**had**
buy	bought	**bought**

22 Die Verlaufsform der Vergangenheit (The past progressive)

a) Bejahte und verneinte Aussagesätze

Das *present progressive* kennst du bereits. Du verwendest es, wenn du sagen möchtest, was jemand gerade tut oder was gerade passiert: *Emma is reading a book.*
Es gibt auch für die Vergangenheit eine *progressive form*, das *past progressive*.
Es drückt aus, ...

- was jemand gerade tat oder was gerade passierte.
- was gerade vor sich ging, als etwas anderes geschah.

So bildest du das *past progressive*:
Simple past*-Form von *be* (*was/were*)** + **Infinitiv des Verbs** + **Endung *-ing.
Rajiv was laughing the whole time.
Rajiv lachte die ganze Zeit.

All the girls were screaming.
Alle Mädchen schrien.

past progressive	*simple past*
Emma was reading a book *Emma las gerade ein Buch,*	when Rajiv called. *als Rajiv anrief.*
The pupils were running around *Die Schüler rannten herum,*	when the teacher came. *als der Lehrer kam.*
was gerade passiert: ***past progressive***	**neues Ereignis:** ***simple past***

Emma was reading a book when her father came to say good night.

Für die Verneinung fügst du einfach ein ***not*** hinter die Form von *be* ein:
Sheree was not singing a song.
Rajiv wasn't screaming with the girls.

b) Fragen und Kurzantworten

Entscheidungsfragen im *past progressive* bildest du, indem du das Subjekt und *was/were* vertauschst:

Was Rajiv **laughing**? – **Yes, he was. / No, he wasn't.**
Were the reporters **asking** many questions? – **Yes, they were. / No, they weren't.**

Bei Fragen mit Fragewörtern stellst du das Fragewort an den Satzanfang:

***What was** the band **doing**?*
***Where were** they **sitting**?*

23 Die Steigerung von Adverbien (Comparison of adverbs)

Du weißt bereits, wie Adjektive gesteigert werden (➔ LiF 16).
Für die Steigerung von Adverbien gelten die gleichen Regeln.
*Greg runs **faster** than his brother.*
Greg rennt schneller als sein Bruder.

*Lara plays the guitar **more beautifully** than her brother.*
Lara spielt schöner Gitarre als ihr Bruder.

Einsilbige Adverbien werden durch das Anhängen von ***-er*** und ***-est*** gesteigert.

Adverb	Komparativ	Superlativ
hard	hard**er**	hard**est**
fast	fast**er**	fast**est**

*He runs **the fastest**.*

Mehrsilbige Adverbien, die auf *-ly* enden, steigerst du mit ***more*** und ***most***.

Adverb	Komparativ	Superlativ
happily	**more** happily	(the) **most** happily
slowly	**more** slowly	(the) **most** slowly
beautifully	**more** beautifully	(the) **most** beautifully

Es gibt auch unregelmäßige Steigerungsformen, die du wie Vokabeln lernen musst:

Adverb	Komparativ	Superlativ
well	**better**	(the) **best**
badly	**worse**	(the) **worst**
much	**more**	(the) **most**

*He plays tennis **better** than his friend Jamie.*

So funktionieren die Wortlisten

Es gibt alphabetische Wortlisten *(Dictionaries)* und Wortlisten nach *Themes*.

Alphabetische Wortlisten *(Dictionaries)*

Camden Market hat zwei *Dictionaries:*
Im *English-German dictionary* ab Seite 243 kannst du nachschlagen, wenn du die Bedeutung von einem englischen Wort aus dem Buch wissen möchtest.
Im *German-English dictionary* ab Seite 269 kannst du nachschlagen, wenn dir mal ein englisches Wort nicht einfällt.

Wortlisten nach *Themes*

In den Wortlisten nach *Themes* ab Seite 203 findest du alle neuen Wörter in der Reihenfolge, in der sie in den *Themes* vorkommen.
Hier siehst du, wie du die Wortlisten benutzen kannst:

Die Lautschrift zeigt dir, wie man ein Wort ausspricht.

Fett gedruckte Wörter solltest du dir merken.

(only pl) bedeutet: Dieses Wort wird nur oder gewöhnlich im Plural (Mehrzahl) benutzt.

(irr) bedeutet: Dieses Verb ist unregelmäßig.

(no pl) bedeutet: Dieses Wort hat keinen Plural (Mehrzahl).

	detective /dɪˈtektɪv/	(Privat)detektiv/in	detective
	statue /ˈstætʃuː/	Statue, Standbild	
	in the middle /ˌɪn ðə ˈmɪdl/	in der Mitte; mitten in / auf	
2	imagine /ɪˈmædʒɪn/	sich vorstellen	
3	part /pɑːt/	Teil	
	each /iːtʃ/	jede(r, s)	
	glass /glɑːs/	Glas	
	high /haɪ/	hoch	
	like /laɪk/	wie	
	underground /ˈʌndəˌgraʊnd/	U-Bahn	underground
	chips *(only pl) (BE)* /tʃɪps/	Pommes frites	chips
5	top /tɒp/	Spitzen-	
6	**weekend** /ˌwiːkˈend/	Wochenende	
	lose *(irr)* /luːz/	verlieren	lose – lost *(simple past)*
	tube *(no pl)* /tjuːb/	*Londoner U-Bahn*	
	full /fʊl/	voll	
	get off	aussteigen	

(BE) bedeutet: *British English*
(AE) bedeutet: *American English*

Kleine Bilder und Beispielsätze helfen dir dabei, dir Wörter besser einzuprägen.

(informal) bedeutet: Dieses Wort ist umgangssprachlich.

Wenn du den *More*-Teil bearbeitest, solltest du dir die grün gedruckten Wörter merken.

(pl leaves) bedeutet: Dieses Wort hat einen unregelmäßigen Plural *(leaves)*.

	doctor /ˈdɒktə/	Arzt/Ärztin	
	medical bag /ˈmedɪkl bæg/	Medikamentenkoffer	
	criminal /ˈkrɪmɪnl/	Verbrecher/in, Kriminelle/r	crimina
	who /huː/	wer; *hier:* der/die/das	
	at that time /æt ˈðæt taɪm/	damals, zu dieser Zeit	
	upstairs /ʌpˈsteəz/	(nach) oben	The children are upstairs in be
	dead /ded/	tot	
	coffin /ˈkɒfɪn/	Sarg	
	weapon /ˈwepən/	Waffe	
	horrible /ˈhɒrəbl/	schrecklich	
	fall *(irr)* /fɔːl/	fallen	
	trapdoor /ˈtræpˌdɔː/	Falltür	
	search /sɜːtʃ/	(durch)suchen	
M5	Africa /ˈæfrɪkə/	Afrika	
	feeding time /ˈfiːdɪŋ ˌtaɪm/	Fütterungszeit	
	leaf *(pl leaves)* /liːf, liːvz/	Blatt	leaf

Folgende Abkürzungen werden noch verwendet: *sb* = *somebody*, *sth* = *something*, etw = etwas, jmd = jemand, jdm/jdn = jemandem / jemanden

English sounds

Im Englischen spricht man Wörter oft anders aus, als man sie schreibt.
Deshalb ist die Lautschrift sehr nützlich: Sie gibt an, wie ein Wort ausgesprochen wird.
Hier ist eine Liste mit Lautschriftzeichen zusammen mit Beispielwörtern, in denen der entsprechende Laut vorkommt.

Vokale

/ɑː/	arm
/ʌ/	but
/e/	desk
/ə/	a, an
/ɜː/	girl, bird
/æ/	apple
/ɪ/	in, it
/i/	every
/iː/	easy, eat
/ɒ/	orange
/ɔː/	all, story
/ʊ/	look
/u/	February
/uː/	food

Doppellaute

/aɪ/	eye, buy
/aʊ/	our
/eə/	there
/eɪ/	take, they
/ɪə/	here
/ɔɪ/	boy
/əʊ/	go, old
/ʊə/	you're

Konsonanten

/b/	bag, club
/d/	duck, card
/f/	fish, laugh
/g/	get, dog
/h/	hot
/j/	you
/k/	can, duck
/l/	lot, small
/m/	more, mum
/n/	now, sun
/ŋ/	song, long
/p/	present, top
/r/	red, right
/s/	sister, class (scharfes **s**)
/t/	time, cat
/z/	nose, dogs (weiches **s**)
/ʒ/	television
/dʒ/	orange
/ʃ/	sure, English
/tʃ/	child, cheese
/ð/	these, mother (weicher Laut)
/θ/	mouth, think (harter Laut)
/v/	very, have
/w/	what, word

Betonungszeichen für die folgende Silbe

/ˈ/	Hauptbetonung
/ˌ/	Nebenbetonung

The English alphabet

a	/eɪ/	**h**	/eɪtʃ/	**o**	/əʊ/	**v**	/viː/
b	/biː/	**i**	/aɪ/	**p**	/piː/	**w**	/ˈdʌbljuː/
c	/siː/	**j**	/dʒeɪ/	**q**	/kjuː/	**x**	/eks/
d	/diː/	**k**	/keɪ/	**r**	/ɑː/	**y**	/waɪ/
e	/iː/	**l**	/el/	**s**	/es/	**z**	/zed/
f	/ef/	**m**	/em/	**t**	/tiː/		
g	/dʒiː/	**n**	/en/	**u**	/juː/		

Ähnliche Wörter im Deutschen und Englischen

Es gibt viele Wörter, die im Englischen und im Deutschen gleich sind. Sie unterscheiden sich oft nur dadurch, dass die meisten von ihnen im Deutschen groß geschrieben werden. Viele dieser Wörter sprechen wir gleich aus.
Diese Wörter stehen nicht in den Wortlisten, weil sie dir ja nicht neu sind. Bei denen, die ein bisschen anders ausgesprochen werden als im Deutschen, ist die Lautschrift farbig hervorgehoben.

adjective /ˈædʒɪktɪv/
adverb /ˈædvɜːb/
anti- /ˈænti/
atlas /ˈætləs/
baby /ˈbeɪbi/
badminton /ˈbædmɪntən/
band /bænd/
bank /bæŋk/
basketball /ˈbɑːskɪtˌbɔːl/
blog /blɒg/
box /bɒks/
burger /ˈbɜːgə/
café /ˈkæfeɪ/
cafeteria /ˌkæfəˈtɪəriə/
camp /kæmp/
CD /ˌsiː ˈdiː/
chat /tʃæt/
clip /klɪp/
clown /klaʊn/
cocktail /ˈkɒkˌteɪl/
collage /ˈkɒlɑːʒ/
comic /ˈkɒmɪk/
computer /kəmˈpjuːtə/
cool /kuːl/
cornflakes /ˈkɔːnˌfleɪks/
cowboy /ˈkaʊˌbɔɪ/
cricket /ˈkrɪkɪt/
darts /dɑːts/
disco /ˈdɪskəʊ/
DJ /ˈdiːˌdʒeɪ/
email /ˈiːmeɪl/
event /ɪˈvent/
fair /feə/
fan /fæn/
feedback /ˈfiːdbæk/
film /fɪlm/
flyer /ˈflaɪə/
form /fɔːm/
gangster /ˈgæŋstə/
geocaching /ˈdʒiːəʊkæʃɪŋ/
gold /gəʊld/
hamburger /ˈhæmˌbɜːgə/
hit /hɪt/
hit song /hɪt sɒŋ/
home page /ˈhəʊm ˌpeɪdʒ/
horror film /ˈhɒrə fɪlm/
hotel /həʊˈtel/
ideal /aɪˈdɪəl/
inline skating /ˌɪnlaɪn ˈskeɪtɪŋ/
intelligent /ɪnˈtelɪdʒənt/
international /ˌɪntəˈnæʃnəl/
Internet /ˈɪntənet/
interview /ˈɪntəˌvjuː/
jeans /dʒiːnz/
judo /ˈdʒuːdəʊ/
karaoke /ˌkæriˈəʊki/
kayak /ˈkaɪæk/
kid /kɪd/
kiwi /ˈkiːwiː/
live /laɪv/
Londoner /ˈlʌndənə/
make-up /ˈmeɪkˌʌp/
manager /ˈmænɪdʒə/
marathon /ˈmærəθn/
material /məˈtɪəriəl/
MP3 player /ˌem piː ˈθriː ˌpleɪə/
museum /mjuːˈziːəm/
musical /ˈmjuːzɪkl/
normal /ˈnɔːml/
OK (= okay) /ˌəʊˈkeɪ/
online /ˈɒnlaɪn/
partner /ˈpɑːtnə/
party /ˈpɑːti/
piñata /piːnˈjɑːtə/
Ping-Pong /ˈpɪŋpɒŋ/
pizza /ˈpiːtsə/
planet /ˈplænɪt/
pool /puːl/
pop (music) /(ˈ)pɒp (ˌmjuːzɪk)/
position /pəˈzɪʃn/
poster /ˈpəʊstə/
puma /ˈpjuːmə/
quiz /kwɪz/
quiz show /ˈkwɪz ʃəʊ/
rafting /ˈrɑːftɪŋ/
rap /ræp/
reporter /rɪˈpɔːtə/
rest /rest/
rose /rəʊz/
sand /sænd/
sandwich /ˈsænwɪdʒ/
science fiction /ˌsaɪəns ˈfɪkʃn/
sheriff /ˈʃerɪf/
sightseeing /ˈsaɪtˌsiːɪŋ/
skateboard /ˈskeɪtˌbɔːd/
snack /snæk/
snooker /ˈsnuːkə/
sofa /ˈsəʊfə/
sound check /ˈsaʊnd tʃek/
souvenir /ˌsuːvəˈnɪə/
spaghetti /spəˈgeti/
star /stɑː/
stunt man /ˈstʌnt mæn/
surfing /ˈsɜːfɪŋ/
sweatshirt /ˈswetˌʃɜːt/
T-shirt /ˈtiːʃɜːt/
talk show /ˈtɔːk ʃəʊ/
taxi /ˈtæksi/
team /tiːm/
teen /tiːn/
teenager /ˈtiːnˌeɪdʒə/
tennis /ˈtenɪs/
text /tekst/
ticket /ˈtɪkɪt/
toast /təʊst/
tolerant /ˈtɒlərənt/
top ten /ˌtɒp ˈten/
tour /tʊə/
tour bus /ˈtʊə bʌs/
tourist /ˈtʊərɪst/
training /ˈtreɪnɪŋ/
unfair /ʌnˈfeə/
uniform /ˈjuːnɪˌfɔːm/
verb /vɜːb/
video /ˈvɪdiəʊ/
website /ˈwebˌsaɪt/
western /ˈwestən/
wild /waɪld/
wind /wɪnd/
wow /waʊ/
zebra /ˈzebrə/

Back to Camden Market!

back /bæk/	zurück	
next door /ˌnekst ˈdɔː/	neben(an)	
India /ˈɪndiə/	Indien	
move /muːv/	sich bewegen; *hier:* umziehen	Caroline moved from Manchester to Camden.
Greece /griːs/	Griechenland	
twin /twɪn/	Zwilling, Zwillings-	
wheelchair /ˈwiːlˌtʃeə/	Rollstuhl	Karla is in a wheelchair.

Theme 1 – After the holidays

I	theme /θiːm/	Thema; Lektion, Kapitel	
1	which /wɪtʃ/	welche(r, s)	
	go with /ˈgəʊ wɪð/	gehören zu, passen zu	
2	**home** /həʊm/	zu Hause; nach Hause	
	title /ˈtaɪtl/	Titel	
	dialogue /ˈdaɪəlɒg/	Gespräch, Dialog	
	I'm fine. /aɪm ˈfaɪn/	Es geht mir gut.	How are you? – I'm fine, thanks.
	a bit /ə ˈbɪt/	ein bisschen	
	with /wɪð/	mit; *hier:* bei	
	so /səʊ/	also	
	the sea *(no pl)* /ðə ˈsiː/	das Meer, die See	
	sight /saɪt/	Sehenswürdigkeit	
	Athens /ˈæθɪnz/	Athen	
	amazing *(informal)* /əˈmeɪzɪŋ/	toll, unglaublich	
	guys *(only pl) (informal)* /gaɪz/	Leute	
	well /wel/	nun (ja), tja	
	wet /wet/	nass	
	Come on! /ˌkʌm‿ˈɒn/	Jetzt hör aber auf!	
	concert /ˈkɒnsət/	Konzert	
	go *(irr)* /gəʊ/	gehen; *hier:* fahren	
	send *(irr)* /send/	(zu)schicken	
	postcard /ˈpəʊstˌkɑːd/	Postkarte	
	beach /biːtʃ/	Strand	
	stay /steɪ/	bleiben; *hier:* untergebracht sein, wohnen	
	campsite /ˈkæmpˌsaɪt/	Campingplatz, Zeltplatz	
	caravan /ˈkærəvæn/	Wohnwagen	
	first /fɜːst/	zuerst, als Erstes	
	Scotland /ˈskɒtlənd/	Schottland	
	castle /ˈkɑːsl/	Burg; Schloss	
	ghost /gəʊst/	Geist, Gespenst	
	walk /wɔːk/	Spaziergang	
	spooky *(informal)* /ˈspuːki/	unheimlich; schaurig	

TIPP

Unregelmäßige Verben *(irregular verbs)* erkennst du im Wörterverzeichnis an der Kennzeichnung *(irr)*. Sie haben eine unregelmäßige Form für die einfache Vergangenheit *(simple past)*, die du dir gut einprägen musst. Eine Liste der unregelmäßigen Verben findest du auf Seite 284 – 285. Hier sind die unregelmäßigen Verben aus Aufgabe 2:

Infinitiv	***simple past***
be *(irr)*	was / were
do *(irr)*	did
go *(irr)*	went
have *(irr)*	had
send *(irr)*	sent
eat *(irr)*	ate
meet *(irr)*	met

	unfortunately / ʌnˈfɔːtʃnətli /	leider, unglücklicherweise	Unfortunately it rained 
	rain / reɪn /	regnen	a lot in Scotland.
	that's a shame / ðæts‿ə ˈʃeɪm /	wie schade	
	Majorca / məˈjɔːkə /	Mallorca	
	take notes / teɪk ˈnəʊts /	(sich) Notizen machen	
	grid / grɪd /	Gitter; *hier:* Tabelle	
	like this / laɪk ˈðɪs /	so	
	note / nəʊt /	Notiz	
	use / juːz /	benutzen	
3	not any / nɒt‿ˈeni /	kein(e)	
	bird / bɜːd /	Vogel	A budgie is a bird.
4	chain / tʃeɪn /	Kette	
5	**diary** / ˈdaɪəri /	Tagebuch	I write in my diary every day. 
	entry / ˈentri /	Eintrag	
	terrible / ˈterəbl /	schrecklich, furchtbar	terrible ↔ great
	how to / haʊ tə /	wie man	
	sb cannot wait (to do sth) / ˌsʌmbədi ˌkænɒt ˈweɪt /	jmd kann es kaum erwarten (, etw zu tun)	
	later / ˈleɪtə /	später	
	cheap / tʃiːp /	billig, preiswert	
	so / səʊ /	deshalb; also	
	take photos / ˌteɪk ˈfəʊtəʊz /	Bilder machen, fotografieren	I like to take photos of my friends.
	feel *(irr)* / fiːl /	(sich) fühlen	
	happy / ˈhæpi /	glücklich; zufrieden; fröhlich	
	when / wen /	wenn; *hier:* als	When I came home, I watched TV.
	yummy *(informal)* / ˈjʌmi /	lecker	
	proud (of sb) / praʊd /	stolz (auf jmd)	
	get *(irr)* / get /	erhalten, bekommen; *hier:* werden	
	customer / ˈkʌstəmə /	Kunde/Kundin	
	angry / ˈæŋgri /	verärgert; zornig; wütend	The boy is very angry.
	unfriendly / ʌnˈfrendli /	unfreundlich	
	lonely / ˈləʊnli /	einsam	
	most / məʊst /	die meisten	
	sad / sæd /	traurig	 happy ↔ sad 
	way / weɪ /	Weg	
	go on holiday / ˌgəʊ‿ɒn ˈhɒlɪdeɪ /	Urlaub machen, in den Urlaub fahren	I went on holiday to England last year.
	correct / kəˈrekt /	korrigieren	
	describe / dɪˈskraɪb /	beschreiben	
	feeling / ˈfiːlɪŋ /	Gefühl	
6	Cologne / kəˈləʊn /	Köln	
	apartment / əˈpɑːtmənt /	Wohnung	
	What's ... like? / wɒts ˈlaɪk /	Wie ist ... ?	What's the weather like? – It's really sunny.
7	present / prɪˈzent /	präsentieren	

	during / ˈdjʊərɪŋ /	während	
8	pair / peə /	Paar	
	share / ʃeə /	teilen	
	remember / rɪˈmembə /	sich erinnern (an)	
	complete / kəmˈpliːt /	vervollständigen	
	another / əˈnʌðə /	noch ein(e, r, s); *hier:* ein anderer/anderes, eine andere	
	put *(irr)* / pʊt /	setzen, legen, stellen; *hier:* anordnen, sortieren	
9	**wonderful** / ˈwʌndəfl /	wunderbar, wundervoll	
	world / wɜːld /	Welt, Erde	There are lots of interesting places in the world.
10	registration / ˌredʒɪˈstreɪʃn /	Anmeldung; *hier:* Überprüfung der Anwesenheit	
	drama / ˈdrɑːmə /	Schauspielerei; *hier:* Theater	
	food technology / ˈfuːd tekˌnɒlədʒi /	Ernährung *(Schulfach)*	
	what else / wɒt‿ˈels /	was noch, was sonst	
	time / taɪm /	(Uhr)zeit; *hier:* Mal	
11	**welcome (to)** / ˈwelkəm /	willkommen (in)	Welcome to my school!
	secondary school / ˈsekəndri skuːl /	*weiterführende Schule für Kinder zwischen 11 und 16/18*	
	than / ðæn /	als	
	closely / ˈkləʊsli /	eng	
	out of / ˈaʊt‿əv /	(her)aus	
	learning *(no pl)* / ˈlɜːnɪŋ /	Lernen; Bildung	
	until / ənˈtɪl /	bis	On Tuesdays we have history until 10 o'clock.
	pm (= post meridiem) / ˌpiːˈem, ˌpəʊst məˈrɪdiəm /	nachmittags, abends *(nur hinter Uhrzeit zwischen 12 Uhr mittags und Mitternacht)*	
	librarian / laɪˈbreəriən /	Bibliothekar/in	
	staff *(no pl)* / stɑːf /	Mitarbeiter, Personal	
	serve / sɜːv /	bedienen	
	morning break / ˈmɔːnɪŋ ˌbreɪk /	Frühstückspause	
	lunchtime / ˈlʌntʃˌtaɪm /	Mittagszeit; Mittagspause	
	selection / sɪˈlekʃn /	Auswahl	
	healthy / ˈhelθi /	gesund	Vegetables are very healthy.
	dish *(pl* **-es***)* / dɪʃ /	Gericht	
	fresh / freʃ /	frisch	
	gym (= gymnasium) / dʒɪm, dʒɪmˈneɪziəm /	Turnhalle	We play basketball in the gym after school.
	take part (in) / ˌteɪk ˈpɑːt /	teilnehmen (an)	
	indoor / ˌɪnˈdɔː /	Hallen-	
	class / klɑːs /	(Schul)klasse; *hier:* Kurs	

	dance /dɑːns/	Tanz	
	wall climbing /ˈwɔːl ˌklaɪmɪŋ/	Klettern an der Kletterwand	
	outdoor /ˌaʊtˈdɔː/	im Freien	
	court /kɔːt/	Platz, Court	
	offer /ˈɒfə/	(an)bieten	
	different /ˈdɪfrənt/	anders, andere(r, s); *hier:* verschieden, unterschiedlich	This shop has a lot of different T-shirts.
	chess *(no pl)* /tʃes/	Schach(spiel)	
	logo /ˈləʊgəʊ/	Abzeichen, Logo	
	blazer /ˈbleɪzə/	Blazer, Jacke	
	tie /taɪ/	Krawatte	tie
	tracksuit /ˈtrækˌsuːt/	Trainingsanzug	
	knee /niː/	Knie	Das „k" wird nicht ausgesprochen.

	length /leŋθ/	Länge	
	personal /ˈpɜːsnəl/	persönlich; privat	
	diary /ˈdaɪəri/	Tagebuch; *hier:* (Termin)kalender	
	planner /ˈplænə/	Kalender zur Arbeitsplanung	
	note down /nəʊt ˈdaʊn/	(sich) notieren	
	set *(irr)* /set/	(fest)setzen, vereinbaren	
	goal /gəʊl/	Ziel	
	guess /ges/	(er)raten	
	meaning /ˈmiːnɪŋ/	Bedeutung	
	look up /lʊk‿ˈʌp/	nachschlagen	
	dictionary /ˈdɪkʃənri/	Wörterbuch	
	page /peɪdʒ/	Seite	
12	**the same** /ðə ˈseɪm/	der-/die-/dasselbe	the same ↔ different
	add /æd/	hinzufügen	
13	**sound** /saʊnd/	Geräusch, Klang; Ton	What a terrible sound!
	write down /raɪt ˈdaʊn/	aufschreiben	
14	correct /kəˈrekt/	richtig, korrekt	
	order /ˈɔːdə/	Ordnung, Reihenfolge	Have you got brothers and sisters?
	brothers and sisters /ˌbrʌðəz‿ænd ˈsɪstəz/	Geschwister	
	think of /ˈθɪŋk‿əv/	denken an; sich ausdenken	
	make up sth /ˌmeɪk‿ˈʌp ˌsʌmθɪŋ/	(sich) etw ausdenken, etw erfinden	Yes, I've got a sister.
	possible /ˈpɒsəbəl/	möglich	
	each other /ˌiːtʃ‿ˈʌðə/	einander	
	answer /ˈɑːnsə/	(be)antworten	
	age /eɪdʒ/	Alter	What's your age? = How old are you?
15	project /ˈprɒdʒekt/	Projekt	
	plan /plæn/	planen	
	on one's own /ɒn wʌnz‿ˈəʊn/	allein(e)	

	presentation /ˌpreznˈteɪʃn/	Präsentation
	already /ɔːlˈredi/	schon
	noticeboard /ˈnəʊtɪsˌbɔːd/	schwarzes Brett
	interview /ˈɪntəˌvjuː/	befragen
	headteacher /ˌhedˈtiːtʃə/	Schulleiter/in, Rektor/in
	make notes /meɪk ˈnəʊts/	(sich) Notizen machen
	topic /ˈtɒpɪk/	Thema
	prepare /prɪˈpeə/	(sich) vorbereiten
	show *(irr)* /ʃəʊ/	zeigen
	edit /ˈedɪt/	bearbeiten, redigieren
	practise /ˈpræktɪs/	üben
	put up /pʊt‿ˈʌp/	aufhängen
P	practice /ˈpræktɪs/	Übung; Training
P2	sort /sɔːt/	sortieren
P3	search /sɜːtʃ/	Suche
	simple past /ˌsɪmpl ˈpɑːst/	einfache Vergangenheit
	try /traɪ/	(aus)probieren; *hier:* versuchen
	ending /ˈendɪŋ/	Ende, Schluss; *hier:* Endung
P5	top /tɒp/	oberes Ende, Spitze; *hier:* Gipfel
	dolphin /ˈdɒlfɪn/	Delfin
	stadium /ˈsteɪdiəm/	Stadion
P6	active /ˈæktɪv/	aktiv
	speak *(irr)* /spiːk/	sprechen, reden
	be about /bi‿əˈbaʊt/	handeln von
	adventure /ədˈventʃə/	Abenteuer, Erlebnis
	will /wɪl/	werden
	kayak /ˈkaɪæk/	Kajakfahren
	am (= ante meridiem) /ˌeɪˈem, ˌænti məˈrɪdiəm/	morgens, vormittags *(nur hinter Uhrzeit zwischen Mitternacht und 12 Uhr mittags)*
	lake /leɪk/	See
	cost /kɒst/	Kosten, Preis
	per /pɜː/	pro
	person /ˈpɜːsn/	Person, Mensch
	swimwear *(no pl)* /ˈswɪmˌweə/	Badebekleidung
	if /ɪf/	wenn, falls
	interested (in sth) /ˈɪntrəstɪd/	interessiert (an etw)
	call /kɔːl/	anrufen
P7	poem /ˈpəʊɪm/	Gedicht
	example /ɪgˈzɑːmpl/	Beispiel
	biology *(no pl)* /baɪˈɒlədʒi/	Biologie
P8	compare /kəmˈpeə/	vergleichen

TIPP

Teamwork
Zu zweit macht das Vokabellernen mehr Spaß. Fragt euch gegenseitig ab. Tauscht euch auch darüber aus, wie ihr am besten Wörter lernt. Wenn ihr Lust habt, könnt ihr selbst Lückentexte, Kreuzwort- oder Buchstabenrätsel für den Partner/die Partnerin erstellen.

TIPP

Probier's mal mit Gemütlichkeit
Nicht nur für das Vokabellernen gilt: Du solltest dich an dem Ort, an dem du arbeitest, wohlfühlen und durch nichts abgelenkt sein! Eine gewisse Ordnung erleichtert das Arbeiten. Mache regelmäßig Pausen, in denen du z. B. das Fenster öffnest, etwas trinkst und dich bewegst. So kannst du dich besser konzentrieren.

P11	play the drums /pleɪ ðə ˈdrʌmz/	Schlagzeug spielen	
	as ... as /əz əz/	(genau)so ... wie ...	
	Chinese /ˌtʃaɪˈniːz/	Chinese/Chinesin; Chinesisch; chinesisch	
P12	get to know sb /get‿tə ˈnəʊ ˌsʌmbədi/	jdn kennenlernen	
	somebody /ˈsʌmbədi/	jemand	
	find out /faɪnd‿ˈaʊt/	herausfinden	
	chips *(only pl) (BE)* /tʃɪps/	Pommes frites	
M1	take turns /ˌteɪk ˈtɜːnz/	sich abwechseln	
	difference /ˈdɪfrəns/	Unterschied	
	fact file /ˈfækt ˌfaɪl/	Steckbrief	
	(three days) ago /əˈgəʊ/	vor (drei Tagen)	John moved to London two years ago.
M2	mysterious /mɪˈstɪəriəs/	geheimnisvoll, mysteriös	
	tale /teɪl/	Geschichte, Erzählung	
	spend *(irr)* /spend/	ausgeben *(Geld)*; verbringen *(Zeit)*	
	Lake Titicaca /leɪk ˌtɪtɪˈkɑːkə/	Titicacasee	
	Bolivia /bəˈlɪviə/	Bolivien	
	South America /ˌsaʊθ‿əˈmerɪkə/	Südamerika	
	its /ɪts/	sein(e), ihr(e)	
	lake /leɪk/	See	
	high /haɪ/	hoch	
	night /naɪt/	Nacht; *hier:* Abend	
	decide /dɪˈsaɪd/	(sich) entscheiden; beschließen	I can't decide what to do today.
	adventure /ədˈventʃə/	Abenteuer, Erlebnis	
	be asleep /bi‿əˈsliːp/	schlafen	
	sneak *(irr)* /sniːk/	schleichen	
	out of /ˈaʊt‿əv/	(her)aus	
	top /tɒp/	oberes Ende, Spitze; *hier:* Gipfel	He is at the top of the mountain.
	hill /hɪl/	Hügel	
	by /baɪ/	bei, in der Nähe	
	on one's way /ɒn wʌnz ˈweɪ/	unterwegs	
	strange /streɪndʒ/	sonderbar, komisch	
	voice /vɔɪs/	Stimme	
	foreign /ˈfɒrɪn/	ausländisch, fremd	
	language /ˈlæŋgwɪdʒ/	Sprache	
	shadow /ˈʃædəʊ/	Schatten	
	moonlight /ˈmuːnˌlaɪt/	Mondlicht	
	be scared (of sth) /biː ˈskeəd/	(vor etw) Angst haben	Are you scared of dogs?
	quick /kwɪk/	schnell	quick = fast
	beard /bɪəd/	Bart	
	huge /hjuːdʒ/	riesig, riesengroß	

surprised /sə'praɪzd/	überrascht	I'm surprised that you don't like chocolate.
in the beginning /ɪn ðə bɪ'gɪnɪŋ/	am Anfang, zu Beginn	
god /gɒd/	Gott	
Inca /'ɪŋkə/	Inka	
people /'pi:pl/	Volk	
rule /ru:l/	Regel	
must not /mʌst 'nɒt/	nicht dürfen	I must not hit my sister. 
climb /klaɪm/	(hinauf)klettern; (hinauf)steigen	
sacred /'seɪkrɪd/	heilig	
burn *(irr)* /bɜ:n/	brennen	
devil /'devl/	Teufel	
sun /sʌn/	Sonne	It's dangerous to look at the sun. 
create /kri'eɪt/	erschaffen; gestalten; *hier:* erzeugen, produzieren	
stone /stəʊn/	Stein	
survive /sə'vaɪv/	überleben	
mean *(irr)* /mi:n/	bedeuten; meinen	What does "tree" mean in German?
stony /'stəʊni/	steinig; steinern	
end /end/	Ende	
sunrise /'sʌnˌraɪz/	Sonnenaufgang	
side /saɪd/	Seite	
not anymore /ˌnɒt eni'mɔ:/	nicht mehr	I don't like bananas anymore. 
seem /si:m/	scheinen	
excited /ɪk'saɪtɪd/	aufgeregt	
any /'eni/	irgendwelche, irgendein(e)	
M3 around the world /əˌraʊnd ðə 'wɜ:ld/	weltweit, auf der ganzen Welt	
country /'kʌntri/	Land	
kind /kaɪnd/	Art, Sorte	What kind of school do you go to?
comprehensive school /ˌkɒmprɪ'hensɪv ˌsku:l/	Gesamtschule	
right /raɪt/	richtig; *hier:* genau, direkt	
primary school /'praɪməri ˌsku:l/	Grundschule	
end /end/	enden	end ↔ begin
quite /kwaɪt/	ziemlich	
strict /strɪkt/	streng	
get into trouble /get‿ɪntə 'trʌbl/	Schwierigkeiten bekommen	Students get into trouble when they forget their homework.
change /tʃeɪndʒ/	(sich) (ver)ändern; *hier:* wechseln	

	another /əˈnʌðə/	noch ein(e, r, s); *hier:* ein anderer/anderes, eine andere	
	otherwise /ˈʌðəˌwaɪz/	sonst, ansonsten	
	repeat /riˈpiːt/	wiederholen	Can you repeat the question, please?
	take notes /teɪk ˈnəʊts/	(sich) Notizen machen	
	that /ðæt/	dass	
	be allowed to do sth /bi‿əˌlaʊd tə ˈduː ˌsʌmθɪŋ/	etw tun dürfen	She is allowed to go to the cinema today.
	prefer /prɪˈfɜː/	vorziehen, bevorzugen, lieber mögen	
	mark /mɑːk/	(Schul)note	I got a good mark in the maths test.
	all day /ˌɔːl ˈdeɪ/	den ganzen Tag	
	too bad /ˌtuː ˈbæd/	wirklich schade	
	piano /piˈænəʊ/	Klavier	piano 
M4	assembly /əˈsembli/	(Schüler)versammlung	
	skateboarding *(no pl)* /ˈskeɪtˌbɔːdɪŋ/	Skateboardfahren	
	evening /ˈiːvnɪŋ/	Abend	evening ↔ morning
M5	**somebody** /ˈsʌmbədi/	jemand	
CC	chronicle /ˈkrɒnɪkl/	Anzeiger	
	the ... way /ðə ˈweɪ/	auf die ... Art	
	get *(irr)* /get/	erhalten, bekommen; *hier:* verstehen	
	kind /kaɪnd/	Art, Sorte	
	colour /ˈkʌlə/	Farbe	
	non- /nɒn/	nicht-	
	yech *(informal)* /jek/	i, igitt	
	put on /pʊt‿ˈɒn/	anziehen; *hier:* sich eincremen mit	
	that /ðæt/	das; der/die/das; *hier:* diese(r, s)	
	sauce /sɔːs/	Soße	
	over /ˈəʊvə/	hinüber; *hier:* vorbei	
	class /klɑːs/	(Schul)klasse; *hier:* Unterricht	
	begin *(irr)* /bɪˈgɪn/	anfangen, beginnen	
	seashell /ˈsiːˌʃel/	Muschel	
	by /baɪ/	bei, an	
	seashore *(no pl)* /ˈsiːˌʃɔː/	Strand, Meeresküste	
	surely /ˈʃɔːli/	sicher(lich)	

TIPP

Nur zehn Minuten
Übe die Vokabeln immer nur fünf bis zehn Minuten, aber dafür regelmäßig! Das ist viel wirkungsvoller als eine ganze Stunde oder nur zweimal im Monat.

Theme 2 – Around London

I	around /əˈraʊnd/	um; *hier:* in, durch	
1	any /ˈeni/	irgendwelche, irgendein(e)	
	match (with) /mætʃ/	zuordnen	
	queen /kwiːn/	Königin	Queen Elizabeth lives in
	palace /ˈpæləs/	Palast	Buckingham Palace in London.
	Changing of the Guard /ˌtʃeɪndʒɪŋ‿əv ðə ˈɡɑːd/	Wachablösung	
	stall /stɔːl/	(Verkaufs)stand	
	juggler /ˈdʒʌɡlə/	Jongleur/in	juggler
	dungeon /ˈdʌndʒn/	Verlies, Kerker	
	travel /ˈtrævl/	reisen	Last summer we travelled around Germany.
	side /saɪd/	Seite	
	scary /ˈskeəri/	Furcht erregend; unheimlich	She often reads scary stories. 
	alone /əˈləʊn/	allein	
	railway /ˈreɪlweɪ/	Gleise, Schienen; *hier:* (Eisen)bahn	
	station /ˈsteɪʃn/	Bahnhof; Station	
	platform /ˈplætˌfɔːm/	Plattform; *hier:* Bahnsteig, Gleis	
	must-see /ˌmʌstˈsiː/	*etw, das man gesehen haben muss*	
	train /treɪn/	Zug, Eisenbahn	train
	leave *(irr)* /liːv/	verlassen; *hier:* abfahren	
	real /rɪəl/	wirklich; echt	
	life *(pl* **lives***)* /laɪf, laɪvz/	Leben	
	about /əˈbaʊt/	ungefähr	
	perfect /ˈpɜːfɪkt/	perfekt	
	relax /rɪˈlæks/	sich entspannen	
	grass *(no pl)* /ɡrɑːs/	Gras; Wiese, Rasen	
	boat /bəʊt/	Boot; Schiff	boat
	sun /sʌn/	Sonne	sun 
	kind /kaɪnd/	Art, Sorte	
	metre /ˈmiːtə/	Meter	
	top /tɒp/	oberes Ende, Spitze	
	view /vjuː/	Sicht; (Aus)blick, Aussicht	
	corner /ˈkɔːnə/	Ecke	corner
	airport /ˈeəˌpɔːt/	Flughafen	
	stadium /ˈsteɪdiəm/	Stadion	
	the (River) Thames /ðə ˈtemz/	die Themse	
	bridge /brɪdʒ/	Brücke	bridge
	wax /wæks/	Wachs	
	king /kɪŋ/	König	
	sportsperson /ˈspɔːtsˌpɜːsn/	Sportler/in	

	even /ˈiːvn/	selbst; sogar	
	wait (for) /weɪt/	warten (auf)	They are waiting for the bus.
	pass /pɑːs/	vorbeikommen	
	tower /ˈtaʊə/	Turm	
	cannon /ˈkænən/	Kanone, Geschütz	
	Crown Jewels *(only pl)* /ˌkraʊn ˈdʒuːəlz/	Kronjuwelen	
	detective /dɪˈtektɪv/	(Privat)detektiv/in	detective 
	statue /ˈstætʃuː/	Statue, Standbild	
	in the middle /ˌɪn ðə ˈmɪdl/	in der Mitte; mitten in/auf	
2	imagine /ɪˈmædʒɪn/	sich vorstellen	
3	part /pɑːt/	Teil	
	each /iːtʃ/	jede(r, s)	
	high /haɪ/	hoch	
	like /laɪk/	wie	
	glass /glɑːs/	Glas	
	underground /ˈʌndəˌgraʊnd/	U-Bahn	underground
	chips *(only pl) (BE)* /tʃɪps/	Pommes frites	chips 
5	top /tɒp/	Spitzen-	
6	**weekend** /ˌwiːkˈend/	Wochenende	
	lose *(irr)* /luːz/	verlieren	lose – lost *(simple past)*
	tube *(no pl)* /tjuːb/	*Londoner U-Bahn*	
	full /fʊl/	voll	
	get off /ˌget‿ˈɒf/	aussteigen	
	not anymore /ˌnɒt eniˈmɔː/	nicht mehr	
	believe (in) /bɪˈliːv/	glauben (an)	I don't believe your story.
	try /traɪ/	(aus)probieren; *hier:* versuchen	
	dead /ded/	tot; *hier:* leer	
	charge /tʃɑːdʒ/	(auf)laden	
	yeah *(informal)* /jeə/	ja	
	reach /riːtʃ/	greifen; *hier:* erreichen	
	explain /ɪkˈspleɪn/	erklären	Can you explain this text to me, please? I don't understand it.
	(three days) ago /əˈgəʊ/	vor (drei Tagen)	
	past /pɑːst/	vorbei/vorüber an	walk past 
	building /ˈbɪldɪŋ/	Gebäude	
	on the/your left /ˌɒn ðə/jɔː ˈleft/	links, auf der linken Seite	on your left 
	queue /kjuː/	Schlange, Reihe	
	along /əˈlɒŋ/	entlang	
	turn /tɜːn/	sich drehen; *hier:* abbiegen	turn right 
	right /raɪt/	(nach) rechts	
	straight (on) /streɪt/	gerade(aus)	walk straight on 
	left /left/	(nach) links	

	get *(irr)* /get/	erhalten, bekommen; *hier:* (an)kommen	
	just a minute /ˌdʒʌst‿ə ˈmɪnɪt/	(einen) Moment (bitte), (einen) Augenblick (bitte)	
	right /raɪt/	richtig; *hier:* genau, direkt	
	read along /ˌriːd‿əˈlɒŋ/	mitlesen	
	below /bɪˈləʊ/	unten	
7	**direction** /dɪˈrekʃn/	Richtung	
	expression /ɪkˈspreʃn/	Ausdruck	
	symbol /ˈsɪmbl/	Symbol, Zeichen	
	on /ɒn/	auf, an; *hier:* weiter	
	on the/your right /ˌɒn ðə/jɔː ˈraɪt/	rechts, auf der rechten Seite	on your right 
	cross /krɒs/	durchqueren; überqueren	cross the street 
	give directions /ˌgɪv dɪˈrekʃnz/	den Weg beschreiben	
8	the next day /ðə ˌnekst ˈdeɪ/	am nächsten Tag	
	follow /ˈfɒləʊ/	folgen	
9	village /ˈvɪlɪdʒ/	Dorf	
	town /taʊn/	Stadt	
	brochure /ˈbrəʊʃə/	Broschüre	
	British /ˈbrɪtɪʃ/	britische(r, s)	
	short /ʃɔːt/	kurz	
	dialogue /ˈdaɪəlɒg/	Gespräch, Dialog	
	English-speaking /ˈɪŋglɪʃ‿ˌspiːkɪŋ/	englischsprachig	
	act out /ækt‿ˈaʊt/	nachspielen	
10	**be frightened (of)** /biː ˈfraɪtnd/	Angst haben, sich fürchten (vor)	Lots of people are frightened of snakes. 
	get together /ˌget‿təˈgeðə/	sich treffen; *hier:* sich sammeln	
	buzz group /ˈbʌz gruːp/	*Form der Gruppenarbeit*	
	result /rɪˈzʌlt/	Ergebnis; Folge	
	at work /æt ˈwɜːk/	auf/bei der Arbeit	
	news *(no pl)* /njuːz/	Neuigkeit; Nachrichten	 My parents always watch the news on TV.
	newsreader /ˈnjuːzˌriːdə/	Nachrichtensprecher/in	
	police *(no pl)* /pəˈliːs/	Polizei	
	keeper /ˈkiːpə/	Tierpfleger/in	keeper 
	must /mʌst/	müssen	must = have to
	somewhere /ˈsʌmweə/	irgendwo	
	perhaps /pəˈhæps/	vielleicht	perhaps = maybe
	outside /ˌaʊtˈsaɪd/	im Freien, draußen; *hier:* (draußen) vor	
	not yet /nɒt ˈjet/	noch nicht	
	that /ðæt/	dass	
	sleepy /ˈsliːpi/	verschlafen, schläfrig	

	its /ɪts/	sein(e), ihr(e)	The bird is in its cage. 
	meal /miːl/	Mahlzeit, Essen	
	Oh dear! /əʊ ˈdɪə/	Du meine Güte!	
	noise /nɔɪz/	Lärm, Krach; Geräusch	
	What's the matter? /ˌwɒts ðə ˈmætə/	Was ist (denn) los?	What's the matter? – I'm tired.
	look /lʊk/	sehen, schauen; *hier:* aussehen	
	quick /kwɪk/	schnell	quick = fast
	Don't be silly! /ˌdəʊnt bi ˈsɪli/	Red(et) keinen Unsinn!	
	news just in /ˌnjuːz dʒʌst‿ˈɪn/	Gerade kommt eine Meldung herein.	
11	**through** /θruː/	durch	Let's walk through the park.
	runaway /ˈrʌnəˌweɪ/	entlaufen	
	call /kɔːl/	anrufen	call = phone
	police officer /pəˈliːs ˌɒfɪsə/	Polizeibeamter/-beamtin	police officer
	away /əˈweɪ/	weg	Polly ran away from the dog.
	canal /kəˈnæl/	Kanal	
12	**adventure** /ədˈventʃə/	Abenteuer, Erlebnis	Do you like adventures?
	reaction (to) /riˈækʃn/	Reaktion (auf)	
	bored /bɔːd/	gelangweilt	Charlie often feels bored at school.
	this afternoon /ðɪs‿ˌɑːftəˈnuːn/	heute Nachmittag	
	ugh *(informal)* /ʌg/	i, igitt	
	let sb in /ˌlet ˌsʌmbədi‿ˈɪn/	jdn hereinlassen	
	That's too bad. /ðæts ˈtuː bæd/	Das ist wirklich schade.	
	what a ... /ˈwɒt‿ə/	was für ein(e) ...	
13	**paw** /pɔː/	Pfote, Tatze	
	predator /ˈpredətə/	Raubtier	
	clever /ˈklevə/	klug, gescheit, schlau	
	stripe /straɪp/	Streifen	
	fur /fɜː/	Fell; Pelz	
	tail /teɪl/	Schwanz	
	Asia /ˈeɪʃə/	Asien	
	fit *(irr)* /fɪt/	passen (zu)	
	which one /ˈwɪtʃ wʌn/	welche(r, s)	
14	test /test/	prüfen, testen	
	insect /ˈɪnsekt/	Insekt	
	apple /ˈæpl/	Apfel	apple
	carrot /ˈkærət/	Möhre, Karotte, Mohrrübe	carrots 
	hippo (= hippopotamus) /ˈhɪpəʊ, ˌhɪpəˈpɒtəməs/	Nilpferd	
	spider /ˈspaɪdə/	Spinne	spider 
15	work /wɜːk/	Arbeit	
	colleague /ˈkɒliːg/	Kollege/Kollegin; Mitarbeiter/in	

	seller /ˈselə/	Verkäufer/in	
	vet (= veterinarian) /vet, ˌvetrɪˈneəriən/	Tierarzt/-ärztin	vet 
	gardener /ˈgɑːdnə/	Gärtner/in	
	director /dəˈrektə/	Direktor/in, Leiter/in	
P1	be the odd one out /biː ði‿ˌɒd wʌn‿ˈaʊt/	aus der Reihe fallen, nicht dazugehören	
	singer /ˈsɪŋə/	Sänger/in	
P3	church /tʃɜːtʃ/	Kirche	
	supermarket /ˈsuːpəˌmɑːkɪt/	Supermarkt	
P5	cost *(irr)* /kɒst/	kosten	
	on your right /ɒn jɔː raɪt/	rechts	
	take a look (at) /teɪk‿ə ˈlʊk/	einen Blick werfen (auf)	
	end /end/	Ende	
P6	sign /saɪn/	Zeichen; (Straßen-/Verkehrs)schild	
	everything /ˈevriθɪŋ/	alles	
	hold *(irr)* /həʊld/	halten	
	handrail /ˈhændˌreɪl/	Geländer	
	keep clear of the edges /kiːp ˌklɪər‿əv ði‿ˈedʒɪz/	sich von den Rändern fernhalten	
	take care /teɪk ˈkeə/	aufpassen	
	extra /ˈekstrə/	besonders	
	carry /ˈkæri/	tragen	
	smoke /sməʊk/	rauchen	
P7	be scared (of sth) /biː ˈskeəd/	(vor etw) Angst haben	
	thin /θɪn/	dünn	
	around /əˈraʊnd/	herum, umher	
	pocket /ˈpɒkɪt/	Tasche	
P9	rhyming pair /ˈraɪmɪŋ peə/	Reimpaar	
	toe /təʊ/	Zeh(e)	
P11	normally /ˈnɔːmli/	normalerweise	
	field /fiːld/	Wiese, Weide, Feld	
	ground /graʊnd/	(Erd)boden, Erde	
	at the moment /æt ðə ˈməʊmənt/	im Moment	
P12	adopt /əˈdɒpt/	adoptieren	
	different /ˈdɪfrənt/	anders, andere(r, s)	
	hut /hʌt/	Hütte	
	African /ˈæfrɪkən/	Afrikaner/in; afrikanisch	
	born /bɔːn/	geboren	
	North Pole /ˌnɔːθ ˈpəʊl/	Nordpol	
	rare /reə/	selten, rar	
	Komodo dragon /kəˌməʊdəʊ ˈdrægən/	Komododrache, Komodowaran	
	Asian /ˈeɪʃn/	Asiat/in; asiatisch	

TIPP

Vergiss es einfach!
Hast du Probleme, dir bestimmte Wörter zu merken? Sind es immer dieselben Vokabeln, die dir nicht einfallen? Dann probiere es doch mal mit Vergessen! Das geht so: Suche fünf oder sechs schwierige Wörter aus, die du unbedingt vergessen willst. Schreibe sie auf Zettel und hänge sie neben dein Bett, über deinen Schreibtisch oder an den Badezimmerspiegel. Lies sie dir bei jeder Gelegenheit durch, damit du dich daran erinnerst, welche Wörter du unbedingt vergessen willst.

M1	tip /tɪp/	Tipp	
	phrase /freɪz/	Satz; Ausdruck, (Rede)wendung	
	church /tʃɜːtʃ/	Kirche	church
	get married /get ˈmærid/	heiraten	They got married today. 
	bury /ˈberi/	begraben	
	department store /dɪˈpɑːtmənt ˌstɔː/	Kaufhaus	Harrods is a famous department store in London.
	Europe /ˈjʊərəp/	Europa	
	medal /ˈmedl/	Medaille	
	former /ˈfɔːmə/	ehemalige(r, s), frühere(r, s)	
M2	**home town** /ˌhəʊm ˈtaʊn/	Heimatort	Karla's home town is London.
	mention /ˈmenʃn/	erwähnen	
	talk /tɔːk/	Gespräch; Unterhaltung; *hier:* Vortrag	
M3	visit /ˈvɪzɪt/	Besuch	
	magnifying glass /ˈmægnɪfaɪɪŋ glɑːs/	Lupe	
	pipe /paɪp/	Pfeife	
	fault /fɔːlt/	Schuld; Fehler	I'm sorry, it's my fault.
	answer /ˈɑːnsə/	(be)antworten	
	belong to sb/sth /bɪˈlɒŋ tə ˌsʌmbədi/ˌsʌmθɪŋ/	jdm/zu etw gehören	Mrs Killmouskey belongs to Gillian.
	person /ˈpɜːsn/	Person, Mensch	
	writer /ˈraɪtə/	Schriftsteller/in, Autor/in	
	create /kriˈeɪt/	erschaffen; gestalten	
	stairs *(only pl)* /steəz/	Treppe	
	narrow /ˈnærəʊ/	eng, schmal	
	study /ˈstʌdi/	Studie; *hier:* Arbeitszimmer	
	doctor /ˈdɒktə/	Arzt/Ärztin	
	medical bag /ˈmedɪkl bæg/	Medikamentenkoffer	
	criminal /ˈkrɪmɪnl/	Verbrecher/in, Kriminelle/r	 criminal
	who /huː/	wer; *hier:* der/die/das	
	at that time /æt ˈðæt taɪm/	damals, zu dieser Zeit	
	upstairs /ʌpˈsteəz/	(nach) oben	The children are upstairs in bed.
	dead /ded/	tot	
	coffin /ˈkɒfɪn/	Sarg	
	weapon /ˈwepən/	Waffe	
	horrible /ˈhɒrəbl/	schrecklich	
	fall *(irr)* /fɔːl/	fallen	
	trapdoor /ˈtræpˌdɔː/	Falltür	
	search /sɜːtʃ/	(durch)suchen	
M5	**Africa** /ˈæfrɪkə/	Afrika	
	feeding time /ˈfiːdɪŋ ˌtaɪm/	Fütterungszeit	
	leaf *(pl* **leaves***)* /liːf, liːvz/	Blatt	leaf 

tortoise /ˈtɔːtəs/	(Land)schildkröte	tortoise
island /ˈaɪlənd/	Insel	island
meerkat /ˈmɪəˌkæt/	Erdmännchen	
information point /ˌɪnfəˈmeɪʃn pɔɪnt/	Informationsstelle	
M6 golden eagle /ˈgəʊldn ˌiːgl/	Goldadler, Steinadler	
eagle /ˈiːgl/	Adler	An eagle is a large bird.
newspaper /ˈnjuːzˌpeɪpə/	Zeitung	
article /ˈɑːtɪkl/	Artikel	
p (= penny, pence) /piː, ˈpenni, pens/	Penny, Centstück	This postcard only costs 60 p.
escape /ɪˈskeɪp/	Flucht	
escape /ɪˈskeɪp/	(ent)fliehen, ausbrechen; entkommen	
home /həʊm/	Zuhause, Heim	
leave *(irr)* /liːv/	verlassen; *hier:* lassen	leave – left *(simple past)*
leave behind /ˌliːv bɪˈhaɪnd/	zurücklassen	
try hard to do sth /ˌtraɪ ˈhɑːd‿tə duː sʌmθɪŋ/	sich sehr bemühen, etw zu tun	Lucy tried hard to do her homework before the party.
The British Navy /ðə ˌbrɪtɪʃ ˈneɪvi/	die britische Marine	
spend *(irr)* /spend/	ausgeben *(Geld)*; verbringen *(Zeit)*	spend – spent *(simple past)*
avoid /əˈvɔɪd/	(ver)meiden, entgehen	
capture /ˈkæptʃə/	Festnahme	
tasty /ˈteɪsti/	lecker	
trap /træp/	Falle	The mouse did not know that the cheese was a trap.
freedom *(no pl)* /ˈfriːdəm/	Freiheit	
naughty /ˈnɔːti/	ungezogen, frech	
time /taɪm/	(Uhr)zeit; *hier:* Mal	2 times = 2 x
CC ever /ˈevə/	jemals; überhaupt	
woolly /ˈwʊli/	Woll-, wollen	
around /əˈraʊnd/	um	
neck /nek/	Hals; Nacken	
wind *(irr)* /waɪnd/	wickeln	
still /stɪl/	(immer) noch, noch immer; trotzdem, dennoch	
trail /treɪl/	schleifen	
upon /əˈpɒn/	auf	
tiny /ˈtaɪni/	winzig	
tomato *(pl -es)* /təˈmɑːtəʊ, təˈmɑːtəʊz/	Tomate	
who /huː/	wer; *hier:* der/die/das	
smile /smaɪl/	lächeln	

TIPP

Mache sie zu deinen Wörtern!
Am besten kannst du dir Wörter merken, die du selbst verwendet hast. Darum: Bilde Sätze mit den Wörtern, die du dir merken willst. Sie können auch lustig sein oder sich reimen:
My mum can make a yummy cake.

	as /əz/	als	
	ride /raɪd/	Fahrt; *hier:* (Aus)ritt	
	inside /ɪnˈsaɪd/	drinnen; innen; *hier:* im Inneren	
	smile /smaɪl/	Lächeln	
	someone /ˈsʌmwʌn/	jemand	
	up /ʌp/	(nach) oben; hinauf	
	mirror /ˈmɪrə/	Spiegel	

Theme 3 – Dreams

1	**star sign** /ˈstɑː saɪn/	Sternzeichen	
	horoscope /ˈhɒrəˌskəʊp/	Horoskop	
2	**(phone) call** /(ˈfəʊn) kɔːl/	(Telefon)anruf	I got a phone call from a friend.
	nothing /ˈnʌθɪŋ/	nichts	
	anything /ˈeniˌθɪŋ/	(irgend)(et)was	Do you know anything about zebras?
	lady /ˈleɪdi/	Frau; Dame	
	Aquarius /əˈkweəriəs/	Wassermann *(Sternzeichen)*	
	lucky /ˈlʌki/	glücklich, glücksbringend, Glücks-	My lucky number is 7.
	take part (in) /ˌteɪk ˈpɑːt/	teilnehmen (an)	
	competition /ˌkɒmpəˈtɪʃn/	Wettbewerb	
	will /wɪl/	werden	will not = won't
	surprise /səˈpraɪz/	Überraschung	
	winner /ˈwɪnə/	Gewinner/in, Sieger/in	
	not any /nɒt‿ˈeni/	kein(e)	There aren't any shops on my street.
	fortune-teller /ˈfɔːtʃən ˌtelə/	Wahrsager/in	
	tell *(irr)* /tel/	erzählen; sagen; *hier:* vorhersagen	
	fortune *(no pl)* /ˈfɔːtʃən/	Schicksal	
	marry /ˈmæri/	heiraten	She wants to marry a pop star.
	not anyone /nɒt‿ˈeniwʌn/	niemand	
	doctor /ˈdɒktə/	Arzt/Ärztin	
	one day /ˈwʌn deɪ/	eines Tages	Charlie wants to be rich one day. 
	rich /rɪtʃ/	reich	
3	**future** /ˈfjuːtʃə/	Zukunft	
4	fortune-telling *(no pl)* /ˈfɔːtʃən ˌtelɪŋ/	Wahrsagen, Wahrsagerei	
5	**pilot** /ˈpaɪlət/	Pilot/in	
	plane /pleɪn/	Flugzeug	plane 
	nurse /nɜːs/	(Kranken)schwester, (Kranken)pfleger	
	technician /tekˈnɪʃn/	Techniker/in	
	driver /ˈdraɪvə/	Fahrer/in	

	builder /ˈbɪldə/	Bauarbeiter/in	
	cook /kʊk/	Koch/Köchin	
	hairdresser /ˈheəˌdresə/	Friseur/in	
	firefighter /ˈfaɪəˌfaɪtə/	Feuerwehrmann/-frau	
	shop assistant /ˈʃɒp‿əˌsɪstənt/	Verkäufer/in	
	cut *(irr)* /kʌt/	schneiden	You can cut an apple with a knife. 
	style /staɪl/	frisieren	
	take care of /teɪk ˈkeər‿əv/	sich kümmern um, versorgen	A nurse takes care of ill people.
	ill /ɪl/	krank	
	cook /kʊk/	kochen	
	repair /rɪˈpeə/	reparieren	
	drive *(irr)* /draɪv/	fahren	drive – drove *(simple past)*
	flower /ˈflaʊə/	Blume	flower 
	plant /plɑːnt/	Pflanze	
	trouble *(no pl)* /ˈtrʌbl/	Schwierigkeiten	
	catch *(irr)* /kætʃ/	fangen; *hier:* festnehmen	catch – caught *(simple past)*
	build *(irr)* /bɪld/	bauen	build – built *(simple past)*
	fight *(irr)* /faɪt/	(be)kämpfen	fight – fought *(simple past)*
	fire /faɪə/	Feuer	
	future /ˈfjuːtʃə/	zukünftig, später	
	grow up /grəʊ‿ˈʌp/	erwachsen werden	
7	**robot** /ˈrəʊbɒt/	Roboter	robot 
	as /əz/	als	
	own /əʊn/	eigene(r, s)	Rajiv has his own bedroom.
	boss /bɒs/	Chef/in	
	moon /muːn/	Mond	 moon
8	whatever /wɒtˈevə/	was (auch immer)	
	language /ˈlæŋgwɪdʒ/	Sprache	
	sing along /ˌsɪŋ‿əˈlɒŋ/	mitsingen	
	just /dʒʌst/	gleich; *hier:* noch	
	pretty /ˈprɪti/	hübsch	Caroline is a pretty girl.
	ours /ˈaʊəz/	unsere(r, s)	
	fall in love (with) /ˌfɔːl‿ɪn ˈlʌv/	sich verlieben (in)	
	sweetheart /ˈswiːtˌhɑːt/	Liebling, Schatz	
	lie ahead /ˌlaɪ‿əˈhed/	bevorstehen, vor jdm liegen	
	rainbow /ˈreɪnˌbəʊ/	Regenbogen	Look at this beautiful rainbow!
	day after day /deɪ‿ɑːftə ˈdeɪ/	Tag für Tag; tagein, tagaus	
	of one's own /əv wʌnz‿ˈəʊn/	eigene(r, s)	„Qué será, será" ist spanisch und bedeutet: „Was kommen wird, wird kommen."
	handsome /ˈhænsm/	gut aussehend, attraktiv	
	tenderly /ˈtendəli/	liebevoll; zärtlich	
	lover /ˈlʌvə/	Liebhaber/in; Liebende(r)	
9	think about (sb/sth) /ˈθɪŋk‿əˌbaʊt/	an (jdn/etw) denken; über (jdn/etw) nachdenken	
	scene /siːn/	Szene	
10	daydream /ˈdeɪˌdriːm/	Tagtraum	

	hero *(pl* **-es***)* /ˈhɪərəʊ, ˈhɪərəʊz/	Held/in	My hero is Uncle Scrooge. (=Onkel Dagobert)
	daydream *(irr)* /ˈdeɪˌdriːm/	tagträumen	
	cattle *(no pl)* /ˈkætl/	Vieh; Rinder	
	hard /hɑːd/	hart; schwer	You have to work hard to make
	make money /meɪk ˈmʌni/	Geld verdienen	lots of money.
	factory /ˈfæktri/	Fabrik; Werk	factory 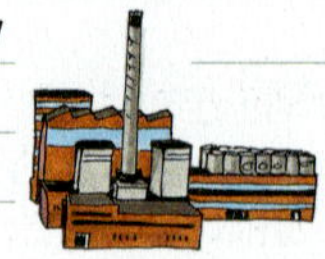
	astronaut /ˈæstrəˌnɔːt/	Astronaut/in	
	well /wel/	gut	
	score a goal /skɔːr‿ə ˈɡəʊl/	ein Tor schießen	
	billion /ˈbɪljən/	Milliarde	
	pound /paʊnd/	Pfund *(brit. Währung)*	one pound (£1) = 100 pence (p)
	past /pɑːst/	Vergangenheit	
	guy *(informal)* /ɡaɪ/	Kerl, Typ	
	the rich *(no pl)* /ðə ˈrɪtʃ/	die Reichen	
	forest /ˈfɒrɪst/	Wald	forest 
	best /best/	am meisten/liebsten/besten	
	person /ˈpɜːsn/	Person, Mensch	
11	corn *(no pl)* /kɔːn/	Getreide, Korn	
	worry /ˈwʌri/	sich Sorgen machen	He worries a lot about his grandparents.
	recognize /ˈrekəɡnaɪz/	(wieder)erkennen	
	far /fɑː/	weit	My school isn't very far away from my home.
	moment /ˈməʊmənt/	Moment, Augenblick	
	dress /dres/	sich kleiden; sich anziehen	
	steal *(irr)* /stiːl/	stehlen, klauen	steal – stole *(simple past)* The boy stole the woman's bag.
	get *(irr)* /ɡet/	erhalten, bekommen; *hier:* steigen	
	remember /rɪˈmembə/	sich erinnern (an); *hier:* (an etw) denken	
	hang /hæŋ/	erhängen	
	loud /laʊd/	laut	
12	keyword /ˈkiːˌwɜːd/	Schlüsselwort	
	let *(irr)* /let/	lassen	let – let *(simple past)*
	finally /ˈfaɪnli/	schließlich, endlich; zum Schluss	
13	dramatic /drəˈmætɪk/	dramatisch	
	reading /ˈriːdɪŋ/	Lesen; Lesung	
	speak *(irr)* /spiːk/	sprechen, reden	speak – spoke *(simple past)*
	excited /ɪkˈsaɪtɪd/	aufgeregt	excited 
	way /weɪ/	Weg; *hier:* Art, Weise	
	character /ˈkærɪktə/	Charakter; Figur	
	role /rəʊl/	Rolle	
	by heart /baɪ ˈhɑːt/	auswendig	

14	**careful** /ˈkeəfl/	vorsichtig; sorgfältig	Please be careful with those plates.
	slow /sləʊ/	langsam	slow ↔ fast, quick
15	record /rɪˈkɔːd/	aufnehmen, aufzeichnen	
	narrator /nəˈreɪtə/	Erzähler/in	
	play /pleɪ/	Spiel; *hier:* (Theater)stück, Hörspiel	
	wanted /ˈwɒntɪd/	gesucht	
P1	name /neɪm/	(be)nennen	
	get down /get ˈdaʊn/	herunterkommen	
	tool /tuːl/	Werkzeug	
	criminal /ˈkrɪmɪnl/	Verbrecher/in, Kriminelle/r	
	hospital /ˈhɒspɪtl/	Krankenhaus	
P2	repeat /rɪˈpiːt/	wiederholen	
	read sth to sb /ˈriːd ˌsʌmθɪŋ tə ˌsʌmbədi/	jdm etw vorlesen	
P4	get married /get ˈmærid/	heiraten	
	take turns /ˌteɪk ˈtɜːnz/	sich abwechseln	
P5	motorbike /ˈməʊtəˌbaɪk/	Motorrad	
P6	Gemini /ˈdʒemɪnaɪ/	Zwilling *(Sternzeichen)*	
	get into action /ˌget‿ɪntə‿ˈækʃn/	loslegen	
	full /fʊl/	voll, gefüllt	
	excitement /ɪkˈsaɪtmənt/	Aufregung, Spannung	
	just /dʒʌst/	gleich; *hier:* genau	
	luck *(no pl)* /lʌk/	Glück	
	happiness *(no pl)* /ˈhæpinəs/	Glück; Zufriedenheit	
	cheerful /ˈtʃɪəfl/	fröhlich, vergnügt, gut gelaunt	
	whole /həʊl/	ganz, gesamt	
P8	tongue twister /ˈtʌŋ ˌtwɪstə/	Zungenbrecher	
	yourself *(pl* yourselves*)* /jəˈself, jəˈselvz/	dich, dir; selbst/ ihr, euch; selbst	
	crazy /ˈkreɪzi/	verrückt	
	race /reɪs/	Rennen	
P9	copy /ˈkɒpi/	abschreiben	
	fill in /fɪl‿ˈɪn/	ausfüllen; *hier:* einsetzen	
P11	move /muːv/	sich bewegen	
	bark /bɑːk/	bellen	
P12	major /ˈmeɪdʒə/	bedeutend, wichtig	
	oak /əʊk/	Eiche	
	hide *(irr)* /haɪd/	(sich) verstecken	
	enemy /ˈenəmi/	Feind/in	
	footpath /ˈfʊtˌpɑːθ/	Fußweg	
	lead *(irr)* /liːd/	führen	

TIPP

Schwierige Wörter
Wenn du merkst, dass du bei der Schreibweise einiger englischer Wörter Schwierigkeiten hast, kannst du Folgendes tun: Schreibe das Wort auf ein großes Blatt und markiere die Stelle, die dir Probleme macht. Hänge das Blatt in deinem Zimmer auf. Du wirst merken, dass du das Wort bald richtig schreiben kannst.

TIPP

Hosentaschenzettel
Schreibe dir kleine Zettel für unterwegs mit den wichtigsten oder schwierigsten Vokabeln. So hast du sie immer bei dir.

M2	Aries /ˈeəriːz/	Widder *(Sternzeichen)*	
	Taurus /ˈtɔːrəs/	Stier *(Sternzeichen)*	
	Cancer /ˈkænsə/	Krebs *(Sternzeichen)*	
	Leo /ˈliːəʊ/	Löwe *(Sternzeichen)*	
	Virgo /ˈvɜːgəʊ/	Jungfrau *(Sternzeichen)*	
	Libra /ˈliːbrə/	Waage *(Sternzeichen)*	
	Scorpio /ˈskɔːpiəʊ/	Skorpion *(Sternzeichen)*	
	Sagittarius /ˌsædʒɪˈteəriəs/	Schütze *(Sternzeichen)*	
	Capricorn /ˈkæprɪˌkɔːn/	Steinbock *(Sternzeichen)*	
	Pisces /ˈpaɪsiːz/	Fische *(Sternzeichen)*	
M3	**spaceship** /ˈspeɪsˌʃɪp/	Raumschiff	spaceship 
	trip /trɪp/	Ausflug; Reise, Fahrt	
M4	timewatch /ˈtaɪmwɒtʃ/	Zeitreise-Uhr	
	Bang! /bæŋ/	Peng!	
	alien /ˈeɪliən/	Außerirdische(r), Alien	This alien looks really strange. 
	silver /ˈsɪlvə/	silbern	
	skyscraper /ˈskaɪˌskreɪpə/	Wolkenkratzer	
	hundred /ˈhʌndrəd/	Hundert	hundred = 100
	thin /θɪn/	dünn	
	wire /ˈwaɪə/	Draht; Leitung, Kabel	
	race /reɪs/	Rennen	
	thousand /ˈθaʊznd/	Tausend	thousand = 1,000
	zip wire /ˈzɪp ˌwaɪə/	Seilrutsche	
	be (great) fun /biː (ˌgreɪt) ˈfʌn/	(viel) Spaß machen	Swimming is great fun.
	worried /ˈwʌrid/	beunruhigt, besorgt	
	go-karting /ˈgəʊˌkɑːtɪŋ/	Gokartfahren	
	century /ˈsentʃəri/	Jahrhundert	We live in the twenty-first century.
	at first /ət ˈfɜːst/	anfangs, zuerst	
	smile /smaɪl/	lächeln	She smiled at me.
	follow /ˈfɒləʊ/	folgen	
	amazed /əˈmeɪzd/	erstaunt, verblüfft	
	...-flavoured /ˈfleɪvəd/	mit ...-Geschmack	
	milkshake /ˈmɪlkˌʃeɪk/	Milchshake	Do you like chocolate milkshake?
	Come on! /ˌkʌm‿ˈɒn/	Auf geht's!, Komm(t) jetzt!	
	broken /ˈbrəʊkən/	zerbrochen, kaputt	The plate is broken.
	wheel /wiːl/	Rad	A bike has got two wheels. 
	flat /flæt/	flach; *hier:* platt	
	going to /ˈgəʊɪŋ tə/	werden	
	win *(irr)* /wɪn/	gewinnen	win – won *(simple past)*
	Let's go! /lets ˈgəʊ/	Los!, Auf geht's!	
	to go /tə ˈgəʊ/	noch	
	take a chance /teɪk‿ə ˈtʃɑːns/	etw wagen, etw riskieren	
	get *(irr)* /get/	erhalten, bekommen; *hier:* steigen	get – got *(simple past)*

	into /ˈɪntʊ/	in	He jumped into the water.
	instead (of) /ɪnˈsted (‿əv)/	stattdessen; (an)statt	
	once /wʌns/	einmal	We visit my uncle
	a year /ə ˈjɪə/	pro/im Jahr	once a year.
	whom /huːm/	wen; wem	
	experience /ɪkˈspɪəriəns/	erleben, erfahren	
M5	word web /ˈwɜːd web/	Wortnetz	
	explore /ɪkˈsplɔː/	erforschen, untersuchen	I like to explore interesting places.
	universe /ˈjuːnɪˌvɜːs/	Universum	
	protect /prəˈtekt/	(be)schützen	It's important to protect wild animals.
	jungle /ˈdʒʌŋgl/	Dschungel, Urwald	
	rainforest /ˈreɪnˌfɒrɪst/	Regenwald	
	author /ˈɔːθə/	Schriftsteller/in, Autor/in	Who is your favourite author?
	discover /dɪˈskʌvə/	entdecken	Who discovered America?
	solo /ˈsəʊləʊ/	allein	
	across /əˈkrɒs/	über	There are bridges across the river.
	the Atlantic (Ocean) /ði‿ətˈlæntɪk(‿ˌəʊʃn)/	der Atlantische Ozean	
	the Pacific (Ocean) /ðə pəˈsɪfɪk(‿ˌəʊʃn)/	der Pazifische Ozean	
	brave /breɪv/	mutig, unerschrocken	
	hospital /ˈhɒspɪtl/	Krankenhaus	Doctors and nurses work in a hospital.
	seriously /ˈsɪəriəsli/	ernst(lich), schwer	
	although /ɔːlˈðəʊ/	obwohl, obgleich	
	American /əˈmerɪkən/	Amerikaner/in; amerikanisch	
	bronze /brɒnz/	Bronze, Bronze-	bronze – silver – gold
	Olympic Games /əˌlɪmpɪk ˈgeɪmz/	Olympische Spiele	
M7	comic strip /ˈkɒmɪk strɪp/	Comic *(in einer Zeitung)*, Comicstreifen	
	speech bubble /ˈspiːtʃ ˌbʌbl/	Sprechblase	
	caption /ˈkæpʃn/	Bildunterschrift, Bildtext	
M8	by /baɪ/	bei, in der Nähe; *hier:* von	
CC	dream *(irr)* /driːm/	träumen	
	wanna (= want to) /ˈwɒnə/	wollen	
	all /ɔːl/	ganz, völlig	
	brightly /ˈbraɪtli/	hell, leuchtend	
	light *(irr)* /laɪt/	erhellen; *hier:* aufleuchten	
	cover /ˈkʌvə/	Titelseite, Cover	
	bar /bɑː/	Lokal, Bar; *hier:* Imbiss	
	so far /ˌsəʊ ˈfɑː/	bisher, bis jetzt	

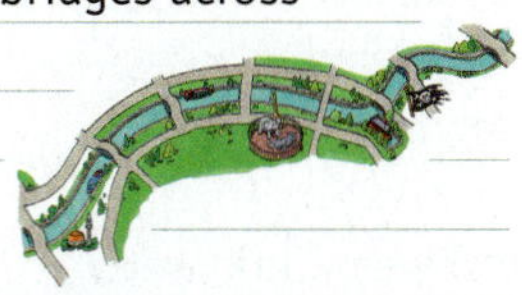

TIPP

Kim's game
Schreibe zehn Wörter auf ein Blatt Papier. Nimm dir drei Minuten Zeit, um sie dir einzuprägen. Dann drehe das Blatt um. Versuche nun, alle Wörter auswendig auf die Rückseite zu schreiben. Wie viele hast du dir gemerkt?

Optional – Writing Stories

Op1	evening /ˈiːvnɪŋ/	Abend
	choir /kwaɪə/	Chor
	nervously /ˈnɜːvəsli/	nervös; aufgeregt
	start /stɑːt/	Anfang, Beginn
	education *(no pl)* /ˌedjʊˈkeɪʃn/	(Aus)bildung
	line /laɪn/	Linie; *hier:* Zeile
	How about ... ? /ˈhaʊ‿əˌbaʊt/	Was ist mit ... ?,
		Wie wäre es mit ... ?
	hide-and-seek /ˌhaɪd‿ən ˈsiːk/	Verstecken
	corridor /ˈkɒrɪdɔː/	Flur, Gang
	empty /ˈempti/	leer
	count /kaʊnt/	zählen
	up to /ˈʌp tuː/	bis (zu)
	hundred /ˈhʌndrəd/	Hundert
	be lost /biː ˈlɒst/	sich verirrt haben,
		sich verlaufen haben
	toward(s) /təˈwɔːd(z)/	in Richtung
	wooden /ˈwʊdn/	hölzern, Holz-
	hall /hɔːl/	Halle; Saal
	anyway /ˈeniˌweɪ/	sowieso, jedenfalls;
		hier: trotzdem
	cobweb /ˈkɒbˌweb/	Spinnennetz, Spinnwebe
	shadow /ˈʃædəʊ/	Schatten
	ghostly /ˈgəʊstli/	geisterhaft; gespenstisch
	voice /vɔɪs/	Stimme
	cry /kraɪ/	weinen; schreien
	joke /dʒəʊk/	Witz
	at night /æt ˈnaɪt/	nachts
	out /aʊt/	nach draußen, (he)raus
	bright /braɪt/	hell
	this way /ˈðɪs weɪ/	hier (ent)lang
	heading /ˈhedɪŋ/	Überschrift, Titel
	get lost /get ˈlɒst/	sich verirren, sich verlaufen
Op2	silly /ˈsɪli/	dumm; albern
	strange /streɪndʒ/	sonderbar, komisch
	beginning /bɪˈgɪnɪŋ/	Anfang
	ending /ˈendɪŋ/	Ende, Schluss
	go out /gəʊ‿ˈaʊt/	ausgehen *(Licht)*
Op4	hiking trip /ˈhaɪkɪŋ trɪp/	Wanderung
	linking word /ˈlɪŋkɪŋ wɜːd/	Bindewort
	connect /kəˈnekt/	verbinden
	enough /ɪˈnʌf/	genügend, ausreichend,
		genug
	swap /swɒp/	tauschen

Theme 4 – Celebrations

I	**celebration** /ˌseləˈbreɪʃn/	Feier, Fest	
1	**festival** /ˈfestɪvl/	Fest; Festival	
	New Year's Eve /ˌnjuː jɪəz‿ˈiːv/	Silvester	New Year's Eve = 31st December
	Eid /iːd/	*islamisches Fest zum Abschluss des Fastenmonats Ramadan*	
	Christmas /ˈkrɪsməs/	Weihnachten	My favourite festival is Christmas.
	Hanukkah /ˈhɑːnəkə/	*jüdisches Lichterfest*	
	Easter /ˈiːstə/	Ostern, Osterfest	
	celebrate /ˈseləˌbreɪt/	feiern	Let's celebrate!
	decorate /ˈdekəˌreɪt/	schmücken, dekorieren	
	church /tʃɜːtʃ/	Kirche	
	set off /set‿ˈɒf/	(an)zünden	
	fireworks *(only pl)* /ˈfaɪəˌwɜːks/	Feuerwerk	
	early /ˈɜːli/	früh, zeitig	early ↔ late
	form /fɔːm/	bilden, formen	
	double circle /ˌdʌbl ˈsɜːkl/	Doppelkreis	
2	**Chinese** /ˌtʃaɪˈniːz/	Chinese/Chinesin; Chinesisch; chinesisch	I love Chinese food.
	Turkish /ˈtɜːkɪʃ/	Türkisch; türkisch	Murat is a Turkish name.
	Great Britain /ˌgreɪt ˈbrɪtn/	Großbritannien	
	Italy /ˈɪtəli/	Italien	Pizza comes from Italy. 
	Italian /ɪˈtæliən/	Italiener/in; Italienisch; italienisch	It's an Italian dish.
	Russian /ˈrʌʃn/	Russe/Russin; Russisch; russisch	Oleg is a Russian name.
	French /frentʃ/	Französisch; französisch	Lily learns French at school.
3	**New Year** /ˌnjuː ˈjɪə/	Neujahr	
	parade /pəˈreɪd/	Parade, Umzug	
	end /end/	Ende	At the end of the day I go to bed.
	Chinatown /ˈtʃaɪnəˌtaʊn/	*Chinesenviertel*	
	colourful /ˈkʌləfl/	farbenfroh, farbenprächtig	
	costume /ˈkɒstjuːm/	Tracht, Kostüm	Children wear scary costumes at Halloween.
	decorated /ˈdekəreɪtɪd/	geschmückt, verziert	
	flag /flæg/	Fahne; Flagge	flag 
	stall /stɔːl/	(Verkaufs)stand	There are lots of stalls at the market.
	prawn crackers *(only pl)* /ˌprɔːn ˈkrækəz/	Krabbenchips	
	noodle /ˈnuːdl/	Nudel	
	delicious /dɪˈlɪʃəs/	köstlich, lecker	delicious = yummy
	shrimp /ʃrɪmp/	Garnele	
	dumpling /ˈdʌmplɪŋ/	Knödel, Kloß; Teigtasche	
	expensive /ɪkˈspensɪv/	teuer	expensive ↔ cheap
	follow /ˈfɒləʊ/	folgen	

	step /step/	treten	
	envelope /ˈenvələʊp/	Briefumschlag, Kuvert	envelope 
	going to /ˈgəʊɪŋ tə/	werden	
	belong to sb/sth /biˈlɒŋ tə ˌsʌmbədi/ˌsʌmθɪŋ/	jdm/zu etw gehören	Fritz the goldfish belongs to Charlie.
	good-luck /ˌgʊd ˈlʌk/	Glücks-	
	no one /ˈnəʊ wʌn/	keiner, niemand	There is no one in the room.
	someone /ˈsʌmwʌn/	jemand	someone ↔ no one
	owner /ˈəʊnə/	Besitzer/in, Eigentümer/in	
5	birth /bɜːθ/	Geburt	
	born /bɔːn/	geboren	My sister was born in 2003.
	sign /saɪn/	Zeichen; (Straßen-/ Verkehrs)schild	sign 
	rat /ræt/	Ratte	rat 
	creative /kriˈeɪtɪv/	kreativ	
	charming /ˈtʃɑːmɪŋ/	bezaubernd, charmant	Rajiv is very charming.
	ox (*pl* -en) /ɒks/	Ochse	
	reliable /rɪˈlaɪəbl/	verlässlich, zuverlässig	
	brave /breɪv/	mutig, unerschrocken	
	optimistic /ˌɒptɪˈmɪstɪk/	optimistisch, zuversichtlich	
	interested (in sth) /ˈɪntrəstɪd/	interessiert (an etw)	Are you interested in music?
	generous /ˈdʒenərəs/	großzügig	
	energy /ˈenədʒi/	Energie, Kraft	
	self-confident /ˌselfˈkɒnfɪdnt/	selbstbewusst, selbstsicher	Caroline is self-confident. She knows that she can do lots of things well.
	independent /ˌɪndɪˈpendənt/	unabhängig; selbstständig	
	rule /ruːl/	Regel	We have lots of rules at school.
	patient /ˈpeɪʃnt/	geduldig	
	active /ˈæktɪv/	aktiv	
	rooster /ˈruːstə/	Hahn	
	hard-working /ˌhɑːdˈwɜːkɪŋ/	fleißig	They are very hard-working.
	proud /praʊd/	stolz	
	honest /ˈɒnɪst/	ehrlich	Das „h" wird nicht ausgesprochen.
	peaceful /ˈpiːsfl/	friedlich	
	argument /ˈɑːgjʊmənt/	Auseinandersetzung, Streit	
6	wedding /ˈwedɪŋ/	Hochzeit	
	Valentine's Day /ˈvæləntaɪnz deɪ/	Valentinstag	
	carnival /ˈkɑːnɪvl/	Karneval	
	St Martin's Day /sənt ˈmɑːtɪnz deɪ/	Martinstag	
	Mother's Day /ˈmʌðəz deɪ/	Muttertag	
7	**Ireland** /ˈaɪələnd/	Irland	Ireland 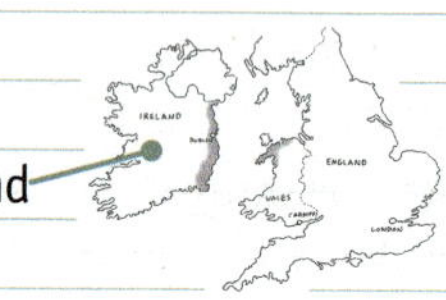
	Irish /ˈaɪrɪʃ/	Irisch; irisch	

8	Diwali /dɪˈwɑːli/	*hinduistisches Lichterfest*	
	Hindu /ˌhɪnˈduː/	Hindu; hinduistisch	
	temple /ˈtempl/	Tempel	
	Indian /ˈɪndiən/	Inder/in; Indianer/in; indisch; indianisch	Rajiv and his family are Indian.
	samosa /səˈməʊsə/	*gefüllte Teigtasche*	
	pakora /pəˈkɔːrə/	*frittiertes Gemüsestück*	
	goddess /ˈgɒdes/	Göttin	
	wealth /welθ/	Reichtum, Wohlstand	
9	quiz sb /ˈkwɪz ˌsʌmbədi/	jdn befragen/prüfen	
11	**chat** /tʃæt/	chatten, sich unterhalten	The girls like to chat about boys at school.
	fine /faɪn/	in Ordnung, gut; *hier:* edel, vornehm	
	department store /dɪˈpɑːtmənt ˌstɔː/	Kaufhaus	Karstadt is a famous department store in Germany.
	just /dʒʌst/	gleich; *hier:* einfach	I just love chocolate.
	stuff *(informal)* /stʌf/	Zeug, Sachen	
	than /ðæn/	als	
	bottle /ˈbɒtl/	Flasche	a bottle
	perfume /ˈpɜːfjuːm/	Parfüm	of perfume
	smell (of) /smel/	riechen (nach)	
	better /ˈbetə/	besser; lieber, mehr	good – better – best
	use /juːz/	benutzen	Can I use your ruler, please?
	a box of chocolates /ə bɒks‿əv ˈtʃɒkləts/	eine Schachtel Pralinen	a box of chocolates
	nonsense /ˈnɒnsns/	Unsinn, Quatsch	
	anyway /ˈeniˌweɪ/	jedenfalls, sowieso	
	fine /faɪn/	in Ordnung, gut	
	earring /ˈɪərɪŋ/	Ohrring	earring
	similar /ˈsɪmɪlə/	ähnlich	
12	brilliant *(informal)* /ˈbrɪljənt/	toll, hervorragend	
	business trip /ˈbɪznəs trɪp/	Dienstreise, Geschäftsreise	
13	**as ... as** /əz əz/	(genau)so ... wie ...	Caroline is as tall as George.
	the same /ðə ˈseɪm/	der-/die-/dasselbe; *hier:* gleich	
14	verse /vɜːs/	Strophe	
	voucher /ˈvaʊtʃə/	Gutschein	
	kiss /kɪs/	Kuss	Do you want a kiss from Charlie?
	bake /beɪk/	backen	
	(I'm) sorry. /ˈsɒri/	Entschuldigung, das tut mir leid.	You're late again! – I'm sorry.
	a little /ə ˈlɪtl/	ein bisschen	
	left /left/	(nach) links; *hier:* übrig	
15	**message** /ˈmesɪdʒ/	Nachricht	
16	broccoli *(no pl)* /ˈbrɒkəli/	Brokkoli	

	now /naʊ/	jetzt; *hier:* also	
	everything /ˈevriθɪŋ/	alles	Is everything OK with you?
	any /ˈeni/	irgendwelche, irgendein(e); *hier:* etwas	Have you got any milk?
	cream *(no pl)* /kriːm/	Sahne	
	potato *(pl* **-es***)* /pəˈteɪtəʊ, pəˈteɪtəʊz/	Kartoffel	one potato – three potatoes
	cupboard /ˈkʌbəd/	Schrank	
	fridge *(informal)* /frɪdʒ/	Kühlschrank	
	sugar *(no pl)* /ˈʃʊgə/	Zucker	sugar
	flour *(no pl)* /ˈflaʊə/	Mehl	
	enough /ɪˈnʌf/	genügend, ausreichend, genug	Do we have enough flour?
	candle /ˈkændl/	Kerze	candles
	still /stɪl/	(immer) noch, noch immer	
	be happy (to do sth) /biː ˈhæpi/	sich freuen (, etw zu tun)	
	shopping list /ˈʃɒpɪŋ lɪst/	Einkaufszettel, Einkaufsliste	
17	**wish** /wɪʃ/	(sich) wünschen	
	waiter/waitress /ˈweɪtə, ˈweɪtrəs/	Bedienung, Kellner/in	He works as a waiter in a restaurant.
	sauce /sɔːs/	Soße	
	while /waɪl/	während	
	set the table /ˌset ðə ˈteɪbl/	den Tisch decken	Do you sometimes set the table?
	dining room /ˈdaɪnɪŋ ˌruːm/	Esszimmer	
	top-class /ˌtɒp ˈklɑːs/	Spitzen-, der Spitzenklasse	
	polite /pəˈlaɪt/	höflich	Students must be polite to the teachers.
	afterwards /ˈɑːftəwədz/	danach, anschließend; später	
	What a pity! /wɒt‿ə ˈpɪti/	Wie schade!	
	once /wʌns/	einmal	We visit my uncle once a year.
	a year /ə ˈjɪə/	pro/im Jahr	
	darling /ˈdɑːlɪŋ/	Liebling, Schatz	
	surprise /səˈpraɪz/	überraschen	
18	for he's a jolly good fellow /fə hiz‿ə ˌdʒɒli gʊd ˈfeləʊ/	weil er so ein prima Kerl ist	
19	gear /gɪə/	Gang	
	crossword puzzle /ˈkrɒswɜːd ˌpʌzl/	Kreuzworträtsel	
	wordsearch /ˈwɜːdsɜːtʃ/	Wortsuchrätsel	
P4	fall *(irr)* /fɔːl/	fallen	
	spill *(irr)* /spɪl/	verschütten	
	climb /klaɪm/	(hinauf)klettern; (hinauf)steigen	
	curtain /ˈkɜːtn/	Vorhang	
	get hurt /get ˈhɜːt/	verletzt werden	

TIPP

Gegensätze
Neue Vokabeln musst du nicht immer in Listen schreiben. Du kannst sie auch anders sortieren, zum Beispiel indem du Gegensätze zusammenstellst. Wie viele Wörter kennst du schon, die sich so zusammenstellen lassen?
girl ↔ boy
black ↔ white
right ↔ wrong

	drop /drɒp/	fallen lassen
	off /ɒf/	herunter, hinunter
P5	tea dance /ˈtiː dɑːns/	Tanztee
	senior citizen /ˌsiːniə ˈsɪtɪzn/	älterer Mensch, Senior/in
	home-baked /ˌhəʊmˈbeɪkt/	selbst gebacken
	serve /sɜːv/	dienen; *hier:* servieren
	including /ɪnˈkluːdɪŋ/	einschließlich
	entertainment /ˌentəˈteɪnmənt/	Unterhaltung
	refreshment /rɪˈfreʃmənt/	Erfrischung
P7	watch out (for) /wɒtʃ‿ˈaʊt/	aufpassen (auf), sich in Acht nehmen (vor)
P8	alphabetical /ˌælfəˈbetɪkl/	alphabetisch
	comparative (form) /kəmˈpærətɪv/	Komparativ
	superlative (form) /sʊˈpɜːlətɪv/	Superlativ
P9	comparison /kəmˈpærɪsn/	Vergleich
P10	short /ʃɔːt/	kurz; *hier:* klein
P11	bread *(no pl)* /bred/	Brot
P12	recipe /ˈresəpi/	Rezept
	cucumber /ˈkjuːˌkʌmbə/	(Salat)gurke
	raita /ˈraɪtə/	*Joghurt mit Gurke und Minze*
	half *(pl* halves*)* /hɑːf, hɑːvz/	Hälfte
	tablespoon /ˈteɪblˌspuːn/	Esslöffel
	mint *(no pl)* /mɪnt/	Minze
	yoghurt *(no pl)* /ˈjɒgət/	Joghurt
	pinch /pɪntʃ/	Prise
	cumin *(no pl)* /ˈkʌmɪn/	Kreuzkümmel
	pepper *(no pl)* /ˈpepə/	Pfeffer
	salt *(no pl)* /sɔːlt/	Salz
	peel /piːl/	schälen
	slice /slaɪs/	in Scheiben schneiden
	chop /tʃɒp/	klein schneiden
	finely /ˈfaɪnli/	fein
	bowl /bəʊl/	Schüssel
	beat *(irr)* /biːt/	schlagen
	mix in /mɪks‿ˈɪn/	untermischen, untermengen
	cool /kuːl/	abkühlen
	taste /teɪst/	schmecken
M1	put up /pʊt‿ˈʌp/	aufhängen; *hier:* aufstellen
	relative /ˈrelətɪv/	Verwandte(r), Angehörige(r) — relatives = aunts, uncles, cousins, ...
	mantelpiece /ˈmæntlˌpiːs/	Kaminsims
	Christmas Eve /ˌkrɪsməs‿ˈiːv/	Heiligabend — Christmas Eve = 24th December
	working day /ˈwɜːkɪŋ deɪ/	Werktag
	mince pie /ˈmɪns paɪ/	*Kuchen gefüllt mit Dörrobst und Sirup*

TIPP

Falsche Freunde
Im Englischen gibt es viele Wörter, die deutschen Wörtern zwar sehr ähnlich sehen, aber eine ganz andere Bedeutung haben. Man nennt sie deshalb *false friends* (falsche Freunde). Für diese Wörter kannst du dir ein Merkblatt „Vorsicht Falle" anlegen.

also = auch (NICHT: also)
map = Karte (NICHT: Mappe)
become = werden (NICHT: bekommen)
kind = Art, Sorte (NICHT: Kind)
stall = (Verkaufs)stand (NICHT: Stall)
brave = mutig (NICHT: brav)

	Father Christmas /ˌfɑːðə ˈkrɪsməs/	Weihnachtsmann	Father Christmas brings presents for the children. 
	reindeer /ˈreɪnˌdɪə/	Rentier	
	chimney /ˈtʃɪmni/	Kamin; Schornstein	The house has a big chimney.
	stocking /ˈstɒkɪŋ/	(Weihnachts)strumpf	
	at night /æt ˈnaɪt/	nachts	It's dark at night.
	Christmas Day /ˌkrɪsməs ˈdeɪ/	erster Weihnachtsfeiertag	Christmas Day = 25th December
	turkey /ˈtɜːki/	Truthahn/-henne, Pute/r	
	cracker /ˈkrækə/	Knallbonbon	
	pull /pʊl/	ziehen	Don't pull the cat's tail. 
	plastic /ˈplæstɪk/	Plastik, Kunststoff	
	crown /kraʊn/	Krone	He is wearing a crown on his head. 
	silly /ˈsɪli/	dumm; albern	
	holiday /ˈhɒlɪdeɪ/	Urlaub, Ferien; *hier:* Feiertag	
	Boxing Day /ˈbɒksɪŋ deɪ/	zweiter Weihnachtsfeiertag	
	leftovers *(only pl)* /ˈleftˌəʊvəz/	Reste	
	year /jɪə/	Jahr; *hier:* Jahrgang(sstufe)	
M2	five-day /ˌfaɪvˈdeɪ/	fünftägig	
	victory /ˈvɪktri/	Sieg	
	darkness /ˈdɑːknəs/	Dunkelheit, Finsternis	The house looks spooky in the darkness. 
	evil /ˈiːvl/	böse	
	highlight /ˈhaɪˌlaɪt/	Höhepunkt, Highlight	
	everybody /ˈevriˌbɒdi/	jede(r); alle	everybody = everyone
	sari /ˈsɑːri/	Sari *(gewickeltes Gewand indischer Frauen)*	
	busy /ˈbɪzi/	beschäftigt; *hier:* arbeitsreich	Christmas is a very busy time.
	oil /ɔɪl/	Öl	
	traditional /trəˈdɪʃnəl/	traditionell	
	exchange /ɪksˈtʃeɪndʒ/	austauschen	
	perform /pəˈfɔːm/	vorführen; aufführen	
M4	reader /ˈriːdə/	Leser/in	
	Australia /ɒˈstreɪliə/	Australien	Kangaroos live in Australia.
	temple /ˈtempl/	Tempel	
	curry /ˈkʌri/	Curry(gericht)	
	rice *(no pl)* /raɪs/	Reis	
	pudding /ˈpʊdɪŋ/	Süßspeise, Nachspeise	
	have a barbecue /ˌhæv‿ə ˈbɑːbɪˌkjuː/	grillen, eine Grillparty feiern	We had a barbecue in our garden on Saturday.
	fairy bread *(no pl)* /ˈfeəri bred/	*Brot mit bunten Zuckerstreuseln*	
	bread *(no pl)* /bred/	Brot	bread 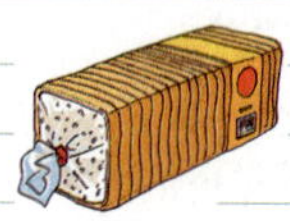
	sprinkles *(only pl)* /ˈsprɪŋkls/	Streusel	
	each /iːtʃ/	jede(r, s)	Each guest has some cake.
	guest /gest/	Gast	

	without /wɪð'aʊt/	ohne	without ↔ with
	mess /mes/	Unordnung, Durcheinander; *hier:* Schweinerei	
	in fact /ɪn 'fækt/	tatsächlich, in Wirklichkeit; sogar	
	turn /tɜːn/	sich drehen; *hier:* werden	
	prize /praɪz/	Preis, Gewinn	The winner will get a prize.
	down /daʊn/	hinunter, hinab	down ↔ up
M6	**throw** *(irr)* /θrəʊ/	werfen	throw – threw *(simple past)*
	drop /drɒp/	fallen lassen	Don't drop the plates!
	elbow /'elbəʊ/	Ellbogen	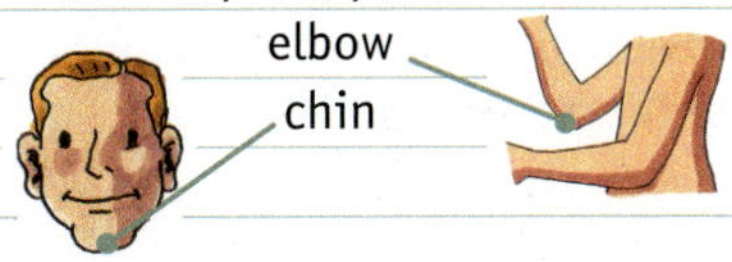
	chin /tʃɪn/	Kinn	
	be out /ˌbi‿'aʊt/	nicht mehr im Spiel sein, draußen sein	
	tag *(no pl)* /tæg/	Fangen *(Spiel)*	
	South Africa /saʊθ‿'æfrɪkə/	Südafrika	
	circle /'sɜːkl/	Kreis	circles 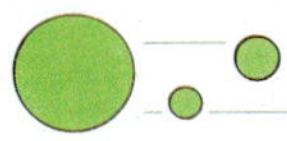
	blindfold /'blaɪnˌfəʊld/	Augenbinde	
	roar /rɔː/	brüllen	The lion roared loudly. 
	squeak /skwiːk/	quieken; *hier:* piepsen	
	continue /kən'tɪnjuː/	weitergehen	
	grocer /'grəʊsə/	Lebensmittelhändler/in	
	act /ækt/	handeln, sich verhalten	
	comment /'kɒment/	Kommentar, Bemerkung	
	such as /sʌtʃ æz/	wie (zum Beispiel)	
	giggle /'gɪgl/	kichern	
	over /'əʊvə/	hinüber; *hier:* vorbei	The race is over now and Benjamin is the winner.
	above /ə'bʌv/	oben	
CC	bed sheet /'bed ʃiːt/	Bettlaken	
	opposite /'ɒpəzɪt/	gegenüberliegend	
	middle /'mɪdl/	Mitte	
	raise /reɪz/	heben	
	lower /'ləʊə/	senken	
	aim /eɪm/	Ziel, Absicht	
	baking powder *(no pl)* /'beɪkɪŋ ˌpaʊdə/	Backpulver	
	cocoa *(no pl)* /'kəʊkəʊ/	Kakao	
	food colouring /'fuːd ˌkʌlərɪŋ/	Lebensmittelfarbe	
	mix /mɪks/	(ver)mischen, anrühren	
	divide /dɪ'vaɪd/	teilen; trennen	
	mixture /'mɪkstʃə/	Mischung	
	baking tin /'beɪkɪŋ tɪn/	Backform	
	stir /stɜː/	rühren	
	melt /melt/	schmelzen	
	cool /kuːl/	kalt, kühl	

TIPP

Für gute Zuhörer
Du kannst dir Vokabeln auch merken, indem du sie dir immer wieder anhörst. Das funktioniert super! Nimm das englische Wort auf, das du lernen willst – aber vergiss die deutsche Übersetzung nicht! Höre dir die Wörter regelmäßig an, und du wirst bald feststellen, dass du sie gelernt hast.

Theme 5 – Dos and don'ts

I	dos and don'ts	was man tun und	
	/ˌduːz‿ən ˈdəʊnts/	was man nicht tun sollte	
1	**spend** *(irr)* /spend/	ausgeben *(Geld)*;	spend – spent *(simple past)*
		verbringen *(Zeit)*	
2	**study** /ˈstʌdi/	studieren; *hier:* lernen	She must study for the English
	test /test/	Prüfung, Test; Klassenarbeit	test on Monday.
	night /naɪt/	Nacht; *hier:* Abend	
	evening /ˈiːvnɪŋ/	Abend	evening ↔ morning
	youth club /ˈjuːθ ˌklʌb/	Jugendzentrum	
	before /bɪˈfɔː/	bevor	I watch TV before I go to bed.
	leave *(irr)* /liːv/	verlassen; *hier:* (weg)gehen	
	by (eight o'clock) /baɪ/	(spätestens) bis (acht Uhr)	Please be back by ten o'clock.
3	know better /nəʊ ˈbetə/	es besser wissen	
	bet *(irr)* /bet/	wetten	
	must not /mʌst ˈnɒt/	nicht dürfen	I must not go to the youth club
			disco.
			must not = mustn't 
	wonder /ˈwʌndə/	sich fragen	
	worse /wɜːs/	schlimmer, schlechter	bad – worse – worst
4	have an argument	(sich) streiten	
	/hæv‿ən‿ˈɑːgjʊmənt/		
	hole /həʊl/	Loch	There's a hole in my sock.
5	**put on make-up**	sich schminken	
	/pʊt‿ˌɒn ˈmeɪkˌʌp/		
	dinner /ˈdɪnə/	Abendessen; Mittagessen	
6	**opinion** /əˈpɪnjən/	Meinung, Ansicht	What's your opinion about John?
			– I think he's really nice.
	strict /strɪkt/	streng	
	strange /streɪndʒ/	sonderbar, komisch	
	salad /ˈsæləd/	Salat	salad
	forget about sb/sth	jdn/etw vergessen	
	/fəˈget‿əˌbaʊt ˌsʌmbədi/		
	ˌsʌmθɪŋ/		
7	top /tɒp/	oberes Ende; *hier:* Top-,	
		Spitzen-	
	singer /ˈsɪŋə/	Sänger/in	singer
	TV series *(only pl)*	Fernsehserie	
	/ˌtiːˈviː ˌsɪəriːz/		
	discuss /dɪˈskʌs/	besprechen; diskutieren	
8	whenever /wenˈevə/	immer wenn,	
		wann (auch) immer	
	don'ting (= not doing)	*nicht tun*	
	/ˈdəʊntɪŋ/		
	slurp /slɜːp/	schlürfen	
	kiss /kɪs/	küssen	Chris and Lana kissed at the
			party.

	butter /ˈbʌtə/	mit Butter bestreichen, buttern	
	like that /laɪk ˈðæt/	so	
	bubble /ˈbʌbl/	blubbern	
	goggle *(informal)* /ˈgɒgl/	starren, glotzen	
	climb /klaɪm/	(hinauf)klettern; (hinauf)steigen	Pat and Mark love climbing mountains.
	curtain /ˈkɜːtn/	Vorhang	
	cut off /kʌt‿ˈɒf/	abschneiden	
	pillow /ˈpɪləʊ/	Kissen	
	change /tʃeɪndʒ/	(sich) (ver)ändern; *hier:* verstellen	
	water /ˈwɔːtə/	gießen	Please water the flowers.
	hide *(irr)* /haɪd/	(sich) verstecken	
	cycle /ˈsaɪkl/	Rad fahren	He often cycles to school.
	upstairs /ʌpˈsteəz/	(nach) oben	
	chew /tʃuː/	kauen	Patch always chews his favourite ball.
	pyjamas *(only pl)* /pəˈdʒɑːməz/	Pyjama, Schlafanzug	
	paint /peɪnt/	(an)malen	The kids want to paint everything red.
	rhyming word /ˈraɪmɪŋ wɜːd/	Reimwort	
9	midnight *(no pl)* /ˈmɪdˌnaɪt/	Mitternacht	
	all day /ˌɔːl ˈdeɪ/	den ganzen Tag	
	pictogram /ˈpɪktəgræm/	Piktogramm	
10	break *(irr)* /breɪk/	(zer)brechen	
	show *(irr)* /ʃəʊ/	zeigen	We must show respect for other students.
	respect *(no pl)* /rɪˈspekt/	Respekt, Achtung	
	report (to sb) /rɪˈpɔːt/	(sich) (bei jdm) melden	
	deputy head /ˈdepjʊti ˌhed/	stellvertretende/r Schulleiter/in, Konrektor/in	
	correct /kəˈrekt/	richtig, korrekt	
	leave *(irr)* /liːv/	verlassen	I must leave the party early – at eight o'clock.
	ground /graʊnd/	(Erd)boden, Erde; *hier:* Gelände	
	(chewing) gum *(no pl)* /(ˈtʃuːɪŋ) gʌm/	Kaugummi	We must not chew gum in class.
	sports kit *(no pl)* /ˈspɔːts kɪt/	Sportkleidung, Sportsachen	
	packed lunch /ˌpækt ˈlʌntʃ/	Lunchpaket	
	property *(no pl)* /ˈprɒpəti/	Eigentum	
	litter *(no pl)* /ˈlɪtə/	Müll, Abfall	
	alarm clock /əˈlɑːm ˌklɒk/	Wecker	alarm clock 
	work /wɜːk/	arbeiten; *hier:* funktionieren	
	miniskirt /ˈmɪniˌskɜːt/	Minirock	
	least /liːst/	am wenigsten	

11	**board** /bɔːd/	Brett; *hier:* Tafel	The teacher wrote the question on the board.
	give reasons /ɡɪv ˈriːznz/	begründen, Gründe angeben	
13	horrible /ˈhɒrəbl/	schrecklich	
	even /ˈiːvn/	sogar; *hier:* noch	
	smart /smɑːt/	schlau; *hier:* schick	
	have a vote /hæv‿ə ˈvəʊt/	abstimmen	
	Hands up! /ˌhændz‿ˈʌp/	Hände hoch!; *hier:* Meldet euch!	
	against /əˈgenst/	gegen	against ↔ for
14	**bus stop** /ˈbʌs ˌstɒp/	Bushaltestelle	bus stop
15	**bullying** *(no pl)* /ˈbʊliɪŋ/	Mobbing	
	article /ˈɑːtɪkl/	Artikel	
	be able to do sth /bi‿ˌeɪbl tə ˈduː ˌsʌmθɪŋ/	etw tun können	I wasn't able to go to school because I was ill.
	parent-teacher meeting /ˌpeərəntˈtiːtʃə ˌmiːtɪŋ/	Elternsprechtag; Elternabend	
	surprised /səˈpraɪzd/	überrascht	She is surprised.
	by /baɪ/	bei, in der Nähe; mit, durch	Claire went to London by train.
	not anymore /ˌnɒt eniˈmɔː/	nicht mehr	He's not my friend anymore.
	mile /maɪl/	Meile	
	on foot /ɒn ˈfʊt/	zu Fuß	We always go to school on foot.
	at first /ət ˈfɜːst/	anfangs, zuerst	
	not anything /nɒt‿ˈeniˌθɪŋ/	nichts	There isn't anything in the bag.
	cry /kraɪ/	weinen; schreien	
	embarrassed /ɪmˈbærəst/	verlegen, peinlich berührt	
	mean /miːn/	gemein, fies	
	be afraid (of sth/sb) /ˌbi‿əˈfreɪd/	(vor etw/jdm) Angst haben	Ali is afraid of his maths teacher.
	bully /ˈbʊli/	Rüpel, Rabauke; *hier:* jemand, der andere drangsaliert	
	report /rɪˈpɔːt/	berichten, melden	
	headteacher /ˌhedˈtiːtʃə/	Schulleiter/in, Rektor/in	
	bully /ˈbʊli/	tyrannisieren, drangsalieren, mobben	She bullies younger children.
	action campaign /ˈækʃn kæmˌpeɪn/	Aktionskampagne, Aktion	
16	**chance** /tʃɑːns/	Chance; Möglichkeit	Sarah got the chance to sing in the concert.
	placemat /ˈpleɪsˌmæt/	Set, Platzdeckchen	
	call /kɔːl/	anrufen; *hier:* rufen	
	decide /dɪˈsaɪd/	(sich) entscheiden; beschließen	
	UK (= United Kingdom) /ˌjuːˈkeɪ, juːˌnaɪtɪd ˈkɪŋdəm/	Vereinigtes Königreich	
	tip /tɪp/	Tipp	This book gives some good tips for learning new words.

	beat *(irr)* /biːt/	schlagen; *hier:* besiegen	
	ignore /ɪɡˈnɔː/	ignorieren	
	on its own /ɒn‿ɪts‿ˈəʊn/	von allein, von selbst	
	contact sb /ˈkɒntækt ˌsʌmbədi/	jdn kontaktieren, sich mit jdm in Verbindung setzen	
	for free /fɔː ˈfriː/	gratis, umsonst	
	fault /fɔːlt/	Schuld; Fehler	It's my fault that we were late.
	safe /seɪf/	sicher	I feel safe when I'm with my friends.
	get into trouble /ɡet‿ɪntə ˈtrʌbl/	Schwierigkeiten bekommen	
17	design /dɪˈzaɪn/	entwerfen	
	label /ˈleɪbl/	beschriften	
P1	opposite /ˈɒpəzɪt/	Gegenteil	
P2	letter /ˈletə/	Brief; Buchstabe	
	underline /ˌʌndəˈlaɪn/	unterstreichen	
P6	mean *(irr)* /miːn/	bedeuten; meinen	
	allowed /əˈlaʊd/	erlaubt	
	keep off /kiːp‿ˈɒf/	wegbleiben; *hier:* nicht betreten	
	clean up /kliːn‿ˈʌp/	sauber machen, reinigen	
	stairs *(only pl)* /steəz/	Treppe	
	attention *(no pl)* /əˈtenʃn/	Achtung, Aufmerksamkeit	
	littering *(no pl)* /ˈlɪtərɪŋ/	Vermüllen	
P7	trainer *(BE)* /ˈtreɪnə/	Turnschuh	
P10	regular /ˈreɡjʊlə/	regelmäßig; *hier:* normal	
P11	workplace /ˈwɜːkˌpleɪs/	Arbeitsplatz	
P12	epal /ˈiːpæl/	*E-Mail-Freund/in*	
	silently /ˈsaɪləntli/	leise	
	enter /ˈentə/	betreten	
	exit /ˈeksɪt/	verlassen	
	seat /siːt/	(Sitz)platz	
	area /ˈeəriə/	Gebiet, Region; *hier:* Bereich	
M1	**still** /stɪl/	(immer) noch, noch immer	All of my friends are thirteen years old but I'm still twelve.
	if /ɪf/	wenn, falls	
	guess /ɡes/	(er)raten; *hier:* vermuten, schätzen	I guess that Mrs Killmouskey will go to the park if it is sunny.
	relaxed /rɪˈlækst/	entspannt; locker, gelassen	
	convince /kənˈvɪns/	überzeugen	
	wedding /ˈwedɪŋ/	Hochzeit	
	earn /ɜːn/	verdienen	Rajiv wants to earn lots of money in the future.
M3	be a mess /ˌbi‿ə ˈmes/	chaotisch/durcheinander sein	
	solve /sɒlv/	lösen, klären	
M4	**letter** /ˈletə/	Brief; Buchstabe	I wrote a letter to my cousin.

TIPP

Wortbilder
Vielleicht kannst du dir Vokabeln besser merken, wenn du daraus Wortbilder machst. Wenn du nicht gerne selbst zeichnest, kannst du auch Bilder aus Zeitschriften und Katalogen ausschneiden und auf ein Blatt Papier kleben. Schreibe die dazugehörigen Vokabeln direkt zum Bild. So kannst du englische Begriffe richtig „sehen."

	first of all /ˌfɜːst‿əv‿ˈɔːl/	erstens, als erstes	First of all, we went shopping. Then we went to the park.
	concentrate /ˈkɒnsnˌtreɪt/	sich konzentrieren	
	take out /ˌteɪk‿ˈaʊt/	hinausbringen; *hier:* herausnehmen	Please take out a pen and start the test.
	warning /ˈwɔːnɪŋ/	Warnung	
	outside /ˌaʊtˈsaɪd/	im Freien, draußen; *hier:* nach draußen, raus	I don't like to go outside when it is rainy.
	cool down /kuːl ˈdaʊn/	sich beruhigen	
	put one's hand up /pʊt wʌnz ˈhænd‿ʌp/	sich melden	
	nearly /ˈnɪəli/	fast, beinahe	Patch ate nearly all the sausages.
	swearword /ˈsweəˌwɜːd/	Schimpfwort, Fluch	
	love /lʌv/	Liebe; *hier:* herzliche Grüße, alles Liebe	
M5	argument /ˈɑːgjʊmənt/	Auseinandersetzung, Streit; *hier:* Argument	
	difference /ˈdɪfrəns/	Unterschied	What is the difference between these boys?
	individual /ˌɪndɪˈvɪdʒuəl/	individuell; eigen	
	discussion /dɪˈskʌʃn/	Diskussion, Besprechung	
	agree (with sb) /əˈgriː/	(jdm) zustimmen	I agree with Paul. I think school uniforms are a good idea, too.
CC	no way /nəʊ ˈweɪ/	keine Chance	
	might /maɪt/	könnte	
	Come on! /ˌkʌm‿ˈɒn/	Auf geht's!, Na los!	
	stand up *(irr)* /ˌstænd‿ˈʌp/	aufstehen	

Theme 6 – Let's go!

I	What's on? *(informal)* /wɒts‿ˈɒn/	Was ist los?, Was steht an?	
1	**sleep over** /sliːp‿ˈəʊvə/	übernachten, über Nacht bleiben	I love sleeping over at my friend's house.
2	**busy** /ˈbɪzi/	beschäftigt	Olivia is always busy because she has a lot of hobbies.
	shed /ʃed/	Schuppen; *hier:* Gartenhäuschen	
	promise /ˈprɒmɪs/	versprechen	
	by /baɪ/	bei, in der Nähe; *hier:* von	"The Hobbit" is a book by J. R. R. Tolkien.
	already /ɔːlˈredi/	schon	Rajiv has already been to a concert.
	not anywhere /nɒt‿ˈeniˌweə/	nirgendwo(hin)	

	chickenpox (*no pl*) /ˈtʃɪkɪnˌpɒks/	Windpocken	Emma has chickenpox. 
	all week /ˌɔːl ˈwiːk/	die ganze Woche	
	may not /meɪ ˈnɒt/	nicht dürfen	
	for /fɔː/	für; *hier:* seit	
	whose /huːz/	wessen	
3	cheer sb up /tʃɪə ˌsʌmbədi‿ˈʌp/	jdn aufmuntern	
	get well card /get ˈwel kɑːd/	Genesungskarte	Gillian is writing a get well card for Charlie.
	request /rɪˈkwest/	Bitte, Anfrage; Wunsch	
	radio station /ˈreɪdiəʊ ˌsteɪʃn/	Radiosender	My favourite radio station always plays great music.
	ever /ˈevə/	jemals	Have you ever been to Italy?
	just /dʒʌst/	gleich; *hier:* nur	
4	**Get well soon.** /get wel ˈsuːn/	Gute Besserung!	
	Cheer up! /tʃɪər‿ˈʌp/	Lass (doch) den Kopf nicht hängen!, Kopf hoch!	
5	who /huː/	wer; *hier:* wen, wem	
	get well /get ˈwel/	gesund werden	
	thanks a lot /ˌθæŋks‿ə ˈlɒt/	vielen Dank	Thanks a lot for your help!
	best wishes /ˌbest ˈwɪʃɪz/	viele Grüße	
	say hello (to sb) /ˌseɪ həˈləʊ/	(jdn) (be)grüßen	
	request sth /rɪˈkwest ˌsʌmθɪŋ/	um etw bitten; *hier:* (sich) etw wünschen	
6	**win** (*irr*) /wɪn/	gewinnen	
7	**programme** /ˈprəʊgræm/	Programm; *hier:* Sendung	
	may /meɪ/	können; *hier:* dürfen	
	soap (opera) /ˈsəʊp (‿ˌɒprə)/	Seifenoper, Soap	
	cartoon /kɑːˈtuːn/	Cartoon, Karikatur; *hier:* Zeichentrickfilm	
	agree (with sb) /əˈgriː/	(jdm) zustimmen	
8	Rome /rəʊm/	Rom	
	T. Rex (= tyrannosaurus rex) /ˈtiː reks, tɪˌrænəsɔːrəs ˈreks/	Tyrannosaurus Rex	
	screen /skriːn/	Leinwand; Bildschirm	
	snail /sneɪl/	Schnecke	
	frog's leg /frɒgz ˈleg/	Froschschenkel	
	backflip /ˈbækflɪp/	Rückwärtssalto, Rolle rückwärts	
10	type /taɪp/	Art; Typ, Sorte	
	channel /ˈtʃænl/	Kanal, Programm	
11	**Britain** /ˈbrɪtn/	Großbritannien	
	nature (*no pl*) /ˈneɪtʃə/	Natur	
	decide /dɪˈsaɪd/	(sich) entscheiden; beschließen	

TIPP

Verknüpfungen herstellen

Bei Wörtern, die überhaupt nicht in deinen Kopf wollen, kannst du:

- dir das Wort bildlich vorstellen,
- ein kleines Bild dazu zeichnen,
- an ein Ereignis denken, das du selbst erlebt hast,
- einen Satz auswendig lernen, in dem das Wort vorkommt,
- dir eine Eselsbrücke (z. B. einen Reim) ausdenken.

	hiking *(no pl)* /ˈhaɪkɪŋ/	Wandern	
	up /ʌp/	(nach) oben; hinauf; *hier:* auf (hinauf)	
	mountain /ˈmaʊntɪn/	Berg	mountain 
	treasure hunt /ˈtreʒə hʌnt/	Schatzsuche; Schnitzeljagd	
	mountain biking *(no pl)* /ˈmaʊntɪn ˌbaɪkɪŋ/	Mountainbiken, Mountainbike fahren	
	fishing *(no pl)* /ˈfɪʃɪŋ/	Angeln, Fischen	
	lover /ˈlʌvə/	Liebende/r; *hier:* Liebhaber/in, Freund/in	
	sailing *(no pl)* /ˈseɪlɪŋ/	Segeln	
	try /traɪ/	(aus)probieren; versuchen	Have you ever tried abseiling?
	abseiling *(no pl)* /ˈæbseɪlɪŋ/	Abseilen	
	programme /ˈprəʊɡræm/	Programm	Yes, but I didn't like it.
	UK (= United Kingdom) /ˌjuːˈkeɪ, juːˌnaɪtɪd ˈkɪŋdəm/	Vereinigtes Königreich	
	technique /tekˈniːk/	Technik, Methode	
	coach /kəʊtʃ/	Trainer	
13	**suitcase** /ˈsuːtˌkeɪs/	Koffer	suitcase 
14	**trip** /trɪp/	Ausflug; Reise, Fahrt	
	Munich /ˈmjuːnɪk/	München	
	Poland /ˈpəʊlənd/	Polen	
15	**fog** /fɒɡ/	Nebel	 It's difficult to see when there is a lot of fog.
	top /tɒp/	oberes Ende, Spitze; *hier:* Gipfel	There is a castle at the top of the mountain. 
	walk /wɔːk/	Spaziergang; *hier:* Aufstieg	
	be out of the question /bi‿ˌaʊt‿əv ðə ˈkwestʃn/	nicht infrage kommen	
	take a picnic /teɪk‿ə ˈpɪknɪk/	etw zum Essen mitnehmen	
	find one's way back /ˌfaɪnd wʌnz weɪ ˈbæk/	zurückfinden	
	time /taɪm/	(Uhr)zeit; *hier:* Mal	2 times = 2 x
	whisper /ˈwɪspə/	flüstern	
	What's up? *(informal)* /wɒts‿ˈʌp/	Was ist los?	
	out of /ˈaʊt‿əv/	(her)aus	Who took my ruler out of my pencil case?
	be scared (of sth) /biː ˈskeəd/	(vor etw) Angst haben	I'm scared of snakes.
	bark /bɑːk/	bellen	The dog barked loudly at the children.
	after /ˈɑːftə/	nach; *hier:* hinterher	
	village /ˈvɪlɪdʒ/	Dorf	Jim lives in a small village.
	turn round /tɜːn ˈraʊnd/	(sich) umdrehen	
	landlady /ˈlænˌleɪdi/	(Gast)wirtin	

	Thank goodness! /ˌθæŋk ˈɡʊdnəs/	Gott sei Dank!	
	incredible /ɪnˈkredəbl/	unglaublich	
	true /truː/	wahr; richtig	Is that story true?
	guess /ɡes/	(er)raten; *hier:* vermuten, schätzen	
	not yet /nɒt ˈjet/	noch nicht	I haven't done my homework yet but I will do it soon.
	master /ˈmɑːstə/	Herr; *hier:* Herrchen	
	walker /ˈwɔːkə/	Fußgänger/in, Spaziergänger/in	
	die /daɪ/	sterben	My goldfish died last year.
16	**snow** *(no pl)* /snəʊ/	Schnee	The kids love playing in the snow. 
18	experience /ɪkˈspɪəriəns/	erleben, erfahren	
	woof /wʊf/	wau	
	foggy /ˈfɒɡi/	neblig	
	no longer /nəʊ ˈlɒŋɡə/	nicht mehr	
19	discussion /dɪˈskʌʃn/	Diskussion	
	travel agency /ˈtrævl‿ˌeɪdʒnsi/	Reisebüro	
	search /sɜːtʃ/	(durch)suchen	
	detail /ˈdiːteɪl/	Detail, Einzelheit	
P1	turn into /ˌtɜːn‿ˈɪntʊ/	umwandeln, verändern	
P2	cooking *(no pl)* /ˈkʊkɪŋ/	Kochen	
P3	go together /ɡəʊ təˈɡeðə/	zusammenpassen	
P4	interview /ˈɪntəˌvjuː/	befragen; *hier:* interviewen	
	coffee /ˈkɒfi/	Kaffee	
P5	spot /spɒt/	entdecken	
	difference /ˈdɪfrəns/	Unterschied	
	change /tʃeɪndʒ/	(sich) (ver)ändern	
	put away /pʊt‿əˈweɪ/	wegräumen	
P6	What's on? *(informal)* /wɒts‿ˈɒn/	Was ist los?; *hier:* Was läuft?	
	Denmark /ˈdenmɑːk/	Dänemark	
	v (= versus) /viː, ˈvɜːsəs/	vs. (= gegen)	
	coverage *(no pl)* /ˈkʌvrɪdʒ/	Berichterstattung	
	emergency room /ɪˈmɜːdʒnsi ruːm/	Notaufnahme	
P10	take a closer look /teɪk‿ə ˌkləʊsə ˈlʊk/	sich (jdn/etw) genauer ansehen	
P11	wake up /weɪk‿ˈʌp/	aufwecken; *hier:* aufwachen	
P12	pick /pɪk/	aussuchen, auswählen	
	nervous /ˈnɜːvəs/	nervös	
P13	make (new) friends /meɪk ˈfrendz/	(neue) Freunde gewinnen	

TIPP

Reimwörter
Damit du dir besser merken kannst, wie bestimmte Wörter ausgesprochen werden, suche Reimwörter für sie. Dir wird auffallen, dass die Reimwörter nicht immer dieselbe Schreibweise haben.
sn<u>ow</u> – g<u>o</u>
s<u>oap</u> – h<u>ope</u>

M1	backstage /ˌbækˈsteɪdʒ/	hinter der Bühne; backstage	
	a few /ə ˈfjuː/	einige	There are only a few cool shops in my town.
	probably /ˈprɒbəbli/	wahrscheinlich	I will probably go to the cinema this weekend.
	few /fjuː/	wenige	Few children like vegetables more than chocolate. 
	after /ˈɑːftə/	nach; *hier:* nachdem	
	hall /hɔːl/	Halle; Saal	
	about /əˈbaʊt/	ungefähr	There are about 500 students at my school.
	make one's way /ˌmeɪk wʌnz ˈweɪ/	gehen	
	crowd /kraʊd/	(Menschen)menge, Zuschauermenge	The crowd watched the race.
	pass /pɑːs/	Pass	
	practise /ˈpræktɪs/	üben	The kids have to practise before the concert. 
	turn out /ˌtɜːn‿ˈaʊt/	sich herausstellen	
	lead singer /liːd ˈsɪŋə/	Leadsänger/in *(seine/ihre Stimme bestimmt den Gesang eines Musikstücks)*	
	copy /ˈkɒpi/	Kopie; *hier:* Exemplar	
	autograph /ˈɔːtəˌgrɑːf/	Autogramm	
	whole /həʊl/	ganz, gesamt	Lizzy ate the whole chocolate cake.
	around /əˈraʊnd/	herum, umher	The dog ran around the park. 
	Time's up! *(informal)* /ˌtaɪmz‿ˈʌp/	Die Zeit ist vorüber!	
	get ready (for sth) /get ˈredi/	sich (für etw) bereit machen	
	stereo /ˈsteriəʊ/	(Stereo)anlage	
	another /əˈnʌðə/	noch ein(e, r, s)	
	at the front /æt ðə ˈfrʌnt/	vorn(e)	
	stage /steɪdʒ/	Bühne	
	scream /skriːm/	schreien; kreischen	I always scream when I see a spider.
	incredible /ɪnˈkredəbl/	unglaublich	
	feeling /ˈfiːlɪŋ/	Gefühl	
	cheer /tʃɪə/	jubeln	He cheered when his favourite team won the football match. 
M4	couch potato *(informal)* /ˈkaʊtʃ pəˌteɪtəʊ/	Couchpotato, Dauerglotzer/in, Stubenhocker/in	
	couch /kaʊtʃ/	Couch, Sofa	couch = sofa
	if /ɪf/	wenn, falls; *hier:* ob	

	English	Deutsch	Example
	tonight /təˈnaɪt/	heute Abend	
	a day /ə ˈdeɪ/	pro/am Tag	I eat three meals a day.
M5	fright *(no pl)* /fraɪt/	Angst, Schrecken	
	tough /tʌf/	robust, zäh, tough	
	thrilling /ˈθrɪlɪŋ/	aufregend	
	ride /raɪd/	Fahrt; *hier:* Fahrgeschäft	
	roller coaster /ˈrəʊlə ˌkəʊstə/	Achterbahn	
	entrance fee /ˈentrəns ˌfiː/	Eintritt(sgeld)	
	adult /ˈædʌlt/	Erwachsene/r	
	save /seɪv/	retten; *hier:* sparen	
	junction /ˈdʒʌŋkʃn/	Kreuzung; *hier:* (Autobahn)abfahrt	
	run *(irr)* /rʌn/	laufen, rennen; *hier:* fahren, verkehren	
	journey /ˈdʒɜːni/	Reise; *hier:* Fahrt	
	available /əˈveɪləbl/	verfügbar; erhältlich	
	opening times *(only pl)* /ˈəʊpnɪŋ ˌtaɪmz/	Öffnungszeiten	
	daily /ˈdeɪli/	täglich	
	dark *(no pl)* /dɑːk/	Dunkelheit	
	closed /kləʊzd/	geschlossen, zu	
	popular /ˈpɒpjʊlə/	beliebt	
M8	**traffic light** /ˈtræfɪk laɪt/	Ampel	traffic light 
	anyway /ˈeniˌweɪ/	jedenfalls	
	view /vjuː/	Sicht; (Aus)blick, Aussicht	There's a great view from the top of the mountain. 
	star /stɑː/	Stern	
	and so on /ænd ˌsəʊ‿ˈɒn/	und so weiter	
	bye for now /ˈbaɪ fə naʊ/	bis bald	
	move /muːv/	sich bewegen	A tiger can move faster than a pig.
	at the moment /æt ðə ˈməʊmənt/	im Moment	
	see you /ˈsiː juː/	bis dann, bis bald	
	motorbike /ˈməʊtəˌbaɪk/	Motorrad	 motorbike
	ferry /ˈferi/	Fähre	You can go from England to France by ferry. 
	means of transport /miːnz‿əv ˈtrænspɔːt/	Verkehrsmittel	
CC	go for a swim /gəʊ fər‿ə ˈswɪm/	schwimmen gehen	
	straight in /streɪt‿ˈɪn/	sofort hinein	
	gasp /gɑːsp/	keuchen; *hier:* nach Luft schnappen	
	splash /splæʃ/	bespritzen	

TIPP

Spell check
Buchstabiere ein Wort für eine/n Partner/in. Wechselt euch ab und kontrolliert anschließend gegenseitig, ob alles richtig geschrieben ist. Für jedes richtige Wort gibt es einen Punkt. Wer ist der *spelling king* oder die *spelling queen*?

skin /skɪn/	Haut
paddle /ˈpædl/	paddeln; *hier:* planschen
across /əˈkrɒs/	hinüber
cling to sth /ˈklɪŋ tə ˌsʌmθɪŋ/	sich an etw klammern/ festhalten
pull /pʊl/	ziehen
myself /maɪˈself/	mich, mir; selbst
slide /slaɪd/	Rutschbahn, Rutsche
if /ɪf/	wenn, falls; *hier:* ob
let go /let ˈgəʊ/	loslassen
splash /splæʃ/	Platschen, Platscher
crash /kræʃ/	stürzen
into /ˈɪntʊ/	in
underwater /ˌʌndəˈwɔːtə/	unter Wasser
sb does not care /ˌsʌmbədi dəz nɒt ˈkeə/	jdm ist es egal
surface /ˈsɜːfɪs/	Oberfläche
breathe in /briːð‿ˈɪn/	einatmen
air *(no pl)* /eə/	Luft
another /əˈnʌðə/	noch ein(e, r, s)
time-saving /ˈtaɪmˌseɪvɪŋ/	Zeit sparend
greetings *(only pl)* /ˈgriːtɪŋz/	Grüße
awful /ˈɔːfl/	furchtbar, schrecklich

TIPP

Unregelmäßige Verben
(irregular verbs) haben eine unregelmäßige Form für das *simple past* und auch für das Partizip Perfekt *(past participle)*. Die Formen solltest du wie Vokabeln lernen. Du findest die Formen in der Liste der unregelmäßigen Verben auf Seite 284 – 285.
Hier einige Beispiele aus *Theme* 6:

Infinitiv	***simple past***	***past participle***
be *(irr)*	was/were	been
take *(irr)*	took	taken
go *(irr)*	went	gone
send *(irr)*	sent	sent
do *(irr)*	did	done

Hier findest du die Wörter, die in deinem Buch vorkommen.

- Die **fett gedruckten** Wörter solltest du dir merken.
- Wenn du den *More*-Teil bearbeitest, solltest du dir auch die grün gedruckten Wörter merken.
- 1/1 bedeutet: Dieses Wort kommt in *Theme* 1, Aufgabe 1 vor.
- I bedeutet: Dieses Wort kommt in Band I (5. Klasse) vor.
- Folgende Abkürzungen werden noch verwendet:
  B = *Back to Camden Market!* P = *Practice* Op = *Optional – Writing Stories*
  M = *More* CC = *Camden Chronicle*

A

a / an /ə, ən/ ein(e) I
a bit /ə ˈbɪt/ ein bisschen 1/2
a day /ə ˈdeɪ/ pro/am Tag 6/M4
a few /ə ˈfjuː/ einige 6/M1
a little /ə ˈlɪtl/ ein bisschen 4/14
a lot (of) /ə ˈlɒt/ sehr; viel(e) I
a year /ə ˈjɪə/ pro/im Jahr 4/17
be able to do sth /bi‿ˌeɪbl tə ˈduː ˌsʌmθɪŋ/ etw tun können 5/15
about /əˈbaʊt/ über I
about /əˈbaʊt/ ungefähr 6/M1
be about /bi‿əˈbaʊt/ handeln von 1/P6
above /əˈbʌv/ oben 4/M6
abseiling *(no pl)* /ˈæbseɪlɪŋ/ Abseilen 6/11
across /əˈkrɒs/ über 3/M5
across /əˈkrɒs/ hinüber 6/CC
act /ækt/ handeln, sich verhalten 4/M6
act out /ækt‿ˈaʊt/ nachspielen 2/9
get into action /ˌget‿ɪntə‿ˈækʃn/ loslegen 3/P6
action campaign /ˈækʃn kæmˌpeɪn/ Aktionskampagne, Aktion 5/15
active /ˈæktɪv/ aktiv 4/5
activity /ækˈtɪvəti/ Aktivität I
actor/actress /ˈæktə, ˈæktrəs/ Schauspieler/in I
add /æd/ hinzufügen 1/12
adopt /əˈdɒpt/ adoptieren 2/P12
adult /ˈædʌlt/ Erwachsene/r 6/M5
adventure /ədˈventʃə/ Abenteuer, Erlebnis 2/12

be afraid (of sth/sb) /ˌbi‿əˈfreɪd/ (vor etw/jdm) Angst haben 5/15
Africa /ˈæfrɪkə/ Afrika 2/M5
African /ˈæfrɪkən/ Afrikaner/in 2/P12
African /ˈæfrɪkən/ afrikanisch 2/P12
after /ˈɑːftə/ nach I
after /ˈɑːftə/ nachdem 6/M1
after /ˈɑːftə/ hinterher 6/15
after that /ˌɑːftə ˈðæt/ anschließend, danach I
afternoon /ˌɑːftəˈnuːn/ Nachmittag I
in the afternoon /ˌɪn ði‿ˈɑːftənuːn/ am Nachmittag, nachmittags I
this afternoon /ðɪs‿ˌɑːftəˈnuːn/ heute Nachmittag 2/12
afterwards /ˈɑːftəwədz/ danach, anschließend; später 4/17
again /əˈgen/ wieder, noch (ein)mal I
against /əˈgenst/ gegen 5/13
age /eɪdʒ/ Alter 1/14
(three days) ago /əˈgəʊ/ vor (drei Tagen) 2/6
agree (with sb) /əˈgriː/ (jdm) zustimmen 6/7
aim /eɪm/ Ziel, Absicht 4/CC
air *(no pl)* /eə/ Luft I
airport /ˈeəˌpɔːt/ Flughafen 2/1
alarm clock /əˈlɑːm ˌklɒk/ Wecker 5/10
alien /ˈeɪliən/ Außerirdische(r), Alien 3/M4
all /ɔːl/ alle(s) I

all /ɔːl/ ganz, völlig 3/CC
all day /ˌɔːl ˈdeɪ/ den ganzen Tag 1/M3
all week /ˌɔːl ˈwiːk/ die ganze Woche 6/2
allowed /əˈlaʊd/ erlaubt 5/P6
be allowed to do sth /bi‿əˌlaʊd tə ˈduː ˌsʌmθɪŋ/ etw tun dürfen 1/M3
alone /əˈləʊn/ allein 2/1
along /əˈlɒŋ/ entlang 2/6
alphabetical /ˌælfəˈbetɪkl/ alphabetisch 4/P8
already /ɔːlˈredi/ schon 6/2
also /ˈɔːlsəʊ/ auch I
although /ɔːlˈðəʊ/ obwohl, obgleich 3/M5
always /ˈɔːlweɪz/ immer I
am (= ante meridiem) /ˌeɪˈem, ˌænti məˈrɪdiəm/ morgens, vormittags *(nur hinter Uhrzeit zwischen Mitternacht und 12 Uhr mittags)* 1/P6
amazed /əˈmeɪzd/ erstaunt, verblüfft 3/M4
amazing *(informal)* /əˈmeɪzɪŋ/ toll, unglaublich 1/2
American /əˈmerɪkən/ Amerikaner/in 3/M5
American /əˈmerɪkən/ amerikanisch 3/M5
and /ænd/ und I
and so on /ænd ˌsəʊ‿ˈɒn/ und so weiter 6/M8
angry /ˈæŋgri/ verärgert; zornig; wütend 1/5
animal /ˈænɪml/ Tier I

another /ə'nʌðə/ ein anderer/ anderes, eine andere 1/M3; noch ein(e, r, s) 6/M1
answer /'ɑ:nsə/ Antwort I
answer /'ɑ:nsə/ (be)antworten 2/M3
any /'eni/ irgendwelche, irgendein(e); etwas 4/16
not any /nɒt‿'eni/ kein(e) 3/2
not anymore /ˌnɒt eni'mɔ:/ nicht mehr 5/15
not anyone /nɒt‿'eniwʌn/ niemand 3/2
anything /'eniˌθɪŋ/ (irgend)(et)was 3/2
not anything /nɒt‿'eniˌθɪŋ/ nichts 5/15
Anything else? /ˌeniθɪŋ‿'els/ Darf es noch etwas sein? I
anyway /'eniˌweɪ/ sowieso, jedenfalls 4/11; trotzdem Op1
not anywhere /nɒt‿'eniˌweə/ nirgendwo(hin) 6/2
apartment /ə'pɑ:tmənt/ Wohnung 1/6
apple /'æpl/ Apfel 2/14
April /'eɪprəl/ April I
Aquarius /ə'kweəriəs/ Wassermann *(Sternzeichen)* 3/2
area /'eəriə/ Gebiet, Region; Bereich 5/P12
argument /'ɑ:gjʊmənt/ Auseinandersetzung, Streit 4/5; Argument 5/M5
have an argument /hæv‿ən‿'ɑ:gjʊmənt/ (sich) streiten 5/4
Aries /'eəri:z/ Widder *(Sternzeichen)* 3/M2
armchair /'ɑ:mˌtʃeə/ Sessel, Lehnstuhl I
around /ə'raʊnd/ um I; herum, umher 6/M1
around /ə'raʊnd/ in, durch 2/I
around the world /əˌraʊnd ðə 'wɜ:ld/ weltweit, auf der ganzen Welt 1/M3
arrive /ə'raɪv/ ankommen I
art /ɑ:t/ Kunst I
article /'ɑ:tɪkl/ Artikel 2/M6
as /əz/ als 3/7
as … as /əz əz/ (genau)so … wie … 4/13
Asia /'eɪʃə/ Asien 2/13
Asian /'eɪʃn/ Asiat/in 2/P12
Asian /'eɪʃn/ asiatisch 2/P2
ask /ɑ:sk/ fragen; bitten I
be asleep /bi‿ə'sli:p/ schlafen 1/M2
assembly /ə'sembli/ (Schüler)versammlung 1/M4
astronaut /'æstrəˌnɔ:t/ Astronaut/in 3/10
at /æt/ auf, an, in, bei; um I
at first /ət 'fɜ:st/ anfangs, zuerst 3/M4
ate /eɪt/ *Vergangenheitsform von „eat"*
Athens /'æθɪnz/ Athen 1/2
the Atlantic (Ocean) /ði‿ətˌlæntɪk(‿'əʊʃn)/ der Atlantische Ozean 3/M5
attack /ə'tæk/ angreifen I
attention *(no pl)* /ə'tenʃn/ Achtung, Aufmerksamkeit 5/P6
August /'ɔ:gəst/ August I
aunt /ɑ:nt/ Tante I
Australia /ɒ'streɪliə/ Australien 4/M4
author /'ɔ:θə/ Schriftsteller/in, Autor/in 3/M5
autograph /'ɔ:təˌgrɑ:f/ Autogramm 6/M1
autumn /'ɔ:təm/ Herbst I
available /ə'veɪləbl/ verfügbar; erhältlich 6/M5
avoid /ə'vɔɪd/ (ver)meiden, entgehen 2/M6
away /ə'weɪ/ weg 2/11
awful /'ɔ:fl/ furchtbar, schrecklich 6/CC

B

back /bæk/ Rücken; Rückseite I
back /bæk/ zurück B
backflip /'bækflɪp/ Rückwärtssalto, Rolle rückwärts 6/8
backstage /ˌbæk'steɪdʒ/ hinter der Bühne; backstage 6/M1
bad /bæd/ schlecht I
too bad /ˌtu: 'bæd/ wirklich schade 1/M3
That's too bad. /ðæts 'tu: bæd/ Das ist wirklich schade. 2/12
bag /bæg/ Tasche I
bake /beɪk/ backen 4/14
baking powder *(no pl)* /'beɪkɪŋ ˌpaʊdə/ Backpulver 4/CC
baking tin /'beɪkɪŋ tɪn/ Backform 4/CC
balloon /bə'lu:n/ Ballon I
banana /bə'nɑ:nə/ Banane I
Bang! /bæŋ/ Peng! 3/M4
bar /bɑ:/ Lokal, Bar; Imbiss 3/CC
have a barbecue /ˌhæv‿ə 'bɑ:bɪˌkju:/ grillen, eine Grillparty feiern 4/M4
bark /bɑ:k/ bellen 6/15
barn /bɑ:n/ Scheune, (Vieh)stall I
basket /'bɑ:skɪt/ Korb I
bathroom /'bɑ:θˌru:m/ Bad(ezimmer) I
be *(irr)* /bi:/ sein I
be out /ˌbi‿'aʊt/ nicht mehr im Spiel sein, draußen sein 4/M6
beach /bi:tʃ/ Strand 1/2
bean /bi:n/ Bohne I
beard /bɪəd/ Bart 1/M2
beat *(irr)* /bi:t/ schlagen 4/P12; besiegen 5/16
beautiful /'bju:təfl/ schön I
became /bɪ'keɪm/ *Vergangenheitsform von „become"*
because /bɪ'kɒz/ weil I
become *(irr)* /bɪ'kʌm/ werden I
bed /bed/ Bett I
bed sheet /'bed ʃi:t/ Bettlaken 4/CC
bedroom /'bedru:m/ Schlafzimmer I
been /bi:n/ *siehe „be"*

before /bɪˈfɔː/ vor I; bevor 5/2

began /bɪˈgæn/ *Vergangenheitsform von „begin"*

begin *(irr)* /bɪˈgɪn/ anfangen, beginnen I

beginning /bɪˈgɪnɪŋ/ Anfang Op2

in the beginning /ɪn ðə bɪˈgɪnɪŋ/ am Anfang, zu Beginn 1/M2

begun /bɪˈgʌn/ *siehe „begin"*

behind /bɪˈhaɪnd/ hinter I

believe (in) /bɪˈliːv/ glauben (an) 2/6

belong to sb/sth /bɪˈlɒŋ tə ˌsʌmbədi/ˌsʌmθɪŋ/ jdm/zu etw gehören 4/3

below /bɪˈləʊ/ unten 2/6

best /best/ beste(r, s) I

best /best/ am meisten/liebsten/besten I

best wishes /ˌbest ˈwɪʃɪz/ viele Grüße 6/5

bet *(irr)* /bet/ wetten 5/3

better /ˈbetə/ besser; lieber, mehr 4/11

between /bɪˈtwiːn/ zwischen I

big /bɪg/ groß I

bike /baɪk/ (Fahr)rad I

ride a bike /ˌraɪd‿ə ˈbaɪk/ (Fahr)rad fahren I

billion /ˈbɪljən/ Milliarde 3/10

bin /bɪn/ Mülleimer, Mülltonne I

biology *(no pl)* /baɪˈɒlədʒi/ Biologie I

bird /bɜːd/ Vogel 1/3

birth /bɜːθ/ Geburt 4/5

birthday /ˈbɜːθdeɪ/ Geburtstag I

Happy birthday! /ˌhæpi ˈbɜːθdeɪ/ Alles Gute zum Geburtstag! I

a bit /ə ˈbɪt/ ein bisschen 1/2

bite *(irr)* /baɪt/ beißen I

black /blæk/ schwarz I

blazer /ˈbleɪzə/ Blazer, Jacke 1/11

blindfold /ˈblaɪnˌfəʊld/ Augenbinde 4/M6

blue /bluː/ blau I

board /bɔːd/ Brett; Tafel 5/11

board game /ˈbɔːd geɪm/ Brettspiel I

boat /bəʊt/ Boot; Schiff 2/1

body /ˈbɒdi/ Körper I

Bolivia /bəˈlɪviə/ Bolivien 1/M2

book /bʊk/ Buch I

bookcase /ˈbʊkˌkeɪs/ Bücherregal, Bücherschrank I

bored /bɔːd/ gelangweilt 2/12

boring /ˈbɔːrɪŋ/ langweilig I

born /bɔːn/ geboren 4/5

boss /bɒs/ Chef/in 3/7

both /bəʊθ/ beide(s) I

bottle /ˈbɒtl/ Flasche 4/11

bought /bɔːt/ *Vergangenheitsform von „buy"*

bowl /bəʊl/ Schüssel 4/P12

a box of chocolates /ə bɒks‿əv ˈtʃɒkləts/ eine Schachtel Pralinen 4/11

Boxing Day /ˈbɒksɪŋ deɪ/ zweiter Weihnachtsfeiertag 4/M1

boy /bɔɪ/ Junge I

boyfriend /ˈbɔɪˌfrend/ (fester) Freund I

brave /breɪv/ mutig, unerschrocken 4/5

bread *(no pl)* /bred/ Brot 4/M4

bread roll /ˈbred rəʊl/ Brötchen I

break /breɪk/ Pause I

break *(irr)* /breɪk/ (zer)brechen 5/10

breakfast /ˈbrekfəst/ Frühstück I

breathe in /briːð‿ˈɪn/ einatmen 6/CC

bridge /brɪdʒ/ Brücke 2/1

bright /braɪt/ hell Op1

brightly /ˈbraɪtli/ hell, leuchtend 3/CC

brilliant *(informal)* /ˈbrɪljənt/ toll, hervorragend 4/12

bring *(irr)* /brɪŋ/ (mit)bringen I

Britain /ˈbrɪtn/ Großbritannien 6/11

British /ˈbrɪtɪʃ/ britische(r, s) I

The British Navy /ðə ˌbrɪtɪʃ ˈneɪvi/ die britische Marine 2/M6

broccoli *(no pl)* /ˈbrɒkəli/ Brokkoli 4/16

brochure /ˈbrəʊʃə/ Broschüre 2/9

broken /ˈbrəʊkən/ zerbrochen, kaputt 3/M4

bronze /brɒnz/ Bronze, Bronze- 3/M5

brother /ˈbrʌðə/ Bruder I

brothers and sisters /ˌbrʌðəz‿ænd ˈsɪstəz/ Geschwister 1/14

brought /brɔːt/ *Vergangenheitsform von „bring"*

brown /braʊn/ braun I

brush /brʌʃ/ bürsten; putzen I

bubble /ˈbʌbl/ blubbern 5/8

budgie (= budgerigar) /ˈbʌdʒi, ˈbʌdʒəriˌgɑː/ Wellensittich I

build *(irr)* /bɪld/ bauen 3/5

builder /ˈbɪldə/ Bauarbeiter/in 3/5

building /ˈbɪldɪŋ/ Gebäude 2/6

bully /ˈbʊli/ Rüpel, Rabauke; jemand, der andere drangsaliert 5/15

bully /ˈbʊli/ tyrannisieren, drangsalieren, mobben 5/15

bullying *(no pl)* /ˈbʊliɪŋ/ Mobbing 5/15

burn *(irr)* /bɜːn/ brennen 1/M2

bury /ˈberi/ begraben 2/M1

bus stop /ˈbʌs ˌstɒp/ Bushaltestelle 5/14

business trip /ˈbɪznəs trɪp/ Dienstreise, Geschäftsreise 4/12

busy /ˈbɪzi/ beschäftigt 6/2

busy /ˈbɪzi/ arbeitsreich 4/M2

but /bʌt/ aber I

butter /ˈbʌtə/ mit Butter bestreichen, buttern 5/8

buy *(irr)* /baɪ/ kaufen I

buzz group /ˈbʌz gruːp/ *Form der Gruppenarbeit* 2/10

by /baɪ/ bei, in der Nähe; mit, durch 5/15; von 6/2; an 1/CC

by (eight o'clock) /baɪ/ (spätestens) bis (acht Uhr) 5/2
bye *(informal)* /baɪ/ tschüss I
bye for now /ˈbaɪ fə naʊ/ bis bald 6/M8

C

cage /keɪdʒ/ Käfig I
cake /keɪk/ Kuchen I
calculator /ˈkælkjʊˌleɪtə/ (Taschen)rechner I
calendar /ˈkælɪndə/ Kalender I
(phone) call /(ˈfəʊn) kɔːl/ (Telefon)anruf 3/2
call /kɔːl/ anrufen 2/11
call /kɔːl/ rufen 5/16
be called /biː ˈkɔːld/ heißen I
came /keɪm/ *Vergangenheitsform von „come"*
campsite /ˈkæmpˌsaɪt/ Campingplatz, Zeltplatz 1/2
can /kæn/ können I
canal /kəˈnæl/ Kanal 2/11
Cancer /ˈkænsə/ Krebs *(Sternzeichen)* 3/M2
candle /ˈkændl/ Kerze 4/16
cannon /ˈkænən/ Kanone, Geschütz 2/1
cap /kæp/ Kappe I
Capricorn /ˈkæprɪˌkɔːn/ Steinbock *(Sternzeichen)* 3/M2
caption /ˈkæpʃn/ Bildunterschrift, Bildtext 3/M7
capture /ˈkæptʃə/ Festnahme 2/M6
car /kɑː/ Auto I
caravan /ˈkærəvæn/ Wohnwagen 1/2
card /kɑːd/ Pappe, Karton; Karte I
get well card /get ˈwel kɑːd/ Genesungskarte 6/3
sb does not care /ˌsʌmbədi dəz nɒt ˈkeə/ jdm ist es egal 6/CC
take care of /teɪk ˈkeər‿əv/ sich kümmern um, versorgen 3/5
careful /ˈkeəfl/ vorsichtig; sorgfältig 3/14
carnival /ˈkɑːnɪvl/ Karneval 4/6
carpet /ˈkɑːpɪt/ Teppich I
carrot /ˈkærət/ Möhre, Karotte, Mohrrübe 2/14
carry /ˈkæri/ tragen 2/P6
cartoon /kɑːˈtuːn/ Cartoon, Karikatur; Zeichentrickfilm 6/7
castle /ˈkɑːsl/ Burg; Schloss 1/2
cat /kæt/ Katze I
catch *(irr)* /kætʃ/ fangen I; festnehmen 3/5
cattle *(no pl)* /ˈkætl/ Vieh; Rinder 3/10
caught /kɔːt/ *Vergangenheitsform von „catch"*
ceiling /ˈsiːlɪŋ/ (Zimmer)decke I
celebrate /ˈseləˌbreɪt/ feiern 4/1
celebration /ˌseləˈbreɪʃn/ Feier, Fest 4/1
centre /ˈsentə/ Zentrum, Center I
century /ˈsentʃəri/ Jahrhundert 3/M4
chain /tʃeɪn/ Kette 1/4
chair /tʃeə/ Stuhl I
chance /tʃɑːns/ Chance; Möglichkeit 5/16
take a chance /teɪk‿ə ˈtʃɑːns/ etw wagen, etw riskieren 3/M4
change /tʃeɪndʒ/ wechseln 1/M3
change /tʃeɪndʒ/ (sich) (ver)ändern 6/P5; verstellen 5/8
Changing of the Guard /ˌtʃeɪndʒɪŋ‿əv ðə ˈgɑːd/ Wachablösung 2/1
channel /ˈtʃænl/ Kanal, Programm 6/10
character /ˈkærɪktə/ Charakter; Figur 3/13
charge /tʃɑːdʒ/ (auf)laden 2/6
charming /ˈtʃɑːmɪŋ/ bezaubernd, charmant 4/5
chat /tʃæt/ chatten, sich unterhalten 4/11
cheap /tʃiːp/ billig, preiswert 1/5
check /tʃek/ überprüfen, kontrollieren I
cheer /tʃɪə/ jubeln 6/M1
cheer sb up /tʃɪə ˌsʌmbədi‿ˈʌp/ jdn aufmuntern 6/3
Cheer up! /tʃɪər‿ˈʌp/ Lass (doch) den Kopf nicht hängen!, Kopf hoch! 6/4
cheerful /ˈtʃɪəfl/ fröhlich, vergnügt, gut gelaunt 3/P6
cheese *(no pl)* /tʃiːz/ Käse I
chemistry /ˈkemɪstri/ Chemie I
chess *(no pl)* /tʃes/ Schach(spiel) 1/11
chew /tʃuː/ kauen 5/8
(chewing) gum *(no pl)* /(ˈtʃuːɪŋ) gʌm/ Kaugummi 5/10
chicken /ˈtʃɪkɪn/ Huhn; Hähnchen I
chickenpox *(no pl)* /ˈtʃɪkɪnˌpɒks/ Windpocken 6/2
child *(pl* **children***)* /tʃaɪld, ˈtʃɪldrən/ Kind I
chimney /ˈtʃɪmni/ Kamin; Schornstein 4/M1
chin /tʃɪn/ Kinn 4/M6
Chinatown /ˈtʃaɪnəˌtaʊn/ *Chinesenviertel* 4/3
Chinese /ˌtʃaɪˈniːz/ Chinese/ Chinesin; Chinesisch 4/2
Chinese /ˌtʃaɪˈniːz/ chinesisch 4/2
chips *(only pl) (BE)* /tʃɪps/ Pommes frites 2/3
chocolate *(no pl)* /ˈtʃɒklət/ Schokolade I
a box of chocolates /ə bɒks‿əv ˈtʃɒkləts/ eine Schachtel Pralinen 4/11
choir /kwaɪə/ Chor Op1
choose *(irr)* /tʃuːz/ auswählen I
chop /tʃɒp/ klein schneiden 4/P12
Christmas /ˈkrɪsməs/ Weihnachten 4/1

Christmas Day /ˌkrɪsməs ˈdeɪ/ erster Weihnachtsfeiertag 4/M1
Christmas Eve /ˌkrɪsməs‿ˈiːv/ Heiligabend 4/M1
chronicle /ˈkrɒnɪkl/ Anzeiger 1/CC
church /tʃɜːtʃ/ Kirche 4/1
cinema /ˈsɪnəmə/ Kino I
circle /ˈsɜːkl/ Kreis 4/M6
city /ˈsɪti/ (Groß)stadt I
class /klɑːs/ (Schul)klasse I
class /klɑːs/ Kurs 1/11; Unterricht 1/CC
classmate /ˈklɑːsˌmeɪt/ Klassenkamerad/in, Mitschüler/in I
classroom /ˈklɑːsˌruːm/ Klassenzimmer I
clean /kliːn/ sauber machen, reinigen, putzen I
clean /kliːn/ sauber I
clean up /kliːn‿ˈʌp/ sauber machen, reinigen 5/P6
clever /ˈklevə/ klug, gescheit, schlau 2/13
climb /klaɪm/ (hinauf)klettern; (hinauf)steigen 5/8
cling to sth /ˈklɪŋ tə ˌsʌmθɪŋ/ sich an etw klammern/ festhalten 6/CC
clock /klɒk/ Uhr I
close /kləʊz/ schließen, zumachen I
closed /kləʊzd/ geschlossen, zu 6/M5
closely /ˈkləʊsli/ eng 1/11
take a closer look /teɪk‿ə ˌkləʊsə ˈlʊk/ sich (jdn/etw) genauer ansehen 6/P10
clothes *(only pl)* /kləʊðz/ Kleider, Kleidung I
cloudy /ˈklaʊdi/ bewölkt, bedeckt I
club /klʌb/ Klub, Verein I
coach /kəʊtʃ/ Trainer 6/11
coast /kəʊst/ Küste I
cobweb /ˈkɒbˌweb/ Spinnennetz, Spinnwebe Op1
cocoa *(no pl)* /ˈkəʊkəʊ/ Kakao 4/CC

coffee /ˈkɒfi/ Kaffee 6/P4
coffin /ˈkɒfɪn/ Sarg 2/M3
cold /kəʊld/ kalt I
colleague /ˈkɒliːg/ Kollege/ Kollegin; Mitarbeiter/in 2/15
collect /kəˈlekt/ sammeln I
Cologne /kəˈləʊn/ Köln 1/6
colour /ˈkʌlə/ Farbe I
colourful /ˈkʌləfl/ farbenfroh, farbenprächtig 4/3
come *(irr)* /kʌm/ kommen I
come in /kʌm‿ˈɪn/ hereinkommen I
Come on! /ˌkʌm‿ˈɒn/ Jetzt hör aber auf! 1/2; Auf geht's!, Komm(t) jetzt! 3/M4; Na los! 5/CC
comedy /ˈkɒmədi/ Komödie I
comfortable /ˈkʌmftəbl/ bequem I
comic strip /ˈkɒmɪk strɪp/ Comic *(in einer Zeitung)*, Comicstreifen 3/M7
comment /ˈkɒment/ Kommentar, Bemerkung 4/M6
comparative (form) /kəmˈpærətɪv/ Komparativ 4/P8
compare /kəmˈpeə/ vergleichen 1/P8
comparison /kəmˈpærɪsn/ Vergleich 4/P9
competition /ˌkɒmpəˈtɪʃn/ Wettbewerb 3/2
complete /kəmˈpliːt/ vervollständigen 1/8
completely /kəmˈpliːtli/ völlig, ganz I
comprehensive school /ˌkɒmprɪˈhensɪv ˌskuːl/ Gesamtschule 1/M3
concentrate /ˈkɒnsnˌtreɪt/ sich konzentrieren 5/M4
concert /ˈkɒnsət/ Konzert 1/2
connect /kəˈnekt/ verbinden Op4
contact sb /ˈkɒntækt ˌsʌmbədi/ jdn kontaktieren, sich mit jdm in Verbindung setzen 5/16
continue /kənˈtɪnjuː/ weitergehen 4/M6

convince /kənˈvɪns/ überzeugen 5/M1
cook /kʊk/ Koch/Köchin 3/5
cook /kʊk/ kochen 3/5
cooking *(no pl)* /ˈkʊkɪŋ/ Kochen 6/P2
do the cooking /ˌduː ðə ˈkʊkɪŋ/ kochen I
cool /kuːl/ abkühlen 4/P12
cool /kuːl/ kalt, kühl 4/CC
cool down /kuːl ˈdaʊn/ sich beruhigen 5/M4
Copenhagen /ˌkəʊpənˈheɪgən/ Kopenhagen 6/P6
copy /ˈkɒpi/ Kopie; Exemplar 6/M1
copy /ˈkɒpi/ abschreiben 3/P9
corn *(no pl)* /kɔːn/ Getreide, Korn 3/11
corner /ˈkɔːnə/ Ecke 2/1
correct /kəˈrekt/ korrigieren 1/5
correct /kəˈrekt/ richtig, korrekt 5/10
corridor /ˈkɒrɪdɔː/ Flur, Gang Op1
cost /kɒst/ Kosten, Preis 1/P6
cost *(irr)* /kɒst/ kosten I
costume /ˈkɒstjuːm/ Tracht, Kostüm 4/3
couch /kaʊtʃ/ Couch, Sofa 6/M4
couch potato *(informal)* /ˈkaʊtʃ pəˌteɪtəʊ/ Couchpotato, Dauerglotzer/in, Stubenhocker/in 6/M4
could /kʊd/ könnte(st, n, t) I
count /kaʊnt/ zählen Op1
country /ˈkʌntri/ Land 1/M3
course /kɔːs/ Kurs I
court /kɔːt/ Platz, Court 1/11
cousin /ˈkʌzn/ Cousin/e I
cover /ˈkʌvə/ Titelseite, Cover 3/CC
coverage *(no pl)* /ˈkʌvrɪdʒ/ Berichterstattung 6/P6
cow /kaʊ/ Kuh I
cracker /ˈkrækə/ Knallbonbon 4/M1
crash /kræʃ/ stürzen 6/CC
crazy /ˈkreɪzi/ verrückt I

go crazy *(informal)* /gəʊ ˈkreɪzi/ durchdrehen, ausflippen I
cream *(no pl)* /kriːm/ Sahne 4/16
create /kriˈeɪt/ erschaffen; gestalten 2/M3
create /kriˈeɪt/ erzeugen, produzieren 1/M2
creative /kriˈeɪtɪv/ kreativ 4/5
criminal /ˈkrɪmɪnl/ Verbrecher/in, Kriminelle/r 2/M3
crisps *(only pl) (BE)* /krɪsps/ Chips I
cross /krɒs/ durchqueren; überqueren 2/7
crossword puzzle /ˈkrɒswɜːd ˌpʌzl/ Kreuzworträtsel 4/19
crowd /kraʊd/ (Menschen)menge, Zuschauermenge 6/M1
crown /kraʊn/ Krone 4/M1
Crown Jewels *(only pl)* /ˌkraʊn ˈdʒuːəlz/ Kronjuwelen 2/1
cry /kraɪ/ weinen; schreien 5/15
cucumber /ˈkjuːˌkʌmbə/ (Salat)gurke 4/P12
cumin *(no pl)* /ˈkʌmɪn/ Kreuzkümmel 4/P12
cup /kʌp/ Tasse I
cupboard /ˈkʌbəd/ Schrank 4/16
curry /ˈkʌri/ Curry(gericht) 4/M4
curtain /ˈkɜːtn/ Vorhang 5/8
cushion /ˈkʊʃn/ Kissen I
customer /ˈkʌstəmə/ Kunde/Kundin 1/5
cut *(irr)* /kʌt/ schneiden 3/5
cut off /kʌt‿ˈɒf/ abschneiden 5/8
cute /kjuːt/ süß, niedlich I
cycle /ˈsaɪkl/ Rad fahren 5/8

D

dad *(informal)* /dæd/ Papa, Vati I
daily /ˈdeɪli/ täglich 6/M5
dance /dɑːns/ Tanz 1/11
dance /dɑːns/ tanzen I
dancing *(no pl)* /ˈdɑːnsɪŋ/ Tanzen I
dangerous /ˈdeɪndʒərəs/ gefährlich I
dark *(no pl)* /dɑːk/ Dunkelheit 6/M5
dark /dɑːk/ dunkel I
darkness /ˈdɑːknəs/ Dunkelheit, Finsternis 4/M2
darling /ˈdɑːlɪŋ/ Liebling, Schatz 4/17
date /deɪt/ Datum I
daughter /ˈdɔːtə/ Tochter I
day /deɪ/ Tag I
day after day /deɪ‿ɑːftə ˈdeɪ/ Tag für Tag; tagein, tagaus 3/8
a day /ə ˈdeɪ/ pro/am Tag 6/M4
all day /ˌɔːl ˈdeɪ/ den ganzen Tag 5/9
one day /ˈwʌn deɪ/ eines Tages 3/2
the next day /ðə ˌnekst‿ˈdeɪ/ am nächsten Tag 2/8
daydream /ˈdeɪˌdriːm/ Tagtraum 3/10
daydream *(irr)* /ˈdeɪˌdriːm/ tagträumen 3/10
dead /ded/ tot 2/M3
dead /ded/ leer 2/6
dear /dɪə/ liebe(r) *(Anrede)* I
Oh dear! /əʊ ˈdɪə/ Du meine Güte! 2/10
December /dɪˈsembə/ Dezember I
decide /dɪˈsaɪd/ (sich) entscheiden; beschließen 6/11
decorate /ˈdekəˌreɪt/ schmücken, dekorieren 4/1
decorated /ˈdekəreɪtɪd/ geschmückt, verziert 4/3
delicious /dɪˈlɪʃəs/ köstlich, lecker 4/3
Denmark /ˈdenmɑːk/ Dänemark 6/P6
department store /dɪˈpɑːtmənt ˌstɔː/ Kaufhaus 4/11
depressed /dɪˈprest/ deprimiert I
deputy head /ˈdepjʊti ˌhed/ stellvertretende/r Schulleiter/in, Konrektor/in 5/10
describe /dɪˈskraɪb/ beschreiben 1/5
design /dɪˈzaɪn/ entwerfen 5/17
desk /desk/ Schreibtisch I
detail /ˈdiːteɪl/ Detail, Einzelheit 6/19
detective /dɪˈtektɪv/ (Privat)detektiv/in 2/1
devil /ˈdevl/ Teufel 1/M2
dialogue /ˈdaɪəlɒg/ Gespräch, Dialog 1/2
diary /ˈdaɪəri/ Tagebuch 1/5
diary /ˈdaɪəri/ (Termin)kalender 1/11
dictionary /ˈdɪkʃənri/ Wörterbuch I
did /dɪd/ *Vergangenheitsform von „do"*
die /daɪ/ sterben 6/15
difference /ˈdɪfrəns/ Unterschied 5/M5
different /ˈdɪfrənt/ verschieden, unterschiedlich 1/11
different /ˈdɪfrənt/ anders, andere(r, s) 2/P12
difficult /ˈdɪfɪklt/ schwierig, schwer I
dining room /ˈdaɪnɪŋ ˌruːm/ Esszimmer 4/17
dinner /ˈdɪnə/ Abendessen; Mittagessen 5/5
direction /dɪˈrekʃn/ Richtung 2/7
give directions /ˌgɪv dɪˈrekʃnz/ den Weg beschreiben 2/7
director /dəˈrektə/ Direktor/in, Leiter/in 2/15
dirty /ˈdɜːti/ dreckig, schmutzig I
disappointed /ˌdɪsəˈpɔɪntɪd/ enttäuscht I
discover /dɪˈskʌvə/ entdecken 3/M5

discuss /dɪˈskʌs/ besprechen; diskutieren 5/7
discussion /dɪˈskʌʃn/ Diskussion, Besprechung 5/M5
dish *(pl* **-es***)* /dɪʃ/ Gericht 1/11
dishwasher /ˈdɪʃˌwɒʃə/ Geschirrspülmaschine I
divide /dɪˈvaɪd/ teilen; trennen 4/CC
Diwali /dɪˈwɑːli/ *hinduistisches Lichterfest* 4/8
do *(irr)* /duː/ machen, tun I
doctor /ˈdɒktə/ Arzt/Ärztin 3/2
dog /dɒg/ Hund I
dolphin /ˈdɒlfɪn/ Delfin 1/P5
Don't be silly! /ˌdəʊnt bi ˈsɪli/ Red(et) keinen Unsinn! 2/10
don'ting (= not doing) /ˈdəʊntɪŋ/ *nicht tun* 5/8
done /dʌn/ *siehe „do"*
door /dɔː/ Tür I
dos and don'ts /ˌduːz‿ən ˈdəʊnts/ was man tun und was man nicht tun sollte 5/I
double circle /ˌdʌbl ˈsɜːkl/ Doppelkreis 4/1
down /daʊn/ hinunter, hinab 4/M4
dragon /ˈdrægən/ Drache I
drama /ˈdrɑːmə/ Schauspielerei; Theater 1/10
dramatic /drəˈmætɪk/ dramatisch 3/13
draw *(irr)* /drɔː/ zeichnen I
dream /driːm/ Traum I
dream *(irr)* /driːm/ träumen 3/CC
dress /dres/ Kleid I
dress /dres/ sich kleiden; sich anziehen 3/11
drink /drɪŋk/ Getränk I
drink *(irr)* /drɪŋk/ trinken I
drive *(irr)* /draɪv/ fahren 3/5
driver /ˈdraɪvə/ Fahrer/in 3/5
drop /drɒp/ fallen lassen 4/M6
play the drums /pleɪ ðə ˈdrʌmz/ Schlagzeug spielen 1/P11
duck /dʌk/ Ente I
dumpling /ˈdʌmplɪŋ/ Knödel, Kloß; Teigtasche 4/3
dungeon /ˈdʌndʒn/ Verlies, Kerker 2/1
during /ˈdjʊərɪŋ/ während I

E

each /iːtʃ/ jede(r, s) 4/M4
each other /ˌiːtʃ‿ˈʌðə/ einander 1/14
eagle /ˈiːgl/ Adler 2/M6
golden eagle /ˈgəʊldn ˌiːgl/ Goldadler, Steinadler 2/M6
ear /ɪə/ Ohr I
early /ˈɜːli/ früh, zeitig 4/1
earn /ɜːn/ verdienen 5/M1
earring /ˈɪərɪŋ/ Ohrring 4/11
east /iːst/ Osten I
Easter /ˈiːstə/ Ostern, Osterfest 4/1
easy /ˈiːzi/ einfach; leicht I
eat *(irr)* /iːt/ essen I
eaten /ˈiːtn/ *siehe „eat"*
keep clear of the edges /kiːp ˌklɪər‿əv ði‿ˈedʒɪz/ sich von den Rändern fernhalten 2/P6
edit /ˈedɪt/ bearbeiten, redigieren 1/15
education *(no pl)* /ˌedjʊˈkeɪʃn/ (Aus)bildung Op1
egg /eg/ Ei I
Eid /iːd/ *islamisches Fest zum Abschluss des Fastenmonats Ramadan* 4/1
elbow /ˈelbəʊ/ Ellbogen 4/M6
elephant /ˈelɪfənt/ Elefant I
what else /wɒt‿ˈels/ was noch, was sonst 1/10
embarrassed /ɪmˈbærəst/ verlegen, peinlich berührt 5/15
emergency room /ɪˈmɜːdʒnsi ruːm/ Notaufnahme 6/P6
empty /ˈempti/ ausräumen, (ent)leeren I
empty /ˈempti/ leer Op1
end /end/ Ende 4/3
end /end/ enden 1/M3
ending /ˈendɪŋ/ Ende, Schluss; Endung 1/P3
enemy /ˈenəmi/ Feind/in 3/P12
energy /ˈenədʒi/ Energie, Kraft 4/5
English /ˈɪŋglɪʃ/ Englisch I
English /ˈɪŋglɪʃ/ englisch I
in English /ˌɪn‿ˈɪŋglɪʃ/ auf Englisch I
English-speaking /ˈɪŋglɪʃ‿ˌspiːkɪŋ/ englischsprachig 2/9
enjoy /ɪnˈdʒɔɪ/ mögen; genießen I
enough /ɪˈnʌf/ genügend, ausreichend, genug 4/16
enter /ˈentə/ betreten 5/P12
entertainment /ˌentəˈteɪnmənt/ Unterhaltung 4/P5
entrance fee /ˈentrəns ˌfiː/ Eintritt(sgeld) 6/M5
entry /ˈentri/ Eintrag 1/5
envelope /ˈenvələʊp/ Briefumschlag, Kuvert 4/3
epal /ˈiːpæl/ *E-Mail-Freund/in* 5/P12
escape /ɪˈskeɪp/ Flucht 2/M6
escape /ɪˈskeɪp/ (ent)fliehen, ausbrechen; entkommen 2/M6
Europe /ˈjʊərəp/ Europa 2/M1
even /ˈiːvn/ selbst; sogar I
even /ˈiːvn/ noch 5/13
evening /ˈiːvnɪŋ/ Abend 5/2
in the evening /ˌɪn ði‿ˈiːvnɪŋ/ am Abend, abends I
ever /ˈevə/ jemals 6/3
ever /ˈevə/ überhaupt 2/CC
every /ˈevri/ jede(r, s) I
everybody /ˈevriˌbɒdi/ jede(r); alle 4/M2
everyone /ˈevriwʌn/ jede(r); alle I
everything /ˈevriθɪŋ/ alles 4/16
evil /ˈiːvl/ böse 4/M2
example /ɪgˈzɑːmpl/ Beispiel I
for example /fər‿ɪgˈzɑːmpl/ zum Beispiel I

exchange /ɪks'tʃeɪndʒ/ austauschen 4/M2
excited /ɪk'saɪtɪd/ aufgeregt 3/13
excitement /ɪk'saɪtmənt/ Aufregung, Spannung 3/P6
exciting /ɪk'saɪtɪŋ/ aufregend; spannend I
excuse /ɪk'skju:s/ Entschuldigung; Ausrede I
Excuse me! /ɪk'skju:z ˌmi/ Entschuldigen Sie bitte!, Entschuldigung! I
exercise book /'eksəsaɪz ˌbʊk/ Heft I
exit /'eksɪt/ verlassen 5/P12
expensive /ɪk'spensɪv/ teuer 4/3
experience /ɪk'spɪəriəns/ erleben, erfahren 3/M4
explain /ɪk'spleɪn/ erklären 2/6
explore /ɪk'splɔ:/ erforschen, untersuchen 3/M5
expression /ɪk'spreʃn/ Ausdruck 2/7
extra /'ekstrə/ besonders 2/P6
extreme /ɪk'stri:m/ extrem I
eye /aɪ/ Auge I

F

face /feɪs/ Gesicht I
in fact /ɪn 'fækt/ tatsächlich, in Wirklichkeit; sogar 4/M4
fact file /'fækt ˌfaɪl/ Steckbrief 1/M1
factory /'fæktri/ Fabrik; Werk 3/10
fairy bread *(no pl)* /'feəri bred/ *Brot mit bunten Zuckerstreuseln* 4/M4
fall *(irr)* /fɔ:l/ fallen 2/M3
fall down /fɔ:l 'daʊn/ hinfallen I
fall in love (with) /ˌfɔ:l‿ɪn 'lʌv/ sich verlieben (in) 3/8
family /'fæmli/ Familie I
famous /'feɪməs/ berühmt I
fantastic *(informal)* /fæn'tæstɪk/ fantastisch, wunderbar I
far /fɑ:/ weit 3/11
so far /'səʊ ˌfɑ:/ bisher, bis jetzt 3/CC
farm /fɑ:m/ Bauernhof I
farmer /'fɑ:mə/ Bauer/ Bäuerin I
fast /fɑ:st/ schnell I
father /'fɑ:ðə/ Vater I
Father Christmas /ˌfɑ:ðə 'krɪsməs/ Weihnachtsmann 4/M1
fault /fɔ:lt/ Schuld; Fehler 5/16
favourite /'feɪvrət/ Lieblings- I
February /'februəri/ Februar I
feed *(irr)* /fi:d/ füttern, zu Essen geben I
feeding time /'fi:dɪŋ ˌtaɪm/ Fütterungszeit 2/M5
feel *(irr)* /fi:l/ (sich) fühlen 1/5
feeling /'fi:lɪŋ/ Gefühl 6/M1
fell /fel/ *Vergangenheitsform von „fall"*
felt /felt/ *Vergangenheitsform von „feel"*
felt tip /'felt‿tɪp/ Filzstift I
ferry /'feri/ Fähre 6/M8
festival /'festɪvl/ Fest; Festival 4/1
a few /ə 'fju:/ einige 6/M1
few /fju:/ wenige 6/M1
field /fi:ld/ Wiese, Weide, Feld 2/P11
fight *(irr)* /faɪt/ (be)kämpfen 3/5
fill in /fɪl‿'ɪn/ ausfüllen; einsetzen 3/P9
finally /'faɪnli/ schließlich, endlich; zum Schluss 3/12
find *(irr)* /faɪnd/ finden I
find one's way back /ˌfaɪnd wʌnz weɪ 'bæk/ zurückfinden 6/15
find out /faɪnd‿'aʊt/ herausfinden 1/P12
fine /faɪn/ in Ordnung, gut 4/11
fine /faɪn/ edel, vornehm 4/11
I'm fine. /aɪm 'faɪn/ Es geht mir gut. I
finely /'faɪnli/ fein 4/P12
finish /'fɪnɪʃ/ beenden, aufhören I
fire /faɪə/ Feuer I
firefighter /'faɪəˌfaɪtə/ Feuerwehrmann/-frau 3/5
fireworks *(only pl)* /'faɪəˌwɜ:ks/ Feuerwerk 4/1
first /fɜ:st/ erste(r, s) I
first /fɜ:st/ zuerst, als Erstes 1/2
at first /ət 'fɜ:st/ anfangs, zuerst 3/M4
first of all /ˌfɜ:st‿əv‿'ɔ:l/ erstens, als erstes 5/M4
fish *(pl* **-** *or* **-es***)* /fɪʃ, fɪʃ, fɪʃɪz/ Fisch I
fish tank /'fɪʃ tæŋk/ Aquarium I
fishing *(no pl)* /'fɪʃɪŋ/ Angeln, Fischen 6/11
fit *(irr)* /fɪt/ passen (zu) 2/13
five-day /ˌfaɪv'deɪ/ fünftägig 4/M2
flag /flæg/ Fahne; Flagge 4/3
flat /flæt/ Wohnung I
flat /flæt/ flach; platt 3/M4
...-flavoured /'fleɪvəd/ mit ...-Geschmack 3/M4
flew /flu:/ *Vergangenheitsform von „fly"*
floor /flɔ:/ Boden I
flour *(no pl)* /'flaʊə/ Mehl 4/16
flower /'flaʊə/ Blume 3/5
fly *(irr)* /flaɪ/ fliegen I
fog /fɒg/ Nebel 6/15
foggy /'fɒgi/ neblig 6/18
folder /'fəʊldə/ Mappe, Schnellhefter I
follow /'fɒləʊ/ folgen 4/3
food colouring /'fu:d ˌkʌlərɪŋ/ Lebensmittelfarbe 4/CC
food *(no pl)* /fu:d/ Essen I
food technology /'fu:d tekˌnɒlədʒi/ Ernährung *(Schulfach)* 1/10
foot *(pl* **feet***)* /fʊt, fi:t/ Fuß I
on foot /ɒn 'fʊt/ zu Fuß 5/15
football /'fʊtbɔ:l/ Fußball I
footpath /'fʊtˌpɑ:θ/ Fußweg 3/P12
for /fɔ:/ für I
for /fɔ:/ seit 6/2
for example /fər‿ɪg'zɑ:mpl/ zum Beispiel I

for free /fɔː ˈfriː/ gratis, umsonst I
for he's a jolly good fellow /fə hiz‿ə ˌdʒɒli gʊd ˈfeləʊ/ weil er so ein prima Kerl ist 4/18
foreign /ˈfɒrɪn/ ausländisch, fremd 1/M2
forest /ˈfɒrɪst/ Wald 3/10
forget *(irr)* /fəˈget/ vergessen I
forget about sb/sth /fəˈget‿əˌbaʊt ˌsʌmbədi/ˌsʌmθɪŋ/ jdn/etw vergessen 5/6
forgot /fəˈgɒt/ *Vergangenheitsform von „forget"*
fork /fɔːk/ Gabel I
form /fɔːm/ bilden, formen 4/1
former /ˈfɔːmə/ ehemalige(r, s), frühere(r, s) 2/M1
fortune *(no pl)* /ˈfɔːtʃən/ Schicksal 3/2
fortune-teller /ˈfɔːtʃən ˌtelə/ Wahrsager/in 3/2
fortune-telling *(no pl)* /ˈfɔːtʃən ˌtelɪŋ/ Wahrsagen, Wahrsagerei 3/4
look forward to sth /ˌlʊk ˈfɔːwəd‿tə ˌsʌmθɪŋ/ sich auf etw freuen I
found /faʊnd/ *Vergangenheitsform von „find"*
France /frɑːnts/ Frankreich I
free /friː/ frei I
for free /fɔː ˈfriː/ gratis, umsonst 5/16
freedom *(no pl)* /ˈfriːdəm/ Freiheit 2/M6
French /frentʃ/ Französisch 4/2
French /frentʃ/ französisch 4/2
fresh /freʃ/ frisch 1/11
Friday /ˈfraɪdeɪ/ Freitag I
fridge *(informal)* /frɪdʒ/ Kühlschrank 4/16
friend /frend/ Freund/in I
friendly /ˈfrendli/ freundlich I
make (new) friends /meɪk ˈfrendz/ (neue) Freunde gewinnen 6/P13
fright *(no pl)* /fraɪt/ Angst, Schrecken 6/M5
be frightened (of) /biː ˈfraɪtnd/ Angst haben, sich fürchten (vor) 2/10
frog's leg /frɒgz ˈleg/ Froschschenkel 6/8
from /frəm/ von, aus I
at the front /æt ðə ˈfrʌnt/ vorn(e) 6/M1
in front of /ɪn ˈfrʌnt‿əv/ vor I
fruit /fruːt/ Frucht; Obst I
frustrated /frʌˈstreɪtɪd/ frustriert; enttäuscht I
full /fʊl/ voll 2/6
full /fʊl/ gefüllt 3/P6
fun *(no pl)* /fʌn/ Spaß I
fun /fʌn/ lustig, witzig, spaßig I
be (great) fun /biː (ˌgreɪt) ˈfʌn/ (viel) Spaß machen 3/M4
make fun of sb /meɪk ˈfʌn‿əv ˌsʌmbədi/ sich über jdn lustig machen I
funny /ˈfʌni/ lustig, witzig, komisch I
fur /fɜː/ Fell; Pelz 2/13
future /ˈfjuːtʃə/ Zukunft 3/3
future /ˈfjuːtʃə/ zukünftig, später 3/5

G

game /geɪm/ Spiel I
garden /ˈgɑːdn/ Garten I
gardener /ˈgɑːdnə/ Gärtner/in 2/15
gasp /gɑːsp/ keuchen; nach Luft schnappen 6/CC
gave /geɪv/ *Vergangenheitsform von „give"*
gear /gɪə/ Gang 4/19
Gemini /ˈdʒemɪnaɪ/ Zwilling *(Sternzeichen)* 3/P6
generous /ˈdʒenərəs/ großzügig 4/5
geography /dʒiːˈɒgrəfi/ Erdkunde, Geografie I
German /ˈdʒɜːmən/ Deutsche/r; Deutsch I
German /ˈdʒɜːmən/ deutsch I
in German /ɪn ˈdʒɜːmən/ auf Deutsch I
Germany /ˈdʒɜːməni/ Deutschland I
get *(irr)* /get/ erhalten, bekommen; holen I; werden 1/5
get *(irr)* /get/ steigen 3/M4
get *(irr)* /get/ verstehen 1/CC; (an)kommen 2/6
get down /get ˈdaʊn/ herunterkommen 3/P1
get hurt /get ˈhɜːt/ verletzt werden 4/P4
get into action /ˌget‿ɪntə‿ˈækʃn/ loslegen 3/P6
get to know sb /get‿tə ˈnəʊ ˌsʌmbədi/ jdn kennenlernen 1/P12
get lost /get ˈlɒst/ sich verirren, sich verlaufen Op1
get married /get ˈmærid/ heiraten 2/M1
get off /ˌget‿ˈɒf/ aussteigen 2/6
get ready (for sth) /get ˈredi/ sich (für etw) bereit machen 6/M1
get together /ˌget‿təˈgeðə/ sich treffen; sich sammeln 2/10
get up /get‿ˈʌp/ aufstehen I
get well /get ˈwel/ gesund werden 6/5
get well card /get ˈwel kɑːd/ Genesungskarte 6/3
Get well soon. /get wel ˈsuːn/ Gute Besserung! 6/4
ghost /gəʊst/ Geist, Gespenst 1/2
ghostly /ˈgəʊstli/ geisterhaft; gespenstisch Op1
giggle /ˈgɪgl/ kichern 4/M6
girl /gɜːl/ Mädchen I
give *(irr)* /gɪv/ geben I
give a talk /ˌgɪv‿ə ˈtɔːk/ einen Vortrag halten 1/7
give directions /ˌgɪv dɪˈrekʃnz/ den Weg beschreiben 2/7

give reasons /gɪv ˈriːznz/ begründen, Gründe angeben 5/11
glad /glæd/ glücklich, froh I
glass /glɑːs/ Glas 2/3
glasses *(only pl)* /ˈglɑːsɪz/ Brille I
glove /glʌv/ Handschuh I
go *(irr)* /gəʊ/ gehen I; fahren 1/2
to go /tə ˈgəʊ/ noch 3/M4
go crazy *(informal)* /gəʊ ˈkreɪzi/ durchdrehen, ausflippen I
go for a walk /ˌgəʊ fər‿ə ˈwɔːk/ spazieren gehen I
go out /gəʊ‿ˈaʊt/ ausgehen *(Licht)* Op2
go shopping /gəʊ ˈʃɒpɪŋ/ einkaufen gehen I
go together /gəʊ təˈgeðə/ zusammenpassen 6/P3
go with /ˈgəʊ wɪð/ gehören zu, passen zu 1/1
go-karting *(no pl)* /ˈgəʊˌkɑːtɪŋ/ Gokartfahren 3/M4
goal /gəʊl/ Ziel 1/11
score a goal /skɔːr‿ə ˈgəʊl/ ein Tor schießen 3/10
goat /gəʊt/ Ziege I
god /gɒd/ Gott 1/M2
goddess /ˈgɒdes/ Göttin 4/8
goggle *(informal)* /ˈgɒgl/ starren, glotzen 5/8
going to /ˈgəʊɪŋ tə/ werden 4/3
golden eagle /ˈgəʊldn ˌiːgl/ Goldadler, Steinadler 2/M6
goldfish *(pl -)* /ˈgəʊldˌfɪʃ/ Goldfisch I
gone /gɒn/ *siehe „go"*
good /gʊd/ gut I
be good at sth /bi ˈgʊd‿æt ˌsʌmθɪŋ/ gut in etw sein; etw gut können I
good-looking /ˌgʊdˈlʊkɪŋ/ gut aussehend I
good-luck /ˌgʊd ˈlʌk/ Glücks- 4/3

got /gɒt/ *Vergangenheitsform von „get"*
grammar /ˈgræmə/ Grammatik 3/14
grandfather /ˈgrænˌfɑːðə/ Großvater I
grandma *(informal)* /ˈgrænˌmɑː/ Oma, Omi I
grandmother /ˈgrænˌmʌðə/ Großmutter I
grandparents *(only pl)* /ˈgrænˌpeərənts/ Großeltern I
grass *(no pl)* /grɑːs/ Gras; Wiese, Rasen 2/1
great /greɪt/ groß, riesig; großartig, wunderbar I
Great Britain /ˌgreɪt ˈbrɪtn/ Großbritannien 4/2
Greece /griːs/ Griechenland B
green /griːn/ grün I
greetings *(only pl)* /ˈgriːtɪŋz/ Grüße 6/CC
grew up /gruː‿ˈʌp/ *Vergangenheitsform von „grow up"*
grey /greɪ/ grau I
grid /grɪd/ Gitter; Tabelle 1/2
grocer /ˈgrəʊsə/ Lebensmittelhändler/in 4/M6
ground /graʊnd/ (Erd)boden, Erde 2/P11; Gelände 5/10
group /gruːp/ Gruppe I
grow up /grəʊ‿ˈʌp/ erwachsen werden 3/5
guess /ges/ vermuten, schätzen 6/15
guess /ges/ (er)raten 1/11
guest /gest/ Gast 4/M4
guinea pig /ˈgɪni ˌpɪg/ Meerschweinchen I
guitar /gɪˈtɑː/ Gitarre I
(chewing) gum *(no pl)* /(ˈtʃuːɪŋ) gʌm/ Kaugummi 5/10
guy *(informal)* /gaɪ/ Kerl, Typ 3/10
guys *(only pl)* *(informal)* /gaɪz/ Leute 1/2

gym (= gymnasium) /dʒɪm, dʒɪmˈneɪziəm/ Turnhalle 1/11

H

had /hæd/ *Vergangenheitsform von „have"*
hair *(no pl)* /heə/ Haar(e) I
hairdresser /ˈheəˌdresə/ Friseur/in 3/5
half past (eight) /ˈhɑːf ˌpɑːst/ halb (neun) I
half *(pl* halves*)* /hɑːf, hɑːvz/ Hälfte 4/P12
hall /hɔːl/ Halle; Saal 6/M1
ham *(no pl)* /hæm/ Schinken I
handrail /ˈhændˌreɪl/ Geländer 2/P6
Hands up! /ˌhændz‿ˈʌp/ Hände hoch!; Meldet euch! 5/13
handsome /ˈhænsm/ gut aussehend, attraktiv 3/8
hang *(irr)* /hæŋ/ (auf)hängen I
hang /hæŋ/ erhängen 3/11
Hanukkah /ˈhɑːnəkə/ *jüdisches Lichterfest* 4/1
happen /ˈhæpən/ geschehen, passieren I
happiness *(no pl)* /ˈhæpinəs/ Glück; Zufriedenheit 3/P6
happy /ˈhæpi/ glücklich; zufrieden; fröhlich 1/5
be happy (to do sth) /biː ˈhæpi/ sich freuen (, etw zu tun) 4/16
Happy birthday! /ˌhæpi ˈbɜːθdeɪ/ Alles Gute zum Geburtstag! I
hard /hɑːd/ hart; schwer 3/10
try hard to do sth /ˌtraɪ ˈhɑːd‿tə duː sʌmθɪŋ/ sich sehr bemühen, etw zu tun 2/M6
hard-working /ˌhɑːdˈwɜːkɪŋ/ fleißig 4/5
hat /hæt/ Hut; Mütze I
hate /heɪt/ hassen, nicht ausstehen können I

have *(irr)* /hæv/ haben; essen I
have got /hæv 'gɒt/ haben I
have to /'hæv tə/ müssen I
he /hi/ er I
head /hed/ Kopf I
heading /'hedɪŋ/ Überschrift, Titel Op1
headteacher /ˌhed'tiːtʃə/ Schulleiter/in, Rektor/in 5/15
healthy /'helθi/ gesund 1/11
hear *(irr)* /hɪə/ hören I
heard /hɜːd/ *Vergangenheitsform von „hear"*
by heart /baɪ 'hɑːt/ auswendig 3/13
hello /hə'ləʊ/ hallo I
say hello (to sb) /ˌseɪ hə'ləʊ/ (jdn) (be)grüßen 6/5
helmet /'helmɪt/ Helm I
help /help/ Hilfe I
help /help/ helfen I
help out /ˌhelp‿'aʊt/ (aus)helfen, unterstützen 1/P6
her /hɜː/ sie; ihr(e, n) I
here /hɪə/ hier(her) I
Here you are. /ˌhɪə ju‿'ɑː/ Hier, bitte!, Bitte schön! I
hero *(pl -es)* /'hɪərəʊ, 'hɪərəʊz/ Held/in 3/10
hi /haɪ/ hallo, hi I
hid /hɪd/ *Vergangenheitsform von „hide"*
hide *(irr)* /haɪd/ (sich) verstecken 5/8
hide-and-seek /ˌhaɪd‿ən 'siːk/ Verstecken Op1
high /haɪ/ hoch 2/3
highlight /'haɪˌlaɪt/ Höhepunkt, Highlight 4/M2
hiking *(no pl)* /'haɪkɪŋ/ Wandern 6/11
hiking trip /'haɪkɪŋ trɪp/ Wanderung Op4
hill /hɪl/ Hügel 1/M2
him /hɪm/ ihm, ihn I
Hindu /ˌhɪn'duː/ Hindu; hinduistisch 4/8

hippo (= hippopotamus) /'hɪpəʊ, ˌhɪpə'pɒtəməs/ Nilpferd 2/14
his /hɪz/ sein(e, r) I
history /'hɪstri/ Geschichte I
hit *(irr)* /hɪt/ schlagen I
hold *(irr)* /həʊld/ halten 2/P6
hole /həʊl/ Loch 5/4
holiday /'hɒlɪdeɪ/ Urlaub, Ferien I
holiday /'hɒlɪdeɪ/ Feiertag 4/M1
go on holiday /ˌgəʊ‿ɒn 'hɒlɪdeɪ/ Urlaub machen, in den Urlaub fahren 1/5
home /həʊm/ Zuhause, Heim 2/M6
home /həʊm/ zu Hause; nach Hause 1/2
at home /ət 'həʊm/ zu Hause I
home town /ˌhəʊm 'taʊn/ Heimatort 2/M2
home-baked /ˌhəʊm'beɪkt/ selbst gebacken 4/P5
homework *(no pl)* /'həʊmˌwɜːk/ Hausaufgaben I
honest /'ɒnɪst/ ehrlich 4/5
honey *(no pl)* /'hʌni/ Honig I
hoover /'huːvə/ staubsaugen I
hope /həʊp/ hoffen I
horoscope /'hɒrəˌskəʊp/ Horoskop 3/1
horrible /'hɒrəbl/ schrecklich 2/M3
horse /hɔːs/ Pferd I
hospital /'hɒspɪtl/ Krankenhaus 3/M5
hot /hɒt/ heiß I
hour /'aʊə/ Stunde I
house /haʊs/ Haus I
how /haʊ/ wie I
How about ... ? /'haʊ‿əˌbaʊt/ Was ist mit ... ?, Wie wäre es mit ... ? Op1
How are you? /haʊ‿'ɑː juː/ Wie geht es dir/Ihnen/euch? I

How much is/are ... ? /ˌhaʊ 'mʌtʃ‿ɪz/ɑː/ Was kostet/kosten ... ? I
How old are you? /haʊ‿'əʊld‿ə jʊ/ Wie alt bist du/seid ihr? I
how to /haʊ tə/ wie man 1/5
huge /hjuːdʒ/ riesig, riesengroß 1/M2
hundred /'hʌndrəd/ Hundert 3/M4
hungry /'hʌŋgri/ hungrig I
hunter /'hʌntə/ Jäger/in I
hurry up /ˌhʌri‿'ʌp/ sich beeilen I
hurt sb /'hɜːt ˌsʌmbədi/ jdn verletzen, jdm wehtun I
husband /'hʌzbənd/ Ehemann I
hut /hʌt/ Hütte 2/P12

I

I /aɪ/ ich I
I'm fine. /aɪm 'faɪn/ Es geht mir gut. 1/2
ice cream /'aɪs ˌkriːm/ Eiskrem I
ICT (= information and communication technology) /ˌaɪ siː 'tiː, ˌɪnfəˌmeɪʃn‿ən kəˌmjuːnɪˌkeɪʃn tek'nɒlədʒi/ Informatik I
idea /aɪ'dɪə/ Idee I
if /ɪf/ wenn, falls 5/M1
if /ɪf/ ob 6/M4
ignore /ɪg'nɔː/ ignorieren 5/16
ill /ɪl/ krank 3/5
imagine /ɪ'mædʒɪn/ sich vorstellen 2/2
important /ɪm'pɔːtnt/ wichtig I
in /ɪn/ in I
in a minute /ˌɪn‿ə 'mɪnɪt/ gleich, sofort I
in fact /ɪn 'fækt/ tatsächlich, in Wirklichkeit; sogar 4/M4
in front of /ɪn 'frʌnt‿əv/ vor I
Inca /'ɪŋkə/ Inka 1/M2
including /ɪn'kluːdɪŋ/ einschließlich 4/P5
incredible /ɪn'kredəbl/ unglaublich 6/M1

independent /ˌɪndɪˈpendənt/ unabhängig; selbstständig 4/5
India /ˈɪndiə/ Indien B
Indian /ˈɪndiən/ Inder/in; Indianer/in 4/8
Indian /ˈɪndiən/ indisch; indianisch 4/8
individual /ˌɪndɪˈvɪdʒuəl/ individuell; eigen 5/M5
indoor /ˌɪnˈdɔː/ Hallen- 1/11
information *(no pl)* /ˌɪnfəˈmeɪʃn/ Information I
information point /ˌɪnfəˈmeɪʃn pɔɪnt/ Informationsstelle 2/M5
insect /ˈɪnsekt/ Insekt 2/14
inside /ɪnˈsaɪd/ drinnen; innen; im Inneren 2/CC
instead (of) /ɪnˈsted (‿əv)/ stattdessen; (an)statt 3/M4
interested (in sth) /ˈɪntrəstɪd/ interessiert (an etw) 4/5
interesting /ˈɪntrəstɪŋ/ interessant I
interview /ˈɪntəˌvjuː/ befragen 1/15; interviewen 6/P4
into /ˈɪntʊ/ in 3/M4
invitation /ˌɪnvɪˈteɪʃn/ Einladung I
invite /ɪnˈvaɪt/ einladen I
Ireland /ˈaɪələnd/ Irland 4/7
Irish /ˈaɪrɪʃ/ Irisch 4/7
Irish /ˈaɪrɪʃ/ irisch 4/7
iron /ˈaɪən/ bügeln I
island /ˈaɪlənd/ Insel 2/M5
it /ɪt/ es I
(it's) your turn /ˈjɔː ˌtɜːn/ du bist dran I
Italian /ɪˈtæliən/ Italiener/in; Italienisch 4/2
Italian /ɪˈtæliən/ italienisch 4/2
Italy /ˈɪtəli/ Italien 4/2
its /ɪts/ sein(e), ihr(e) 2/10

J

jacket /ˈdʒækɪt/ Jacke I
jam /dʒæm/ Marmelade I
January /ˈdʒænjuəri/ Januar I
join /dʒɔɪn/ mitmachen bei; beitreten I
joke /dʒəʊk/ Witz Op1
journey /ˈdʒɜːni/ Reise; Fahrt 6/M5
juggler /ˈdʒʌɡlə/ Jongleur/in 2/1
juice /dʒuːs/ Saft I
July /dʒʊˈlaɪ/ Juli I
jump /dʒʌmp/ springen I
junction /ˈdʒʌŋkʃn/ Kreuzung; (Autobahn)abfahrt 6/M5
June /dʒuːn/ Juni I
jungle /ˈdʒʌŋɡl/ Dschungel, Urwald 3/M5
just /dʒʌst/ gleich; einfach 4/11
just /dʒʌst/ noch 3/8; genau 3/P6; nur 6/3
just a minute /ˌdʒʌst‿ə ˈmɪnɪt/ (einen) Moment (bitte), (einen) Augenblick (bitte) 2/6

K

kangaroo /ˌkæŋɡəˈruː/ Känguru I
kayak /ˈkaɪæk/ Kajakfahren 1/P6
keep *(irr)* /kiːp/ (be)halten; aufbewahren I
keep clear of the edges /kiːp ˌklɪər‿əv ði‿ˈedʒɪz/ sich von den Rändern fernhalten 2/P6
keep off /kiːp‿ˈɒf/ wegbleiben; nicht betreten 5/P6
keeper /ˈkiːpə/ Tierpfleger/in 2/10
key /kiː/ Schlüssel I
keyword /ˈkiːˌwɜːd/ Schlüsselwort 3/12
kind /kaɪnd/ Art, Sorte 2/1
king /kɪŋ/ König 2/1
kiss /kɪs/ Kuss 4/14
kiss /kɪs/ küssen 5/8
kitchen /ˈkɪtʃən/ Küche I
knee /niː/ Knie 1/11
knew /njuː/ *Vergangenheitsform von „know"*
knife *(pl* **knives***)* /naɪf, naɪvz/ Messer I
know *(irr)* /nəʊ/ wissen; kennen I
know better /nəʊ ˈbetə/ es besser wissen 5/3
get to know sb /get‿tə ˈnəʊ ˌsʌmbədi/ jdn kennenlernen 1/P12
Komodo dragon /kəˌməʊdəʊ ˈdræɡən/ Komododrache, Komodowaran 2/P12

L

label /ˈleɪbl/ beschriften 5/17
lady /ˈleɪdi/ Frau; Dame 3/2
lake /leɪk/ See 1/M2
Lake Titicaca /leɪk ˌtɪtɪˈkɑːkə/ Titicacasee 1/M2
lamb /læm/ Lamm I
lamp /læmp/ Lampe I
landlady /ˈlænˌleɪdi/ (Gast)wirtin 6/15
language /ˈlæŋɡwɪdʒ/ Sprache 1/M2
large /lɑːdʒ/ groß I
last /lɑːst/ letzte(r, s) I
late /leɪt/ (zu) spät I
be late /biː ˈleɪt/ (zu) spät kommen, sich verspäten I
later /ˈleɪtə/ später 1/5
laugh /lɑːf/ lachen I
lead *(irr)* /liːd/ führen 3/P12
lead singer /liːd ˈsɪŋə/ Leadsänger/in *(seine/ihre Stimme bestimmt den Gesang eines Musikstücks)* 6/M1
leaf *(pl* **leaves***)* /liːf, liːvz/ Blatt 2/M5
learn *(irr)* /lɜːn/ lernen I
learning *(no pl)* /ˈlɜːnɪŋ/ Lernen; Bildung 1/11
least /liːst/ am wenigsten 5/10
leave *(irr)* /liːv/ verlassen 5/10
leave *(irr)* /liːv/ lassen 2/M6
leave *(irr)* /liːv/ abfahren 2/1; (weg)gehen 5/2
leave behind /ˌliːv bɪˈhaɪnd/ zurücklassen 2/M6

left /left/ (nach) links 2/6
left /left/ übrig 4/14
left /left/ *Vergangenheitsform von „leave"*
on the/your left /ˌɒn ðə/jɔː ˈleft/ links, auf der linken Seite 2/6
leftovers *(only pl)* /ˈleftˌəʊvəz/ Reste 4/M1
leg /leg/ Bein I
lemonade /ˌleməˈneɪd/ Limonade I
length /leŋθ/ Länge 1/11
Leo /ˈliːəʊ/ Löwe *(Sternzeichen)* 3/M2
lesson /ˈlesn/ Stunde I
let *(irr)* /let/ lassen 3/12
let go /let ˈgəʊ/ loslassen 6/CC
let sb in /ˌlet ˌsʌmbədi‿ˈɪn/ jdn hereinlassen 2/12
let's (= let us) /lets, ˈlet‿əs/ lass(t) uns I
Let's go! /lets ˈgəʊ/ Los!, Auf geht's! 3/M4
letter /ˈletə/ Brief; Buchstabe 5/M4
Libra /ˈliːbrə/ Waage *(Sternzeichen)* 3/M2
librarian /laɪˈbreəriən/ Bibliothekar/in 1/11
library /ˈlaɪbrəri/ Bibliothek, Bücherei I
lie ahead /ˌlaɪ‿əˈhed/ bevorstehen, vor jdm liegen 3/8
life *(pl* **lives***)* /laɪf, laɪvz/ Leben 2/1
light /laɪt/ Licht I
light *(irr)* /laɪt/ erhellen; aufleuchten 3/CC
like /laɪk/ mögen I
like /laɪk/ wie 2/3
What's ... like? /wɒts ˈlaɪk/ Wie ist ... ? 1/6
like that /laɪk ˈðæt/ so 5/8
like this /laɪk ˈðɪs/ so 1/2
line /laɪn/ Linie; Zeile Op1
linking word /ˈlɪŋkɪŋ wɜːd/ Bindewort Op4
lion /ˈlaɪən/ Löwe I
list /lɪst/ Liste I
listen (to) /ˈlɪsn/ (zu)hören I
litter *(no pl)* /ˈlɪtə/ Müll, Abfall 5/10
littering *(no pl)* /ˈlɪtərɪŋ/ Vermüllen 5/P6
little /ˈlɪtl/ klein I
a little /ə ˈlɪtl/ ein bisschen 4/14
live /lɪv/ leben, wohnen I
living room /ˈlɪvɪŋ ˌruːm/ Wohnzimmer I
logo /ˈləʊgəʊ/ Abzeichen, Logo 1/11
lonely /ˈləʊnli/ einsam 1/5
long /lɒŋ/ lang I
no longer /nəʊ ˈlɒŋgə/ nicht mehr 6/18
look /lʊk/ sehen, schauen I; aussehen 2/10
take a closer look /teɪk‿ə ˌkləʊsə ˈlʊk/ sich (jdn/etw) genauer ansehen 6/P10
take a look (at) /teɪk‿ə ˈlʊk/ einen Blick werfen (auf) 2/P5
look after /ˌlʊk‿ˈɑːftə/ sich kümmern um I
look at /ˈlʊk‿ət/ betrachten, sehen, anschauen I
look for /ˈlʊk fɔː/ suchen (nach) I
look forward to sth /ˌlʊk ˈfɔːwəd‿tə ˌsʌmθɪŋ/ sich auf etw freuen I
look up /lʊk‿ˈʌp/ nachschlagen 1/11
lose *(irr)* /luːz/ verlieren 2/6
be lost /biː ˈlɒst/ sich verirrt haben, sich verlaufen haben Op1
get lost /get ˈlɒst/ sich verirren, sich verlaufen Op1
a lot (of) /ə ˈlɒt/ sehr; viel(e) I
lots of /ˈlɒts‿əv/ viel, jede Menge I
loud /laʊd/ laut 3/11
love /lʌv/ Liebe I
love /lʌv/ herzliche Grüße, alles Liebe 5/M4
love /lʌv/ lieben; sehr gern mögen I
fall in love (with) /ˌfɔːl‿ɪn ˈlʌv/ sich verlieben (in) 3/8
lovely /ˈlʌvli/ schön, hübsch I
lover /ˈlʌvə/ Liebhaber/in; Liebende(r) 3/8; Freund(in) 6/11
lower /ˈləʊə/ senken 4/CC
luck *(no pl)* /lʌk/ Glück 3/P6
lucky /ˈlʌki/ glücklich, glücksbringend, Glücks- 3/2
be lucky /biː ˈlʌki/ Glück haben I
lunch /lʌntʃ/ Mittagessen I
lunchtime /ˈlʌntʃˌtaɪm/ Mittagszeit; Mittagspause 1/11

M

machine /məˈʃiːn/ Maschine I
made /meɪd/ *Vergangenheitsform von „make"*
magazine /ˌmægəˈziːn/ Zeitschrift, Magazin I
magnifying glass /ˈmægnɪfaɪɪŋ glɑːs/ Lupe 2/M3
major /ˈmeɪdʒə/ bedeutend, wichtig 3/P12
Majorca /məˈjɔːkə/ Mallorca 1/2
make *(irr)* /meɪk/ machen I
make fun of sb /meɪk ˈfʌn‿əv ˌsʌmbədi/ sich über jdn lustig machen I
make money /meɪk ˈmʌni/ Geld verdienen 3/10
make (new) friends /meɪk ˈfrendz/ (neue) Freunde gewinnen 6/P13
make notes /meɪk ˈnəʊts/ (sich) Notizen machen 1/15
make one's way /ˌmeɪk wʌnz ˈweɪ/ gehen 6/M1

make up sth /ˌmeɪk‿ˈʌp ˌsʌmθɪŋ/ (sich) etw ausdenken, etw erfinden 1/14
put on make-up /pʊt‿ˌɒn ˈmeɪkˌʌp/ sich schminken 5/5
man *(pl* **men***)* /mæn, men/ Mann I
mantelpiece /ˈmæntlˌpiːs/ Kaminsims 4/M1
many /ˈmeni/ viele I
map /mæp/ (Land)karte I
March /mɑːtʃ/ März I
mark /mɑːk/ (Schul)note 1/M3
market /ˈmɑːkɪt/ Markt I
get married /get ˈmærid/ heiraten 2/M1
marry /ˈmæri/ heiraten 3/2
master /ˈmɑːstə/ Herr; Herrchen 6/15
match /mætʃ/ Spiel I
match /mætʃ/ Streichholz, Zündholz I
match (with) /mætʃ/ zuordnen 2/1
maths /mæθs/ Mathe I
What's the matter? /ˌwɒts ðə ˈmætə/ Was ist (denn) los? 2/10
May /meɪ/ Mai I
may /meɪ/ können; dürfen 6/7
may not /meɪ ˈnɒt/ nicht dürfen 6/2
maybe /ˈmeɪbi/ vielleicht, möglicherweise I
me /miː/ mir, mich I
meal /miːl/ Mahlzeit, Essen 2/10
mean *(irr)* /miːn/ bedeuten; meinen 1/M2
mean /miːn/ gemein, fies 5/15
meaning /ˈmiːnɪŋ/ Bedeutung 1/11
means of transport /miːnz‿əv ˈtrænspɔːt/ Verkehrsmittel 6/M8
meat *(no pl)* /miːt/ Fleisch I
medal /ˈmedl/ Medaille 2/M1
medical bag /ˈmedɪkl bæg/ Medikamentenkoffer 2/M3
meerkat /ˈmɪəˌkæt/ Erdmännchen 2/M5
meet *(irr)* /miːt/ (sich) treffen; kennenlernen I
Nice to meet you. /ˌnaɪs tə ˈmiːt jə/ Es freut mich, Sie/dich kennenzulernen. I
melt /melt/ schmelzen 4/CC
member /ˈmembə/ Mitglied I
mention /ˈmenʃn/ erwähnen 2/M2
mess /mes/ Unordnung, Durcheinander; Schweinerei 4/M4
be a mess /ˌbi‿ə ˈmes/ chaotisch/durcheinander sein 5/M3
message /ˈmesɪdʒ/ Nachricht 4/15
met /met/ *Vergangenheitsform von „meet"*
metre /ˈmiːtə/ Meter 2/1
middle /ˈmɪdl/ Mitte 4/CC
in the middle /ˌɪn ðə ˈmɪdl/ in der Mitte; mitten in/auf 2/1
midnight *(no pl)* /ˈmɪdˌnaɪt/ Mitternacht 5/9
might /maɪt/ könnte 5/CC
mile /maɪl/ Meile 5/15
milk *(no pl)* /mɪlk/ Milch I
milkshake /ˈmɪlkˌʃeɪk/ Milchshake 3/M4
mince pie /ˈmɪns paɪ/ *Kuchen gefüllt mit Dörrobst und Sirup* 4/M1
miniskirt /ˈmɪniˌskɜːt/ Minirock 5/10
mint *(no pl)* /mɪnt/ Minze 4/P12
minute /ˈmɪnɪt/ Minute I
in a minute /ˌɪn‿ə ˈmɪnɪt/ gleich, sofort I
just a minute /ˌdʒʌst‿ə ˈmɪnɪt/ (einen) Moment (bitte), (einen) Augenblick (bitte) 2/6
mirror /ˈmɪrə/ Spiegel 2/CC
miss /mɪs/ vermissen, verpassen I
mix /mɪks/ (ver)mischen, anrühren 4/CC
mix in /mɪks‿ˈɪn/ untermischen, untermengen 4/P12
mixture /ˈmɪkstʃə/ Mischung 4/CC
mobile (= mobile phone) /ˈməʊbaɪl, ˌməʊbaɪl ˈfəʊn/ Mobiltelefon, Handy I
moment /ˈməʊmənt/ Moment, Augenblick 3/11
at the moment /æt ðə ˈməʊmənt/ im Moment 6/M8
Monday /ˈmʌndeɪ/ Montag I
money *(no pl)* /ˈmʌni/ Geld I
make money /meɪk ˈmʌni/ Geld verdienen 3/10
monkey /ˈmʌŋki/ Affe I
month /mʌnθ/ Monat I
moon /muːn/ Mond 3/7
moonlight /ˈmuːnˌlaɪt/ Mondlicht 1/M2
more /mɔː/ (noch) mehr I
morning /ˈmɔːnɪŋ/ Morgen I
in the morning /ˌɪn ðə ˈmɔːnɪŋ/ morgens, am Morgen, vormittags I
morning break /ˈmɔːnɪŋ ˌbreɪk/ Frühstückspause 1/11
most /məʊst/ die meisten 1/5
mother /ˈmʌðə/ Mutter I
Mother's Day /ˈmʌðəz deɪ/ Muttertag 4/6
motorbike /ˈməʊtəˌbaɪk/ Motorrad 6/M8
mountain /ˈmaʊntɪn/ Berg 6/11
mountain biking *(no pl)* /ˈmaʊntɪn ˌbaɪkɪŋ/ Mountainbiken, Mountainbike fahren 6/11
mouse *(pl* **mice***)* /maʊs, maɪs/ Maus I
mouth /maʊθ/ Mund I
move /muːv/ sich bewegen; umziehen B
Mr /ˈmɪstə/ Herr *(Anrede)* I
Mrs /ˈmɪsɪz/ Frau *(Anrede)* I
much /mʌtʃ/ viel; sehr I
muesli *(no pl)* /ˈmjuːzli/ Müsli I
mum *(informal)* /mʌm/ Mama, Mutti I

Munich /ˈmjuːnɪk/ München 6/14
music *(no pl)* /ˈmjuːzɪk/ Musik I
must /mʌst/ müssen 2/10
must not /mʌst ˈnɒt/ nicht dürfen 5/3
must-see /ˌmʌstˈsiː/ *etw, das man gesehen haben muss* 2/1
my /maɪ/ mein(e) I
my name is /maɪ ˈneɪm‿ˌɪz/ ich heiße I
myself /maɪˈself/ mich, mir; selbst 6/CC
mysterious /mɪˈstɪəriəs/ geheimnisvoll, mysteriös 1/M2

N

name /neɪm/ Name I
name /neɪm/ (be)nennen 3/P1
my name is /maɪ ˈneɪm‿ˌɪz/ ich heiße I
What's your name? /ˌwɒts jə ˈneɪm/ Wie heißt du?, Wie heißen Sie? I
narrator /nəˈreɪtə/ Erzähler/in 3/15
narrow /ˈnærəʊ/ eng, schmal 2/M3
nature *(no pl)* /ˈneɪtʃə/ Natur 6/11
naughty /ˈnɔːti/ ungezogen, frech 2/M6
near /nɪə/ nah(e) I
nearly /ˈnɪəli/ fast, beinahe 5/M4
neck /nek/ Hals; Nacken 2/CC
need /niːd/ brauchen I
neighbour /ˈneɪbə/ Nachbar/in I
nervous /ˈnɜːvəs/ nervös 6/P12
nervously /ˈnɜːvəsli/ nervös; aufgeregt Op1
never /ˈnevə/ nie(mals) I
new /njuː/ neu I
New Year /ˌnjuː ˈjɪə/ Neujahr 4/3
New Year's Eve /ˌnjuː jɪəz‿ˈiːv/ Silvester 4/1
news *(no pl)* /njuːz/ Neuigkeit; Nachrichten 2/10
news just in /ˌnjuːz dʒʌst‿ˈɪn/ Gerade kommt eine Meldung herein. 2/10
newspaper /ˈnjuːzˌpeɪpə/ Zeitung 2/M6
newsreader /ˈnjuːzˌriːdə/ Nachrichtensprecher/in 2/10
next /nekst/ nächste(r, s) I
the next day /ðə ˌnekst ˈdeɪ/ am nächsten Tag 2/8
next door /ˌnekst ˈdɔː/ neben(an) B
next to /ˈnekst‿tə/ neben I
nice /naɪs/ schön, angenehm; nett, freundlich I
Nice to meet you. /ˌnaɪs tə ˈmiːt jə/ Es freut mich, Sie/dich kennenzulernen. I
night /naɪt/ Nacht I
night /naɪt/ Abend 1/M2
at night /æt ˈnaɪt/ nachts 4/M1
no /nəʊ/ nein; kein(e) I
no longer /nəʊ ˈlɒŋgə/ nicht mehr 6/18
no one /ˈnəʊ wʌn/ keiner, niemand 4/3
no way /nəʊ ˈweɪ/ keine Chance 5/CC
noise /nɔɪz/ Lärm, Krach; Geräusch 2/10
non- /nɒn/ nicht- 1/CC
nonsense /ˈnɒnsns/ Unsinn, Quatsch 4/11
noodle /ˈnuːdl/ Nudel 4/3
normally /ˈnɔːmli/ normalerweise I
north /nɔːθ/ Norden I
North Pole /ˌnɔːθ ˈpəʊl/ Nordpol 2/P12
nose /nəʊz/ Nase I
not /nɒt/ nicht I
not any /nɒt‿ˈeni/ kein(e) 3/2
not anymore /ˌnɒt eniˈmɔː/ nicht mehr 1/M2
not anyone /nɒt‿ˈeniwʌn/ niemand 3/2
not anywhere /nɒt‿ˈeniˌweə/ nirgendwo(hin) 6/2
not yet /nɒt ˈjet/ noch nicht 6/15
note /nəʊt/ Notiz 1/2
note down /nəʊt ˈdaʊn/ (sich) notieren 1/11
make notes /meɪk ˈnəʊts/ (sich) Notizen machen 1/15
take notes /teɪk ˈnəʊts/ (sich) Notizen machen 1/M3
nothing /ˈnʌθɪŋ/ nichts 3/2
notice /ˈnəʊtɪs/ bemerken I
noticeboard /ˈnəʊtɪsˌbɔːd/ schwarzes Brett 1/15
November /nəʊˈvembə/ November I
now /naʊ/ jetzt I
now /naʊ/ also 4/16
number /ˈnʌmbə/ Zahl; Ziffer, Nummer I
nurse /nɜːs/ (Kranken)schwester, (Kranken)pfleger 3/5

O

(seven) o'clock /əˈklɒk/ (sieben) Uhr I
oak /əʊk/ Eiche 3/P12
October /ɒkˈtəʊbə/ Oktober I
be the odd one out /biː ði‿ˌɒd wʌn‿ˈaʊt/ aus der Reihe fallen, nicht dazugehören 2/P1
of /əv/ von I
of course /əv ˈkɔːs/ natürlich I
off /ɒf/ herunter, hinunter 4/P4
offer /ˈɒfə/ (an)bieten 1/11
office /ˈɒfɪs/ Büro I
often /ˈɒfn/ oft, häufig I
Oh dear! /əʊ ˈdɪə/ Du meine Güte! 2/10
oil /ɔɪl/ Öl 4/M2
old /əʊld/ alt I
How old are you? /haʊ‿ˈəʊld‿ə jʊ/ Wie alt bist du/seid ihr? I
Olympic Games /əˌlɪmpɪk ˈgeɪmz/ Olympische Spiele 3/M5
on /ɒn/ auf, an; in; am I
on /ɒn/ im I

on /ɒn/ weiter 2/7
on its own /ɒn‿ɪts‿ˈəʊn/ von allein, von selbst 5/16
on one's own /ɒn wʌnz‿ˈəʊn/ allein(e) 1/15
once /wʌns/ einmal 4/17
one /wʌn/ eins; ein(e) I
one day /ˈwʌn deɪ/ eines Tages 3/2
only /ˈəʊnli/ nur I
open /ˈəʊpən/ (sich) öffnen I
open /ˈəʊpən/ offen, geöffnet I
opening times *(only pl)* /ˈəʊpnɪŋ ˌtaɪmz/ Öffnungszeiten 6/M5
opinion /əˈpɪnjən/ Meinung, Ansicht 5/6
opposite /ˈɒpəzɪt/ Gegenteil 5/P1
opposite /ˈɒpəzɪt/ gegenüberliegend 4/CC
optimistic /ˌɒptɪˈmɪstɪk/ optimistisch, zuversichtlich 4/5
or /ɔː/ oder I
orange /ˈɒrɪndʒ/ Orange, Apfelsine I
orange /ˈɒrɪndʒ/ orange(farben) I
order /ˈɔːdə/ Ordnung, Reihenfolge 1/14
other /ˈʌðər/ andere(r, s) I
otherwise /ˈʌðəˌwaɪz/ sonst, ansonsten 1/M3
our /aʊə/ unser(e) I
ours /ˈaʊəz/ unsere(r, s) 3/8
out /aʊt/ nach draußen, (he)raus Op1
be out /ˌbi‿ˈaʊt/ nicht mehr im Spiel sein, draußen sein 4/M6
out of /ˈaʊt‿əv/ (her)aus 6/15
be out of the question /bi‿ˌaʊt‿əv ðə ˈkwestʃn/ nicht infrage kommen 6/15
outdoor /ˌaʊtˈdɔː/ im Freien 1/11
outside /ˌaʊtˈsaɪd/ im Freien, draußen I
outside /ˌaʊtˈsaɪd/ nach draußen, raus 5/M4
outside /ˌaʊtˈsaɪd/ (draußen) vor 2/10
over /ˈəʊvə/ über I
over /ˈəʊvə/ hinüber; vorbei 4/M6
over there /ˌəʊvə ˈðeə/ dort (drüben) I
own /əʊn/ eigene(r, s) 3/7
on its own /ɒn‿ɪts‿ˈəʊn/ von allein, von selbst 5/16
on one's own /ɒn wʌnz‿ˈəʊn/ allein(e) 1/15
owner /ˈəʊnə/ Besitzer/in, Eigentümer/in 4/3
ox *(pl -en)* /ɒks/ Ochse 4/5

P

p (= penny, pence) /piː, ˈpeni, pens/ Penny, Centstück 2/M6
the Pacific (Ocean) /ðə pəˌsɪfɪk(‿ˈəʊʃn)/ der Pazifische Ozean 3/M5
pack /pæk/ packen I
packed lunch /ˌpækt ˈlʌntʃ/ Lunchpaket 5/10
paddle /ˈpædl/ paddeln; planschen 6/CC
page /peɪdʒ/ Seite 1/11
paint /peɪnt/ (an)malen 5/8
pair /peə/ Paar 1/8
pakora /pəˈkɔːrə/ *frittiertes Gemüsestück* 4/8
palace /ˈpæləs/ Palast 2/1
paper *(no pl)* /ˈpeɪpə/ Papier I
parade /pəˈreɪd/ Parade, Umzug 4/3
parent-teacher meeting /ˌpeərəntˈtiːtʃə ˌmiːtɪŋ/ Elternsprechtag; Elternabend 5/15
parents *(only pl)* /ˈpeərənts/ Eltern I
parrot /ˈpærət/ Papagei I
part /pɑːt/ Teil 2/3
take part (in) /ˌteɪk ˈpɑːt/ teilnehmen (an) 1/11
pass /pɑːs/ Pass 6/M1
pass /pɑːs/ vorbeikommen 2/1
past /pɑːst/ Vergangenheit 3/10
past /pɑːst/ vorbei/vorüber an 2/6
patient /ˈpeɪʃnt/ geduldig 4/5
paw /pɔː/ Pfote, Tatze 2/13
pay /peɪ/ bezahlen I
PE (= physical education) /ˌpi‿ˈiː, ˌfɪzɪkl‿ˌedjʊˈkeɪʃn/ Sport(unterricht) I
peaceful /ˈpiːsfl/ friedlich 4/5
peel /piːl/ schälen 4/P12
pen /pen/ Stift I
pencil /ˈpensl/ Bleistift I
pencil case /ˈpensl ˌkeɪs/ (Feder)mäppchen I
pencil sharpener /ˈpensl ˌʃɑːpnə/ (Bleistift)spitzer I
penguin /ˈpeŋgwɪn/ Pinguin I
people *(no pl)* /ˈpiːpl/ Leute, Menschen I
people /ˈpiːpl/ Volk 1/M2
pepper *(no pl)* /ˈpepə/ Pfeffer 4/P12
per /pɜː/ pro 1/P6
perfect /ˈpɜːfɪkt/ perfekt 2/1
perform /pəˈfɔːm/ vorführen; aufführen 4/M2
perfume /ˈpɜːfjuːm/ Parfüm 4/11
perhaps /pəˈhæps/ vielleicht 2/10
person /ˈpɜːsn/ Person, Mensch 3/10
personal /ˈpɜːsnəl/ persönlich; privat 1/11
pet /pet/ Haustier I
pet /pet/ streicheln I
phone /fəʊn/ Telefon I
phone /fəʊn/ anrufen I
(phone) call /(ˈfəʊn) kɔːl/ (Telefon)anruf 3/2
photo /ˈfəʊtəʊ/ Foto I
take photos /ˌteɪk ˈfəʊtəʊz/ Bilder machen, fotografieren 1/5
phrase /freɪz/ Satz; Ausdruck, (Rede)wendung 2/M1
piano /piˈænəʊ/ Klavier 1/M3

pick /pɪk/ aussuchen, auswählen 6/P12
take a picnic /teɪk‿ə 'pɪknɪk/ etw zum Essen mitnehmen 6/15
pictogram /'pɪktəgræm/ Piktogramm 5/9
picture /'pɪktʃə/ Bild, Foto I
pig /pɪg/ Schwein I
pillow /'pɪləʊ/ Kissen 5/8
pilot /'paɪlət/ Pilot/in 3/5
pinch /pɪntʃ/ Prise 4/P12
pink /pɪŋk/ rosa, pink I
pipe /paɪp/ Pfeife 2/M3
pirate /'paɪrət/ Pirat, Seeräuber I
Pisces /'paɪsi:z/ Fische *(Sternzeichen)* 3/M2
What a pity! /wɒt‿ə 'pɪti/ Wie schade! 4/17
place /pleɪs/ Ort; Platz I
placemat /'pleɪs,mæt/ Set, Platzdeckchen 5/16
plan /plæn/ planen 1/15
plane /pleɪn/ Flugzeug 3/5
planner /'plænə/ Kalender zur Arbeitsplanung 1/11
plant /plɑ:nt/ Pflanze 3/5
plastic /'plæstɪk/ Plastik, Kunststoff 4/M1
plate /pleɪt/ Teller I
platform /'plæt,fɔ:m/ Plattform; Bahnsteig, Gleis 2/1
play /pleɪ/ (Theater)stück I
play /pleɪ/ Spiel; Hörspiel 3/15
play /pleɪ/ spielen I
player /'pleɪə/ Spieler/in I
playground /'pleɪ,graʊnd/ Spielplatz I
please /pli:z/ bitte I
pm (= post meridiem) /,pi:'em, ,pəʊst mə'rɪdiəm/ nachmittags, abends *(nur hinter Uhrzeit zwischen 12 Uhr mittags und Mitternacht)* 1/11
pocket /'pɒkɪt/ Tasche 2/P7
poem /'pəʊɪm/ Gedicht 1/P7

Poland /'pəʊlənd/ Polen 6/14
police *(no pl)* /pə'li:s/ Polizei 2/10
police officer /pə'li:s ,ɒfɪsə/ Polizeibeamter/-beamtin 2/11
polite /pə'laɪt/ höflich 4/17
poor /pɔ:/ arm I
popular /'pɒpjʊlə/ beliebt 6/M5
portfolio /pɔ:t'fəʊliəʊ/ (Akten)mappe 1/7
possible /'pɒsəbəl/ möglich 1/14
postcard /'pəʊst,kɑ:d/ Postkarte 1/2
potato *(pl* **-es***)* /pə'teɪtəʊ, pə'teɪtəʊz/ Kartoffel 4/16
pound /paʊnd/ Pfund *(brit. Währung)* 3/10
practice /'præktɪs/ Übung; Training 1/P
practise /'præktɪs/ üben 6/M1
prawn crackers *(only pl)* /,prɔ:n 'krækəz/ Krabbenchips 4/3
predator /'predətə/ Raubtier 2/13
prefer /prɪ'fɜ:/ vorziehen, bevorzugen, lieber mögen 1/M3
prepare /prɪ'peə/ (sich) vorbereiten 1/15
present /'preznt/ Geschenk I
present /prɪ'zent/ präsentieren 1/7
presentation /,prezn'teɪʃn/ Präsentation 1/15
pretty /'prɪti/ hübsch 3/8
price /praɪs/ Preis I
primary school /'praɪməri ,sku:l/ Grundschule 1/M3
prize /praɪz/ Preis, Gewinn 4/M4
probably /'prɒbəbli/ wahrscheinlich 6/M1
programme /'prəʊgræm/ Programm 6/11; Sendung 6/7
project /'prɒdʒekt/ Projekt 1/15
promise /'prɒmɪs/ versprechen 6/2
property *(no pl)* /'prɒpəti/ Eigentum 5/10

protect /prə'tekt/ (be)schützen 3/M5
proud /praʊd/ stolz 4/5
pudding /'pʊdɪŋ/ Süßspeise, Nachspeise 4/M4
pull /pʊl/ ziehen 4/M1
purple /'pɜ:pl/ violett, lila(farben) I
put *(irr)* /pʊt/ setzen, legen, stellen I
put *(irr)* /pʊt/ anordnen, sortieren 1/8
put away /pʊt‿ə'weɪ/ wegräumen 6/P5
put on /pʊt‿'ɒn/ anziehen; sich eincremen mit 1/CC
put on make-up /pʊt‿,ɒn 'meɪk,ʌp/ sich schminken 5/5
put one's hand up /pʊt wʌnz 'hænd‿ʌp/ sich melden 5/M4
put up /pʊt‿'ʌp/ aufhängen 1/15; aufstellen 4/M1
pyjamas *(only pl)* /pə'dʒɑ:məz/ Pyjama, Schlafanzug 5/8

Q

quarter (to/past) /'kwɔ:tə/ Viertel (vor/nach) I
queen /kwi:n/ Königin 2/1
question /'kwestʃn/ Frage I
be out of the question /bi‿,aʊt‿əv ðə 'kwestʃn/ nicht infrage kommen 6/15
queue /kju:/ Schlange, Reihe 2/6
quick /kwɪk/ schnell 2/10
quiet /'kwaɪət/ leise, ruhig I
quite /kwaɪt/ ziemlich 1/M3
quiz sb /'kwɪz ,sʌmbədi/ jdn befragen/prüfen 4/9

R

rabbit /'ræbɪt/ Kaninchen I
race /reɪs/ Rennen 3/M4
radio station /'reɪdiəʊ ,steɪʃn/ Radiosender 6/3
railway /'reɪlweɪ/ Gleise, Schienen; (Eisen)bahn 2/1

rain /reɪn/ regnen 1/2
rainbow /ˈreɪnˌbəʊ/ Regenbogen 3/8
rainforest /ˈreɪnˌfɒrɪst/ Regenwald 3/M5
rainy /ˈreɪni/ regnerisch I
raise /reɪz/ heben 4/CC
raita /ˈraɪtə/ *Joghurt mit Gurke und Minze* 4/P12
ran /ræn/ *Vergangenheitsform von „run"*
rare /reə/ selten, rar 2/P12
rat /ræt/ Ratte 4/5
RE (= religious education) /ˌɑː(r)‿ˈiː, rəˌlɪdʒəs‿ˌedjʊˈkeɪʃn/ Religion(sunterricht) I
reach /riːtʃ/ greifen; erreichen 2/6
reaction (to) /riˈækʃn/ Reaktion (auf) 2/12
read *(irr)* /riːd/ lesen I
read along /ˌriːd‿əˈlɒŋ/ mitlesen 2/6
read sth to sb /ˈriːd ˌsʌmθɪŋ tə ˌsʌmbədi/ jdm etw vorlesen 3/P2
reader /ˈriːdə/ Leser/in 4/M4
reading /ˈriːdɪŋ/ Lesen; Lesung 3/13
ready /ˈredi/ fertig, bereit I
get ready (for sth) /get ˈredi/ sich (für etw) bereit machen 6/M1
real /rɪəl/ wirklich; echt 2/1
really /ˈrɪəli/ wirklich I
give reasons /gɪv ˈriːznz/ begründen, Gründe angeben 5/11
recipe /ˈresəpi/ Rezept 4/P12
recognize /ˈrekəgnaɪz/ (wieder)erkennen 3/11
record /rɪˈkɔːd/ aufnehmen, aufzeichnen 3/15
red /red/ rot I
refreshment /rɪˈfreʃmənt/ Erfrischung 4/P5
registration /ˌredʒɪˈstreɪʃn/ Anmeldung; Überprüfung der Anwesenheit 1/10
regular /ˈregjʊlə/ regelmäßig; normal 5/P10
reindeer /ˈreɪnˌdɪə/ Rentier 4/M1
relative /ˈrelətɪv/ Verwandte(r), Angehörige(r) 4/M1
relax /rɪˈlæks/ sich entspannen 2/1
relaxed /rɪˈlækst/ entspannt; locker, gelassen 5/M1
reliable /rɪˈlaɪəbl/ verlässlich, zuverlässig 4/5
remember /rɪˈmembə/ (an etw) denken 3/11
remember /rɪˈmembə/ sich erinnern (an) I
repair /rɪˈpeə/ reparieren 3/5
repeat /riˈpiːt/ wiederholen 1/M3
report /rɪˈpɔːt/ Bericht I
report /rɪˈpɔːt/ berichten, melden 5/15
report (to sb) /rɪˈpɔːt/ (sich) (bei jdm) melden 5/10
request /rɪˈkwest/ Bitte, Anfrage; Wunsch 6/3
request sth /rɪˈkwest ˌsʌmθɪŋ/ um etw bitten; (sich) etw wünschen 6/5
respect *(no pl)* /rɪˈspekt/ Respekt, Achtung 5/10
result /rɪˈzʌlt/ Ergebnis; Folge 2/10
rhyming pair /ˈraɪmɪŋ peə/ Reimpaar 2/P9
rhyming word /ˈraɪmɪŋ wɜːd/ Reimwort 5/8
rice *(no pl)* /raɪs/ Reis 4/M4
rich /rɪtʃ/ reich 3/2
the rich *(no pl)* /ðə ˈrɪtʃ/ die Reichen 3/10
ride /raɪd/ Fahrt; (Aus)ritt 2/CC; Fahrgeschäft 6/M5
ride *(irr)* /raɪd/ fahren; reiten I
ride a bike /ˌraɪd‿ə ˈbaɪk/ (Fahr)rad fahren I
riding *(no pl)* /ˈraɪdɪŋ/ Reiten I
right /raɪt/ richtig I
right /raɪt/ (nach) rechts 2/6
right /raɪt/ genau, direkt 1/M3
be right /biː ˈraɪt/ Recht haben I
on the/your right /ˌɒn ðə/jɔː ˈraɪt/ rechts, auf der rechten Seite 2/7
river /ˈrɪvə/ Fluss I
road /rəʊd/ Straße I
roar /rɔː/ brüllen 4/M6
robot /ˈrəʊbɒt/ Roboter 3/7
rode /rəʊd/ *Vergangenheitsform von „ride"*
role /rəʊl/ Rolle 3/13
roller coaster /ˈrəʊlə ˌkəʊstə/ Achterbahn 6/M5
Rome /rəʊm/ Rom 6/8
room /ruːm/ Zimmer I
rooster /ˈruːstə/ Hahn 4/5
rope /rəʊp/ Seil I
rubber *(BE)* /ˈrʌbə/ Radiergummi I
rubbish *(no pl)* /ˈrʌbɪʃ/ Müll I
rule /ruːl/ Regel 4/5
ruler /ˈruːlə/ Lineal I
run *(irr)* /rʌn/ laufen, rennen I
run *(irr)* /rʌn/ fahren, verkehren 6/M5
runaway /ˈrʌnəˌweɪ/ entlaufen 2/11
runner /ˈrʌnə/ Läufer/in I
Russia /ˈrʌʃə/ Russland I
Russian /ˈrʌʃn/ Russe/Russin; Russisch 4/2
Russian /ˈrʌʃn/ russisch 4/2

S

sacred /ˈseɪkrɪd/ heilig 1/M2
sad /sæd/ traurig 1/5
safe /seɪf/ sicher 5/16
Sagittarius /ˌsædʒɪˈteəriəs/ Schütze *(Sternzeichen)* 3/M2
said /sed/ *Vergangenheitsform von „say"*
sailing *(no pl)* /ˈseɪlɪŋ/ Segeln 6/11
salad /ˈsæləd/ Salat 5/6
salt *(no pl)* /sɔːlt/ Salz 4/P12
the same /ðə ˈseɪm/ der-/die-/dasselbe 1/12

the same /ðə 'seɪm/ gleich 4/13
samosa /sə'məʊsə/ *gefüllte Teigtasche* 4/8
sari /'sɑːri/ Sari *(gewickeltes Gewand indischer Frauen)* 4/M2
Saturday /'sætədeɪ/ Samstag I
sauce /sɔːs/ Soße 4/17
sausage /'sɒsɪdʒ/ Wurst, Würstchen I
save /seɪv/ retten; sparen 6/M5
saw /sɔː/ *Vergangenheitsform von „see"*
say *(irr)* /seɪ/ sagen I
say hello (to sb) /ˌseɪ hə'ləʊ/ (jdn) (be)grüßen 6/5
be scared (of sth) /biː 'skeəd/ (vor etw) Angst haben 6/15
scarf *(pl* **-s** *or* **scarves***)* /skɑːf, skɑːvz/ Schal I
scary /'skeəri/ Furcht erregend; unheimlich 2/1
scene /siːn/ Szene 3/9
school /skuːl/ Schule I
schoolbag /'skuːlbæg/ Schultasche I
science /'saɪəns/ Naturwissenschaft I
(pair of) scissors *(only pl)* /'sɪzəz/ Schere I
score a goal /skɔːr‿ə 'gəʊl/ ein Tor schießen 3/10
Scorpio /'skɔːpiəʊ/ Skorpion *(Sternzeichen)* 3/M2
Scotland /'skɒtlənd/ Schottland 1/2
scream /skriːm/ schreien; kreischen 6/M1
screen /skriːn/ Leinwand; Bildschirm 6/8
the sea *(no pl)* /ðə 'siː/ das Meer, die See 1/2
search /sɜːtʃ/ Suche 1/P3
search /sɜːtʃ/ (durch)suchen 2/M3
seashell /'siːˌʃel/ Muschel 1/CC
seashore *(no pl)* /'siːˌʃɔː/ Strand, Meeresküste 1/CC
seat /siːt/ (Sitz)platz 5/P12

second /'sekənd/ zweite(r, s) I
secondary school /'sekəndri skuːl/ *weiterführende Schule für Kinder zwischen 11 und 16/18* 1/11
secretary /'sekrətri/ Sekretär/in I
see *(irr)* /siː/ sehen I
see you /'siː juː/ bis dann, bis bald 6/M8
seem /siːm/ scheinen 1/M2
seen /siːn/ *siehe „see"*
selection /sɪ'lekʃn/ Auswahl 1/11
self-confident /ˌself'kɒnfɪdnt/ selbstbewusst, selbstsicher 4/5
sell *(irr)* /sel/ verkaufen I
seller /'selə/ Verkäufer/in 2/15
send *(irr)* /send/ (zu)schicken 1/2
senior citizen /ˌsiːniə 'sɪtɪzn/ älterer Mensch, Senior/in 4/P5
sent /sent/ *Vergangenheitsform von „send"*
sentence /'sentəns/ Satz I
September /sep'tembə/ September I
seriously /'sɪəriəsli/ ernst(lich), schwer 3/M5
serve /sɜːv/ bedienen 1/11; dienen; servieren 4/P5
set *(irr)* /set/ (fest)setzen, vereinbaren 1/11
set off /set‿'ɒf/ (an)zünden 4/1
set the table /ˌset ðə 'teɪbl/ den Tisch decken 4/17
shadow /'ʃædəʊ/ Schatten 1/M2
that's a shame /ðæts‿ə 'ʃeɪm/ wie schade 1/2
share /ʃeə/ teilen 1/8
she /ʃiː/ sie I
shed /ʃed/ Schuppen; Gartenhäuschen 6/2
sheep *(pl -)* /ʃiːp/ Schaf I
shelf *(pl* **shelves***)* /ʃelf, ʃelvz/ Regal I
ship /ʃɪp/ Schiff I
shirt /ʃɜːt/ Hemd; Bluse I

shoe /ʃuː/ Schuh I
shop /ʃɒp/ Geschäft, Laden I
shop assistant /'ʃɒp‿əˌsɪstənt/ Verkäufer/in 3/5
do the shopping /ˌduː ðə 'ʃɒpɪŋ/ einkaufen (gehen) I
go shopping /gəʊ 'ʃɒpɪŋ/ einkaufen gehen I
shopping list /'ʃɒpɪŋ lɪst/ Einkaufszettel, Einkaufsliste 4/16
short /ʃɔːt/ kurz 2/9; klein 4/P10
should /ʃʊd/ sollte/müsste I
shout /ʃaʊt/ schreien, rufen I
show *(irr)* /ʃəʊ/ zeigen 5/10
shrimp /ʃrɪmp/ Garnele 4/3
side /saɪd/ Seite 2/1
sight /saɪt/ Sehenswürdigkeit 1/2
sign /saɪn/ Zeichen; (Straßen-/Verkehrs)schild 4/5
silently /'saɪləntli/ leise 5/P12
silly /'sɪli/ dumm; albern 4/M1
Don't be silly! /ˌdəʊnt bi 'sɪli/ Red(et) keinen Unsinn! 2/10
silver /'sɪlvə/ silbern 3/M4
similar /'sɪmɪlə/ ähnlich 4/11
simple past /ˌsɪmpl 'pɑːst/ einfache Vergangenheit 1/P3
sing *(irr)* /sɪŋ/ singen I
sing along /ˌsɪŋ‿ə'lɒŋ/ mitsingen 3/8
singer /'sɪŋə/ Sänger/in 5/7
sister /'sɪstə/ Schwester I
brothers and sisters /ˌbrʌðəz‿ænd 'sɪstəz/ Geschwister 1/14
sit *(irr)* /sɪt/ sitzen I
skateboarding *(no pl)* /'skeɪtˌbɔːdɪŋ/ Skateboardfahren 1/M4
skin /skɪn/ Haut 6/CC
skirt /skɜːt/ Rock I
skyscraper /'skaɪˌskreɪpə/ Wolkenkratzer 3/M4
sleep *(irr)* /sliːp/ schlafen I
sleep over /sliːp‿'əʊvə/ übernachten, über Nacht bleiben 6/1

sleepy /ˈsliːpi/ verschlafen, schläfrig 2/10
slept /slept/ *Vergangenheitsform von „sleep"*
slice /slaɪs/ in Scheiben schneiden 4/P12
slide /slaɪd/ Rutschbahn, Rutsche 6/CC
slow /sləʊ/ langsam 3/14
slurp /slɜːp/ schlürfen 5/8
small /smɔːl/ klein I
smart /smɑːt/ schlau; schick 5/13
smell /smel/ Geruch; Duft; Gestank I
smell (of) /smel/ riechen (nach) 4/11
smile /smaɪl/ Lächeln 2/CC
smile /smaɪl/ lächeln 3/M4
smoke /sməʊk/ rauchen 2/P6
snail /sneɪl/ Schnecke 6/8
snake /sneɪk/ Schlange I
sneak *(irr)* /sniːk/ schleichen 1/M2
snow *(no pl)* /snəʊ/ Schnee 6/16
snowy /ˈsnəʊi/ schneereich; verschneit I
snuck /snʌk/ *Vergangenheitsform von „sneak"*
so /səʊ/ so I
so /səʊ/ deshalb; also 1/5
so far /ˌsəʊ ˈfɑː/ bisher, bis jetzt 3/CC
soap (opera) /ˈsəʊp (‿ɒprə)/ Seifenoper, Soap 6/7
sock /sɒk/ Socke I
solo /ˈsəʊləʊ/ allein 3/M5
solve /sɒlv/ lösen, klären 5/M3
some /sʌm/ einige; etwas I
somebody /ˈsʌmbədi/ jemand 1/M5
someone /ˈsʌmwʌn/ jemand 4/3
something /ˈsʌmθɪŋ/ etwas I
sometimes /ˈsʌmtaɪmz/ manchmal I
somewhere /ˈsʌmweə/ irgendwo 2/10
son /sʌn/ Sohn I

soon /suːn/ bald I
sorry /ˈsɒri/ Verzeihung!, Entschuldigung!; Wie bitte? I
(I'm) sorry. /ˈsɒri/ Entschuldigung, das tut mir leid. 4/14
sort /sɔːt/ Art, Sorte I
sort /sɔːt/ sortieren 1/P2
sound /saʊnd/ Geräusch, Klang; Ton 1/13
sound /saʊnd/ klingen, sich anhören I
south /saʊθ/ Süden I
South Africa /saʊθ‿ˈæfrɪkə/ Südafrika 4/M6
South America /ˌsaʊθ‿əˈmerɪkə/ Südamerika 1/M2
spaceship /ˈspeɪsˌʃɪp/ Raumschiff 3/M3
Spain /speɪn/ Spanien I
Spanish /ˈspænɪʃ/ Spanisch I
Spanish /ˈspænɪʃ/ spanisch I
speak *(irr)* /spiːk/ sprechen, reden 3/13
special /ˈspeʃl/ besondere(r, s); speziell I
speech bubble /ˈspiːtʃ ˌbʌbl/ Sprechblase 3/M7
spell *(irr)* /spel/ buchstabieren I
spend *(irr)* /spend/ ausgeben *(Geld)*; verbringen *(Zeit)* 5/1
spent /spent/ *Vergangenheitsform von „spend"*
spider /ˈspaɪdə/ Spinne 2/14
spill *(irr)* /spɪl/ verschütten 4/P4
spit *(irr)* /spɪt/ spucken I
splash /splæʃ/ Platschen, Platscher 6/CC
splash /splæʃ/ bespritzen 6/CC
spoke /spəʊk/ *Vergangenheitsform von „speak"*
spoken /ˈspəʊkən/ *siehe „speak"*
spooky *(informal)* /ˈspuːki/ unheimlich; schaurig 1/2
spoon /spuːn/ Löffel I
sports *(only pl)* /spɔːts/ Sport; Sportart I

sports ground /ˈspɔːts ˌgraʊnd/ Sportplatz I
sports kit *(no pl)* /ˈspɔːts kɪt/ Sportkleidung, Sportsachen 5/10
sportsperson /ˈspɔːtsˌpɜːsn/ Sportler/in 2/1
spot /spɒt/ entdecken 6/P5
spring /sprɪŋ/ Frühling I
sprinkles *(only pl)* /ˈsprɪŋkls/ Streusel 4/M4
squeak /skwiːk/ quieken; piepsen 4/M6
St Martin's Day /sənt ˈmɑːtɪnz deɪ/ Martinstag 4/6
stadium /ˈsteɪdiəm/ Stadion 2/1
staff *(no pl)* /stɑːf/ Mitarbeiter, Personal 1/11
stage /steɪdʒ/ Bühne 6/M1
stairs *(only pl)* /steəz/ Treppe 2/M3
stall /stɔːl/ (Verkaufs)stand 4/3
stamp /stæmp/ Briefmarke I
stand *(irr)* /stænd/ ertragen, ausstehen, aushalten I
stand up *(irr)* /ˌstænd‿ˈʌp/ aufstehen 5/CC
star /stɑː/ Stern 6/M8
star sign /ˈstɑː saɪn/ Sternzeichen 3/1
start /stɑːt/ Anfang, Beginn Op1
start /stɑːt/ anfangen, beginnen I
station /ˈsteɪʃn/ Bahnhof; Station 2/1
radio station /ˈreɪdiəʊ ˌsteɪʃn/ Radiosender 6/3
statue /ˈstætʃuː/ Statue, Standbild 2/1
stay /steɪ/ bleiben I; untergebracht sein, wohnen 1/2
stay up /ˌsteɪ‿ˈʌp/ aufbleiben, wach bleiben I
steal *(irr)* /stiːl/ stehlen, klauen 3/11
step /step/ treten 4/3
stereo /ˈsteriəʊ/ (Stereo)anlage 6/M1

stick /stɪk/ Stock I
still /stɪl/ (immer) noch, noch immer 5/M1
still /stɪl/ trotzdem, dennoch 2/CC
stir /stɜː/ rühren 4/CC
stocking /ˈstɒkɪŋ/ (Weihnachts)strumpf 4/M1
stole /stəʊl/ *Vergangenheitsform von „steal"*
stone /stəʊn/ Stein 1/M2
stony /ˈstəʊni/ steinig; steinern 1/M2
stop /stɒp/ aufhören; beenden; anhalten I
story /ˈstɔːri/ Geschichte, Erzählung I
straight in /streɪt‿ˈɪn/ sofort hinein 6/CC
straight (on) /streɪt/ gerade(aus) 2/6
strange /streɪndʒ/ sonderbar, komisch 5/6
street /striːt/ Straße I
strict /strɪkt/ streng 5/6
stripe /straɪp/ Streifen 2/13
strong /strɒŋ/ stark I
student /ˈstjuːdnt/ Student/in, Studierende/r; Schüler/in I
study /ˈstʌdi/ Studie; Arbeitszimmer 2/M3
study /ˈstʌdi/ studieren; lernen 5/2
stuff *(informal)* /stʌf/ Zeug, Sachen 4/11
stupid /ˈstjuːpɪd/ dumm, blöd I
style /staɪl/ frisieren 3/5
subject /ˈsʌbdʒɪkt/ Thema; (Schul)fach I
such as /sʌtʃ æz/ wie (zum Beispiel) 4/M6
suddenly /ˈsʌdnli/ plötzlich, auf einmal I
sugar *(no pl)* /ˈʃʊɡə/ Zucker 4/16
suitcase /ˈsuːtˌkeɪs/ Koffer 6/13
summer /ˈsʌmə/ Sommer I
sun /sʌn/ Sonne 2/1
Sunday /ˈsʌndeɪ/ Sonntag I
sunglasses *(only pl)* /ˈsʌnˌɡlɑːsɪz/ Sonnenbrille I
sunny /ˈsʌni/ sonnig I
sunrise /ˈsʌnˌraɪz/ Sonnenaufgang 1/M2
superlative (form) /sʊˈpɜːlətɪv/ Superlativ 4/P8
supermarket /ˈsuːpəˌmɑːkɪt/ Supermarkt I
sure /ʃɔː/ sicher I
surely /ˈʃɔːli/ sicher(lich) 1/CC
surface /ˈsɜːfɪs/ Oberfläche 6/CC
surprise /səˈpraɪz/ Überraschung 3/2
surprise /səˈpraɪz/ überraschen 4/17
surprised /səˈpraɪzd/ überrascht 5/15
survive /səˈvaɪv/ überleben 1/M2
swap /swɒp/ tauschen Op4
swearword /ˈsweəˌwɜːd/ Schimpfwort, Fluch 5/M4
sweet /swiːt/ Süßigkeit I
sweet /swiːt/ süß I
sweetheart /ˈswiːtˌhɑːt/ Liebling, Schatz 3/8
swim *(irr)* /swɪm/ schwimmen I
go for a swim /ɡəʊ fər‿ə ˈswɪm/ schwimmen gehen 6/CC
swimming /ˈswɪmɪŋ/ Schwimmen I
swimming pool /ˈswɪmɪŋ puːl/ Schwimmbecken, -bad I
swimwear *(no pl)* /ˈswɪmˌweə/ Badebekleidung 1/P6
symbol /ˈsɪmbl/ Symbol, Zeichen 2/7

T

T. Rex (= tyrannosaurus rex) /ˈtiː reks, tɪˌrænəsɔːrəs ˈreks/ Tyrannosaurus Rex 6/8
table /ˈteɪbl/ Tisch I
set the table /ˌset ðə ˈteɪbl/ den Tisch decken 4/17
table tennis *(no pl)* /ˈteɪbl ˌtenɪs/ Tischtennis I
tablespoon /ˈteɪblˌspuːn/ Esslöffel 4/P12
tag *(no pl)* /tæɡ/ Fangen *(Spiel)* 4/M6
tail /teɪl/ Schwanz 2/13
take *(irr)* /teɪk/ (mit)nehmen; bringen I
take a chance /teɪk‿ə ˈtʃɑːns/ etw wagen, etw riskieren 3/M4
take a look (at) /teɪk‿ə ˈlʊk/ einen Blick werfen (auf) 2/P5
take a picnic /teɪk‿ə ˈpɪknɪk/ etw zum Essen mitnehmen 6/15
take care /teɪk ˈkeə/ aufpassen 2/P6
take care of /teɪk ˈkeər‿əv/ sich kümmern um, versorgen 3/5
take notes /teɪk ˈnəʊts/ (sich) Notizen machen 1/M3
take out /ˌteɪk‿ˈaʊt/ hinausbringen I
take out /ˌteɪk‿ˈaʊt/ herausnehmen 5/M4
take part (in) /ˌteɪk ˈpɑːt/ teilnehmen (an) 3/2
take photos /ˌteɪk ˈfəʊtəʊz/ Bilder machen, fotografieren 1/5
take turns /ˌteɪk ˈtɜːnz/ sich abwechseln 1/M1
taken /ˈteɪkən/ *siehe „take"*
tale /teɪl/ Geschichte, Erzählung 1/M2
talk /tɔːk/ Gespräch; Unterhaltung; Vortrag 2/M2
give a talk /ˌɡɪv‿ə ˈtɔːk/ einen Vortrag halten 1/7
talk (to) /tɔːk/ sprechen/reden/sich unterhalten (mit) I
tall /tɔːl/ hoch; groß I
taste /teɪst/ schmecken 4/P12
tasty /ˈteɪsti/ lecker 2/M6
Taurus /ˈtɔːrəs/ Stier *(Sternzeichen)* 3/M2
tea /tiː/ Tee I

tea dance /ˈtiː dɑːns/ Tanztee 4/P5
teach *(irr)* /tiːtʃ/ unterrichten I
teacher /ˈtiːtʃə/ Lehrer/in I
tear /tɪə/ Träne I
technician /tekˈnɪʃn/ Techniker/in 3/5
technique /tekˈniːk/ Technik, Methode 6/11
tell *(irr)* /tel/ erzählen; sagen I
tell *(irr)* /tel/ vorhersagen 3/2
temple /ˈtempl/ Tempel 4/M4
tenderly /ˈtendəli/ liebevoll; zärtlich 3/8
terrible /ˈterəbl/ schrecklich, furchtbar 1/5
test /test/ Prüfung, Test; Klassenarbeit 5/2
test /test/ prüfen, testen 2/14
the (River) Thames /ðə ˈtemz/ die Themse 2/1
than /ðæn/ als 4/11
Thank goodness! /ˌθæŋk ˈgʊdnəs/ Gott sei Dank! 6/15
thank you /ˈθæŋk juː/ danke I
thanks /θæŋks/ danke I
thanks a lot /ˌθæŋks‿ə ˈlɒt/ vielen Dank 6/5
that /ðæt/ das; der/die/das I
that /ðæt/ dass 1/M3
that /ðæt/ diese(r, s) 1/CC
at that time /æt ˈðæt taɪm/ damals, zu dieser Zeit 2/M3
That's too bad. /ðæts ˈtuː bæd/ Das ist wirklich schade. 2/12
that's why /ˈðæts waɪ/ deshalb; das ist der Grund, warum I
the /ðə/ der/die/das I
the ... way /ðə ˈweɪ/ auf die ... Art 4/CC
their /ðeə/ ihr(e) I
them /ðem/ sie, ihnen I
theme /θiːm/ Thema; Lektion, Kapitel 1/I
then /ðen/ dann I
then /ðen/ danach I
there /ðeə/ dort, da I
over there /ˌəʊvə ˈðeə/ dort (drüben) I
there are /ðear‿ˈɑː/ es gibt, da sind I
there is /ðear‿ˈɪz/ es gibt, da ist I
these *(pl of* **this***)* /ðiːz/ diese I
they /ðeɪ/ sie I
thin /θɪn/ dünn 3/M4
thing /θɪŋ/ Ding, Gegenstand, Sache I
think *(irr)* /θɪŋk/ denken, glauben, meinen I
think about (sb/sth) /ˈθɪŋk‿əˌbaʊt/ an (jdn/etw) denken; über (jdn/etw) nachdenken 3/9
think of /ˈθɪŋk‿əv/ denken an; sich ausdenken 1/14
this /ðɪs/ diese(r, s); das I
this way /ˈðɪs weɪ/ hier (ent)lang 0p1
those *(pl of* **that***)* /ðəʊz/ diese; jene I
thought /θɔːt/ *Vergangenheitsform von „think"*
thousand /ˈθaʊznd/ Tausend 3/M4
thriller /ˈθrɪlə/ Krimi, Thriller I
thrilling /ˈθrɪlɪŋ/ aufregend 6/M5
through /θruː/ durch 2/11
throw *(irr)* /θrəʊ/ werfen 4/M6
Thursday /ˈθɜːzdeɪ/ Donnerstag I
tidy up /ˌtaɪdi‿ˈʌp/ aufräumen I
tie /taɪ/ Krawatte 1/11
time /taɪm/ (Uhr)zeit I; Mal 6/15
at that time /æt ˈðæt taɪm/ damals, zu dieser Zeit 2/M3
What time is it? /wɒt‿ˈtaɪm ˌɪz‿ɪt/ Wie spät/Wie viel Uhr ist es? I
Time's up! *(informal)* /ˌtaɪmz‿ˈʌp/ Die Zeit ist vorüber! 6/M1
time-saving /ˈtaɪmˌseɪvɪŋ/ Zeit sparend 6/CC
timetable /ˈtaɪmteɪbl/ Stundenplan I
timewatch /ˈtaɪmwɒtʃ/ Zeitreise-Uhr 3/M4
tiny /ˈtaɪni/ winzig 2/CC
tip /tɪp/ Tipp 5/16
tired /ˈtaɪəd/ müde I
title /ˈtaɪtl/ Titel 1/2
to /tə/ in, nach, zu, an; vor; bis I
today /təˈdeɪ/ heute I
toe /təʊ/ Zeh(e) 2/P9
together /təˈgeðə/ zusammen, gemeinsam I
get together /ˌget‿təˈgeðə/ sich treffen; sich sammeln 2/10
go together /gəʊ təˈgeðə/ zusammenpassen 6/P3
told /təʊld/ *Vergangenheitsform von „tell"*
tomato *(pl* **-es***)* /təˈmɑːtəʊ, təˈmɑːtəʊz/ Tomate I
tomorrow /təˈmɒrəʊ/ morgen I
tongue twister /ˈtʌŋ ˌtwɪstə/ Zungenbrecher 3/P8
tonight /təˈnaɪt/ heute Abend 6/M4
too /tuː/ zu; auch I
too bad /ˌtuː ˈbæd/ wirklich schade 1/M3
took /tʊk/ *Vergangenheitsform von „take"*
tool /tuːl/ Werkzeug 3/P1
tooth *(pl* **teeth***)* /tuːθ, tiːθ/ Zahn I
top /tɒp/ oberes Ende, Spitze 2/1; Gipfel 6/15
top /tɒp/ Top-, Spitzen- 5/7
top-class /ˌtɒp ˈklɑːs/ Spitzen-, der Spitzenklasse 4/17
topic /ˈtɒpɪk/ Thema 1/15
tortoise /ˈtɔːtəs/ (Land)schildkröte 2/M5
touch /tʌtʃ/ berühren I
tough /tʌf/ robust, zäh, tough 6/M5

toward(s) /tə'wɔ:d(z)/ in Richtung Op1
towel /'taʊəl/ Handtuch I
tower /'taʊə/ Turm 2/1
town /taʊn/ Stadt I
toy /tɔɪ/ Spielzeug I
tracksuit /'træk,su:t/ Trainingsanzug 1/11
tractor /'træktə/ Traktor I
traditional /trə'dɪʃnəl/ traditionell 4/M2
traffic light /'træfɪk laɪt/ Ampel 6/M8
trail /treɪl/ schleifen 2/CC
train /treɪn/ Zug, Eisenbahn 2/1
trainer *(BE)* /'treɪnə/ Turnschuh 5/P7
means of transport /mi:nz‿əv 'trænspɔ:t/ Verkehrsmittel 6/M8
trap /træp/ Falle 2/M6
trapdoor /'træp,dɔ:/ Falltür 2/M3
travel /'trævl/ reisen 2/1
travel agency /'trævl‿,eɪdʒnsi/ Reisebüro 6/19
treasure hunt /'treʒə hʌnt/ Schatzsuche; Schnitzeljagd 6/11
tree /tri:/ Baum I
trip /trɪp/ Ausflug; Reise, Fahrt 6/14
trouble *(no pl)* /'trʌbl/ Schwierigkeiten 3/5
get into trouble /get‿ɪntə 'trʌbl/ Schwierigkeiten bekommen 1/M3
trousers *(only pl)* /'traʊzəz/ Hose I
true /tru:/ wahr; richtig 6/15
try /traɪ/ (aus)probieren; versuchen 2/6
try hard to do sth /,traɪ 'ha:d‿tə du: sʌmθɪŋ/ sich sehr bemühen, etw zu tun 2/M6
tube *(no pl)* /tju:b/ *Londoner U-Bahn* 2/6
Tuesday /'tju:zdeɪ/ Dienstag I
Turkey /'tɜ:ki/ Türkei I
turkey /'tɜ:ki/ Truthahn/-henne, Pute/r 4/M1
Turkish /'tɜ:kɪʃ/ Türkisch 4/2
Turkish /'tɜ:kɪʃ/ türkisch 4/2
turn /tɜ:n/ sich drehen; abbiegen 2/6
turn /tɜ:n/ werden 4/M4
(it's) your turn /'jɔ: ,tɜ:n/ du bist dran I
turn into /,tɜ:n‿'ɪntʊ/ umwandeln, verändern 6/P1
turn out /,tɜ:n‿'aʊt/ sich herausstellen 6/M1
turn round /tɜ:n 'raʊnd/ (sich) umdrehen 6/15
take turns /,teɪk 'tɜ:nz/ sich abwechseln 5/P9
turtle /'tɜ:tl/ Schildkröte I
watch TV /,wɒtʃ ,ti: 'vi:/ fernsehen I
TV (= television) /,ti:'vi:, 'telɪ,vɪʒn/ Fernseher; Fernsehen I
TV series *(only pl)* /,ti:'vi: ,sɪəri:z/ Fernsehserie 5/7
twin /twɪn/ Zwilling, Zwillings- B
type /taɪp/ Art; Typ, Sorte 6/10

U

ugh *(informal)* /ʌg/ i, igitt 2/12
ugly /'ʌgli/ hässlich I
UK (= United Kingdom) /,ju:'keɪ, ju:,naɪtɪd 'kɪŋdəm/ Vereinigtes Königreich 6/11
uncle /'ʌŋkl/ Onkel I
under /'ʌndə/ unter I
underground /'ʌndə,graʊnd/ U-Bahn 2/3
underline /,ʌndə'laɪn/ unterstreichen 5/P2
understand *(irr)* /,ʌndə'stænd/ verstehen I
underwater /,ʌndə'wɔ:tə/ unter Wasser 6/CC
unfortunately /ʌn'fɔ:tʃnətli/ leider, unglücklicherweise 1/2
unfriendly /ʌn'frendli/ unfreundlich 1/5
universe /'ju:nɪ,vɜ:s/ Universum 3/M5
until /ən'tɪl/ bis 1/11
up /ʌp/ (nach) oben; hinauf 2/CC; auf (hinauf) 6/11
get up /get‿'ʌp/ aufstehen I
up to /'ʌp tu:/ bis (zu) Op1
upon /ə'pɒn/ auf 2/CC
upstairs /ʌp'steəz/ (nach) oben 5/8
us /ʌs/ uns I
use /ju:z/ benutzen 4/11
usually /'ju:ʒʊəli/ gewöhnlich, normalerweise I

V

v (= versus) /vi:, 'vɜ:səs/ vs. (= gegen) 6/P6
Valentine's Day /'væləntaɪnz deɪ/ Valentinstag 4/6
vegetable /'vedʒtəbl/ Gemüse I
verse /vɜ:s/ Strophe 4/14
very /'veri/ sehr I
vet (= veterinarian) /vet, ,vetrɪ'neəriən/ Tierarzt/-ärztin 2/15
victory /'vɪktri/ Sieg 4/M2
view /vju:/ Sicht; (Aus)blick, Aussicht 6/M8
village /'vɪlɪdʒ/ Dorf 6/15
Virgo /'vɜ:gəʊ/ Jungfrau *(Sternzeichen)* 3/M2
visit /'vɪzɪt/ Besuch 2/M3
visit /'vɪzɪt/ besuchen I
voice /vɔɪs/ Stimme 1/M2
volunteer /,vɒlən'tɪə/ Freiwillige/r I
have a vote /hæv‿ə 'vəʊt/ abstimmen 5/13
voucher /'vaʊtʃə/ Gutschein 4/14

W

wait (for) /weɪt/ warten (auf) 2/1

sb cannot wait (to do sth) /ˌsʌmbədi ˌkænɒt ˈweɪt/ jmd kann es kaum erwarten (, etw zu tun) 1/5
waiter/waitress /ˈweɪtə, ˈweɪtrəs/ Bedienung, Kellner/in 4/17
wake up /weɪk‿ˈʌp/ aufwecken; aufwachen I
walk /wɔːk/ Spaziergang 1/2
walk /wɔːk/ Aufstieg 6/15
walk /wɔːk/ (zu Fuß) gehen, laufen I
go for a walk /ˌgəʊ fər‿ə ˈwɔːk/ spazieren gehen I
walker /ˈwɔːkə/ Fußgänger/in, Spaziergänger/in 6/15
wall /wɔːl/ Wand I
wall climbing *(no pl)* /ˈwɔːl ˌklaɪmɪŋ/ Klettern an der Kletterwand 1/11
wanna (= want to) /ˈwɒnə/ wollen 3/CC
want /wɒnt/ wollen I
want to do sth /ˌwɒnt‿tə ˈduː ˌsʌmθɪŋ/ etw tun wollen I
wanted /ˈwɒntɪd/ gesucht 3/15
wardrobe /ˈwɔːdrəʊb/ Kleiderschrank I
warning /ˈwɔːnɪŋ/ Warnung 5/M4
was /wɒz/ *Vergangenheitsform von „be"*
wash /wɒʃ/ (sich) waschen I
watch /wɒtʃ/ beobachten; anschauen; zusehen I
watch out (for) /wɒtʃ‿ˈaʊt/ aufpassen (auf), sich in Acht nehmen (vor) 4/P7
watch TV /ˌwɒtʃ ˌtiː ˈviː/ fernsehen I
water *(no pl)* /ˈwɔːtə/ Wasser I
water /ˈwɔːtə/ gießen 5/8
wax /wæks/ Wachs 2/1
way /weɪ/ Weg 1/5
way /weɪ/ Art, Weise 3/13
find one's way back /ˌfaɪnd wʌnz weɪ ˈbæk/ zurückfinden 6/15
make one's way /ˌmeɪk wʌnz ˈweɪ/ gehen 6/M1
no way /nəʊ ˈweɪ/ keine Chance 5/CC
the ... way /ðə ˈweɪ/ auf die ... Art 1/CC
this way /ˈðɪs weɪ/ hier (ent)lang Op1
on one's way /ɒn wʌnz ˈweɪ/ unterwegs 1/M2
we /wiː/ wir I
wealth /welθ/ Reichtum, Wohlstand 4/8
weapon /ˈwepən/ Waffe 2/M3
wear *(irr)* /weə/ tragen I
weather /ˈweðə/ Wetter I
wedding /ˈwedɪŋ/ Hochzeit 5/M1
Wednesday /ˈwenzdeɪ/ Mittwoch I
week /wiːk/ Woche I
weekend /ˌwiːkˈend/ Wochenende 2/6
at the weekend /æt ðə ˈwiːkˌend/ am Wochenende I
welcome (to) /ˈwelkəm/ willkommen (in) 1/11
well /wel/ gut 3/10
well /wel/ nun (ja), tja 1/2
went /went/ *Vergangenheitsform von „go"*
were /wɜː/ *Vergangenheitsform von „be"*
west /west/ Westen I
wet /wet/ nass 1/2
what /wɒt/ was; welche(r, s) I
what a ... /ˈwɒt‿ə/ was für ein(e) ... 2/12
What a pity! /wɒt‿ə ˈpɪti/ Wie schade! 4/17
What about ... ? *(informal)* /ˈwɒt‿əˌbaʊt/ Was ist mit ... ?, Wie wäre es mit ... ? I
what else /wɒt‿ˈels/ was noch, was sonst 1/10
What time is it? /wɒt‿ˈtaɪm ˌɪz‿ɪt/ Wie viel Uhr ist es? I
What's ... like? /wɒts ˈlaɪk/ Wie ist ... ? 1/6
What's on? *(informal)* /wɒts‿ˈɒn/ Was ist los?, Was steht an? 6/I; Was läuft? 6/P6
What's the matter? /ˌwɒts ðə ˈmætə/ Was ist (denn) los? 2/10
What's up? *(informal)* /wɒts‿ˈʌp/ Was ist los? 6/15
What's your name? /ˌwɒts jə ˈneɪm/ Wie heißt du?, Wie heißen Sie? I
whatever /wɒtˈevə/ was (auch immer) 3/8
wheel /wiːl/ Rad 3/M4
wheelchair /ˈwiːlˌtʃeə/ Rollstuhl B
when /wen/ wann; wenn I; als 1/5
whenever /wenˈevə/ immer wenn, wann (auch) immer 5/8
where /weə/ wo(hin) I
Where are you from? /ˌweər‿ɑː jə ˈfrɒm/ Wo kommst du her? I
which /wɪtʃ/ welche(r, s) 1/1
which one /ˈwɪtʃ wʌn/ welche(r, s) 2/13
while /waɪl/ während 4/17
whisper /ˈwɪspə/ flüstern 6/15
white /waɪt/ weiß I
who /huː/ wer I
who /huː/ der/die/das 2/M3; wen, wem 6/5
whole /həʊl/ ganz, gesamt 6/M1
whom /huːm/ wen; wem 3/M4
whose /huːz/ wessen 6/2
why /waɪ/ warum I
that's why /ˈðæts waɪ/ deshalb; das ist der Grund, warum I
wife *(pl* **wives***)* /waɪf, waɪvz/ Ehefrau I
will /wɪl/ werden 3/2
win *(irr)* /wɪn/ gewinnen 6/6
wind *(irr)* /waɪnd/ wickeln 2/CC
window /ˈwɪndəʊ/ Fenster I
windy /ˈwɪndi/ windig I
winner /ˈwɪnə/ Gewinner/in, Sieger/in 3/2

wire /ˈwaɪə/ Draht; Leitung, Kabel 3/M4
wish /wɪʃ/ (sich) wünschen 4/17
best wishes /ˌbest ˈwɪʃɪz/ viele Grüße 6/5
with /wɪð/ mit I
with /wɪð/ bei 1/2
go with /ˈgəʊ wɪð/ gehören zu, passen zu 2/13
without /wɪðˈaʊt/ ohne 4/M4
woman *(pl* **women)** /ˈwʊmən, ˈwɪmɪn/ Frau I
won /wʌn/ *Vergangenheitsform von „win"*
wonder /ˈwʌndə/ sich fragen 5/3
wonderful /ˈwʌndəfl/ wunderbar, wundervoll 1/9
wooden /ˈwʊdn/ hölzern, Holz- Op1
woof /wʊf/ wau 6/18
woolly /ˈwʊli/ Woll-, wollen, aus Wolle 2/CC
word /wɜːd/ Wort I
word web /ˈwɜːd web/ Wortnetz 3/M5
wordbank /ˈwɜːdbæŋk/ Wortfeld 1/6
wordsearch /ˈwɜːdsɜːtʃ/ Wortsuchrätsel 4/19
work /wɜːk/ Arbeit 2/15
work /wɜːk/ arbeiten I
work /wɜːk/ funktionieren 5/10
at work /æt ˈwɜːk/ auf/bei der Arbeit 2/10
working day /ˈwɜːkɪŋ deɪ/ Werktag 4/M1
workplace /ˈwɜːkˌpleɪs/ Arbeitsplatz 5/P11
world /wɜːld/ Welt, Erde 1/9
around the world /əˌraʊnd ðə ˈwɜːld/ weltweit, auf der ganzen Welt 4/M4
worn /wɔːn/ *siehe „wear"*
worried /ˈwʌrid/ beunruhigt, besorgt 3/M4
worry /ˈwʌri/ sich Sorgen machen 3/11
worse /wɜːs/ schlimmer, schlechter 5/3
worst /wɜːst/ schlechteste(r, s), schlimmste(r, s) I
would /wʊd/ würde(st, n, t) I
sb would like (to) /wʊd ˈlaɪk/ jmd möchte (gern) I
wound /waʊnd/ *Vergangenheitsform von „wind"*
write *(irr)* /raɪt/ schreiben I
write down /raɪt ˈdaʊn/ aufschreiben 1/13
writer /ˈraɪtə/ Schriftsteller/in, Autor/in 2/M3
wrong /rɒŋ/ falsch I
wrote /rəʊt/ *Vergangenheitsform von „write"*

Y

yeah *(informal)* /jeə/ ja 2/6
year /jɪə/ Jahr I
year /jɪə/ Jahrgang(sstufe) 4/M1
a year /ə ˈjɪə/ pro/im Jahr 4/17
yech *(informal)* /jek/ i, igitt 1/CC
yellow /ˈjeləʊ/ gelb I
yes /jes/ ja I
yesterday /ˈjestədeɪ/ gestern I
not yet /nɒt ˈjet/ noch nicht 6/15
yoghurt *(no pl)* /ˈjɒgət/ Joghurt I
you /juː/ du; dich; dir; Sie; Ihnen; ihr; euch I
young /jʌŋ/ jung I
your /jɔː/ dein(e); euer/eure; Ihr(e) I
yourself *(pl* yourselves*)* /jəˈself, jəˈselvz/ dich; dir; selbst/ihr; euch; selbst 3/P8
youth club /ˈjuːθ ˌklʌb/ Jugendzentrum 5/2
yummy *(informal)* /ˈjʌmi/ lecker 1/5

Z

zip wire /ˈzɪp ˌwaɪə/ Seilrutsche 3/M4

DICTIONARY GERMAN-ENGLISH

A

abbiegen turn
Abend evening
am Abend in the evening
heute Abend tonight
Abendessen dinner
abends in the evening
Abenteuer adventure
aber but
Abzeichen logo
Achtung respect *(no pl)*
Adler eagle
(sich) (ver)ändern change
Affe monkey
Afrika Africa
aktiv active
Aktivität activity
albern silly
alle everyone, everybody
allein alone
alle(s) all
alles everything
Alles Gute zum Geburtstag! Happy birthday!
als as; than; when
als Erstes first, first of all
also so
alt old
Wie alt bist du/seid ihr? How old are you?
Alter age
am on
am besten best
am liebsten best
am meisten best
Amerikaner/in American
amerikanisch American
Ampel traffic light
an on; at; to
(an)bieten offer
andere(r, s) other; different
ein anderer/anderes, eine andere another
anders different
am Anfang in the beginning
anfangen start, begin
anfangs at first, first
Angehörige(r) relative
angenehm nice
angreifen attack
Angst haben (vor etw) be frightened (of sth), be scared (of sth), be afraid (of sth)
anhalten stop
sich anhören sound
ankommen arrive
(an)malen paint
(Telefon)anruf (phone) call
anrufen phone, call
anschauen watch, look at
anschließend after that, afterwards
Ansicht opinion
(an)statt instead (of)
Antwort answer
(be)antworten answer
Apfel apple
Apfelsine orange
April April
Aquarium fish tank
arbeiten work
arbeitsreich busy
arm poor
Art sort, kind
Arzt/Ärztin doctor
Astronaut/in astronaut
auch also, too
auf on; at
auf Deutsch in German
auf einmal suddenly
auf Englisch in English
Auf geht's! Let's go!
aufbewahren keep
aufbleiben stay up
aufgeregt excited
(auf)hängen hang
aufhören stop, finish
aufräumen tidy up
aufregend exciting
aufstehen get up
aufwachen wake up
aufwecken wake up
Auge eye
Augenblick moment
August August
aus from
(her)aus out of
(Aus)blick view
ausbrechen escape
ausflippen go crazy *(informal)*
Ausflug trip
ausgeben *(Geld)* spend
aushalten stand
(aus)probieren try
ausräumen empty
Ausrede excuse
ausreichend enough
aussehen look
gut aussehend good-looking
Außerirdische(r) alien
Aussicht view
ausstehen stand
nicht ausstehen können hate
Australien Australia
auswählen choose
Auto car
Autogramm autograph
Autor/in author, writer

B

backen bake
Bad(ezimmer) bathroom
Bahnhof station
bald soon
Ballon balloon
Banane banana
Bart beard
Bauarbeiter/in builder
bauen build
Bauer/Bäuerin farmer
Bauernhof farm
Baum tree
(be)antworten answer
bedeckt cloudy
bedeuten mean
Bedienung waiter/waitress
sich beeilen hurry up
beenden finish, stop
zu Beginn in the beginning
beginnen begin, start
(be)halten keep
bei by; at
beide(s) both

Bein leg
beinahe nearly
Beispiel example
zum Beispiel for example
beißen bite
beitreten join
(be)kämpfen fight
bekommen get
bellen bark
bemerken notice
sich sehr bemühen, etw zu tun try hard to do sth
benutzen use
beobachten watch
bequem comfortable
bereit ready
Berg mountain
Bericht report
berühmt famous
berühren touch
sich beruhigen cool down
beschäftigt busy
beschließen decide
(be)schützen protect
besondere(r, s) special
besorgt worried
besser better
Gute Besserung! Get well soon.
beste(r, s) best
am besten best
besuchen visit
betrachten look at
Bett bed
beunruhigt worried
bevor before
bevorzugen prefer
sich bewegen move
bewölkt cloudy
bezahlen pay
bezaubernd charming
Bibliothek library
(an)bieten offer
Bild picture
Bilder machen take photos
billig cheap
Biologie biology
bis to, until
(spätestens) bis (acht Uhr) by (eight o'clock)
bis bald bye for now, see you
bis dann see you
bitte please
Bitte schön! Here you are.
bitten ask
Blatt leaf *(pl leaves)*
blau blue
bleiben stay
Bleistift pencil
(Bleistift)spitzer pencil sharpener
(Aus)blick view
blöd stupid
Blume flower
Bluse shirt
Boden floor
Bohne bean
Boot boat
brauchen need
braun brown
brennen burn
Brett board
Brettspiel board game
Brief letter
Briefmarke stamp
Briefumschlag envelope
Brille glasses *(only pl)*
bringen take
(mit)bringen bring
britische(r, s) British
Bronze bronze
Brot bread *(no pl)*
Brötchen bread roll
Brücke bridge
Bruder brother
brüllen roar
Buch book
Bücherei library
Bücherregal bookcase
Bücherschrank bookcase
Buchstabe letter
buchstabieren spell
bügeln iron
Bühne stage
Burg castle
Büro office
bürsten brush
Bushaltestelle bus stop

C

Campingplatz campsite
Centstück p (= penny, pence)
Chance chance
charmant charming
chatten chat
Chef/in boss
Chemie chemistry
Chinese/Chinesin Chinese
Chinesisch Chinese
chinesisch Chinese
Chips crisps *(only pl) (BE)*
Couch couch
Cousin/e cousin

D

da there
da ist there is
da sind there are
Dame lady
danach afterwards, after that, then
vielen Dank thanks a lot
danke thanks, thank you
dann then
Darf es noch etwas sein? Anything else?
das the; that, this
dasselbe the same
Datum date
(Zimmer)decke ceiling
den Tisch decken set the table
dein(e) your
dekorieren decorate
denken think
(an etw) denken remember
deprimiert depressed
der the; that
derselbe the same
deshalb so; that's why
(Privat)detektiv/in detective
Deutsch German
deutsch German
auf Deutsch in German

Deutsche/r German
Deutschland Germany
Dezember December
dich you
die the; that
Dienstag Tuesday
diese these *(pl of* this*)*, those *(pl of* that*)*
diese(r, s) this
dieselbe the same
Ding thing
dir you
Direktor/in director
Donnerstag Thursday
Dorf village
dort there
dort (drüben) over there
Drache dragon
Draht wire
du bist dran (it's) your turn
drangsalieren bully
draußen outside
nach draußen outside
dreckig dirty
sich drehen turn
Dschungel jungle
du you
Duft smell
dumm stupid; silly
dunkel dark
Dunkelheit darkness
dünn thin
durch through; by
durchdrehen go crazy *(informal)*
durchqueren cross
dürfen may
etw tun dürfen be allowed to do sth
nicht dürfen must not, may not

E

echt real
Ecke corner
Ehefrau wife *(pl* wives*)*
Ehemann husband
ehrlich honest
Ei egg
eigene(r, s) own
ein(e) a/an; one
ein bisschen a bit, a little
eines Tages one day
einfach easy; just
einige a few, some
einkaufen (gehen) do the shopping
einkaufen gehen go shopping
einladen invite
Einladung invitation
einmal once
einsam lonely
Eisenbahn train
Eiskrem ice cream
Elefant elephant
Ellbogen elbow
Eltern parents *(only pl)*
Ende end
enden end
endlich finally
Energie energy
eng narrow
Englisch English
englisch English
auf Englisch in English
entdecken discover
Ente duck
(ent)fliehen escape
entkommen escape
(ent)leeren empty
(sich) entscheiden decide
Entschuldigen Sie bitte! Excuse me!
Entschuldigung excuse
Entschuldigung! Excuse me!, Sorry!
Entschuldigung, das tut mir leid. (I'm) sorry.
sich entspannen relax
entspannt relaxed
enttäuscht disappointed, frustrated
er he
Erde world
Erdkunde geography
erforschen explore
erhalten get
sich erinnern (an) remember
erklären explain
Erlebnis adventure
(er)raten guess
erschaffen create
erste(r, s) first
erstens first of all
erster Weihnachtsfeiertag Christmas Day
als Erstes first, first of all
ertragen stand
erwachsen werden grow up
erzählen tell
Erzählung story
es it
Es freut mich, Sie/dich kennenzulernen. Nice to meet you.
Es geht mir gut. I'm fine.
es gibt there is, there are
Essen food *(no pl)*; meal
essen eat; have
zu Essen geben feed
etwas something; some; any
(irgend)(et)was anything
euch you
euer your
eure your
Europa Europe
extrem extreme

F

Fabrik factory
(Schul)fach subject
Fahne flag
Fähre ferry
fahren drive; ride; go
Fahrer/in driver
(Fahr)rad bike
(Fahr)rad fahren ride a bike
Fahrt trip
Falle trap
fallen fall
fallen lassen drop
falls if
falsch wrong
Familie family

fangen catch
fantastisch fantastic *(informal)*
Farbe colour
farbenfroh colourful
farbenprächtig colourful
fast nearly
Februar February
(Feder)mäppchen pencil case
Fehler fault
Feier celebration
feiern celebrate
Fell fur
Fenster window
Ferien holiday
Fernsehen TV (= television)
fernsehen watch TV
Fernseher TV (= television)
Fernsehserie TV series *(only pl)*
fertig ready
Fest celebration; festival
festnehmen catch
Feuer fire
Feuerwehrmann/-frau firefighter
fies mean
Filzstift felt tip
finden find
Finsternis darkness
Fisch fish *(pl - or -es)*
flach flat
Flagge flag
Flasche bottle
Fleisch meat *(no pl)*
fleißig hard-working
fliegen fly
(ent)fliehen escape
Flucht escape
Flughafen airport
Flugzeug plane
Fluss river
flüstern whisper
folgen follow
Foto photo, picture
fotografieren take photos
Frage question
fragen ask
Frankreich France
Französisch French
französisch French
Frau woman *(pl* women*)*, lady
Frau *(Anrede)* Mrs
frech naughty
frei free
im Freien outside
Freiheit freedom *(no pl)*
Freitag Friday
Freiwillige/r volunteer
sich auf etw freuen look forward to sth
Freund/in friend
(fester) Freund boyfriend
freundlich friendly, nice
frisch fresh
Friseur/in hairdresser
frisieren style
froh glad
fröhlich happy
Frucht fruit
früh early
Frühling spring
Frühstück breakfast
Frühstückspause morning break
frustriert frustrated
(sich) fühlen feel
für for
Furcht erregend scary
furchtbar terrible
sich fürchten (vor) be frightened (of)
Fuß foot *(pl* feet*)*
zu Fuß on foot
(zu Fuß) gehen walk
Fußball football
füttern feed

G

Gabel fork
ganz whole; completely
Garten garden
Gärtner/in gardener
Gast guest
Gebäude building
geben give
geboren born
Geburtstag birthday
Alles Gute zum Geburtstag! Happy birthday!
gefährlich dangerous
Gefühl feeling
gegen against
Gegenstand thing
gehen go
(zu Fuß) gehen walk
jdm/zu etw gehören belong to sb/sth
Wie geht es dir/Ihnen/euch? How are you?
Es geht mir gut. I'm fine.
Geist ghost
gelangweilt bored
gelassen relaxed
gelb yellow
Geld money *(no pl)*
Geld verdienen make money
gemein mean
gemeinsam together
Gemüse vegetable
(genau)so ... wie ... as ... as
Genesungskarte get well card
genießen enjoy
genug enough
genügend enough
geöffnet open
Geografie geography
gerade(aus) straight (on)
Geräusch sound; noise
Gericht dish *(pl -es)*
Geruch smell
gesamt whole
Gesamtschule comprehensive school
Geschäft shop
geschehen happen
gescheit clever
Geschenk present
Geschichte history; story
Geschirrspülmaschine dishwasher
Geschwister brothers and sisters
Gesicht face

Gespenst ghost
gestalten create
Gestank smell
gestern yesterday
gesund healthy
gesund werden get well
Getränk drink
Gewinn prize
gewinnen win
Gewinner/in winner
gewöhnlich usually
es gibt there is, there are
gießen water
Gipfel top
Gitarre guitar
Glas glass
glauben think; believe
glauben (an) believe (in)
gleich in a minute; just
Glück haben be lucky
glücklich glad; lucky; happy
Glücks- lucky
glücksbringend lucky
Goldfisch goldfish *(pl -)*
Gott god
Gras grass *(no pl)*
gratis for free
grau grey
Griechenland Greece
grillen have a barbecue
eine Grillparty feiern have a barbecue
groß big; large; tall; great
großartig great
Großbritannien Great Britain
Großeltern grandparents *(only pl)*
Großmutter grandmother
(Groß)stadt city
Großvater grandfather
grün green
das ist der Grund, warum that's why
Grundschule primary school
Gruppe group
herzliche Grüße love
viele Grüße best wishes
gut good; well; fine
gut aussehend good-looking
gut in etw sein be good at sth
etw gut können be good at sth
Gute Besserung! Get well soon.

H

Haar(e) hair *(no pl)*
haben have, have got
Hähnchen chicken
halb (neun) half past (eight)
Halle hall
hallo hello, hi
(be)halten keep
Handschuh glove
Handtuch towel
Handy mobile (= mobile phone)
(auf)hängen hang
hart hard
hassen hate
hässlich ugly
häufig often
Haus house
Hausaufgaben homework *(no pl)*
nach Hause home
zu Hause at home; home
Haustier pet
Heft exercise book
Heiligabend Christmas Eve
Heim home
Heimatort home town
heiraten get married, marry
heiß hot
heißen be called
ich heiße my name is
Wie heißen Sie? What's your name?
Wie heißt du? What's your name?
Held/in hero *(pl -es)*
helfen help
Helm helmet
Hemd shirt
(her)aus out of
herausnehmen take out
Herbst autumn
hereinkommen come in
Herr *(Anrede)* Mr
herum around
heute today
heute Abend tonight
heute Nachmittag this afternoon
Hier, bitte! Here you are.
hier(her) here
Hilfe help
hinab down
(hinauf)klettern climb
(hinauf)steigen climb
hinausbringen take out
hinfallen fall down
hinter behind
hinüber over
hinunter down
hoch high; tall
Hochzeit wedding
hoffen hope
höflich polite
Höhepunkt highlight
holen get
Honig honey *(no pl)*
hören hear
(zu)hören listen (to)
Horoskop horoscope
Hose trousers *(only pl)*
hübsch pretty, lovely
Hügel hill
Huhn chicken
Hund dog
hungrig hungry
Hut hat

I

ich I
ich heiße my name is
Idee idea
ihm him
ihn him
ihnen them
Ihnen you
ihr you
ihr(e) their; its

Ihr(e) your
ihr(e, n) her
im Freien outside
immer always
(immer) noch still
in in; into; at; on; to
Inder/in Indian
Indianer/in Indian
indianisch Indian
Indien India
Indisch Indian
indisch Indian
Informatik ICT (= information and communication technology)
Information information *(no pl)*
Insekt insect
Insel island
interessant interesting
interessiert (an etw) interested (in sth)
irgendein(e) any
(irgend)(et)was anything
irgendwelche any
irgendwo somewhere
Irisch Irish
irisch Irish
Irland Ireland
Italien Italy
Italiener/in Italian
Italienisch Italian
italienisch Italian

J

ja yes
Jacke jacket
Jäger/in hunter
Jahr year
Jahrhundert century
Januar January
jede(r) everyone, everybody
jede(r, s) every, each
jemals ever
jemand someone, somebody
jene those *(pl of* that*)*
jetzt now
Joghurt yoghurt *(no pl)*
Jongleur/in juggler
jubeln cheer
Jugendzentrum youth club
Juli July
jung young
Junge boy
Juni June

K

Kabel wire
Käfig cage
Kalender calendar
kalt cold
Kamin chimney
(be)kämpfen fight
Känguru kangaroo
Kaninchen rabbit
Kappe cap
kaputt broken
Karikatur cartoon
Karotte carrot
Karte card
(Land)karte map
Kartoffel potato *(pl -es)*
Karton card
Käse cheese *(no pl)*
Katze cat
kauen chew
kaufen buy
Kaufhaus department store
Kaugummi (chewing) gum *(no pl)*
kein(e) no; not any
keiner no one
Kellner/in waiter/waitress
kennen know
kennenlernen meet
Es freut mich, Sie/dich kennenzulernen. Nice to meet you.
Kerze candle
Kind child *(pl* children*)*
Kinn chin
Kino cinema
Kirche church
Kissen cushion
Klang sound
(Schul)klasse class
Klassenarbeit test
Klassenkamerad/in classmate
Klassenzimmer classroom
klauen steal
Klavier piano
Kleid dress
Kleider clothes *(only pl)*
Kleiderschrank wardrobe
Kleidung clothes *(only pl)*
klein small, little
Klettern an der Kletterwand wall climbing
(hinauf)klettern climb
klingen sound
Klub club
klug clever
Knie knee
Koch/Köchin cook
kochen cook, do the cooking
Koffer suitcase
komisch strange; funny
kommen come
(zu) spät kommen be late
Wo kommst du her? Where are you from?
Komödie comedy
König king
Königin queen
können can; may
etw gut können be good at sth
etw tun können be able to do sth
könnte(st, n, t) could
kontrollieren check
sich konzentrieren concentrate
Konzert concert
Kopf head
Korb basket
Körper body
korrekt correct
kosten cost
Was kostet/kosten ... ? How much is/are ... ?
köstlich delicious
Kostüm costume
Krach noise

Kraft energy
krank ill
Krankenhaus hospital
(Kranken)pfleger nurse
(Kranken)schwester nurse
Krawatte tie
kreativ creative
Kreis circle
kreischen scream
Krimi thriller
Kriminelle(r) criminal
Krone crown
Küche kitchen
Kuchen cake
Kuh cow
Kühlschrank fridge *(informal)*
sich kümmern um look after, take care of
Kunde/Kundin customer
Kunst art
Kunststoff plastic
Kurs course
Kuss kiss
küssen kiss
Küste coast
Kuvert envelope

L

lächeln smile
lachen laugh
Laden shop
Lamm lamb
Lampe lamp
Land country
(Land)karte map
(Land)schildkröte tortoise
lang long
langsam slow
langweilig boring
Lärm noise
lassen let; leave
lass(t) uns let's (= let us)
laufen walk; run
Läufer/in runner
laut loud
Leben life *(pl lives)*
leben live
lecker delicious, yummy *(informal)*
(ent)leeren empty
legen put
Lehnstuhl armchair
Lehrer/in teacher
leicht easy
leider unfortunately
leise quiet
Leiter/in director
Leitung wire
lernen learn; study
lesen read
letzte(r, s) last
Leute people *(no pl)*
Licht light
Liebe love
alles Liebe love
lieben love
liebe(r) *(Anrede)* dear
lieber better
lieber mögen prefer
Lieblings- favourite
am liebsten best
lila(farben) purple
Limonade lemonade
Lineal ruler
auf der linken Seite on the/your left
links on the/your left
(nach) links left
Liste list
Loch hole
locker relaxed
Löffel spoon
Los! Let's go!
Löwe lion
Luft air
lustig funny; fun
sich über jdn lustig machen make fun of sb

M

machen make; do
Mädchen girl
Magazin magazine
Mahlzeit meal
Mai May
Mal time
(an)malen paint
Mama mum *(informal)*
manchmal sometimes
Mann man *(pl men)*
(Feder)mäppchen pencil case
Mappe folder
Markt market
Marmelade jam
März March
Maschine machine
Mathe maths
Maus mouse *(pl mice)*
Medaille medal
das Meer the sea *(no pl)*
Meerschweinchen guinea pig
Mehl flour
mehr better
(noch) mehr more
mein(e) my
meinen mean; think
Meinung opinion
am meisten best
die meisten most
jede Menge lots of
Mensch person
Menschen people *(no pl)*
(Menschen)menge crowd
Messer knife *(pl knives)*
Meter metre
mich me
Milch milk *(no pl)*
Milchshake milkshake
Minirock miniskirt
Minute minute
mir me
mit with; by
(mit)bringen bring
Mitglied member
mitmachen bei join
(mit)nehmen take
Mitschüler/in classmate
Mittagessen lunch; dinner
Mittagspause lunchtime
Mittagszeit lunchtime
in der Mitte in the middle

mitten in/auf in the middle
Mittwoch Wednesday
mobben bully
Mobbing bullying *(no pl)*
Mobiltelefon mobile (= mobile phone)
jmd möchte (gern) sb would like (to)
mögen like; enjoy
lieber mögen prefer
sehr gern mögen love
möglicherweise maybe
Möglichkeit chance
Möhre carrot
Mohrrübe carrot
Moment moment
im Moment at the moment
Monat month
Mond moon
Mondlicht moonlight
Montag Monday
Morgen morning
am Morgen in the morning
morgen tomorrow
morgens in the morning
Motorrad motorbike
müde tired
Müll rubbish *(no pl)*
Mülleimer bin
Mülltonne bin
München Munich
Mund mouth
Musik music *(no pl)*
Müsli muesli *(no pl)*
müssen have to, must
müsste should
mutig brave
Mutter mother
Mutti mum *(informal)*
Mütze hat

N

nach after; to
(nach) links left
(nach) oben upstairs
(nach) rechts right
Nachbar/in neighbour
nachdem after
Nachmittag afternoon
am Nachmittag in the afternoon
heute Nachmittag this afternoon
nachmittags in the afternoon
Nachricht message
Nachrichten news *(no pl)*
nächste(r, s) next
Nacht night
über Nacht bleiben sleep over
nachts at night
nah(e) near
in der Nähe by
Name name
Nase nose
nass wet
Natur nature *(no pl)*
natürlich of course
Naturwissenschaft science
Nebel fog
neben next to
neblig foggy
(mit)nehmen take
nein no
nett nice
neu new
Neuigkeit news *(no pl)*
Neujahr New Year
nicht not
nicht dürfen must not, may not
nicht mehr not anymore
nichts nothing; not anything
niedlich cute
nie(mals) never
niemand no one
Nilpferd hippo (= hippopotamus)
(immer) noch still
noch ein(e, r, s) another
noch (ein)mal again
noch immer still
(noch) mehr more
noch nicht not yet
Norden north
normalerweise normally, usually
(Schul)note mark
(sich) Notizen machen take notes
November November
Nummer number
nur only

O

(nach) oben upstairs
oberes Ende top
Obst fruit
oder or
offen open
(sich) öffnen open
oft often
ohne without
Ohr ear
Ohrring earring
Oktober October
Öl oil
Olympische Spiele Olympic Games
Oma grandma *(informal)*
Omi grandma *(informal)*
Onkel uncle
optimistisch optimistic
Orange orange
orange(farben) orange
in Ordnung fine
Ort place
Osten east
Osterfest Easter
Ostern Easter

P

packen pack
Palast palace
Papa dad *(informal)*
Papagei parrot
Papier paper *(no pl)*
Pappe card
Parfüm perfume
passieren happen
Pause break
peinlich berührt embarrassed

Pelz fur
perfekt perfect
Person person
Pferd horse
Pflanze plant
(Kranken)pfleger nurse
Pfote paw
Pfund *(engl. Währung)* pound
Pilot/in pilot
Pinguin penguin
Pirat pirate
Plastik plastic
platt flat
Platz place
plötzlich suddenly
Polen Poland
Polizei police *(no pl)*
Polizeibeamter/-beamtin police officer
Pommes frites chips *(only pl)* *(BE)*
Postkarte postcard
eine Schachtel Pralinen a box of chocolates
Preis price; prize
preiswert cheap
(Privat)detektiv/in detective
pro/am Tag a day
pro/im Jahr a year
(aus)probieren try
Programm programme
Prüfung test
Pute/r turkey
putzen clean; brush

R

Rabauke bully
Rad wheel
(Fahr)rad bike
(Fahr)rad fahren ride a bike, cycle
Radiergummi rubber *(BE)*
Radiosender radio station
Rasen grass *(no pl)*
(er)raten guess
Ratte rat
Raumschiff spaceship
raus outside
(Taschen)rechner calculator
Recht haben be right
auf der rechten Seite on the/your right
rechts on the/your right
(nach) rechts right
reden speak; talk (to)
Regal shelf *(pl* shelves*)*
Regel rule
Regenbogen rainbow
Regenwald rainforest
regnen rain
regnerisch rainy
reich rich
Reihe queue
reinigen clean
Reis rice *(no pl)*
Reise trip
reisen travel
Reiten riding *(no pl)*
reiten ride
Rektor/in headteacher
Religion(sunterricht) RE (= religious education)
Rennen race
rennen run
reparieren repair
Respekt respect
richtig right, correct; true
Richtung direction
riechen (nach) smell (of)
riesengroß huge
riesig huge; great
Roboter robot
Rock skirt
Rollstuhl wheelchair
rosa pink
rot red
Rücken back
Rückseite back
rufen shout
ruhig quiet
Rüpel bully
Russe/Russin Russian
Russisch Russian
russisch Russian
Russland Russia

S

Saal hall
Sache thing
Saft juice
sagen say; tell
Sahne cream *(no pl)*
Salat salad
sammeln collect
Samstag Saturday
Sänger/in singer
Sarg coffin
Satz sentence
sauber clean
sauber machen clean
Schach(spiel) chess *(no pl)*
eine Schachtel Pralinen a box of chocolates
Schaf sheep *(pl -)*
Schal scarf *(pl* -s *or* scarves*)*
Schatten shadow
schätzen guess
schauen look
schaurig spooky *(informal)*
Schauspieler/in actor/actress
Schere (pair of) scissors *(only pl)*
Scheune barn
(zu)schicken send
Schiff ship, boat
(Straßen)schild sign
Schildkröte turtle
(Land)schildkröte tortoise
Schinken ham *(no pl)*
schlafen sleep
Schlafzimmer bedroom
schlagen hit
Schlange snake; queue
schlau clever
schlecht bad
schlechter worse
schlechteste(r, s) worst
schließen close
schließlich finally
schlimmer worse

schlimmste(r, s) worst
Schloss castle
zum Schluss finally
Schlüssel key
schmal narrow
sich schminken put on make-up
schmücken decorate
schmutzig dirty
Schnee snow *(no pl)*
schneereich snowy
schneiden cut
schnell fast, quick
Schnellhefter folder
Schokolade chocolate *(no pl)*
schon already
schön beautiful; nice; lovely
Schornstein chimney
Schottland Scotland
Schrank cupboard
schrecklich horrible, terrible
schreiben write
Schreibtisch desk
schreien shout; cry
Schriftsteller/in writer, author
Schuh shoe
Schuld fault
Schule school
Schüler/in student
(Schul)fach subject
(Schul)klasse class
Schulleiter/in headteacher
(Schul)note mark
Schultasche schoolbag
(be)schützen protect
Schwanz tail
schwarz black
Schwein pig
schwer hard, difficult
Schwester sister
(Kranken)schwester nurse
schwierig difficult
Schwierigkeiten bekommen get into trouble
Schwimmbad swimming pool
Schwimmbecken swimming pool
Schwimmen swimming
schwimmen swim
See lake
die See the sea *(no pl)*
Seeräuber pirate
sehen see; look (at)
Sehenswürdigkeit sight
sehr very; much; a lot (of)
Seifenoper soap (opera)
Seil rope
sein be
sein(e) its
sein(e, r) his
Seite side
auf der linken Seite on the/ your left
auf der rechten Seite on the/ your right
Sekretär/in secretary
selbst even
selbstbewusst self-confident
selbstsicher self-confident
Sendung programme
September September
Sessel armchair
setzen put
sicher safe; sure
Sicht view
sie she; her; they; them
Sie you
Sieger/in winner
silbern silver
Silvester New Year's Eve
singen sing
sitzen sit
so so
(genau)so ... wie ... as ... as
Socke sock
Sofa couch
sofort in a minute
sogar even
Sohn son
sollte should
Sommer summer
sonderbar strange
Sonne sun
Sonnenaufgang sunrise
Sonnenbrille sunglasses *(only pl)*
sonnig sunny
Sonntag Sunday
sich Sorgen machen worry
sorgfältig careful
Sorte sort, kind
Soße sauce
Spanien Spain
Spanisch Spanish
spanisch Spanish
spannend exciting
Spaß fun *(no pl)*
(viel) Spaß machen be (great) fun
(zu) spät late
(zu) spät kommen be late
Wie spät ist es? What time is it?
später later; afterwards
(spätestens) bis (acht Uhr) by (eight o'clock)
spazieren gehen go for a walk
Spaziergang walk
speziell special
Spiel game, match, play
spielen play
Spieler/in player
Spielplatz playground
Spielzeug toy
Spinne spider
Spitze top
(Bleistift)spitzer pencil sharpener
Sport sports *(only pl)*
Sportplatz sports ground
Sport(unterricht) PE (= physical education)
Sprache language
sprechen (mit) speak, talk (to)
springen jump
spucken spit
Stadion stadium
Stadt town

(Groß)stadt city
(Vieh)stall barn
(Verkaufs)stand stall
stark strong
Station station
(an)statt instead (of)
stattdessen instead (of)
staubsaugen hoover
stehen stand
stehlen steal
steigen get
(hinauf)steigen climb
Stein stone
stellen put
sterben die
(Stereo)anlage stereo
Stern star
Sternzeichen star sign
Stift pen
Stimme voice
Stock stick
stolz (auf jmd) proud (of sb)
Strand beach
Straße street, road
(Straßen)schild sign
streicheln pet
Streichholz match
streng strict
(Theater)stück play
Student/in student
studieren study
Studierende/r student
Stuhl chair
Stunde hour; lesson
Stundenplan timetable
suchen (nach) look for
Südafrika South Africa
Süden south
Supermarkt supermarket
süß sweet; cute
Süßigkeit sweet

T

Tafel board
Tag day
eines Tages one day
Tagebuch diary
Tante aunt
Tanz dance
Tanzen dancing *(no pl)*
tanzen dance
Tasche bag
(Taschen)rechner calculator
Tasse cup
Tatze paw
Techniker/in technician
Tee tea
teilnehmen (an) take part (in)
Telefon phone
(Telefon)anruf (phone) call
Teller plate
Tempel temple
Teppich carpet
Test test
teuer expensive
Teufel devil
(Theater)stück play
Thema subject
die Themse the (River) Thames
Tier animal
Tierarzt/-ärztin vet (= veterinarian)
Tierpfleger/in keeper
Tipp tip
Tisch table
den Tisch decken set the table
Tischtennis table tennis *(no pl)*
Tochter daughter
toll amazing *(informal)*
Tomate tomato *(pl -es)*
Ton sound
tot dead
Tracht costume
traditionell traditional
tragen wear *(Kleidung)*
Traktor tractor
Träne tear
Traum dream
traurig sad
(sich) treffen meet
Treppe stairs *(only pl)*
trinken drink
Truthahn/-henne turkey
tschüss bye *(informal)*
tun do
Tür door
Türkei Turkey
Türkisch Turkish
türkisch Turkish
Turm tower
Turnhalle gym (= gymnasium)
tyrannisieren bully

U

U-Bahn underground
üben practise
über over; about; across
über Nacht bleiben sleep over
überleben survive
übernachten sleep over
überprüfen check
überqueren cross
überrascht surprised
Überraschung surprise
Uhr clock
(sieben) Uhr (seven) o'clock
Wie viel Uhr ist es? What time is it?
(Uhr)zeit time
um around; at *(Uhrzeit)*
umher around
umsonst for free
umziehen move
und and
unerschrocken brave
unfreundlich unfriendly
ungefähr about
ungezogen naughty
unglaublich incredible, amazing *(informal)*
unglücklicherweise unfortunately
unheimlich scary, spooky *(informal)*
Universum universe
uns us

unser(e) our
unter under
untergebracht sein stay
sich unterhalten (mit) chat, talk (to)
unterrichten teach
Unterschied difference
unterschiedlich different
untersuchen explore
Urlaub holiday
Urlaub machen go on holiday
in den Urlaub fahren go on holiday
Urwald jungle

V

Vater father
Vati dad *(informal)*
(sich) (ver)ändern change
verärgert angry
Verbrecher/in criminal
verbringen *(Zeit)* spend
verdienen earn
Geld verdienen make money
Verein club
Vereinigtes Königreich UK (= United Kingdom)
vergessen forget
verkaufen sell
Verkäufer/in seller, shop assistant
(Verkaufs)stand stall
(Verkehrs)schild sign
verlassen leave
verlegen embarrassed
jdn verletzen hurt sb
verlieren lose
vermissen miss
vermuten guess
verpassen miss
verrückt crazy
verschieden different
verschneit snowy
versorgen take care of
sich verspäten be late
versprechen promise
(sich) verstecken hide
verstehen understand
versuchen try
Verwandte(r) relative
Verzeihung! Sorry.
(Vieh)stall barn
(viel) Spaß machen be (great) fun
viel much, lots of
viel(e) a lot (of)
viele many
viele Grüße best wishes
vielen Dank thanks a lot
vielleicht perhaps, maybe
Viertel (vor/nach) quarter (to/past)
violett purple
Vogel bird
voll full
völlig completely
von of; by; from
vor before; in front of; to *(Uhrzeit)*
vor (drei Tagen) (three days) ago
vorbei (an) past; over
Vorhang curtain
vorher before
vormittags in the morning
vorsichtig careful
vorüber (an) past
vorziehen prefer

W

wach bleiben stay up
Waffe weapon
wahr true
während during
wahrscheinlich probably
Wald forest
Wand wall
Wandern hiking *(no pl)*
wann when
Warnung warning
warten (auf) wait (for)
warum why
was what
(irgend)(et)was anything
Was ist (denn) los? What's the matter?
Was ist mit ... ? What about ... ? *(informal)*
Was kostet/kosten ... ? How much is/are ... ?
(sich) waschen wash
Wasser water *(no pl)*
wechseln change
Wecker alarm clock
weg away
Weg way
weg away
jdm wehtun hurt sb
Weihnachten Christmas
erster Weihnachtsfeiertag Christmas Day
Weihnachtsmann Father Christmas
weil because
weinen cry
weiß white
weit far
welche(r, s) what
Wellensittich budgie (= budgerigar)
Welt world
wenige few
wenn when; if
wer who
werden become; get; will; going to
werfen throw
Werk factory
Westen west
Wettbewerb competition
Wetter weather
wichtig important
wie how; like
Wie alt bist du/seid ihr? How old are you?
Wie bitte? Sorry?
Wie geht es dir/Ihnen/euch? How are you?
Wie heißen Sie? What's your name?

Wie heißt du? What's your name?
Wie ist ... ? What's ... like?
Wie spät ist es? What time is it?
Wie viel Uhr ist es? What time is it?
Wie wäre es mit ... ? What about ... ? *(informal)*
wieder again
wiederholen repeat
Wiese grass *(no pl)*
willkommen (in) welcome (to)
windig windy
Windpocken chickenpox *(no pl)*
wir we
wirklich real; really
wissen know
witzig funny
Wo kommst du her? Where are you from?
Woche week
Wochenende weekend
am Wochenende at the weekend
wo(hin) where
wohnen live; stay
Wohnung flat, apartment
Wohnwagen caravan
Wohnzimmer living room
wollen want
etw tun wollen want to do sth
Wort word
Wörterbuch dictionary
wunderbar wonderful, great, fantastic *(informal)*
wundervoll wonderful
(sich) wünschen wish
würde(st, n, t) would
Wurst sausage
Würstchen sausage
wütend angry

Z

Zahl number
Zahn tooth *(pl* teeth*)*
Zeichen sign
Zeichentrickfilm cartoon
zeichnen draw
zeigen show
(Uhr)zeit time
zeitig early
Zeitschrift magazine
Zeltplatz campsite
Zentrum centre
zerbrochen broken
Ziege goat
ziehen pull
ziemlich quite
Ziffer number
Zimmer room
(Zimmer)decke ceiling
zornig angry
zu to; too
zu Fuß on foot
(zu Fuß) gehen walk
zu Hause at home; home
(zu) spät late
(zu) spät kommen be late
Zucker sugar *(no pl)*
zuerst first, at first
zufrieden happy
Zug train
Zuhause home
(zu)hören listen (to)
Zukunft future
zum Beispiel for example
zumachen close
Zündholz match
zurück back
zusammen together
Zuschauermenge crowd
(zu)schicken send
zusehen watch
(jdm) zustimmen agree (with sb)
zuversichtlich optimistic
zuvor before
zweite(r, s) second
Zwilling twin
Zwillings- twin
zwischen between

Girls / Women

Abby /ˈæbi/
Anna /ˈænə/
Caroline /ˈkærəlaɪn/
Cerys /ˈkærɪs/
Claire /kleə/
Daisy /ˈdeɪzi/
Geraldine /ˈdʒerəldiːn/
Gillian /ˈdʒɪliən/
Grace /greɪs/
Hannah /ˈhænə/
Hilda /ˈhɪldə/
Jennifer /ˈdʒenɪfə/
Josephine /ˈdʒəʊzɪfiːn/
Karla /ˈkɑːlə/
Kate /keɪt/
Katie /ˈkeɪti/
Lana /ˈlɑːnə/
Leanne /liˈæn/
Mary /ˈmeəri/
Matilda /məˈtɪldə/
Mena /ˈmiːnə/
Michelle /mɪˈʃel/
Nasaar /nəˈsɑː/
Neela /ˈniːlə/
Nina /ˈniːnə/
Olivia /əˈlɪviə/
Paula /ˈpɔːlə/
Rebecca /riˈbekə/
Regina /rɪˈdʒaɪnə/
Safia /ˈsɑːfiə/
Samantha /səˈmænθə/
Sarah /ˈseərə/
Sharon /ˈʃærən/
Shelby /ˈʃelbi/
Sheree /ˈʃeri/
Sonya /ˈsɒnjə/
Sue /suː/
Zoe /ˈzəʊi/

Boys / Men

Alex /ˈælɪks/
Andrew /ˈændruː/
Austin /ˈɒstɪn/
Bobby /ˈbɒbi/
Charlie /ˈtʃɑːli/
Daniel /ˈdænjəl/
David /ˈdeɪvɪd/
Fritz /frɪts/
George /dʒɔːdʒ/
Gerret /ˈdʒerət/
Hugo /ˈhjuːgəʊ/
Jason /ˈdʒeɪsən/
Joe /dʒəʊ/
Joel /ˈdʒəʊəl/
John /dʒɒn/
Josh /dʒɒʃ/
Julian /ˈdʒuːliən/
Ken /ken/
Louis /ˈluːis/
Mark /mɑːk/
Martin /ˈmɑːtɪn/
Mo /məʊ/
Murat /ˈmurɑːt/
Nick /nɪk/
Noah /ˈnəʊə/
Oleg /ˈəʊleg/
Oliver /ˈɒlɪvə/
Onur /ˈəʊnʊə/
Pete /piːt/
Rajiv /rɑːˈdʒiːv/
Rick /rɪk/
Rob /rɒb/
Robin /ˈrɒbɪn/
Sam /sæm/
Selim /ˈselɪm/
Serkan /ˈserkɑːn/
Simon /ˈsaɪmən/
Tariq /ˈtærɪk/
Taylor /ˈteɪlə/
Tim /tɪm/
Will /wɪl/
William /ˈwɪljəm/
Yusuf /ˈjʊsʊf/

Families

Batson /ˈbætsən/
Collins /ˈkɒlɪnz/
Griff /grɪf/
Jones /dʒəʊnz/
Killmouskey /kɪlˈmaʊski/
Lambraki /læmˈbrɑːki/
MacHowl /məkˈhaʊl/
Marshall /ˈmɑːʃəl/
Miller /ˈmɪlə/
Mutt /mʌt/
Patel /pəˈtel/
Perkins /ˈpɜːkɪnz/
Perrin /ˈperɪn/
Pratt /præt/
Smale /smeɪl/
Watson /ˈwɒtsən/
Williams /ˈwɪljəmz/

Other Names

the Acropolis /ðiˌəˈkrɒpəlɪs/
Amelia Earhart /əˌmiːliəˌˈeəhɑːt/
Arsenal /ˈɑːsnl/
Arsenal FC /ˌɑːsnlˌef ˈsiː/
Auld Lang Syne /ˌɔːld læŋ ˈzaɪn/
BBC (= British Broadcasting Corporation) /ˌbiː biː ˈsiː, ˌbrɪtɪʃ ˈbrɔːdkɑːstɪŋ ˌkɔːpəˌreɪʃn/
BBC1 /ˌbiː biː ˌsiː ˈwʌn/
BBC2 /ˌbiː biː ˌsiː ˈtuː/
Beam House Adventure Centre /ˌbiːm haʊsˌədˈventʃə ˌsentə/
Big Ben /ˌbɪg ˈben/
Blue Peter /ˌbluː ˈpiːtə/
Boxing Day /ˈbɒksɪŋ deɪ/
Buckingham Palace /ˌbʌkɪŋəm ˈpælɪs/
Buzz Aldrin /ˌbʌz ˈɔːldrɪn/
the Camden Chronicle /ðə ˌkæmdən ˈkrɒnɪkl/
Camden Market /ˌkæmdən ˈmɑːkɪt/
CBBC (= Children's BBC) /ˌsiː biː biː ˈsiː, ˈtʃɪldrənz ˌbiː biː ˌsiː/
Channel 4 /ˌtʃænl ˈfɔː/
ChildLine /ˈtʃaɪldlaɪn/
Coldy /ˈkəʊldi/
Coldy School /ˈkəʊldi skuːl/
Covent Garden /ˌkɒvənt ˈgɑːdn/
the Daily Post /ðə ˌdeɪli ˈpəʊst/
Delphi /ˈdelfaɪ/
Denbigh School /ˈdenbi skuːl/
DJ Rasta /ˌdiːˌdʒeɪ ˈræstə/
Doctor Watson /ˌdɒktə ˈwɒtsən/
Doctor Who /ˌdɒktə ˈhuː/
Donald Duck /ˌdɒnəld ˈdʌk/
EastEnders /ˈiːstendəz/

Fairfield High School /ˌfeəfi:əld ˈhaɪ sku:l/
Gary Lineker /ˌgæri ˈlɪnɪkə/
the Gherkin /ðə ˈgɜ:kɪn/
Goldie /ˈgəʊldi/
Halloween /ˌhæləʊˈi:n/
Harrods /ˈhærədz/
Harry Potter /ˌhæri ˈpɒtə/
Havafax /ˈhævəfæks/
Haverstock /ˈhævəstɒk/
Haverstock School /ˈhævəstɒk sku:l/
HMS Belfast /ˌeɪtʃ‿em‿ˌes ˈbelˌfɑ:st/
Hogwarts /ˈhɒgwɔ:ts/
Hollywood /ˈhɒliˌwʊd/
Hoppity /ˈhɒpəti/
Inti /ˈɪnti/
Jack the Ripper /ˌdʒæk ðə ˈrɪpə/
Jupiter /ˈʤu:pɪtə/
Kenny Hoover /ˌkeni ˈhu:və/
Lakshmi /ˈlʌkʃmi/
Linus May /ˌlaɪnəs ˈmeɪ/
London City Hall /ˌlʌndən ˈsɪti hɔ:l/
London Dungeon /ˌlʌndən ˈdʌndʒn/
the London Eye /ðə ˌlʌndən‿ˈaɪ/
London Zoo /ˌlʌndən ˈzu:/
Madame Tussauds /məˌdɑ:m təˈsɔ:dz/
the Magic Boys /ðə ˌmædʒɪk ˈbɔɪz/
the Major Oak /ðə ˌmeɪdʒər‿ˈəʊk/
Manchester United /ˌmæntʃɪstə ju:ˈnaɪtɪd/
Millennium Bridge /mɪˈleniəm brɪdʒ/
Nessie /ˈnesi/
Newsround /ˈnju:zˌraʊnd/
Parken Stadium /ˈpɑ:kən ˌsteɪdiəm/
Patch /pætʃ/
Radio Camden /ˌreɪdiəʊ ˈkæmdən/
Radio Junior Europe /ˌreɪdiəʊ ˌdʒu:niə ˈjʊərəp/
Rama /ˈrɑ:mə/
Rangers /ˈreɪndʒəz/
Richard Edwards /ˌrɪtʃəd‿ˈedwədz/
Roald Dahl /ˌrəʊəld ˈdɑ:l/
Robert Earl of Huntingdon /ˌrɒbət‿ɜ:l‿əv ˈhʌntɪŋdən/
Robin Hood /ˌrɒbɪn ˈhʊd/
Selfridges /ˈselfrɪdʒɪz/
Sherlock Holmes /ˌʃɜ:lɒk ˈhəʊmz/
Shrove Tuesday /ˌʃrəʊv ˈtju:zdeɪ/
the Simpsons /ðə ˈsɪmpsənz/
Sir Arthur Conan Doyle /sɜ:r‿ˌɑ:θə ˌkəʊnən ˈdɔɪəl/
Snowdonia /snəʊˈdəʊniə/
South West Trains /ˌsaʊθ ˈwest treɪnz/
Speaker's Corner /ˌspi:kəz ˈkɔ:nə/
St Patrick's Day /sənt ˈpætrɪks deɪ/
St Paul's Cathedral /sənt ˌpɔ:lz kəˈθi:drəl/
Supermouse /ˈsu:pəmaʊs/
TARDIS /ˈtɑ:dɪs/
Tarzan /ˈtɑ:zən/
Tate Modern /ˌteɪt ˈmɒdən/
Terry Pratchett /ˌteri ˈprætʃɪt/
Thorpe Park /ˌθɔ:p ˈpɑ:k/
Tony Mitton /ˌtəʊni ˈmɪtən/
Tower Bridge /ˌtaʊə ˈbrɪdʒ/
the Tower of London /ðə ˌtaʊər‿əv ˈlʌndən/
Uncle Scrooge /ˌʌŋkl ˈskru:dʒ/
Valentine's Day /ˈvæləntaɪnz deɪ/
Vitaly Fridzon /ˌvi:təli ˈfrɪzdən/
Walk of Fame /ˌwɔ:k‿əv ˈfeɪm/
Waterloo Station /ˌwɔ:təlu: ˈsteɪʃn/
Westminster Abbey /westmɪnstər‿ˈæbi/

Geographical names

Africa /ˈæfrɪkə/
America /əˈmerɪkə/
Arlington Road /ˈɑ:lɪŋtən rəʊd/
Asia /ˈeɪʃə/
Athens /ˈæθɪnz/
the Atlantic (Ocean) /ði‿ətˌlæntɪk(‿ˈəʊʃn)/
Australia /ɒˈstreɪliə/
Baker Street /ˈbeɪkə stri:t/
Barbados /bɑ:ˈbeɪdɒs/
Belfast /ˌbelˈfɑ:st/
Berlin /ˌbɜ:ˈlɪn/
Bolivia /bəˈlɪviə/
Bristol /ˈbrɪstl/
Britain /ˈbrɪtn/
Camden /ˈkæmdən/
Camden High Street /ˌkæmdən ˈhaɪ stri:t/
Camden Town /ˌkæmdən ˈtaʊn/
Cardiff /ˈkɑ:dɪf/
Carol Street /ˈkærəl stri:t/
Central Camden /ˌsentrəl ˈkæmdən/
Cerro Calvario /ˌserəʊ ˌkælˈveəriəʊ/
Chertsey /ˈtʃɜ:tsi/
China /ˈtʃaɪnə/
Cologne /kəˈləʊn/
Copenhagen /ˌkəʊpənˈheɪgən/
Cornwall /ˈkɔrnwəl/
Denmark /ˈdenmɑ:k/
Edinburgh /ˈedɪnbərə/
England /ˈɪŋglənd/
Eton Road /ˈi:tən rəʊd/
Europe /ˈjʊərəp/
Euston /ˈju:stən/
France /frɑ:nts/
Galapagos Islands /gəˈlæpəgəs‿ˌaɪləndz/
Germany /ˈdʒɜ:məni/
Glasgow /ˈglɑ:zgəʊ/
Great Britain /ˌgreɪt ˈbrɪtn/
Great Torrington /ˌgreɪt ˈtɒrɪŋtən/
Greece /gri:s/
Hamburg /ˈhæmbɜ:g/

Haverstock Hill /ˈhævəstɒk hɪl/
Hyde Park /ˌhaɪd ˈpɑːk/
India /ˈɪndiə/
Ireland /ˈaɪələnd/
Italy /ˈɪtəli/
Japan /dʒəˈpæn/
Kensington Gardens /ˌkenzɪŋtən ˈgɑːdnz/
King's Cross /ˌkɪŋz ˈkrɒs/
Lake Titicaca /leɪk ˌtɪtɪˈkɑːkə/
Leicester /ˈlestə/
Loch Ness /ˌlɒk ˈnes/
London /ˈlʌndən/
Los Angeles /lɒs‿ˈændʒəliːz/
Luxborough Street /ˈlʌksbərə striːt/
Majorca /məˈjɔːkə/
Manchester /ˈmæntʃɪstə/
Marylebone High Street /ˌmærələbən ˈhaɪ striːt/
Marylebone Road /ˈmærələbən rəʊd/
Mexico /ˈmeksɪˌkəʊ/
Milton Keynes /ˌmɪltən ˈkiːnz/
Mount Snowdon /ˌmaʊnt ˈsnəʊdən/
Munich /ˈmjuːnɪk/
New Mexico /njuː ˈmeksɪkəʊ/
New York /njuː ˈjɔːk/
North Devon /ˌnɔːθ ˈdevən/
North Pole /ˌnɔːθ ˈpəʊl/
Northern Ireland /ˌnɔːðn‿ˈaɪələnd/
Nottingham /ˈnɒtɪŋəm/
Nottingham Street /ˈnɒtɪŋəm striːt/
Oxford Street /ˈɒksfəd striːt/
the Pacific (Ocean) /ðə pəˌsɪfɪk(‿ˈəʊʃn)/
Paris /ˈpærɪs/
Piccadilly Circus /ˌpɪkəˌdɪli ˈsɜːkəs/
Regent's Park /ˌriːdʒənts ˈpɑːk/
Riga /ˈriːgə/
Rome /rəʊm/
Russia /ˈrʌʃə/
Scotland /ˈskɒtlənd/
Sherwood Forest /ˌʃɜːwʊd ˈfɒrɪst/
Snowdonia National Park /snəʊˌdəʊniə ˌnæʃnəl ˈpɑːk/
South Africa /saʊθ‿ˈæfrɪkə/
South America /ˌsaʊθ‿əˈmerɪkə/
Spain /speɪn/
Staines Road /ˈsteɪnz rəʊd/
Tottenham Court Road /ˌtɒtənəm ˌkɔːt ˈrəʊd/
Turkey /ˈtɜːki/
UK (= United Kingdom) /ˌjuːˈkeɪ, juːˌnaɪtɪd ˈkɪŋdəm/
USA (= United States of America) /ˌjuːesˈeɪ, juːˌnaɪtɪd ˌsteɪts‿əv‿əˈmerɪkə/
Wales /weɪlz/

Numbers

Cardinal numbers

0 zero /ˈzɪərəʊ/
1 one /wʌn/
2 two /tuː/
3 three /θriː/
4 four /fɔː/
5 five /faɪv/
6 six /sɪks/
7 seven /ˈsevn/
8 eight /eɪt/
9 nine /naɪn/
10 ten /ten/
11 eleven /ɪˈlevn/
12 twelve /twelv/
13 thirteen /ˌθɜːˈtiːn/
14 fourteen /ˌfɔːˈtiːn/
15 fifteen /ˌfɪfˈtiːn/
16 sixteen /ˌsɪksˈtiːn/
17 seventeen /ˌsevnˈtiːn/
18 eighteen /ˌeɪˈtiːn/
19 nineteen /ˌnaɪnˈtiːn/
20 twenty /ˈtwenti/
21 twenty-one /ˌtwentiˈwʌn/
...
30 thirty /ˈθɜːti/
40 forty /ˈfɔːti/
50 fifty /ˈfɪfti/
...
90 ninety /ˈnaɪnti/
100 one hundred /ˈwʌn ˌhʌndrəd/
...
900 nine hundred /ˈnaɪn ˌhʌndrəd/
1,000 one thousand /ˈwʌn ˌθauznd/

Ordinal numbers

1st first /fɜːst/
2nd second /ˈsekənd/
3rd third /θɜːd/
4th fourth /fɔːθ/
5th fifth /fɪfθ/
6th sixth /sɪksθ/
7th seventh /ˈsevnθ/
8th eighth /eɪtθ/
9th ninth /naɪnθ/
10th tenth /tenθ/
11th eleventh /ɪˈlevnθ/
12th twelfth /twelfθ/
13th thirteenth /ˌθɜːˈtiːnθ/
14th fourteenth /ˌfɔːˈtiːnθ/
15th fifteenth /ˌfɪfˈtiːnθ/
16th sixteenth /ˌsɪksˈtiːnθ/
...
20th twentieth /ˈtwentiəθ/
21st twenty-first /ˌtwentiˈfɜːst/
22nd twenty-second /ˌtwentiˈsekənd/
23rd twenty-third /ˌtwentiˈθɜːd/
24th twenty-fourth /ˌtwentiˈfɔːθ/
...
30th thirtieth /ˈθɜːtiəθ/
31st thirty-first /ˌθɜːtiˈfɜːst/
...
40th fortieth /ˈfɔːtiəθ/
50th fiftieth /ˈfɪftiəθ/
60th sixtieth /ˈsɪkstiəθ/
70th seventieth /ˈsevntiəθ/
80th eightieth /ˈeɪtiəθ/
90th ninetieth /ˈnaɪntiəθ/
100th hundredth /ˈhʌndrədθ/

infinitive	simple past	past participle	German
be /biː/	was/were /wɒz/wɜː/	been /biːn/	sein
beat /biːt/	beat /biːt/	beaten /ˈbiːtn/	schlagen; besiegen
become /bɪˈkʌm/	became /bɪˈkeɪm/	become /bɪˈkʌm/	werden
begin /bɪˈɡɪn/	began /bɪˈɡæn/	begun /bɪˈɡʌn/	anfangen, beginnen
bite /baɪt/	bit /bɪt/	bitten /ˈbɪtn/	beißen
break /breɪk/	broke /brəʊk/	broken /ˈbrəʊkən/	(zer)brechen
bring /brɪŋ/	brought /brɔːt/	brought /brɔːt/	(mit)bringen
build /bɪld/	built /bɪlt/	built /bɪlt/	bauen
burn /bɜːn/	burnt/burned /bɜːnt/bɜːnd/	burnt/burned /bɜːnt/bɜːnd/	brennen
buy /baɪ/	bought /bɔːt/	bought /bɔːt/	kaufen
catch /kætʃ/	caught /kɔːt/	caught /kɔːt/	fangen; festnehmen
choose /tʃuːz/	chose /tʃəʊz/	chosen /ˈtʃəʊzn/	auswählen
come /kʌm/	came /keɪm/	come /kʌm/	kommen
cost /kɒst/	cost /kɒst/	cost /kɒst/	kosten
cut /kʌt/	cut /kʌt/	cut /kʌt/	schneiden
do /duː/	did /dɪd/	done /dʌn/	machen, tun
draw /drɔː/	drew /druː/	drawn /drɔːn/	zeichnen
dream /driːm/	dreamt/dreamed /dremt/driːmd/	dreamt/dreamed /dremt/driːmd/	träumen
drink /drɪŋk/	drank /dræŋk/	drunk /drʌŋk/	trinken
drive/ draɪv/	drove /drəʊv/	driven /ˈdrɪvn/	fahren
eat /iːt/	ate /eɪt/	eaten /ˈiːtn/	essen
fall /fɔːl/	fell /fel/	fallen /ˈfɔːlən/	fallen
feed /fiːd/	fed /fed/	fed /fed/	füttern, zu Essen geben
feel /fiːl/	felt /felt/	felt /felt/	(sich) fühlen
fight /faɪt/	fought /fɔːt/	fought /fɔːt/	(be)kämpfen
find /faɪnd/	found /faʊnd/	found /faʊnd/	finden
fit /fɪt/	fit/fitted /fɪt/ˈfɪtɪd/	fit/fitted /fɪt/ˈfɪtɪd/	passen (zu)
fly /flaɪ/	flew /fluː/	flown /fləʊn/	fliegen
forget /fəˈɡet/	forgot /fəˈɡɒt/	forgotten /fəˈɡɒtn/	vergessen
get /ɡet/	got /ɡɒt/	got/gotten /ɡɒt/ˈɡɒtn/	erhalten, bekommen; (an)kommen; verstehen; holen; werden
give /ɡɪv/	gave /ɡeɪv/	given /ˈɡɪvn/	geben
go /ɡəʊ/	went /went/	gone /ɡɒn/	gehen; fahren
hang /hæŋ/	hung /hʌŋ/	hung /hʌŋ/	(auf)hängen
have /hæv/	had /hæd/	had /hæd/	haben; essen
hear /hɪə/	heard /hɜːd/	heard /hɜːd/	hören
hide /haɪd/	hid /hɪd/	hidden /ˈhɪdn/	(sich) verstecken
hit /hɪt/	hit /hɪt/	hit /hɪt/	schlagen
hold /həʊld/	held /held/	held /held/	halten
keep /kiːp/	kept /kept/	kept /kept/	(be)halten; aufbewahren
know /nəʊ/	knew /njuː/	known /nəʊn/	wissen; kennen
lead /liːd/	led /led/	led /led/	führen

infinitive	simple past	past participle	German
learn /lɜ:n/	learnt/learned /lɜ:nt/lɜ:nd/	learnt/learned /lɜ:nt/lɜ:nd/	lernen
leave /li:v/	left /left/	left /left/	verlassen; lassen; (weg)gehen; abfahren
let /let/	let /let/	let /let/	lassen
lose /lu:z/	lost /lɒst/	lost /lɒst/	verlieren
make /meɪk/	made /meɪd/	made /meɪd/	machen
mean /mi:n/	meant /ment/	meant /ment/	bedeuten; meinen
meet /mi:t/	met /met/	met /met/	(sich) treffen; kennenlernen
put /pʊt/	put /pʊt/	put /pʊt/	setzen, legen, stellen
read /ri:d/	read /red/	read /red/	lesen
ride /raɪd/	rode /rəʊd/	ridden /ˈrɪdn/	fahren; reiten
run /rʌn/	ran /ræn/	run /rʌn/	laufen, rennen; fahren, verkehren
say /seɪ/	said /sed/	said /sed/	sagen
see /si:/	saw /sɔ:/	seen /si:n/	sehen
sell /sel/	sold /səʊld/	sold /səʊld/	verkaufen
send /send/	sent /sent/	sent /sent/	(zu)schicken
show /ʃəʊ/	showed /ʃəʊd/	shown /ʃəʊn/	zeigen
sing /sɪŋ/	sang /sæŋ/	sung /sʌŋ/	singen
sit /sɪt/	sat /sæt/	sat /sæt/	sitzen
sleep /sli:p/	slept /slept/	slept /slept/	schlafen
sneak /sni:k/	snuck /snʌk/	snuck /snʌk/	schleichen
speak /spi:k/	spoke /spəʊk/	spoken /ˈspəʊkən/	sprechen, reden
spell /spel/	spelt/spelled /spelt/speld/	spelt/spelled /spelt/speld/	buchstabieren
spend /spend/	spent /spent/	spent /spent/	ausgeben *(Geld)*; verbringen *(Zeit)*
spit /spɪt/	spit/spat /spɪt/spæt/	spit/spat /spɪt/spæt/	spucken
stand /stænd/	stood /stʊd/	stood /stʊd/	stehen; ertragen, aushalten
steal /sti:l/	stole /stəʊl/	stolen /ˈstəʊlən/	stehlen, klauen
swim /swɪm/	swam /swæm/	swum /swʌm/	schwimmen
take /teɪk/	took /tʊk/	taken /ˈteɪkən/	(mit)nehmen; bringen
teach /ti:tʃ/	taught /tɔ:t/	taught /tɔ:t/	unterrichten
tell /tel/	told /təʊld/	told /təʊld/	erzählen; sagen; vorhersagen
think /θɪŋk/	thought /θɔ:t/	thought /θɔ:t/	denken, glauben, meinen
throw /θrəʊ/	threw /θru:/	thrown /θrəʊn/	werfen
understand /ˌʌndəˈstænd/	understood /ˌʌndəˈstʊd/	understood /ˌʌndəˈstʊd/	verstehen
wear /weə/	worn /wɔ:/	worn /wɔ:n/	tragen *(Kleidung)*
win /wɪn/	won /wʌn/	won /wʌn/	gewinnen
write /raɪt/	wrote /rəʊt/	written /ˈrɪtn/	schreiben

Bildquellen

|adpic Bildagentur, Köln: Wodicka 72 1. |alamy images, Abingdon/Oxfordshire: 85 wedding, 125 A; 67photo 109 o. r.; Adrian Sherratt 109 o. l.; Alan Jeffery 144 u.; Alex Segre 35 5; Arco Images / De Meester, J 63 l.; BL Images Ltd 37 Buckingham Palace; Bob Turner 34 10; Bower, Jon 36 Big Ben; Caro 58 car technician; Danny Yanai / PhotoStock-Israel 80 F; Ford, Rob 35 2; grzegorz knec 35 u. r.; Henn Photography / Cultura Creative 121, 127 o. l.; Hipix 139 u. r.; Holmes Garden Photos 37 Tower; Hurst, D. 80 E; Image Source 109 u. l.; Jan Csernoch 29; JGI/Jamie Grill / Blend Images 84 Valentine's Day; Johnson, Betty 132 Serkan; Jon Wilson 144 o.; Jordan, Peter 34 1; Kelly Redinger / Design Pics Inc. 109 u. r.; Loop Images Ltd 36 Underground; Michael Cullen 125 G; Mickael David - Author's Image 35 9; OJO Images Ltd 79, 80; one-image photography 50 m.; PCL 34 3; Pegaz 80 C; Pens Forms 21 r.; Peter Scholey 37 City Hall, 37 Tate Modern; Russell Kord / 50 o. l.; Steve Vidler 13, 21 o.; SuperStock / Purestock 84 birthday; Trinity Mirror / Mirrorpix 53; © Blend Images 85 Mother's Day; © David Ball 16 r.; © Janine Wiedel Photolibrary 85 Christmas; © KAKIMAGE 81 r.; © Pawel Libera 37 shop; © Tetra Images 132 Martin. |altro - die fotoagentur, Regensburg: 55, 58. |Avenue Images GmbH, Hamburg: Wendy Connett / agefotostock 16 l.. |Barker, Ruth, Plauen: 17, 65 u., 91 u., 106, 106, 106, 111; Eiffelturm: fotolia.com (Marco Bonan); Pyramide: istockphoto.com (Ingenui); Notre Dame:fotolia.com (anshar73) 131; Karte: Technisch-Grafische Abteilung, Westermann; Zug: Shutterstock.com (hans engbers) 131. |BBC Photo Library, London: 121 B, 125, 125 u. l.; Hutton, Colin 125 F. |Bildagentur Schapowalow, Hamburg: Robert Harding 69. |bildagentur-online GmbH, Burgkunstadt: TIPS/Mitch Diamond 127 u. u.. |BilderBox Bildagentur GmbH, Breitbrunn/Hörsching: Erwin Wodicka 38 r.. |Callaghan, Valerie, Braunschweig: 101. |Caro Fotoagentur, Berlin: Sorge 14 2. |CartoonStock.com, Bath: 120; Loren Fishman 32; Tony Neat 74. |Corgi Yearling Books: Wilson, Jacqueline: Cliffhanger, illustrated by Nick Sharratt, 1995 142, 142, 143, 143, 143, 143. |ddp images GmbH, Hamburg: Lennart Preiss 125 C. |Design Pics, Berlin: 58 bus driver. |Douglas, Matthew: 113 3. |dreamstime.com, Brentwood: Jesse 36 Gherkin; Kaphoto 86 u.; Peter Lovás 34 4. |dsphotos.de, Hamburg: Titel. |Eckart-Scheurig, Jutta, Wiesbaden: 38 l.. |Egbert, Martin, Tecklenburg: 27. |F1online digitale Bildagentur GmbH, Frankfurt/M.: Maskot 132 Grace. |Fischer, Knoblauch & Co. Medienproduktionsgesellschaft mbH, München: 19, 20 homework, 36 o., 84 Daniel, 84 Leanne, 84 Rebecca, 114 Safia, 114 Shelby, 114 Taylor, 114 Yusuf. |Focus Photo- u. Presseagentur GmbH, Hamburg: Sturrock, Alex 58 police. |fotolia.com, New York: air 63 r.; AndiPu 132 Sue; Ben Chams 113 5; jeff gynane 113 4; Kurhan 93; Marina Zlochin 33 u.; tungphoto 52 giraffe. |Getty Images, München: David Ball 50 o. r.; Francesco Ruggeri 58 cook; Fuse 86 m.; I-593-0137 58 shop assistant; Jeff J Mitchell 81 l.; Mark Scoggins 30; New York Times Co./Kontributor 72 4; Rex Butcher 37 Covent Garden; © Rune Hellestad 72 6. |Hammersen, Bettina, Braunschweig: 105. |Interfoto, München: 140; Travel Library / Grant Pritchard 85 Chinese New Year. |iStockphoto.com, Calgary: abbesses 37 St Paul's; idildemir 72; raclro 139 o. r.; Rich Legg 91 o.. |JOKER: Fotojournalismus, Bonn: Gloger, Marcus 58 vet. |kes-online, Berlin: 36 London Eye. |Kobal Collection, Berlin: MGM 72 2. |Laudanna, Saba, Berlin: 50 u.. |mauritius images GmbH, Mittenwald: Mallaun 80 D; Rosenfeld 58 builder; Steve Vidler 34 8; SuperStock 25; Vidler 34 7, 35 12. |Mohm, Julia, Braunschweig: 20 clubs, 20 library, 20 sports, 20 uniforms, 119. |Moore, Inga, Gloucestershire: 54 l.. |OKAPIA KG - Michael Grzimek & Co., Frankfurt/M.: Staffan Widstrand/Naturbild 52 tortoise. |ONLY FRANCE.FR, Berlin: HENRI TABARANT 14 5. |PantherMedia GmbH (panthermedia.net), München: kapu 168. |Pearson, Carol, Paris: 35 6, 36 Theatre. |Picture-Alliance GmbH, Frankfurt/M.: 58 pilot; Bildagentur Huber/R. Schmid 85 St. Martin's Day; Boris Rössler 52 meerkats; dpa 14 4, 58 firefighter; dpa / ABC Television Network 125 H; dpa/Karl-Josef Hildenbrand 80 A; dpa/R. Vennenbernd 37 Tower Bridge; epa Handout © dpa 125 E; epa/Geoff Caddick 49; maxppp/van Montagu, Philippe 33 o. l.; NASA/AFP 72; Schindler 58 gardener; ZB / Killig, Oliver 58 hairdresser; ZB, Martin Schutt 85 carnival; ZB/Büttner, Jens 35 11. |Quandt, Susanne, Bremen: 57, 65 o.. |Random House UK Limited, London: Good Housekeeping: Kid's Cookbook: A First Step-By-Step Book for Young Cooks by Janet Smith 1993, published by Ebury Press 100, 100, 100, 100, 100, 100. |Reuter, Christoph, Detmold: 20 cafeteria, 106, 113 2. |REUTERS, Berlin: Stephen Hird 125 u. r.. |Schmidt, Andreas, Hannover: 95. |Schmidt-Brücken, Frank, Weiterstadt: 47. |Shutterstock.com, New York: Fabrizio Andrea Bertani 72; Nick Beer 113. |stock.adobe.com, Dublin: ©Dotan 72; ©Phil Cardamone 139; ©rimmdream 72; ©Roman Stetsyk 72. |THORPE PARK: 138. |Tönnies, Frauke, Laatzen: 14 1, 52 penguin. |TopicMedia Service, Mehring-Öd: Lacz 44. |transit - Fotografie und -Archiv, Leipzig: Hirth, Peter 14 3. |ullstein bild, Berlin: United Archives 125 D. |vario images, Bonn: 86 o.. |wikimedia.commons: 98, 98. |www.roggenthin.de, Nürnberg: 127 u. o.. |© Arsenal/SammlungRichter, Wetzlar: 51.

Wir arbeiten sehr sorgfältig daran, für alle verwendeten Abbildungen die Rechteinhaberinnen und Rechteinhaber zu ermitteln. Sollte uns dies im Einzelfall nicht vollständig gelungen sein, werden berechtigte Ansprüche selbstverständlich im Rahmen der üblichen Vereinbarungen abgegolten.

Textquellen

54 „Geraldine Giraffe", Colin West;

60 „Qué Será, Será (Whatever Will Be, Will Be)", Ray Evans

74 „I wanna be a star", Tony Mitton

106 „Don't", Richard Edwards © Simon & Schuster Education, Hampstead

140 „Going for a swim", John Foster

142/143 from Cliffhanger by Jacqueline Wilson, published by Corgi Yearling. Reprinted by permission of The Random House Group Ltd.

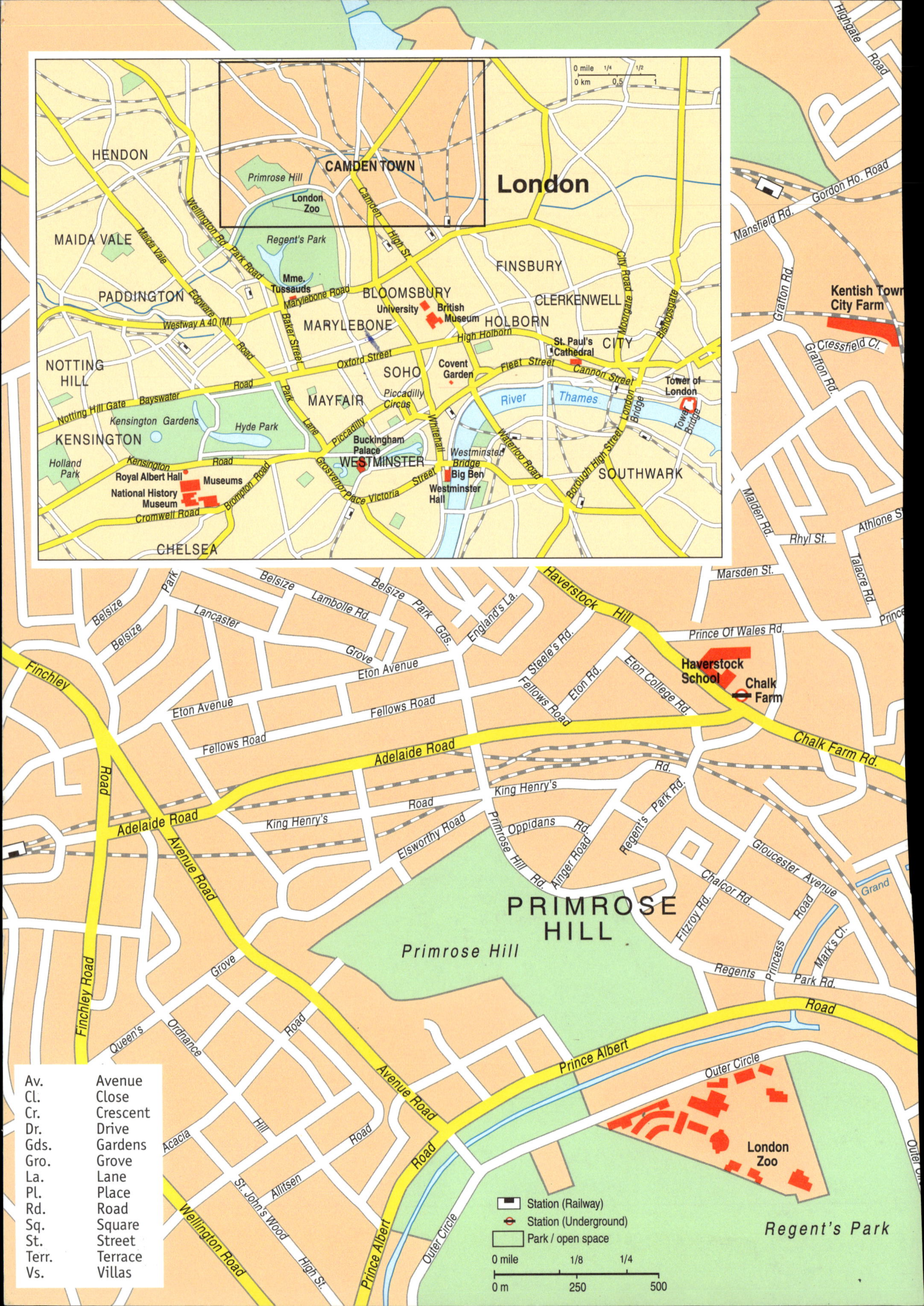
London
HENDON
CAMDEN TOWN
Primrose Hill
London Zoo
Regent's Park
MAIDA VALE
Maida Vale
Wellington Rd
Park Road
PADDINGTON
Edgware Road
Mme. Tussauds
Marylebone Road
Westway A 40 (M)
BLOOMSBURY
University
British Museum
MARYLEBONE
Baker Street
Camden High St
FINSBURY
CLERKENWELL
City Road
Moorgate
Bishopsgate
HOLBORN
High Holborn
St. Paul's Cathedral
CITY
NOTTING HILL
Oxford Street
SOHO
Covent Garden
Fleet Street
Cannon Street
Tower of London
Tower Bridge
London Bridge
River Thames
MAYFAIR
Piccadilly Circus
Piccadilly
Park Lane
Notting Hill Gate
Bayswater Road
Kensington Gardens
Hyde Park
KENSINGTON
Holland Park
Kensington Road
Buckingham Palace
WESTMINSTER
Whitehall
Westminster Bridge
Waterloo Road
Borough High Street
SOUTHWARK
Royal Albert Hall
Museums
National History Museum
Brompton Road
Cromwell Road
Grosvenor Place
Victoria Street
Big Ben
Westminster Hall
CHELSEA
0 mile 1/4 1/2
0 km 0,5 1
Highgate Road
Gordon Ho. Road
Mansfield Rd.
Grafton Rd.
Kentish Town City Farm
Cressfield Cl.
Grafton Rd.
Malden Rd.
Rhyl St.
Athlone St.
Talacre Rd.
Marsden St.
Prince
Haverstock Hill
Prince Of Wales Rd.
Belsize
Belsize Park
Belsize
Belsize Park Gds.
Lamble Rd.
Lancaster Grove
England's La.
Steele's Rd.
Eton Rd.
Eton College Rd.
Haverstock School
Chalk Farm
Finchley Road
Eton Avenue
Eton Avenue
Fellows Road
Fellows Road
Fellows Road
Chalk Farm Rd.
Adelaide Road
Adelaide Road
King Henry's Road
King Henry's Road
Elsworthy Road
Primrose Hill Rd.
Oppidans Rd.
Ainger Road
Regent's Park Rd.
Gloucester Avenue
Chalcot Rd.
Grand
Avenue Road
PRIMROSE HILL
Primrose Hill
Fitzroy Rd.
Princess Road
Mark's Cl.
Regents Park Rd.
Grove
Queen's Grove
Ordnance Hill
Road
Prince Albert Road
Outer Circle
Avenue Road
London Zoo
Road
Acacia Road
Allitsen Road
St. John's Wood High St.
Wellington Road
Prince Albert Road
Outer Circle
Station (Railway)
Station (Underground)
Park / open space
0 mile 1/8 1/4
0 m 250 500
Regent's Park
Outer Circle
Av. Avenue
Cl. Close
Cr. Crescent
Dr. Drive
Gds. Gardens
Gro. Grove
La. Lane
Pl. Place
Rd. Road
Sq. Square
St. Street
Terr. Terrace
Vs. Villas